PHONETIC READINGS OF SONGS and ARIAS

Second edition, with revised German transcriptions

BERTON COFFIN

RALPH ERROLLE

WERNER SINGER

PIERRE DELATTRE

The Scarecrow Press, Inc.
Metuchen, N.J., & London • 1982

Library of Congress Cataloging in Publication Data

Main entry under title:

Phonetic readings of songs and arias.

   Bibliography: p.
   Includes index.
   1. Singing--Diction. 2. Italian language--
Phonetics. 3. German language--Phonetics.
4. French language--Phonetics. I. Coffin, Berton.
II. Coffin, Berton. Singer's repertoire.
MT883.P5   1981   784.3'05   82-874
ISBN 0-8108-1533-8   AACR2

TABLE OF CONTENTS

ACKNOWLEDGMENTS

Acknowledgments for counsel and valued assistance should be made to Clara Regnoni-Macera, Assistant Professor of Italian at the University of Colorado-Boulder, formerly of St. Cecilia, Rome; Lola Martini, Tuscan Italian, and Dr. Anton Burzle, phonetician and Professor of German at the University of Kansas and Director of the German Summer Institute, Holz-kirchen O. B. B. Germany.

Without the assistance and permission of the following publishers to use copyrighted lyrics, the extent of the reper-toire included would have been seriously limited: Associated Music Publishers, Inc.; Boston Music Company; Durand et Cie; Elkan-Vogel Co., Inc.; Chas. H. Homeyer and Co., Inc.; Theodore Presser Company; G. Ricordi and Co.; and G. Schirmer, Inc. Vera Tugel, copyright owner of "Wiegenlied" granted permission for the use of that lyric.

A grant from the Council on Research and Creative Work at the University of Colorado-Boulder made this study possible.

FOREWORD

"Phonetic Readings of Songs and Arias" is Volume VI of "The Singer's Repertoire" series of aids for the singer and teacher of singing.

The teacher of singing is faced with many, many challenges - the forming of an individual voice for each of his students, the appropriate use of repertoire for each voice, the teaching of individualized diction of songs in various languages, and the stimulation of vocal artistry. Few fields are larger in scope and more challenging than that faced by the serious teacher of singing.

One of the most persistent problems is that of diction in the four principal languages of singing. Molding the pronunciation of lyrics of the basic repertoire of the young singer may be relatively easy but the need for teaching the same pronunciation of the same songs to students over a period of years can easily become a devitalizing activity. This text has been partially directed to this problem.

Another problem is involved with the song needs of the advanced singer. Each individual voice will need its own repertoire. A teacher may not use certain songs for years, but when the time comes, it is urgent that these songs be taught correctly and efficiently as a language. Furthermore, the burden of proof is upon the teacher. He, and he alone, must form the diction, for teachers of languages in the classes of our colleges and universities have little time to serve the individual language needs of students of singing. Also the shortage of time necessitates that the singer must do as much learning on his own as possible.

Oral assignments can now be made in the text "Phonetic Readings of Songs and Arias" before actual singing of a song is begun. Psychologically it is easier to do one thing at a time - learn the language - read it with the accent of the word - and then place it to music. Many teachers recommend the learning of a lyric prior to the preparation of a song as being an efficient memory device. A fabled teacher was known for her desire to have her students read aloud the poetry of their songs early in the day as an inflective and interpretative device for preparing songs and arias. It was with the above concept in mind that this book of phonetic transcriptions was formed as a reader.

Many students want to hurry the process of learning to sing. Time may be gained in the area of language work faster than in other areas. And, if a language can be learned from the first without the necessity of correcting mistakes, learning can indeed be fast, and the attention of the teacher directed to the use of the language art as it relates to the use of vocal resources and interpretation. Instrumentalists usually observe long practice hours but the singer's work must be accomplished in a shorter length of time because of the nature of the vocal instrument. With the procedure of learning the diction of songs and arias through phonetics, more work can be accomplished in a limited time and a larger and more dependable repertoire should evolve.

The singer today is faced with the problem that his art is more international than ever before. Hundreds of American singers are active in Europe. With the advent of fast transportation a singer is frequently called upon to sing in several countries and several languages within a very short time. Furthermore, he is expected to sing each language with standardized diction. The singer who performs only in the United States is faced with the singing of several languages, and wherever he appears can be relatively sure that several persons in his audience will know correct pronunciation of languages due to our traveling, sophisticated culture and to the enormous influence of recordings by world renowned artists. Now, as never before, the student must sing well and with correct diction.

As one travels through such countries as Italy, Germany, France, England and the United States, he is constantly aware of the changing of language within each nation. Almost any area of a country may be represented by our language teachers. But as far as singing is concerned, there is a standard to be used and the standards are subtley changing - witness Webster's Dictionary in this country. Suffice it to say that the transcriptions found in this text have been made according to the most recent techniques of phonetic transcriptions and accepted standards of language. The phonetics used are those of the International Phonetic Association of which at least half of the symbols are already known to the singer. With the memorization of the remaining symbols the pronunciation of the basic lyric repertoire will be easily available to every singer. A clear statement concerning the symbols of each of the languages is found in the foreword of each of the divisions.

The Italian standard, used by Italian radio announcers and actors, is Zingarelli - "Vocabulario della Lingua Italiana." Although this reference does not use the International Phonetic Alphabet, pronunciation is clearly marked and is in this text transferred to I. P. A. symbols with few changes.

The German standard used has been Siebs - "Deutsche Hochsprache," 1958 Edition, the use of which has been further strengthened by the reference "Deutsche Phonetik" by Martens. These sources differ from earlier use of I. P. A. transcriptions primarily in the treatment of diphthongs.

Eis	is now	ae	rather than	aɪ	
Leute	is now	ɔø	rather than	ɔɪ	
Haus	is now	ɑo	rather than	au or ao	

French, the most standardized of the languages, is written in open syllabification for better flow of the language in this text, designed as a phonetic reader. French is essentially a language of open syllables (consonants do not close them). In this reference the closing consonant has been transposed to the right, becoming a part of the consonant cluster at the beginning of the next syllable. Americans have the tendency of closing the syllables, thus anglicizing the French. The standard for the French transcription has been Fouché - "Traite de Prononciation Française."

THE RELATIONSHIP of PHONETIC
READINGS and SINGING

For the experienced singer who kinesthetically knows the following modifications or for the teacher of singing or coach with a sensitive ear, the phenomena herein described have probably been observed but not categorized. For the untrained singer, the teacher of singing, and coach with limited experience, a definition of vowel modification is probably necessary in a book of phonetic transcription to avoid a forced, uniform phonetic forming of vowels in singing. Inflexible language treatment tends to impare the musicality, expressiveness, and survival of voices.

My studies into acoustic phonetics, to better explain this paragraph, have led me to the publication of two texts, "Sounds of Singing" (1977) and "Overtones of Bel Canto" (1980), both with Vowel Charts. My revised and simplified explanation of the relationship of Phonetic Readings and Singing at this time would be as follows:

1. Spoken vowels are caused by two cavities, the cavity behind the tongue hump and the cavity in front of the tongue hump. In good singing the tongue hump is reduced in height in order that the vocal tract can act more as one resonator which allows an instrumental standing wave between the vocal cords and the front of the mouth.

2. The resonant frequencies of these cavities are approximately 15% higher (1 1/2 steps) for women than for men.

3. The high resonance of vowels, in front of the tongue hump, R^2, can be heard by whispering the vowels.

4. The low resonance of vowels, R^1, can be heard by forming the vowel and thumping the side of the throat just above the larynx. This resonance frequency can only be heard when the glottis is closed (as before the explosion of a cough). The vowels i-e-a-o-u will give a rising and falling pattern of pitches. R^1 can also be heard by stopping the ears and whispering the different vowels.

5. R^1 frequencies for the various vowels in male and female voices are as high as

æ	a	ɑ (750 cps)	roughly g^2
ɛ	œ	ɔ (600 cps)	roughly d^2
e	ø	o (456 cps)	roughly a^1
i	y	u (350 cps)	roughly f^1
I	II	III	Series (Modified from Howie and Delattre.)

6. Three vowel series are shown, I - Front vowels, II - Umlaut vowels, and III - Back vowels. In "Sounds of Singing" and "Overtones of Bel Canto" I have introduced a Neutral vowel series for use in vocalization and the singing of songs and arias.

7. There is a loss of understandability of a given vowel when it is sung on a pitch above its R^1 frequency and it will tend to sound like the vowel in its series on that particular note.

8. Vowels sung on pitches higher than the pitches indicated in No. 5 will tend to be distuned, harsh, unfocused, and unstable in vibrato when an unmodified form is forced upon the voice, and conversely, the voice becomes musical and the vibrato even when correct resonance is used. The crux of the matter is--the vocal tract becomes a resonator for sung pitch in singing--vowels must be modified for the resonator to work efficiently, and vice-versa, when the resonator adjusts to amplify the sung pitch, vowels are automatically modified.

9. Basically, language study and the pronunciation of texts should precede the modifications of vowels in singing. The Yersin sisters, the famous teachers of French diction said (1924, p. 13), "One ought to be able to read a song at first sight in a foreign language prior to singing it so that the whole attention may be concentrated upon the singing itself. "

10. There is no rule of thumb on the modification of vowels except that in an ascending scale they will tend to open until the voice is spread, and in a descending scale the voice will close until it is muted (when in the same register). If vowel positions are kept in a steady state the voice will run into and out of resonance points (change registers). A study of video tapes in repetition, slow motion, and stop frame will reveal what good singers do to stay in resonance. Again, learn the pronunciation of songs and arias first and then use the Vowel Charts in singing to find the modification nearest to good linguistic pronunciation.

11. Again, if the resonance phenomenon is disregarded (without intuitive change) there may be difficulty with timbre, pitch, agility, and flexibility in dynamics. When things are right the vibrato will spin. Good critics will point out vocal deficiencies sooner than they will mention slight modifications of language values--in fact, they will usually not notice the latter.

12. It has been found that the extremes of the vowel tri-
angle /i/, /a/, and /u/ must be modified in singing for
a standing wave to occur in the throat. Albert Bach in
"Musical Education and Vocal Culture" quotes Anna
Maria Celoni as saying, "le vocali l'i ed l'u si devono
evitare a lasciarle a coloro che avessero la mania
al'imitare i cavalli ed i lupi." (The vowel /i/ and /u/
should be left for those who desire to imitate horses and
wolves.) The younger Garcia says of /a/ that in the
tenor voice the "/a/ in clear timbre on the notes g' to
b' will always appear shrill . . . and resembling a boy
chorister's voice; therefore they should never be used
except in closed timbre." The closed timbre is a
change into another register. My continued observa-
tions have indicated that where teaching is done entirely
on /a/ breaks occur at certain points, so in general,
pure forms of /i/, /u/, and /a/ should not be used
except in recitative and soft passages. This means that
the Italian pure vowel concept should be replaced by the
Italian pure tone concept--watch while listening to the
Italian singers on video tapes.

13. Since female voices sing nearer to the resonance frequency of vowels, they must have a great deal of modification in their singing. Also for acoustical reasons
there will be greater visual evidence of it.

14. Since male voices are playing the pitch of vowels by
overtones most of the time, there tends to be less need
of vowel modification, especially below c^1. However,
there is a basic modification in male voices utilized by
Caruso. The vowels should be modified towards the
open on the low notes and rounded towards the closed on
the top (Coffin 1980, p. 97).

15. The exact meaning of each word should be known for
expression and word emphasis before singing. These
meanings may be found for the most usual songs and
arias in "Word-for-Word Translations" (1966 and 1972).

16. Vowels vary their modification with emotional coloring--
when notes are fast there is less need to be concerned
about vowel modification. In slower passages when joy
is to be depicted the vowels become brighter (higher
overtones used). When sadness is to be depicted the

face drops and the highest overtones are reduced so that the vowels tend towards the Back and Umlaut vowels.

For application of vowel modifications in singing see "Overtones of Bel Canto"--but precede that study by reading your songs and arias phonetically, and knowing the meaning of the words. Thus, there is a high art with which the wedding of language and cantilena (vocal line) must be accomplished. Traditionally this has occurred quite late in study and is the mark of an artist. Why can it not occur earlier if the above phenomena are understood and observed in the study of languages through phonetics?

I believe that this volume of "The Singer's Repertoire" series was most fortunate in the selection of its co-authors.

Ralph Errolle, was a leading tenor of the Metropolitan, Chicago and San Francisco opera companies, and was the author of "Italian Diction for Singers," Pruett Press, 1963. He was Professor of Music and Director of Opera at Louisiana State University, and Director of the Opera Arts Association of Atlanta, Georgia. He taught Italian and French Diction at several National Association of Teachers of Singing Workshops. He later taught singing in Chicago and Los Angeles.

Werner Singer, Coach-Accompanist of New York City, was German-born and trained at the Staatliche Hochschule für Musik, Berlin. He conducted operas at the Hamburg Volksoper and the Theatro Municipal, Rio de Janeiro, Brazil. In this country he was widely known, having been a coach and/or accompanist to Mmes. Barbieri, Berger, Leider, Loevberg, Tebaldi, and Yeend, and Messrs. Bernac, de Luca, Gedda, London, Svanholm, Tagliavini, and Vinay. In the academic field, Mr. Singer established and held summer classes in "Repertoire for Singers" at the University of Colorado-Boulder.

Pierre Delattre, Professor of French at the University of Colorado-Boulder and the University of California-Santa Barbara, was a French-born specialist in phonetics. He was trained at the University of Paris and the University of Michigan. He was Head of the Department of Phonetics at Middlebury summer schools for 20 years and was phonetics editor of the French Review. He built outstanding experimental phonetics laboratories for the analysis of accents in foreign languages and the acoustic analysis of vowels and consonants in Boulder and Santa Barbara. He contributed two articles to the National Association of Teachers of Singing Bulletin Vol. XV No. 1, October 1958, "Vowel Color and Voice Quality" (most important for comparison of speech and singing vowel qualities and vocal positions); Vol. XVIII No. 4, May 1962, "Effect of Pitch on the Intelligibility of Vowels. " Lecturer at NATS Workshops. French editor for Webster Dictionaries 1941-1969.

FOREWORD BIBLIOGRAPHY

Bach, Albert.	Musical Education and Vocal Culture. Kegan, Paul and Trench. London, 1898.
Cartier, Frances A.	The Phonetic Alphabet. Wm. C. Brown. Dubuque, Iowa, 1954. (English vowels.)
Coffin, Berton.	Overtones of Bel Canto. The Scarecrow Press, Metuchen, New Jersey, 1980.
	The Singer's Repertoire. Vol. I. Coloratura, Lyric and Dramatic Soprano. Vol. II. Mezzo Soprano and Contralto. Vol. III. Lyric and Dramatic Tenor. Vol. IV. Baritone and Bass. The Scarecrow Press, Metuchen, New Jersey, 1960.
	Sounds of Singing. The Scarecrow Press, Metuchen, New Jersey, 1977.
Coffin, Berton and Werner Singer.	Program Notes for the Singer's Repertoire. The Scarecrow Press, Metuchen, New Jersey, 1962.
Coffin, Berton, Werner Singer, and Pierre Delattre.	Word-By-Word Translations of Songs and Arias. Part I - German and French. The Scarecrow Press, Metuchen, New Jersey, 1966.
Garcia, Manuel P. R.	The Art of Singing, Part I. Oliver Ditson, Boston, ab. 1855.
Gray, Giles Wilkerson and Claude M. Wise.	The Bases of Speech. Harper, New York, 1946.
Howie, John and Pierre Delattre.	"An Experimental Study of the Effect of Pitch on the Intelligibility of Vowels, " Bulletin, National Association of Teachers of Singing, Vol. XVIII, No. 4, May 15, 1962.

Kantner, Claude and Robert West.	<u>Phonetics</u>. Harper, New York, 1941.
Schoep, Arthur and Daniel Harris.	<u>Word-By-Word Translations of Songs and Arias</u>. Part II - Italian (a companion to <u>The Singer's Repertoire</u>). The Scarecrow Press, Metuchen, New Jersey, 1972.
Wise, Claude M.	<u>Introduction to Phonetics</u>. Prentice Hall, New York, 1958.
Witherspoon, Herbert.	<u>Singing</u>. G. Schirmer, New York, 1925.

ITALIAN BIBLIOGRAPHY

Bianchi, Enrico.	<u>Come si dice, Come si scrive</u>. Casa Editrice. Adriano, Salani, Firenze, 1947.
Edgren, Hjalmor.	<u>An Italian and English Dictionary</u>. Henry Holt & Co., New York 1929. (Contains many words used in songs not found in other works.)
Errolle, Ralph.	<u>Italian Diction for Singers</u>. Third Edition. Pruett Press, Boulder, Colorado, 1963. (Adjustments from speech to singing explained.) Recommended by Dr. Riccardo Picozzi, Teatro alla Scala, Milano and Teatro dell'Opera di Roma.
Grandgent & Wilkens.	<u>Italian Grammar</u>. D. C. Heath Co., New York, 1915.
Hoare, Alfred.	<u>A Short Italian Dictionary</u>. Cambridge University Press, 1950.
Russo, Joseph Louis.	<u>Present Day Italian</u>. D. C. Heath Co., Boston, 1947.

Zingarelli,
    Nicola.

Vocabolario Della Lingua Italiana.
Eighth Edition. Nicola Zanichelli
Editore, Bologna, 1959.

GERMAN BIBLIOGRAPHY

Bithell, Jethro.

German Pronunciation and Pho-
nology. Methuen and Co., London,
1952.

Martens, Carl and
    Peter.

Phonetik der Deutschen Sprache.
Hueber Berlag, Munchen, 1961.
(Excellent photographs of pronunciation of German vowels and consonants.)

Siebs, Theodore.

Deutsche Hochsprache Bühnen-
aussprache. Stage pronunciation in
phonetics. Gruyter and Co., Berlin,
1961. (Called by some, "the bible.")

Wardale, W. L.

German Pronunciation. Edinburgh
University Press, Edinburgh, 1955.

Wilcke, Eva.

German Diction in Singing. Tr. and
ed. by Bainbridge Crist. Dutton,
New York, 1930.

FRENCH BIBLIOGRAPHY

Barbeau, Alfred &
    Émile Rodhe.

Dictionnaire Phonétique de la
Langue Française. 1930.

Coustenoble, Hélène.

A Pronunciation Dictionary of the
French Language, Based Upon
Gasc's Concise Dictionary. 1929.

Delattre, Pierre.

An Introduction to French Speech
Habits. 1947.

Delattre, Pierre.

Les Difficultés Phonétiques du
Français. 1948.

Delattre, Pierre.   Advanced Training in French Pronunciation, 1949.

Delattre, Pierre.   Principes de Phonétique Française,
à l'usage des Etudiants Anglo-
Américains. 1951.

Delattre, Pierre.   "Les Modes Phonétiques du
Français." The French Review,
27: 59-63. Oct. 1953.

Fouché, Pierre.   Traité de Prononciation Française.
1956.

Mansion's   French and English Dictionary.
(in America, D. C. Heath and
Company, Boston).

PHONETIC TRANSCRIPTION OF ITALIAN SONGS AND ARIAS

Ralph Errolle and Berton Coffin

Vocal coaches in Italy are striving to limit the concessions in pronunciation asked for by singers and to keep the pronunciation in singing as nearly as possible to recognized academic rules. This text is the transcription of classic Italian with permissible concessions to singing.

PROBLEMS OF ITALIAN DICTION

The basic problems of Italian diction are concerned with the pronunciation of orthographic e, o, s, z, and zz. The mispronouncing of accented e and o may affect meaning:

> venti... vẹnti--winds, but vẹnti--twenty
>
> dei.....dẹi---gods, but dẹi----of the
>
> mezzo...mẹd:zo--medium, but mẹt:so--over-ripe

Stressed e and o

1. The principle problems in Italian diction are concerned with the open and close e, ɛ and e, and open and close o, ɔ and o. Dictionaries do not always agree on the close and open e and o in accented syllables. In such cases the vowel most conducive to vocal emission has been indicated. Please see Bibliography.

2. Accented finale e - e has been transcribed close and accented final o-o has been transcribed open according to present usage.

> perchè......pɛrkẹ   salpò....salpọ
>
> fè.........fe   farò....farọ

Unaccented e and o

According to accepted academic rules <u>the orthographic e and o are always close when not the vowel of the tonic syllable.</u> The following concessions to singing are included in this transcription.

1. e in apocopation (the dropping of the final vowel) tends to open to ɛ and is so transcribed - della...del:la, del.....dɛl. But, since there is a more marked difference between e and ɛ than o and ɔ, the o in apocopation remains close.

1

2. In singing, unstressed e tends to open before m, l, n, r when followed by another consonant and is transcribed ɛ.

M	L	N	R
ɛmblɛma	bɛltà	ɛntità	vɛrbɛna
tɛmperare	dɛlfin	sɛntire	cɛrvɛllo

3. The unstressed o tends to open before r when followed by another consonant and is transcribed as follows:

mortal.....mɔrtal   sortire.....sɔrtire

Note that the following is <u>not</u> an exception: unaccented final e may sound to some persons as a change in value to an intermediate vowel or even the open vowel. This is incorrect. Final e should be considered as <u>the close sound in unstressed form</u>, and should never be pronounced ɛ. Hence unstressed <u>final</u> e is always transcribed e.

Intervocalic s

Intervocalic s is pronounced soft z -even when pronounced s in speech, because the American singer will tend to emphasize the s so much that it will be heard as ss. If s follows a prefix, it is pronounced s.

Intervocalic	rosa...rɔza	pisa...piza
With prefix	disegno...diseɲo	risuonò...riswonɔ

Pronunciation of z and zz

The two pronunciations of z and zz, which are almost without rules, are indicated in this text by ts, dz, and when doubled t:s and d:z.

danza....dantsa	bonzo....bɔndzo
pazzo....pat:so	mezzo....mɛd:zo

Tonic accent

In this transcription the tonic accent or elevation of the tone is indicated by the vowel being underlined (bɛl:la) rather than accented (ˋbɛl:la) for easier reading and for a clearer indication of the lengthening of the syllable.

Textual Diphthongs

When the final vowel of a word is tied to the initial vowel of the succeeding word and is sung on a single note, the combination

2

is referred to as a textual diphthong. The textual diphthong is indicated by a tie and the stressed vowel is underlined.

ch<u>e</u>‿un   che‿<u>a</u>i   cento‿<u>e</u>

Each such cluster must be uttered with one impulse of the breath and should never be broken into separate sounds - the composer would have written separate notes had he so desired. (Errolle)

Double Consonants

Double consonants are stressed in articulation and the sound is <u>prolonged</u>. Since the double consonant is of such importance in Italian and is so frequently neglected by American singers, all double consonants have been separated in this text by a colon to remind the singer that the utterance of the consonant should be prolonged.

letto – l<u>ɛ</u>t:to	bocca – b<u>o</u>k:ka	giammai – dʒam:m<u>a</u>i
legge – l<u>ɛ</u>d:ʒe	mezzo – m<u>ɛ</u>d:zo	prezzo – pr<u>ɛ</u>t:so

Value of the phonetic symbols used in the
transcription of Italian

Phonetic Symbol	Sound as derived from English sounds	As found in Italian words
	VOWELS	
a*	father (in middle west)	casa. . . . .k<u>a</u>za
ɛ	pet	ecco. . . . .<u>ɛ</u>k:ko
e	pate, without the diphthong vanish ei	che. . . . .ke
i	me	mi. . . . .mi
o	loan, roll, without diphthong glide ou to u	voce. . . . .v<u>o</u>tʃe
ɔ	orphan	oggi. . . . .<u>ɔ</u>dʒi
u	rule	muto. . . . .m<u>u</u>to

*Do not confuse this IPA symbol with the a used in French where it represents a sound acoustically between æ and ɑ.

CONSONANTS

b	bond	banco.....baŋko
d	<u>d</u>ental, with tongue touching the upper front teeth	dente.....dɛnte
dʒ	Affricate of d and ʒ as in ju<u>dge</u>	gioja.....dʒɔ̯ja
f	fat	fatto.....fat:to
g	gamble	gamba.....gamba
j	yes	ieri.....jɛri
k	keel	caro.....karo
l	love dentalized, with tongue touching upper front teeth	lunga.....luŋga
ʎ	mil<u>l</u>ion li or lj becomes ʎ when tongue touches lower front teeth	gli.....ʎi
m	mine	mio.....mi̯o
n	dent dentalized, with tongue touching upper front teeth	notte.....nɔt:te
ŋ	ring	anche.....aŋke
ɲ	pinion, ni becomes ɲ when tongue touches lower front teeth	ogni.....oɲi
p	pull	pace.....patʃe
r	rock – but always rolled in Italian	riso.....rizo
s	sell	sapete.....sapete
t	try – dentalized with the tongue touching upper front teeth	testa.....tɛsta
tʃ	Affricate of t and ʃ as in <u>ch</u>ess	voce.....vɔtʃe
v	vine	vino.....vino
w	went	guerra.....gwɛr:ra
z	zoo	rosa.....rɔza

4

Beethoven   In questa tomba oscura
                  in kwesta tomba oskura

In questa tomba oscura lasciami riposar;
in kwesta tomba oskura laʃami ripozar;

quando vivevo, ingrata, dovevi a me pensar.
kwando vivevo, iŋgrata, dovevi a me pɛnsar.*

Lascia che l'ombre ignude godansi pace almen,
laʃa ke lombre iɲude godansi patʃe almɛn,

e non bagnar mie ceneri d'inutile velen.
e non baɲar mie tʃeneri dinutile velɛn.*

Bellini   Casta Diva, from "Norma"
bel:lini   kasta diva norma

Casta Diva, che inargenti
kasta diva, ke inardʒɛnti

queste sacre, antiche piante,
kweste sakre, antike pjante,

a noi volgi il bel sembiante,
a noi voldʒi il bɛl sɛmbjante,

senza nube e senza vel, si.
sɛntsa nube e sɛntsa vel, si.

Tempra, o Diva, tempra tu de' cori ardenti,
tɛmpra, o diva, tɛmpra tu de kori ardɛnti,

tempra ancora, tempra ancor lo zelo audace,
tɛmpra aŋkora, tɛmpraŋkor lo dzɛlo audatʃe,

spargi in terra, ah, quella pace,
spardʒin tɛr:ra, a, kwɛl:la patʃe,

che regnar tu fai nel ciel.
ke reɲar tu fai nɛl tʃɛl.

Bencini   Tanto sospirerò
bentʃini   tanto sospirerɔ

Tanto sospirerò, tanto mi lagnerò,
tanto sospirerɔ, tanto mi laɲerɔ,

*See page 1 for unusual openings of unaccented vowels.

che intender le farò, che per lei moro!
ke intɛndɛr le faro̞, ke per lɛi mo̞ro!

Pur l'alma le dirà: "Cara, t'adoro"!
pur la̞lma le dira̞: "ka̞ra tado̞ro"!

Boïto   L'altra notte in fondo al mare, from "Mefistofele"
bo̞ito   la̞ltra no̞t:te in fo̞ndo al ma̞re   mefisto̞fele

L'altra notte in fondo al mare
la̞ltra no̞t:te in fo̞ndo a̞l ma̞re

il mio bimbo hanno gittato,
il mi̞o bi̞mbo a̞n:no dʒit:ta̞to,

or per farmi delirare diconch'io
ɔr per fa̞rmi delira̞re dikoŋki̞o

l'abbia affogato.
la̞b:bjaf:fo̞ga̞to.

L'aura è fredda, il carcer fosco,
la̞ura̞ ɛ frɛd:da, il ka̞rtʃɛr fo̞sko,

e la mesta anima mia
e la mɛsta a̞nima mi̞a

come il passero del bosco
ko̞me̞ il pa̞s:sero dɛl bo̞sko

vola via. Ah! di me pietà!
vo̞la vi̞a. a di me pjeta̞!

In funereo sopore è mia madre addormentata
in funɛreo sopo̞re ɛ mi̞a ma̞dre ad:do̞rmenta̞ta*

e per colmo dell'orrore diconch'io
e per ko̞lmo del:lor:ro̞re dikoŋki̞o

l'abbia attoscata.
la̞b:bjat:tosko̞ta.

Bononcini   L'esperto nocchiero
bonontʃini lespɛrto nok:kje̞ro

L'esperto nocchiero perchè torna al lido, appena partì?
lespɛrto nok:kje̞ro pɛrke̞ to̞rnal li̞do, ap:pe̞na partì

* See pages 1 and 2 for unusual openings of unaccented vowels.

6

Del vento cangiato, del flutto turbato s'accorse e fuggì!
dɛl vɛnto kandʒato, dɛl flut:to turbato sak:korse fud:ʒi!

Se il mar lusinghiero sapea ch'era infido,
se il mar luziŋgjero sapɛa kɛra infido,

perchè mai salpò? Salpò ma ingannato,
pɛrke mai salpo? salpo ma ingan:nato,

al lido lasciato in breve tornò!
al lido laʃato in brɛve torno!

Bononcini   Per la gloria
bonontʃini   per la glorja

Per la gloria d'adorarvi
per la glorja dadorarvi

voglio amarvi, o luci care.
voʎo amarvi, o lutʃi kare.

Amando penerò, ma sempre v'amerò,
amando penero, ma sɛmpre vamero,

sì, sì, nel mio penare.
si, si, nɛl mio penare.

Penerò, v'amerò luci care.
penero, vamero lutʃi kare.

Senza speme di diletto vano affetto
sɛntsa spɛme di dilɛt:to vano af:fɛt:to

è sospirare, ma i vostri dolci rai
ɛ sospirare, ma i vostri doltʃi rai

chi vagheggiar può mai, e non v'amare?
ki vaged:ʒar pwo mai, e non vamare?

Penerò, v'amerò, luci care!
penero, vamero, lutʃi kare!

Caccini   Amarilli, mia bella
kat:ʃini   amaril:li, mia bɛl:la

Amarilli, mia bella,
amaril:li, mia bɛl:la,

non credi, o del mio cor
non kredi, o dɛl mio kɔr

dolce desío, d' esser tu l' amor mio?
doltʃe dezio, dɛs:ser tu lamor mio?

Credilo pur: e se timor t' assale,
kredilo pur: e se timor tas:sale,

dubitar non ti vale.
dubitar non ti vale.

Aprimi il petto
apri mil pɛt:to

E vedrai scritto in core:
e vedrai skrit:to in kɔre

Amarilli è il mio amore.
amaril:li ɛ il mio amore.

Caldara   Alma del core
kaldara   alma dɛl kɔre

Alma del core, spirto dell' alma,
alma dɛl kɔre, spirto del:lalma,

sempre costante t' adorerò.
sɛmpre kostante tadorerɔ.

Sarò contento nel mio tormento
sarɔ kontɛnto nɛl mio tormɛnto

se quel bel labbro baciar potrò.
se kwel bɛl lab:bro batʃar potrɔ.

Caldara   Come raggio di sol
kaldara   kome rad:ʒo di sol

Come raggio di sol mite e sereno,
kome rad:ʒo di sol mite sereno,

sovra placidi flutti si riposa,
sovra plat∫idi flut:ti si ripoza,

mentre del mare nel profondo seno
mɛntre dɛl mare nɛl profondo sɛno

sta la tempesta ascosa:
sta la tempɛsta askoza:

così riso talor gaio e pacato di contento,
kozi rizo talor gajo e pakato di kontɛnto,

di gioia un labbro infiora,
di dʒoja un lab:bro infjora,

mentre nel suo segreto il cor piagato
mɛntre nɛl suo segrɛto il kor pjagato

s' angoscia e si martora.
saŋgo∫a   e si martora.

Caldara   Sebben, crudele
kaldara   seb:bɛn krudɛle

Sebben, crudele, mi fai languir,
seb:bɛn, krudɛle, mi fai laŋgwir,

sempre fedele ti voglio amar.
sɛmpre fedɛle ti voʎo amar.

Con la lunghezza del mio servir
kon la luŋget:sa dɛl mio sɛrvir

la tua fierezza saprò stancar.
la tua fjerɛt:sa sapro staŋkar.

Caldara   Selve amiche
kaldara   sɛlve amike

Selve amiche, ombrose piante
sɛlve amike, ombroze pjante,

fido albergo del mio core,
fido albɛrgo dɛl mio kore,

9

chiede a voi quest' alma amante
kjede a voi kwestalma amante

qualche pace al suo dolore.
kwalke patʃe al suo dolore.

Carissimi   Vittoria, mio core!
karis:simi   vit:torja, mio kore!

Vittoria, mio core!   non lagrimar più,
vit:torja, mio kore!   non lagrimar pju,

è sciolta d' Amore la vil servitù.
ɛ ʃolta damore la vil servitu.

Già l' empia a' tuoi danni
dʒa lempja twoi dan:ni

fra stuolo di sguardi,
fra stwolo di zgwardi,

con vezzi bugiardi dispose gl' inganni;
kon vet:si budʒardi dispoze ʎiŋgan:ni;

le frode, gli affanni non hanno più loco,
le frode, ʎaf:fan:ni non an:no pju loko,

del crudo suo foco è spento l' ardore!
dɛl krudo suo foko ɛ spento lardore!

Da luci ridenti non esce più strale,
da lutʃi ridɛnti non ɛʃe pju strale,

che piaga mortale nel petto m' avventi:
ke pjaga mortale nɛl pɛt:to mav:vɛnti,

nel duol, ne' tormenti io più non mi sfaccio
nɛl dwol, ne tormɛnti io pju non mi sfat:ʃo

è rotto ogni laccio, sparito il timore!
ɛ rot:toɲi   lat:ʃo, sparito il timore!

10

Catalani   Ebben, ne andrò lontana, from "La Wally"
katalani   eb:bɛn, ne andrↄ lontana la val:li

Ebben, ne andrò lontana,
eb:bɛn, ne andrↄ lontana,

come va l'eco della pia campana,
kome va lɛko del:la pia kampana,

là, fra la neve bianca, là, fra le nubi d'ôr,
la, fra la neve bjaŋka, la, fra le nubi dↄr,

laddove la speranza è rimpianto, è dolor!
lad:dove la sperantsa ɛ rimpjanto, ɛ dolↄr!

O della madre mia casa gioconda,
o del:la madre mia kaza dʒokonda,

la Wally ne andrà da te,
la val:li ne andra da te,

da te lontana assai,
da te lontanas:sai,

e forse a te non farà mai più ritorno,
e forse a te non fara mai pju ritↄrno,

nè più la rivedrai! mai più.
ne pju la rivedrai! mai pju.

Ne andrò sola e lontana
ne andrↄ sola e lontana

come l'eco della pia campana,
kome lɛko del:la pia kampana

là fra la neve bianca, n'andrò,
la, fra la neve bjaŋka, nandrↄ,

n'andrò sola e lontana
nandrↄ sola e lontana

e fra le nubi d'ôr!
e fra le nubi dↄr!

Ma fermo è il pie'! n'andiam,
ma fermo ɛ il pje! nandjam,

chè lunga è la via, n'andiam.
ke lunga ɛ la via, nandjam.

Cavalli   Donzelle, fuggite
kaval:li   dondzɛl:le, fud:ʒite

Donzelle, fuggite procace beltà! Fuggite!
dondzɛl:le, fud:ʒite prokatʃe bɛlta! fud:ʒite!

Se lucido sguardo vi penetra il core,
se lutʃido zgwardo vi pɛnetra il kɔre,

Lasciate quel' dardo del perfido amore,
laʃate kwɛl dardo dɛl pɛrfido amore,

Che insidie scaltrite tramando vi sta!
ke insidje skaltrite tramando vi sta!

Cesti   Intorno all'idol mio, from "Il Pomo d'Oro"
tʃɛsti   intorno al:lidol mio   "il pomo dɔro"

Intorno all' idol mio spirate pur,
intorno al:lidol mio spirate pur,

aure soavi e grate, e nelle guancie elette
aure soavi e grate, e nɛl:le gwan tʃe lɛt:te

baciatelo per me, cortesi aurette!
batʃatelo per me, kortezi auret:te!

Al mio ben, che riposa su l'ali della
al mio bɛn, ke ripɔza su lali dɛl:la

quiete, grati sogni assistete
kwiɛte, grati soɲi as:sistɛte

E il mio racchiuso ardore
e il mio rak:juzo ardore

svelategli per me, o larve d'amore!
zvelateʎi per me, o larve damore!

Cesti   Tu mancavi a tormentarmi
tʃɛsti   tu maŋkavi a tormentarmi

Tu mancavi a tormentarmi
tu maŋkavi a tormentarmi,

crudelissima speranza,
krudelis:sima sperantsa,

12

e con dolce rimembranza vuoì
e kon dɔltʃe rimɛmbrantsa vwɔi

di nuovo avvelenarmi.
di nwɔvo av:velenarmi.

Ancor dura la sventura
aŋkɔr dura la zventura

d'una fiamma incenerita,
duna fjam:ma intʃenerita,

la ferita ancora aperta par
la ferita aŋkɔra apɛrta par

m'avverta nuove pene.
mav:vɛrta nwɔve pɛne.

Dal rumor delle catene
dal rumɔr del:le katene

mai non vedo allontanarmi.
mai non vedo al:lontanarmi.

Cilea   Il Lamento di Federico, from "L'Arlesiana"
tʃilɛa   il lamento di federiko larlezjana

È la solita storia del pastore
ɛ la sɔlita stɔrja del pastore

Il povero ragazzo voleva raccontarla e s'addormì
il pɔvero ragat:so voleva rak:kontarla e sad:dormi

C'è nel sonno l'oblio come l'invidio!
tʃe nɛl sɔn:no loblio kɔme linvidjo!

Anch'io vorrei dormir così
aŋkio   vor:rɛi dormir kozi

Nel sonno almen l'oblio trovar!
nɛl sɔn:no almɛn loblio trovar!

La pace sol cercando io vo.
la patʃe sol tʃerkando io vo.

Vorrei poter tutto scordar!
vor:rɛi potɛr tut:to skordar!

Ma ogni sforzo è vano ;
ma ɔɲi sfɔrtso ɛ vano ;

Davanti ho sempre di lei
davanti ɔ sɛmpre di lɛi

il dolce sembiante.
il dolt͡ʃe sɛmbjante.

La pace tolta è solo a me!
la pat͡ʃe tɔlta ɛ sɔlo a me!

Perchè degg' io tanto penar?
pɛrke ded:d͡ʒio tanto penar?

Lei sempre lei mi parla al cor...
lɛi sɛmpre lɛi mi par lal kɔr...

Mi fai tanto male!   ahimè!   Fatale vision, mi lascia!
mi fai tanto male!   aimɛ!   fatale vizjɔn, mi laʃa!

Cimara   Fiocca la neve
t͡ʃimara   fjɔk:ka la neve

Lenta la neve fiocca, fiocca, fiocca.
lɛnta la neve fjɔk:ka, fjɔk:ka, fjɔk:ka.

Senti, una zana dondola pian piano.
sɛnti, una dzana dondola pjan pjano.

Un bimbo piange, il piccol dito in bocca.
un bimbo pjand͡ʒe, il pik:kol dito in bɔk:ka.

Canta una vecchia, il mento sulla mano.
kanta una vɛk:kja, il mento sul:la mano.

La vecchia canta: "Intorno al tuo lettino
la vɛk:kja kanta: "intɔrno al tuo let:tino

c'è rose e gigli come un bel giardino."
t͡ʃɛ rɔze   d͡ʒiʎi kome un bɛl d͡ʒardino."

Nel bel giardino il bimbo s'addormenta,
nɛl bɛl d͡ʒardino il bimbo sad:dormɛnta,

fiocca la neve lenta, fiocca la neve.
fjɔk:ka la neve lɛnta, fjɔk:ka la neve.

14

Donaudy   O del mio amato ben
donaudi   o dɛl mio amato bɛn

O del mio amato ben perduto incanto!
o dɛl mio amato bɛn pɛrduto iŋkanto!

Lungi è dagli occhi miei chi m'era gloria e vanto!
lundʒi ɛ da ʎɔk:ki mjɛi ki mɛra glɔrja e vanto!

Or per le mute stanze sempre la cerco e chiamo
or per le mute stantse sɛmpre la tʃerko e kjamo

con pieno il cor di speranze ma cerco invan,
kon pjɛno il kor di sperantse ma tʃerko invan,

chiamo invan! E il pianger m'è sì caro,
kjamo invan! e il pjandʒɛr mɛ si karo,

che di pianto sol nutro il cor.
ke di pjanto sol nutro il kor.

Mi sembra, senza lei, triste ogni loco.
mi sɛmbra, sɛntsa lɛi, triste ɔni lɔko.

Notte mi sembra il giorno, mi sembra gelo il foco.
nɔt:te mi sɛmbra il dʒɔrno, mi sɛmbra dʒɛlo il fɔko.

Se pur tal volta spero di darmi ad altra cura,
se pur tal vɔlta spɛro di darmi ad altra kura,

sol mi tormenta un pensiero: ma, senza lei, che farò?
sol mi tormɛnta un pɛnsjero, ma, sɛntsa lɛi, ke farɔ?

Mi par così la vita vana cosa senza il mio ben.
mi par kozi la vita vana kɔza sɛntsa il mio bɛn.

By permission of G. Ricordi & Co.,
Milan, Copyright Owner

Donizetti   O mio Fernando, from "La Favorita"
donidzet:ti o mio fɛrnando la favorita

Fia dunque vero.. oh Ciel! desso Fernando
fia duŋkwe vɛro o tʃɛl! des:so fɛrnando

lo sposo di Leonora! Ah!
lo spɔzo di leonɔra! a!

Tutto mel dice.. e dubbia l'alma ancora
tut:to mel ditʃe e dub:bja lalma aŋkɔra

all' inattesa gioja.
al:linat:teza dʒɔja.

15

Oh Dio!   sposarlo... Oh mia vergogna estrema...
o   dio   spozarlo   o mia vergoɲa estrema...

in doteal prode recar il diʂonor!
in doteal prode rekar il dizonor!

no... mai dovessi esecrarmi...fuggir!
no mai doves:si ezekrarmi, fud:ʒir!

saprà in brev' ora chi sia la donna che cotanto adora.
saprа in brevora ki sia la don:na ke kotanto adora.

O mio Fernando!   della terra il trono
o mio fernando!   del:la ter:ra il trono

A possederti avrai donato il cor;
a pos:sederti avrai donato il kor;

Ma puro l'amor mio come il perdono,
ma puro lamor mio kome il perdono,

Dannato ahì lassa! e a disperato orror...
dan:nato ai las:sa! e a disperator:ror...

Il ver fia noto, e in tuo dispregio estremo
il ver fia noto, e in tuo dispredʒo estremo

La pena avrommi che maggior si de'! ah!
la pena avrom:mi ke mad:ʒor si de! a!

Se il giusto tuo disdegno allor, allor fia scemo.
se il dʒusto tuo dizdeɲo al:lor, al:lor fia ʃemo.

Piombi, gran Dio, ... la folgor tua su me.
pjombi, gran dio,   la folgor tua su me.

Ah, se fia scemo il tuo disdegno, piombi, o Dio,
a, se fia ʃemo il tuo dizdeɲo, pjombi, o dio,

la folgor tua su me!
la folgor tua su me!

Su, crudeli... e chi v'arresta?
su krudeli.... e ki var:resta?

Scritto è in cielo il mio dolor!
skrit:to e in tʃelo il mio dolor!

Su, venite, ell' è una festa, Sparsa l'ara sia di fior,
su, venite, el:le una festa,   sparsa lara sia di fjor,

Già la tomba a me s'appresta, E coperta in negro vel.
dʒa la tomba a me sap:presta, e koperta in negro vel.

Sia la trista fidanzata,
sia la trista fidantsata,

Che rejetta, disperata, Non avrà perdono in ciel
ke rejɛt:ta disperata, non avra pɛrdono in tʃɛl

maledetta, disperata, non avrà perdono in ciel!
maledɛt:ta, disperata, non avra pɛrdono in tʃɛl!

Donizetti   Regnava nel silenzio, from "Lucia di Lammermoor"
donidzɛt:ti reɲava nɛl silɛntsjo   lutʃia di lam:mermur

Regnava nel silenzio alta la notte bruna,
reɲava nɛl silɛntsjo alta la nɔt:te bruna,

colpía la fonte un pallido raggio di tetra Luna,
kolpia la fɔnte un pal:lido rad:ʒo di tɛtra luna,

quando un sommesso gemito fra l'aure udir si fe',
kwando un som:mes:so dʒɛmito fra laure udir si fe,

ed ecco su quel margine l'ombra mostrarsi a me, ah!
ed ɛk:ko su kwɛl mardʒine lombra mostrarsi a me, a!

qual di chi parla muoversi il labbro suo vedea,
kwal di ki parla mwɔvɛrsi il lab:bro suo vedea,

e con la mano esanime chiamarmi a sé parea;
e kon la mano ezanime kjamarmi a se parea;

stette un momento immobile, poi ratta dileguò
stɛt:te un momɛnto im:mobile, pɔɪ rat:ta dilegwɔ

e l'onda pria si limpida di sangue rosseggiò.
e londa pria si limpida di saŋgwe ros:sed:ʒɔ.

Quando rapita in estasi del più cocente ardore
kwando rapita in ɛstazi dɛl pju kotʃɛnte ardore

col favellar del core mi giura eterna fé
kol favel:lar dɛl kɔre mi dʒura etɛrna fe

gli affanni miei dimentico gioja diviene il pianto,
ʎaf:fan:ni mjɛi dimɛntiko dʒɔja divjɛne il pjanto,

parmi, che a lui d'accanto si schiuda il ciel per me, ah!
parmi, ke a lui dak:kanto si skjuda il tʃɛl per me, a!

Donizetti   Spirto gentil, from " La Favorita"
donidzɛt:ti   spirto dʒɛntil   la favorita

Spirto gentil, ne' sogni miei
spirto dʒɛntil, ne soɲi mjɛi

brillasti un dì, ma ti perdei,
bril:lasti un di, ma ti pɛrdei,

fuggi dal cor mentita speme,
fud:ʒi dal kɔr mɛntita spɛme,

larve d'amor, fuggite insieme, larve d'amor!
larve damɔr, fud:ʒite insjɛme, larve damɔr!

A te d'accanto del genitore
a te dak:kanto dɛl dʒenitɔre

scordava il pianto, la patria, il Ciel!
skɔrdava il pjanto, la patria, il tʃɛl!

donna sleal, in tanto amore,
dɔn:na zleal, in tanto amɔre,

segnasti il core d'onta mortal, ahimè!
seɲastil   kɔre dɔnta mortal, aimɛ!

Donizetti   Una furtiva lagrima, from "L'Elisir d'Amore"
donidzɛt:ti una furtiva lagrima   lelizir damɔre

Una furtiva lagrima negl' occhi suoi spuntò:
Una furtiva lagrima neʎɔk:ki   swɔi spuntɔ,

quelle festose giovani, invidiar sembrò;
kwɛl:le festɔze dʒɔvani, invidiar sɛmbrɔ;

che più cercando io vo? m'ama, si m'ama, lo vedo!
ke pju tʃɛrkando io vo? mama, si mama, lo vedo!

un solo istante i palpiti del suo bel cor sentir;
un sɔlo istante i palpiti dɛl suo bɛl kɔr sɛntir;

i miei sospir confondere, per poco a' suoi sospir,
i mjɛi sospir konfɔndere, per pɔko a swɔi sospir,

i palpiti sentir, confondere i miei, coi suoi sospir.
i palpiti sɛntir, konfɔndere i mjɛi, kɔi swɔi sospir.

Cielo si può morir; di più non chiedo!
tʃɛlo si pwɔ morir; di pju non kjɛdo!

18

Durante   Danza, danza, fanciulla
durante   dᵃntsa, dᵃntsa, fantʃul:la

Danza, fanciulla, al mio cantar;
dᵃntsa, fantʃul:la, al mi̯o kantar̪;

danza, fanciulla gentile, al mio cantar.
dᵃntsa, fantʃul:la dʒentile, al mi̯o kantar̪.

Gira leggera, sottile al suono,
dʒira led:ʒera, sot:tile al swono,

al suono dell'onde del mar.
al swono del:londe del mar.

Senti il vago rumore dell' aura scherzosa
sɛn til vago rumore del:laura skɛrtsoza

che parla al core con languido suon,
ke par lal kore kon laŋgwido swon,

e che invita a danzar, senza posa,
e ke invita dantsar, sɛntsa poza,

che invita a danzar.
ke invita dantsar̪.

Durante   Vergin, tutta amor
durante   vɛrdʒin, tut:tamor

Vergin, tutta amor, O Madre di bontade,
vɛrdʒin, tut:tamor, o madre di bontade,

o Madre pia, ascolta, dolce Maria,
o madre pi̯a, askolta, doltʃe maria,

la voce del peccator.
la votʃe dɛl pek:kator.

Il pianto suo ti muova,
il pi̯anto su̯o ti mwova,

giungano a te i suoi lamenti,
dʒuŋgano a te i swoi lamenti,

suo duol, suoi tristi accenti
su̯o dwol, swoi tristi at:ʃenti

oda pietoso quel tuo cor.
oda pi̯etozo kwɛl tu̯o kor.

Flotow   M' apparì tutt' amor, from "Martha"
floto   map:pari tut:tamor   marta

M' apparì tutt' amor, il mio sguardo l' incontrò;
map:pari tut:tamor, il mio zgwardo liŋkontro;

bella si che il mio cor ansioso a lei volò;
bel:la si ke il mio kor anzjozo a lei volo;

mi ferì, m'invaghì quell' angelica beltà,
mi feri, miŋvagi kwel:landʒelika belta,

sculta in cor dall' amor, cancellarsi non potrà:
skulta in kor dal:lamor, kantʃel:larsi non potra:

il pensier di poter palpitar con lei d' amor,
il pensjer di poter palpitar kon lei damor,

può sopir il martir che m' affanna e strazia il cor,
pwo sopir il martir ke maf:fan:na e stratsja il kor,

Marta, Marta, tu sparisti, e il mio cor col tuo n' andò!
marta, marta, tu sparisti, e il mio kor kol tuo nando!

tu la pace mi rapisti, di dolor io morirò,
tu la patʃe mi rapisti, di dolor io moriro,

ah, di dolor morrò, si, morrò!
a, di dolor mor:ro, si, mor:ro!

Flotow   Qui sola vergin rosa, from "Martha"
floto   kwi sola verdʒin roza   marta

Qui sola vergin rosa, come puoi tu fiorir?
kwi sola verdʒin roza, kome pwoi tu fjorir?

Ancora mezzo ascosa e presso già morir!
aŋkora med:ʒo askoza e pres:so dʒa morir!

Non ha per te rugiade, già colta sei dal gel!
non a per te rudʒade, dʒa kolta sei dal dʒel!

Il capo tuo già cade, chino sul verde stel.
il kapo tuo dʒa kade, kino sul verde stel.

Perchè sola ignorata languir nel tuo giardin,
perke sola iɲorata laŋgwir nel tuo dʒardin,

dal vento tormentata in preda a un rio destin.
dal vento tormentata in preda un rio destin.

Sul cespite tremante ti colgo, giovin fior!
sul t∫ɛspite tremante ti kɔlgo, dʒovin fjor!

Su questo core amante così morrai d'amor.
su kwesto kɔre amante kozi mor:rai damor.

Giordani   Caro mio ben
dʒordani   karo mio bɛn

Caro mio ben, credimi almen,
karo mio bɛn, kredimi almɛn,

senza di te languisce il cor.
sɛntsa di te laŋgwi∫e il kɔr.

Il tuo fedel sospira ognor.
il tuo fedɛl sospira ɔŋɔr.

Cessa, crudel, tanto rigor!
t∫ɛs:sa, krudɛl, tanto rigɔr!

Giordano   Nemico della patria? from "Andrea Chenier"
dʒordano   nemiko del:la patria   andrɛa ∫eɲe

Nemico della patria?! È vecchia fiaba che beatamente
nemiko del:la patria! ɛ vɛk:kja fjaba ke beatamente

ancor la beve il popolo. Nato a Castantinopoli?
aŋkɔr la bɛve il pɔpolo. nato a kostantinɔpoli?

Straniero! Studiò a Saint Cyr?
stranjero! studjɔ a sɛn sir?

Soldato! Traditore! Di Dumouriez un complice!
soldato! traditɔre! di dumurje un kɔmplit∫e!

È poeta? Sovvertitor di cuori e di costumi!
ɛ pɔɛta? sov:vɛrtitɔr di kwɔri e di kostumi!

Un dì m'era di gioia passar fra gli odî e le vendette,
un di mɛra di dʒɔja pas:sar fra ʎɔdi e le vɛndet:te,

puro, innocente e forte! Gigante, mi credea!
puro, in:not∫ɛnte forte! dʒigante, mi kredea!

21

Son sempre un servo!   Ho mutato padrone!
son sɛmpre un sɛrvo!   ɔ mutato padrone!

Un servo obbediente di violenta passione!   Ah, peggio!
un sɛrvob:bedjɛnte di vjolɛnta pas:sjɔne!   a, pɛd:ʒo!

Uccido e tremo, e mentre uccido, io piango!
ut:ʃido e trɛmo, e mɛntre ut:ʃido, io pjaŋgo!

Io della Redentrice figlio pel primo ho udito il grido
io del:la redɛntritʃe fiʎo pel pri mo udito il grido

suo pel mondo ed ho al suo il mio grido unito. . . .
suo pel mondo ed ɔ al suo il mio grido unito . . .

Or smarrita ho la fede nel sognato destino?
or zmar:rita ɔ la fɛde nɛl soɲato destino?

Com' era irradiato di gloria il mio cammino!
komɛra ir:radjato di glɔrja il mio kam:mino!

La coscienza nei cuor ridestar de le genti!
la koʃɛntsa nei kwor ridestar de le dʒɛnti!

Raccogliere le lagrime dei vinti e sofferenti!
rak:koʎere le lagrime dei vinti e sof:ferɛnti!

Fare del mondo un Pantheon!   Gli uomini in dii mutare
fare dɛl mondo un panteon!   ʎi womini in dii mutare

e in un sol bacio e abbraccio tutte le genti amar!
e in un sol batʃo e ab:brat:ʃo tut:te le dʒɛnti amar!

Gluck   Che farò senza Eudidice, from "Orfeo"
gluk   ke farɔ sɛntsa euriditʃe   orfɛo

Ahimè!   dove trascorsi, ove mi spinse un delirio d' amor?
aimɛ!   dove traskorsi, ɔve mi spinse un delirjo damɔr?

Sposa Euridice Consorte
spɔza euriditʃe konsɔrte

Ah! più non vive la chiamo invan!
a! pju non vive la kjamo invan!

Misero me! la perdo e di nuovo e per sempre! oh legge!
mizero me! la pɛrdo e di nwɔvo e per sɛmpre! o led:ʒe!

oh morte! oh ricordo crudel!
o mɔrte! o rikɔrdo krudɛl!

Non ho soccorso non m' avanza consiglio io veggo solo
non ɔ sok:kɔrso non mavantsa konsiʎo io vɛg:go sɔlo

(Oh fiera vista!)
o fjɛra vista!

il luttoso aspetto dell' orrido mio stato!
il lut:tɔzo aspɛt:to del:lɔr:rido mio stato!

Saziati, sorte rea son disperato!
satsjati, sɔrte rɛa son disperato!

Che farò senza Euridice? Dove andrò senza il mio ben?
ke farɔ sɛntsa euriditʃe? dove andrɔ sɛntsa il mio bɛn?

Euridice! oh Dio! rispondi.
euriditʃe! o dio rispɔndi.

Io son pur il tuo fedele,
io son pur il tuo fedɛle,

Ah! non m' avanza più soccorso,
a! non mavantsa pju sok:kɔrso,

più speranza nè dal mondo, nè dal ciel!
pju sperantsa ne dal mɔndo, ne dal tʃɛl!

Gluck	O del mio dolce ardor, from "Paride ed Elena"
gluk	o dɛl mio dɔltʃe ardɔr paride ed ɛlena

O del mio dolce ardor bramato oggetto,
o dɛl mio dɔltʃe ardɔr bramato od:ʒɛt:to,

L' aura che tu respiri, alfin respiro,
laura ke tu respiri, alfin respiro,

Ovunque il guardo io giro,
ovuŋkwe il gwardo io dʒiro,

Le tue vaghe   sembianze Amore in me dipinge:
le tue vage sɛmbjantse amore in me dipindʒe,

Il mio pensier si finge
il mio pɛnsjɛr si findʒe

Le più liete speranze;
le pju ljɛte sperantse;

23

E nel desio che così m'empie il petto
e nɛl dezi̯o ke kozi mempi̯e il pɛt:to

Cerco te, chiamo te, spero e sospiro. Ah!
tʃɛrko te, kjamo te, spɛro e sospiro. a!

Gluck   Spiagge amate, from "Paride ed Elena"
gluk   spi̯ad:ʒe amate   paride ed ɛlena

Spiagge amate ove talora
spi̯ad:ʒe amate ɔve talɔra

l'idol mio lieto s'aggira,
lidol mi̯o li̯eto sad:ʒira,

ruscelletti, ove si mira
ruʃel:let:ti, ɔve si mira

quando infiora il crine o il sen,
kwando infjɔra il krine ɔ il sen,

chiari fonti, ove si bagna,
kjari fɔnti, ɔve si baɲa,

erbe in cui posa le piante,
ɛrbe in kui pɔza le pi̯ante,

voi pietose a un core amante,
vɔi pi̯etɔze a un kɔre amante,

dite voi che fa il mio ben,
dite vɔi ke fa il mi̯o bɛn,

chiari fonti, ruscelletti.
kjari fɔnti, ruʃel:let:ti.

Handel   Ah! mio cor!, from "Alcina"
             a mi̯o kɔr   altʃina

Ah! mio cor, schernito sei.
a mi̯o kɔr, skɛrnito sɛi.

Stelle, Dei, Nume d'amore! traditore,
stɛl:le, dɛi, nume damɔre! traditɔre,

24

t' amo tanto, puoi lasciarmi sola in pianto?
ta̱mo ta̱nto, pwo̱i la∫armi so̱la in pja̱nto?

Oh!Dei! puoi lasciarmi, perchè?
o de̱i! pwo̱i la∫armi, pɛrke̱?

Handel   Alma mia (Aria di Floridante from Floridante)
            a̱lma mi̱a   floridante

Alma mia, sì, sol tu sei la mia gloria, il mio diletto.
a̱lma mi̱a, si sol tu se̱i la mi̱a glo̱rja, il mi̱o dilɛ̱t:to.

Dal poter de' sommi Dei più bel dono io non aspetto.
dal potɛ̱r de so̱m:mi de̱i pju bɛl do̱no i̱o non aspɛ̱t:to.

Handel   Care selve, from "Atalanta"
            ka̱re se̱lve   atala̱nta

Care selve, ombre beate,
ka̱re se̱lve, o̱mbre bea̱te,

vengo in traccia del mio cor.
vɛ̱ngo̱ in tra̱t:∫a dɛl mi̱o kɔr.

Handel   Lascia ch' io pianga, from "Rinaldo"
            la∫a   ki̱o pja̱nga   rina̱ldo

Armida, dispietata colla forza d' abisso rapimmi
armi̱da, dispjeta̱ta ko̱l:la fo̱rtsa dabi̱s:so rapi̱m:mi

al caro ciel de' miei contenti,
al ka̱ro t∫ɛl de mjɛ̱i kontɛ̱nti,

e qui, con duolo eterno,
e kwi, kon dwo̱lo etɛ̱rno,

vivo mi tiene in tormentoso inferno!
vi̱vo mi tjɛ̱ne in tormento̱zo infɛ̱rno!

Signor, deh! per pietà, lasciami piangere!
si̱nor, dɛ! per pjeta̱, la∫ami pja̱ndʒere!

25

Lascia ch' io pianga la cruda sorte,
laʃa kio pjaŋga la kruda sɔrte,

e che sospiri la libertà,
e ke sospiri la liberta,

Il duolo infranga queste ritorte,
il dwɔlo infraŋga kweste ritɔrte,

de' miei martiri sol per pietà
de mjɛi martiri sol per pjeta!

Lusinghe più care, from " Alessandro "
           luziŋge pju kare   ales:sandro

Ne trionfa d' Alessandro, trionfa ancor quest' alma,
ne trionfa dales:sandro, trionfaŋkor kwestalma,

ma funesta Zisaura ogni mia palma ma sentirò
ma funɛsta tsizaura oɲi mia palma ma sentiro

tutte d' amor le vie, perchè allettato il vincitore
tut:te damor le vie, pɛrke al:let:tato il vintʃitɔre

amante, infido altrui, sia solo a me costante.
amante, infido altrui, sia solo a me kostante.

Lusinghe più care, d' amor veri dardi, vezzose volate
luziŋge pju kare, damor veri dardi, vet:sɔze volate

sul labbro, nei guardi, e tutta involate l' altrui libertà,
sul lab:bro, nei gwardi, e tut:ta involate laltrui libɛrta,

Gelosi sospetti, diletti con pene, fra gioie e tormenti,
dʒelozi sospɛt:ti, dilɛt:ti kon pene, fra dʒɔje tormɛnti,

momenti di spene voi l' armi sarete di vaga beltà.
momɛnti di spɛne voi larmi sarete di vaga bɛlta.

Handel   Ombra mai fu, from " Serse "
           ombra mai fu   sɛrse

Frondi tenere e belle
frondi tɛnere e bɛl:le

del mio platano amato, per voi risplende il fato
dɛl mio platano amato, per vɔi risplɛnde il fato

26

tuoni, lampi e procelle non v'oltraggino mai
twọni, lampi e protʃɛl:le non voltradːʒino mai

la cara pace, nè giunga a profanarvi,
la kạra pạtʃe, ne dʒụṇga profanạrvi,

austro rapace!
ạustro rapạtʃe!

Ombra mai fu di vegetabile,
ọmbra mại fu di vedʒetạbile,

cara ed amabile, soave più.
kạra ed amạbile, soạve pju.

Handel   Sì, tra i ceppi, from "Berenice"
               si, trại tʃep:pi   berenịtʃe

Sì tra i ceppi e le ritorte
si, trại tʃep:pi e le ritọrte

La mia fè tra le ritorte,
la mịa fe tra le ritọrte,

La mia fè risplenderà.
la mịa fe risplɛnderạ.

Nò, nè pur la stessa morte
nɔ, ne pur la stɛs:sa mọrte

Il mio foco estinguerà.
il mịo fọkọ estiṇgwerạ.

Legrenzi   Che fiero costume
legrɛntsi   ke fjẹro kostụme

Che fiero costume d'aligero nume,
ke fjẹro kostụme dalịdʒero nụme,

che a forza di pene si faccia adorar!
ke ạ fọrtsa di pẹne si fatːʃadorạr!

E pur nell'ardore il dio traditore
e pur nel:lardọre il dịo traditọre

un vago sembiante mi fe' idolatrar.
un vago sɛmbjante mi fe idolatrar.

Che crudo destino che un cieco bambino
ke krudo destino ke un tʃeko bambino

con bocca di latte si faccia stimar!
kon bok:ka di lat:te si fat:ʃa stimar!

Ma questo tiranno con barbaro inganno,
ma kwɛsto tir:rano kon barbaro ingan:no,

entrando per gli occhi, mi fe' sospirar.
ɛntrando per ʎok:ki mi fe sospirar.

Leoncavallo Prologue, from ''Pagliacci''
leonkaval:lo   paʎat:ʃi

Si può? Si può? Signore! Signori!
si pwɔ si pwɔ siɲore   siɲori

Scusatemi se da sol mi presento.
skuzatemi se da sol mi prezɛnto.

Io sono il Prologo:
io sono il prɔlogo,

Poichè in iscena ancor
poike in iʃɛnaŋkor

le antiche maschere mette l'autore;
le antike maskere mɛt:te lautore;

in parte ei vuol riprendere le vecchie usanze,
in partei   vwol riprɛndere le vɛk:kje uzantse,

e a voi di nuovo inviami.
e a voi di nwɔvo inviami.

Ma non per dirvi come pria:
ma non per dirvi kome pria:

''Le lacrime che noi versiam son false!
le lakrime ke noi vɛrsjam son false!

Degli spasimi e de' nostri martir non allarmatevi.''
deʎi spazimi e de nostri martir non al:larmatevi.''

No! No! L'autore ha cercato
nɔ! nɔ! lautore a tʃɛrkato

28

invece pingervi uno squarcio di vita.
invetʃe pindʒɛrvi uno skwartʃo di vita.

Egli ha per massima sol che l'artista è un uom
eʎa   per mas:sima sol ke lartista ɛ un wom

e che per gli uomini scrivere ei deve.
e ke per   ʎwomini skriverei deve.

Ed al vero ispiravasi.
ed al vero ispiravasi.

Un nido di memorie in fondo a l'anima cantava un giorno,
un nido di memorje in fondo a lanima kantava un dʒorno,

ed ei con vere lacrime scrisse,
ed ei kon vere lakrime skris:se,

e i singhiozzi il tempo gli battevano!
e i siŋgjot:si il tɛmpo ʎi bat:tevano!

Dunque, vedrete amar sì come s'amano gli esseri umani;
duŋkwe, vedrete amar si kome samano ʎɛs:seri umani;

vedrete de l'odio i tristi frutti, Del dolor gli spasimi,
vedrete de lodjo i tristi frut:ti, dɛl dolor ʎi spazimi,

urli di rabbia, udrete e risa ciniche!
urli di rab:bja udrete e riza tʃinike!

E voi, piuttosto, che le vostre povere gabbane d'istrioni,
e voi, pjut:tosto, ke le vostre povere gab:bane distrjoni,

le nostr'anime considerate,
le nostranime konsiderate,

poichè siam uomini di carne e d'ossa,
poike sjam womini di karne e dos:sa,

e che di quest'orfano mondo
e ke di kwestorfano mondo

al pari di voi spiriamo l'aere!
al pari di voi spirjamo laere!

Il concetto vi dissi...Or ascoltate com'egli è svolto.
il kontʃɛt:to vi dis:si, or askoltate komeʎɛ zvolto.

Andiam, Incominciate!
andjam, iŋkomintʃate!

Leoncavallo   Vesti la giubba, from "Pagliacci"
leonkavaˈl:lo   vesti la dʒubˈba   paˈʎatˈʃi

Vesti la giubba e la faccia infarina.
vesti la dʒubˈba e la fatˈʃa infarina.

La gente paga e rider vuole qua.
la dʒɛnte paga e ridɛr vwole kwa.

E se Arlecchin t'invola Colombina,
e se arlekˈkin tinvola kolombina,

ridi, Pagliaccio e ognun applaudirà!
ridi, paˈʎatˈʃo e oɲun apˈplaudira!

Tramuta in lazzi lo spasmo ed il pianto;
tramuta in ladˈzi lo spazmo ed il pjanto;

in una smorfia il singhiozzo e'l dolor Ah!
in una zmorfja il siŋgjotˈso el dolor a!

Ridi, Pagliaccio, sul tuo amore infranto!
ridi, paˈʎatˈʃo,   sul tuo amore infranto!

Ridi del duol che t'avvelena il cor!
ridi dɛl dwol ke   tavˈvelena il kor!

Lotti   Pur dicesti, o bocca bella
lotˈti   pur ditʃesti, o bokˈka bɛlˈla

Pur dicesti, o bocca, bocca bella,
pur ditʃesti, o bokˈka, bokˈka bɛlˈla,

quel soave e caro sì,
kwɛl soave karo si.

sì, che fa tutto il mio piacer.
si, ke fa tutˈto il mio pjatʃɛr.

Per onor di sua facella
per onor di sua fatʃɛlˈla

con un bacio Amor t'aprì,
kon un batʃo amor tapri,

dolce fonte del goder, ah!
doltʃe fonte dɛl godɛr, a!

Marcello   Il mio bel foco
martʃɛl:lo   il mi̯o bɛl fɔko

Il mio bel foco, o lontano o vicino
il mi̯o bɛl fɔko, o lontano vitʃino

ch' esser poss' io, senza cangiar mai tempre
kɛs:ser pɔs:si̯o, sɛntsa kandʒar mai tɛmpre

per voi, care pupille, arderà sempre.
per vo̯i, kare pupil̯:le, ardera̯ sɛmpre.

Quella fiamma che m' accende,
kwɛl:la fi̯am:ma ke matʃɛnde,

piace tanto all' alma mia,
pi̯atʃe ta̯nto‿al:lalma mi̯a,

che giammai s' estinguerà.
ke dʒam:mai̯ sestiŋgwera̯.

E se il fato a voi mi rende,
e se‿il fato‿a vo̯i mi rɛnde,

vaghi rai del mio bel sole,
vagi ra̯i dɛl mi̯o bɛl sɔle,

altra luce ella non vuole
a̯ltra lutʃɛl:la non vwɔle

nè voler giammai potrà.
ne volɛr dʒam:mai̯ potra̯.

Mascagni   Voi lo sapete, from "Cavalleria Rusticana"
maskaɲi   vo̯i lo sapɛte   kaval:leri̯a rustika̯na

Voi lo sapete, o mamma, prima d' andar soldato
vo̯i lo sapɛte̯, o̯ ma̯m:ma, pri̯ma dandar soldato

Turiddu aveva a Lola eterna fè giurato.
turid̯:du ave̯va lo̯la etɛrna fe dʒurato.

Tornò, la seppe sposa;
tornɔ, la sep̯:pe spɔza;

e con un nuovo amore volle spegner la fiamma
e kon un nwɔvo‿amo̯re vɔl:le speɲer la fi̯a̯m:ma

che gli bruciava il core m' amò, l' amai, ah!
ke ʎi brutʃava̯ il kɔre mamo̯, lama̯i, a!

31

Quell' invida d'ogni delizia mia,
kwel:l̲invida d̲o̲ɲi delit̲sja mi̲a,

del suo sposo dimentica,
dɛl su̲o spo̲zo dime̲ntika,

arse di gelosia, Me l'ha rapito.
a̲rse di d̲zelozi̲a, me la rapi̲to.

Priva dell' onor mio rimango:
pri̲va del:lono̲r mi̲o rima̲ŋgo,

Lola e Turiddu s'amano, io piango!
lo̲la̲ e turid̲:du sa̲mano, i̲o pja̲ŋgo!

Monteverdi   Lasciatemi morire
monteve̲rdi   laʃa̲temi mori̲re

Lasciatemi morire!
laʃa̲temi mori̲re!

e che volete che mi conforte
e ke vole̲te ke mi konfo̲rte

in così dura sorte,
in kozi̲ du̲ra so̲rte,

in così gran martire?
in kozi̲ gran marti̲re?

Mozart   Aprite un po' quegl'occhi, from "Le Nozze di Figaro"
              apri̲te̲ u̲n pɔ kweʎɔ̲k:ki   le nɔ̲t:se di fi̲garo

Aprite un po' quegl'occhi, Uomini incauti e schiocchi,
apri̲te̲ un pɔ kweʎɔ̲k:ki, wo̲miniŋka̲uti̲ e ʃɔ̲k:ki,

Guardate queste femmine, guardate cosa son!
gwarda̲te kwe̲ste fe̲m:mine, gwarda̲te kɔ̲za son!

Queste chiamate dee, Dagli ingannati sensi,
kwe̲ste kjama̲te dɛɛ, daʎingan:na̲ti sɛ̲nsi,

A cui tributa incensi La debole ragion.
a ku̲i tribu̲ta̲ intʃɛ̲nsi la de̲bole radzo̲n.

Son streghe che incantano per farci penar,
son strege ke iŋkantano per fartʃi penar,

Sirene che cantano per farci affogar,
sirɛne ke kantano per fartʃi af:fogar,

Civette che allettano per trarci le piume,
tʃivɛt:te ke al:let:tano per trartʃi le pjume,

Comete che brillano per toglierci il lume,
komɛte ke bril:lano per toʎɛrtʃil lume,

Son rose spinose, Son volpi vezzose,
son roze spinoze, son vɔlpi vet:soze,

Son orse benigne, Colombe, maligne, Maestre d'inganni,
son ɔrse beniɲe, kolombe, maliɲe, maɛstre diŋgan:ni,

Amiche d'affanni, Che fingono, mentono, amore
amike daf:fani, ke fiŋgono, mentono, amore

Non senton pietà, non senton pietà, no.
non sɛnton pjeta, non sɛnton pjeta, nɔ.

Il resto nol dico, già ognuno lo sa.
il rɛsto nol diko, dʒa oɲuno lo sa.

Mozart   Batti, batti, o bel Masetto, from "Don Giovanni"
              bat:ti, bat:ti, o bɛl mazet:to   don dʒovan:ni

Batti, batti, o bel Masetto, la tua povera Zerlina:
bat:ti, bat:ti, o bɛl mazet:to, la tua pɔvera dzɛrlina,

starò qui come agnellina le tue botte ad aspettar.
starɔ kwi kome aɲel:lina le tue bɔt:te ad aspet:tar.

Lascierò straziarmi il crine,
laʃerɔ stratsjarmil krine,

lascierò cavarmi gli occhi,
laʃerɔ kavarmi ʎɔk:ki,

le care tue manine lieta poi saprò baciar.
le kare tue manine ljeta pɔi saprɔ batʃar.

Ah, lo vedo non hai core.
a, lo vedo non ai kore.

33

Pace, pace, o vita mia!
patʃe, patʃe, o vita mia!

In contento ed allegria notte e dì vogliam passar.
in kontɛnto ed al:legria nɔt:te di voʎam pas:sar.

Mozart   Dalla sua pace, from "Don Giovanni"
                dal:la sua patʃe   don dʒovan:ni

Dalla sua pace la mia dipende,
dal:la sua patʃe la mia dipɛnde,

quel che a lei piace vita mi rende,
kwɛl ke a lɛi pjatʃe vita mi rɛnde,

quel che le incresce, morte mi dà,
kwɛl ke le iŋkreʃe, mɔrte mi da,

S'ella sospira, sospiro anch'io,
sɛl:la sospira, sospiro aŋkio,

è mia quell'ira, quel pianto è mio;
ɛ mia kwel:lira, kwɛl pjanto ɛ mio;

e non ho bene, s'ella non l'ha!
e non ɔ bɛne, sɛl:la non la!

Mozart   Deh vieni alla finestra, from "Don Giovanni"
                dɛ vjɛni al:la finɛstra   don dʒovan:ni

Deh vieni alla finestra, o mio tesoro,
dɛ, vjɛni al:la finɛstra, o mio tezɔro,

Deh vieni a consolar il pianto mio!
de vjɛni a konsolar il pjanto mio!

Se neghi a me di dar qualche ristoro,
se nɛgi a me di dar kwalke ristɔro,

Davanti agli occhi tuoi morir vogl'io!
davanti a ʎɔk:ki twɔi morir voʎio!

Tu ch'hai la bocca dolce più del miele,
tu kai la bɔk:ka dɔltʃe pju dɛl mjɛle,

34

Tu che il zucchero porti in mezzo al core!
tu ke il dzuk:kero pọrti in mɛd:zọ al kọre!

Non esser, gioja mia, con me crudele!
non ɛs:ser, dʒọja mịa, kon me krudɛle!

Lasciati almen veder, mio bell' amore!
laʃati almɛn vedɛr, mịo bɛl:lamọre!

Mozart   Deh, vieni, non tardar, from "Le Nozze di Figaro"
          dɛ, vjɛni non tardạr   le nọt:se di fịgaro

Giunse alfin il momento che godrò senza affanno
dʒunse alfịn il momẹnto ke godrọ sɛntsaf:fạn:no

in braccio all' idol mio!   Timide cure!
in brạt:ʃo al:lịdol mịo!   tịmide kụre!

uscite dal mio petto:
uʃịte dal mịo pɛt:to,

a turbar non venite il mio diletto!
a turbạr non venịtẹ il mịo dilɛt:to!

Oh! come par, che all' amoroso foco
o, kọme par, ke al:lamorọzo fọko

l' amenità del loco, la terra e il ciel risponda!
lamenitạ dɛl lọko, la tɛr:rạ e ịl tʃɛl rispọnda!

Come la notte i furti miei seconda!
kọme la nọt:te i fụrti mjẹi sekọnda!

Deh, vieni, non tardar, o gioja bella!
dɛ, vjɛni, non tardạr, o dʒọja bɛl:la!

vieni ove amore per goder t' appella
vjɛni ọve amọre per godẹr tap:pɛl:la

finchè non splende in ciel notturna face,
fiŋkẹ non splɛndẹ in tʃɛl nọt:turna fatʃe,

finchè l' aria è ancor bruna, e il mondo tace.
fiŋkẹ larjạ ɛ aŋkor brụna, ẹ il mọndo tạtʃe.

Qui mormora il ruscel quì scherza l' aura,
kwi mọrmorạ ịl ruʃɛl kwi skɛrtsa lạura,

che col dolce sussurro il cor ristaura;
ke kol dọltʃe sus:sụr:rọ il kọr ristạura,

Qui ridono i fioretti, e l'erba è fresca!
kwi ridono i fjorɛt:ti, e lɛrba ɛ freska!

ai piaceri d'amor qui tutto adesca.
ai pjatʃeri damor kwi tut:to adeska.

Vieni, ben mio! tra queste piante ascose.
vjɛni, bɛn mio! tra kweste pjante askoze.

ti vo' la fronte incoronar di rose.
ti vɔ la fronte iŋkoronar di roze!

Mozart   Dove sono, from "Le Nozze di Figaro"
              dove sono   le nɔt:se di figaro

Dove sono i bei momenti Di dolcezza, e di piacer!
dove sono i bɛi momenti di doltʃet:sa, e di pjatʃɛr!

Dove andaro i giuramenti Di quel labbro menzogner!
dove andaro i dʒuramenti di kwɛl:lab:bro mɛntsoɲɛr!

Perchè mai se in pianti, e in pene
pɛrke mai se in pjanti, e in pene

Per me tutto si cangiò. La memoria di quel bene
per me tut:to si kandʒo. la memɔrja di kwɛl bɛne

Dal mio sen non trapassò!
dal mio sen non trapas:so!

Ah! se almen la mia costanza Nel languire amando ognor
a   se almɛn la mia kostantsa nɛl laŋgwire amando oɲor

Mi portasse una speranza Di cangiar l'ingrato cor!
mi portas:se una sperantsa di kandʒar liŋgrato kor!

Mozart   Finch' han dal vino, from "Don Giovanni"
              fiŋkan dal vino   dɔn dʒovan:ni

Finch' han dal vino calda la testa,
fiŋkan   dal vino kalda la tɛsta,

una gran festa fa preparar!
una gran fɛsta fa preparar!

Se trovi in piazza qualche ragazza,
se trọ vin pjạt:sa kwạlke ragạt:sa,

teco ancor quella cerca menar.
tẹko ạŋkọr kwẹl:la tʃɛrka menạr.

Senza alcun ordine la danza sia,
sẹntsa alkụn ọrdine la dạntsa sịa,

chi'l menuetto, chi la follia,
kil menuẹt:to, ki la fol:lịa,

chi l'alemana farai ballar!
ki lalemạna farại bal:lạr!

Ed io frattanto dall' altro canto
ed ịo frat:tạnto dal:lạltro kạnto

con questa e quella vo' amoreggiar;
kon kwẹstạ e kwẹl:la vọ ạmored:ʒạr;

Ah, la mia lista doman mattina
a, la mịa lịsta domạn mat:tịna

d'una decina devi aumentar.
dụna detʃịna dẹvị ạumɛntạr.

Mozart   Il mio tesoro, from "Don Giovanni"
          il mịo tezọro   dɔn dʒovạn:ni

Il mio tesoro intanto, andate, a consolar!
il mịo tezọro intạnto, andạte, a konsolạr!

e del bel ciglio il pianto cercate di asciugar, cercate,
e dɛl bɛl tʃịʎọ il pjạnto tʃɛrkạte di aʃugạr, tʃɛrkạte,

Ditele che i suoi torti a vendicar io vado,
dịtele kẹ i swọi tọrti a vɛndikạr ịo vạdo,

che sol di stragi e morti Nunzio vogl'io tornar.
ke sol di strạdʒi e mọrti nụntsjo voʎịo tornạr.

Mozart   Madamina, from "Don Giovanni"
          madamịna   dɔn dʒovạn:ni

Madamina!   Il catalogo è questo,
madamịna!   il katạlogọ ɛ kwẹsto,

delle belle, che amò il padron mio
del:le bɛl:le, ke amɔ il padrɔn mio

un catalogo è gli è, che ho fatto io,
un katalogo ɛ ʎɛ,　ke ɔ fat:to io,

osservate, leggete con me!
os:sɛrvate, led:ʒete kon me!

In Italia sei cento e quaranta;
in italja sɛi tʃɛnto e kwaranta;

in Almagna due cento e trent' una,
in almaɲa due tʃɛnto e trɛntuna,

cento in Francia, in Turchia novant' una;
tʃɛnto in frantʃa, in turkia novant una;

ma in Ispagna son già mille e tre!
ma in ispaɲa son dʒa mil:le tre!

V'han fra queste contadine, cameriere, cittadine.
van　fra kwɛste kontadine, kamɛrjere, tʃit:tadine,

V'han contesse, baronesse, marchesane,
van kɔntes:se, barones:se, markezane,

principesse, e v'han donne d'ogni grado,
printʃipes:se, e van dɔn:ne doɲi grado

d'ogni forma, d'ogni età.
doɲi fɔrma, doɲi eta.

Nella bionda egli ha l'usanza
nel:la bjɔnda eʎa luzantsa

di lodar la gentilezza, nella bruna
di lodar la dʒɛntilet:sa, nel:la bruna

la costanza nella bianca la dolcezza.
la kostantsa, nel:la bjaŋka la doltʃet:sa.

Vuol d'inverno la grassotta,
vwɔl dinvɛrno la gras:sɔt:ta,

vuol d'estate la magrotta, e la grande maestosa
vwɔl destate la magrɔt:ta, e la grande maestoza

La piccina è ognor vezzosa,
la pit:ʃina, ɛ oɲɔr vet:soza,

delle vecchie fa conquista pel piacer di porle in lista
del:le vɛk:kje fa koŋkwista pel pjatʃɛr di pɔrle in lista

sua passion predominante è la giovin principiante;
sua pas:sjɔn predominante ɛ la dʒovin printʃipjante;

non si picca se sia ricca, se sia brutta,
non si pik:ka se sia rik:ka, se sia brut:ta,

se sia bella, se sia ricca, brutta, se sia bella,
se sia bɛl:la, se sia rik:ka, brut:ta, se sia bɛl:la,

purchè porti la gonella, voi sapete quel che fa,
purke pɔrti la gonɛl:la, voi sapete kwɛl ke fa.

Mozart   Non più andrai, from "Le Nozze di Figaro"
           non pju andrai   le nɔt:se di figaro

Non più andrai farfallone amoroso,
non pju andrai farfal:lone amorozo,

notte e giorno d'intorno girando,
nɔt:te dʒorno dintorno dʒirando,

delle belle turbando il riposo,
del:le bɛl:le turbando il ripozo,

Narcisetto, Adoncino d'amor!
nartʃizet:to, adontʃino d' amor!

Non più avrai questi bei pennacchini,
non pju avrai kwesti bɛi pen:nak:kini,

quel cappello leggiero e galante,
kwɛl kap:pɛl:lo led:ʒero e galante,

quella chioma, quell'aria brillante,
kwɛl:la kjoma, kwel:larja bril:lante,

quel vermiglio donnesco color!
kwɛl vermiʎo don:nesko kolor!

Fra guerrieri, poffar Bacco!
fra gwer:rjeri, pɔf:far bak:ko!

gran mustacchi, stretto sacco,
gran mustak:ki, stret:to sak:ko,

schioppo in spalla, sciabla al fianco,
skjɔp:po in spal:la, ʃa blal fjaŋko,

collo dritto, muso franco;
kɔl:lo drit:to, muzo fraŋko;

un gran casco, o un gran turbante,
un gran kasko, o un gran turbante,

39

molto onor, poco contante!
molto onọr, pọko kontante!

Ed in vece del fandango
ed in vẹtʃe dɛl fandaŋgo

una marcia per il fango,
una martʃa per il faŋgo,

per montagne, per valloni,
per montaɲe, per val:lọni,

colle nevi, e i sollioni,
kọl:le nẹvi, e i sol:ljọni,

al concerto di tromboni,
al kontʃɛrto di trombọni,

di bombarde, di cannoni,
di bombarde, di kan:nọni,

che le palle in tutti i tuoni
ke le pạl:lẹ in tụt:ti twọni

all'orecchio fan fischiar!
al:lorẹk:kjo fan fiskjạr!

Cherubino, alla vittoria!   alla gloria militar!
kerubịno, ạl:la vit:tọrja! ạl:la glọrja militạr!

Mozart   Non so più cosa son, from "Le Nozze di Figaro"
            non so pju kọza son   le nọt:se di fịgaro

Non so più cosa son, cosa faccio
non so pju kọza son, kọza fạt:ʃo

or di foco, ora sono di ghiaccio,
or di fọkọra   sọno di gjạt:ʃo,

ogni donna cangiar di colore,
ọɲi dọn:na kandʒạr di kolọre,

ogni donna mi fa palpitar.
ọɲi dọn:na mi fa palpitạr.

Solo ai nomi d'amor di diletto
sọlo ại nọmi damọr di dilɛt:to

mi si turbami s'altera il petto;
mi si tụrbami sạltera il pɛt:to;

e a parlare mi sforza d' amore
e a parlare mi sfɔrtsa damore

un desío ch' io non posso spiegar.
un dezio kio non pɔs:so spjegar.

Parlo d' amor vegliando, parlo d' amor sognando,
parlo damɔr veʎando, parlo damɔr soɲando,

all' acqua, all' ombra, ai monti,
al:lak:kwa, al:lom brai mɔnti,

ai fiori, all' erbe, ai fonti,
ai fjɔrjal:lɛrbe, ai fɔnti,

all' eco, all' aria, ai venti,
al:lɛko, al:larjai vɛnti,

che il suon de' vani accenti
ke il swɔn devani at:ʃɛnti

portano via con sé
pɔrtano via kon se

E se non ho chi m' oda,
e se non ɔ ki mɔda,

parlo, d' amor con me.
parlo, damɔr kon me.

Mozart   Porgi amor, from "Le Nozze di Figaro"
        pɔrdʒi amɔr   le nɔt:se di figaro

Porgi amor qualche ristoro al mio duolo,
pɔrdʒi amɔr kwalke ristɔro al mio dwɔlo,

a miei sospir! O mi rendi il mio tesoro,
a mjɛi sospir! o mi rɛndil mio tezɔro,

o mi lascia almen morir!
o mi laʃalmɛn morir!

Mozart   Se vuol ballare, from "Le Nozze di Figaro"
        se vwɔl bal:lare   le nɔt:se di figaro

Se vuol ballare, Signor contino,
se vwɔl bal:lare siɲor kontino,

il chitarrino le suonerò, sì, le suonerò.
il kitar:rino le swonerǫ, si, le swonerǫ.

Se vuol venire nella mia scuola,
se vwol venịre nɛl:la mịa skwǫla,

la capriola le insegnerò.
la kaprịǫla lɛ inseɲerǫ.

Saprò, ma piano, meglio ogni arcano
saprǫ, ma pjạno, mɛʎoɲi arkạno

dissimulando scoprir potrò.
dis:simulạndo skoprịr potrǫ.

L'arte schermendo, l'arte adoprando,
lạrte skɛrmɛndo, lạrte adoprạndo,

di qua pungendo, di là scherzando,
di kwa pundʒɛndo, di la skɛrtsạndo,

tutte le macchine rovescierò!
tụt:te le mạk:kine roveʃerǫ!

Mozart   Vedrai, carino, from "Don Giovanni"
              vedrại, karịno   don dʒovạn:ni

Vedrai, carino, se sei buonino,
vedrại, karịno, se sɛi bwonịno,

che bel rimedio ti voglio dar.
ke bɛl rimɛdjo ti vǫʎo dar.

È naturale, non dà disgusto
ɛ naturạle, non da dizgụsto

e lo speziale non lo sa far.
e lo spetsjạle non lo sa far.

È un certo balsamo che porto addosso,
ɛ un tʃɛrto bạlsamo ke pǫrto ad:sǫs:so,

dare t'el posso, se il vuoi provar.
dạre tɛl pǫs:so, se il vwǫi provạr.

Saper vorresti dove mi sta?
sạper vor:rɛsti dǫve mi sta?

Sentilo battere, toccami qua.
sɛntilo bạt:tere, tǫk:kami kwa.

42

Mozart   Voi, che sapete, from "Le Nozze di Figaro"
              voi, ke sapete   le nɔt:se di figaro

Voi, che sapete che cosa è amor,
voi, ke sapete ke kɔza ɛ amor,

donne, vedete, s' io l' ho nel cor,
dɔn:ne vedete, sio lo nɛl kɔr,

Quello ch' io provo, vi ridirò,
kwɛl:lo kio prɔvo, vi ridirɔ,

è per me nuovo capir nol so.
ɛ per me nwɔvo kapir nol sɔ.

Sento un affetto pien di desir,
sɛnto un af:fɛt:to pjɛn di dezir,

ch' ora è diletto, ch' ora è martir.
kɔra ɛ dilɛt:to kɔra ɛ martir.

Gelo, e poi sento l' alma avvampar,
dzɛlo, e pɔi sɛnto lal mav:vampar,

e in un momento torno a gelar!
e in un momɛnto tɔrno a dzelar!

Ricerco un bene fuori di me,
ritʃɛrko un bɛne fwɔri di me,

non so chi il tiene, non so cos' è,
non so kil tjɛne, non sɔ kɔzɛ,

sospiro e gemo senza voler,
sospiro e dzɛmo sɛntsa volɛr,

palpito e tremo senza saper,
palpito e trɛmo sɛntsa sapɛr,

non trovo pace notte, nè dì,
non trɔvo patʃe nɔt:te, ne di,

ma pur mi piace languir così.
ma pur mi pjatʃe laŋgwir kozi.

Paisiello   Chi vuol la zingarella
paizjɛl:lo   ki vwɔl la tsiŋgarɛl:la

Chi vuol la zingarella graziosa, accorta e bella?
ki vwɔl la tsiŋgarɛl:la gratsjɔ zak:kɔrta e bɛl:la?

43

Signori, eccola qua, signori, eccola qua.
siɲori, ɛk:kola kwa, siɲori, ɛk:kola kwa

Le donne sul balcone ṣo bene indovinar.
le dɔn:ne sul balkone sɔ bɛne indovinar.

I giovani al cantone so meglio stuzzicar.
i dʒovan:ni al kantone sɔ mɛʎo stut:tsikar.

A vecchi innamorati scaldar fo le cervella.
a vɛk:kin:namorati skaldar fo le tʃɛrvɛl:la.

Paisiello   Nel cor più non mi sento
paizjɛl:lo   nɛl kor pju non mi sɛnto

Nel cor più non mi sento brillar la gioventù;
nɛl kor pju non mi sɛnto bril:lar la dʒoventu,

cagion del mio tormento, amor, sei colpa tu.
kadʒon dɛl mio tormɛnto, amor, sɛi kolpa tu.

Mi pizzichi, mi stuzzichi, mi pungichi, mi mastichi;
mi pit:siki, mi stut:siki, mi pundʒiki, mi mastiki;

che cosa è questo, ahimè?   Pietà, pietà, pietà!
ke kɔza ɛ kwesto, aimɛ?   pjeta, pjeta, pjeta!

Amore è un certo che disperar mi fa.
amore ɛ un tʃɛrto che disperar mi fa.

Pergolesi   Se tu m'ami
pergolɛzi   se tu mami

Se tu m'ami, se tu sospiri Sol per me, gentil pastor,
se tu mami, se tu sospiri sol per me dʒentil pastor,

Ho dolor de' tuoi martiri, Ho diletto del tuo amor,
ɔ dolor de twoi martiri, ɔ dilɛt:to dɛl tuo amor,

Ma se pensi che soletto Io ti debba riamar,
ma se pɛnsi ke solɛt:to io ti deb:ba riamar,

Pastorello, sei soggetto Facilmente a t'ingannar.
pastorɛl:lo, sɛi sod:ʒɛt:to fatʃilmente a tiŋgan:nar.

Bella rosa porporina Oggi Silvia sceglierà,
bɛl:la rọza porporịna ọd:ʒi sịlvja ʃeʎera,

Con la scusa della spina Doman poi la sprezzerà.
kon la skụza dẹl:la spịna domạn pọi la spret:serạ.

Ma degli uomini il consiglio Io per me non seguirò.
ma deʎi wọmini il konsịʎo ịo per me non segwirọ.

Non perchè mi piace il giglio
non pɛrkẹ mi pjatʃẹ il dʒịʎo

Gli altri fiori sprezzerò.
ʎaltri fjọri spret:serọ.

Pergolesi   Stizzoso, mio stizzoso, from "La Serva Padrona"
pergolẹzi   stit:sọzo, miọ stit:sọzo   la sɛrva padrọna

Stizzoso, mio stizzoso, voi fate il borioso, ma no,
stit:sọzo miọ stit:sọzo, vọi fatẹ il boriọzo, ma nɔ,

ma non vi può giovare;
ma non vi pwɔ dʒovarẹ;

bisogna al mio divieto star cheto;
bizọɲal   miọ divjẹto star kẹto;

e non parlare, zit Serpina vuol così.
e non parlarẹ, tsit sɛrpịna vwɔl kozị.

Cred' io che m' intendete, sì.
kredịo ke mintɛndẹte, si,

da che mi conoscete son molti e molti dì.
da ke mi konoʃẹte son mọlti e mọlti di.

Pergolesi   Tre giorni son che Nina
pergolẹzi   tre dʒọrni son ke nịna

Tre giorni son che Nina
tre dʒọrni son ke nịna

a letto se ne sta.
a lɛt:to se ne sta.

Pifferi, cembali, timpani,
pif:feri, tʃembali, timpani,

svegliatemi Ninetta, acciò non dorma più.
zveʎatemi ninet:ta,   at:ʃọ non dọrma pju.

Peri   Invocazione di Orfeo, from "Euridice"
peri   invokatsjọne di orfẹo   euriditʃe

Gioite al canto mio, selve frondose,
dʒọite al kanto mịo, selve frondọze,

Gioite amati colli, e d'ogn' intorno.
dʒọite amati kọl:li, e dọnintọrno.

Eco rimbombi dalle valli ascose.
ẹko rimbọmbi dal:le val:li askọze,

Risorto è il mio bel sol di raggi adorno
rizọrtọ ẹ il mịo bẹl sol di rad:ʒi adọrno

E coi begli occhi, onde fa scorno a Delo,
e kọi beʎọk:ki,   ọnde fa skọrnọ a dẹlo,

Raddoppia fuoco all' alme e luce al giorno,
rad:dọp:pja fwọkọ al:lalme e lutʃe al dʒọrno,

E fa servi d' amor la terra e il cielo.
e fa sẹrvi damọr   la tẹr:ra e il tʃẹlo.

Ponchielli   Cielo e mar, from "La Gioconda"
poŋkjẹl:li   tʃẹlo e mar   la dʒokọnda

Cielo e mar!   l' etereo velo splende come un santo altar.
tʃẹlo e mar!   letẹreo velo splẹnde kọme un santo altar.

L' angiol mio verrà dal cielo?   l' angiol mio verrà dal mare?
landʒol mịo ver:ra dal tʃẹlo?   landʒol mịo ver:ra dal mare?

Qui l' attendo; ardente spira oggi il vento dell' amor
kwi lat:tẹndo; ardẹnte spira ọd:ʒil vẹnto del:lamọr

Ah! quell' uom che vi sospira vi conquide, o sogni d' ôr,
a! kwẹl:lwọm ke vi sospịra vi koŋkwịde, soɲi dọr,

46

Per l'aura fonda non appar nè suol, nè monte,
per laura fonda non ap:par ne swɔl, ne mǫnte,

L'orizzonte bacia l'onda! l'onda bacia l'orizzonte!
lorid:zǫnte batʃa lǫnda! lǫnda batʃa lorid:zǫnte!

Qui nell'onda ov'io mi giaccio coll'anelito del cor,
kwi nel:lǫnda, ovịo mi dʒat:ʃo kol:lanẹlito dɛl kɔr,

vieni, o donna, vieni al bacio della vita e dell'amor,
vjɛni, o dǫn:na, vjɛni al batʃo dɛl:la vịta e dɛl:lamǫr,

vieni, o donna, qui t'attendo coll'anelito del cor
vjɛni, ǫ dǫn:na, kwi tat:tɛndo kol:lanẹlito dɛl kɔr

vieni al bacio della vita e dell'amor ah! vien!
vjɛni ạl batʃo dɛl:la vịta e dɛl:lamǫr, a vjɛn!

Ponchielli   Suicidio! from "La Gioconda"
poŋkjɛl:li   suitʃidjo   la dʒokǫnda

Suicidio! In questi fieri momenti tu sol mi resti,
suitʃidjo! in kwẹsti fjẹri momẹnti tu sol mi rɛsti,

e il cor mi tenti. Ultima voce del mio destino,
ẹ il kɔr mi tɛnti. ụltima vǫtʃe dɛl mịo destịno,

ultima croce del mio cammin!
ụltima krǫtʃe dɛl mịo kam:mịn!

E un dì leggiadre volavan l'ore, perdei la madre,
ẹ un di led:ʒadre volạvan lǫre, pɛrdẹi la mạdre,

perdei l'amore, vinsi l'infausta gelosa febbre!
pɛrdẹi lamǫre, vịnsi linfạusta dʒelǫza fɛb:bre!

or piombo esausta, fra le tenebre!
or pjǫmbo ezạusta, fra le tɛnebre!

Tocco alla meta,
tǫk:ko ạl:la mɛta,

domando al cielo di dormir queta dentro l'avel.
domạndo ạl tʃɛlo di dormịr kwẹta dɛntro lavɛl.

Ponchielli   Voce di donna, from "La Gioconda"
poŋkjɛl:li   vọtʃe di dọn:na   la dʒokọnda

Voce di donna o d'angelo
vọtʃe di dọn:na ọ da̰ndʒelo

le mie catene ha sciolto;
le miẹ katẹne a ʃọlto;

Mi vietan le mie tenebre
mi vjetan le miẹ tẹnebre

di quella santa il volto.
di kwẹl:la sa̰ntạ il vọlto.

Pure da me non partasi,
pu̱re da me non pa̱rtasi,

senza un pietoso don, no! no!
sẹntsạ ụn pjetọzo don, nɔ! nɔ!

A te questo rosario che le preghiere aduna,
a te kwẹsto rozạrjo ke le pregjẹrẹ a̰du̱na,

Io te lo porgo, accettalo, ti porterà fortuna.
iọ te lo pọrgọ, a̰t:ʃɛt:talo, ti pọrtera̱ fortu̱na.

Sulla tua testa vigili la mia benedizion.
su̱l:la tụa tẹsta vi̱dʒili la miạ beneditsjọn.

Puccini   Che gelida manina, from "La Bohême"
put:ʃini   ke dʒẹlida mani̱na   la boẹm

Che gelida manina, se la lasci riscaldar.
ke dʒẹlida mani̱na, se la lạʃi riskaldạr.

Cercar che giova? - Al buio non si trova.
tʃẹrkạr ke dʒọva? - al bu̱jo non si trọva.

Ma per fortuna è una notte di luna,
ma per fortu̱na ɛ u̱na nọt:te di lu̱na,

e qui la luna l'abbiamo vicina.
e kwi la lu̱na lab:bjạmo vitʃi̱na.

Aspetti, signorina, le dirò con due parole
aspɛt:ti, siɲori̱na, le dirọ kon du̱e parọle

chi son, e che faccio, come vivo.   Vuole?
ki son, e ke fạt:ʃo, kọme vi̱vo.   vwọle?

Chi son? - Sono un poeta.
ki son? - sọnọ un poẹta.

48

Che cosa faccio? – Scrivo.
ke kɔza fat:ʃo? – skrivo.

E come vivo? – Vivo.
e kɔme vivo? – vivo.

In povertà mia lieta scialo da gran signore
in povɛrta mia ljeta ʃalo da gran siɲore

rime ed inni d'amore.
rime din:ni damore.

Per sogni e per chimere e per castelli in aria
per soɲi e per kimɛre e per kastɛl:lin arja

l'anima ho milionaria.
lanima ɔ miʎonaria.

Talor dal mio forziere ruban tutti i gioielli
talor dal mio fɔrtsjere ruban tut:ti dʒojɛl:li

due ladri: gli occhi belli.
due ladri, ʎɔk:ki bɛl:li.

V'entrar con voi pur ora, ed i miei sogni usati
vɛntrar kon voi pur ɔra, ed i mjɛi soɲi uzati

e i bei sogni miei tosto si dileguar!
e i bɛi soɲi mjɛi tɔsto si dilegwar!

Ma il furto non m'accora poichè vi ha preso stanza
ma il furto non mak:kɔra poikɛ vi a prɛzo stantsa

la dolce speranza!
la dɔltʃe sperantsa!

Or che mi conoscete parlate voi. Chi siete?
or ke mi konoʃete parlate voi. ki sjete?

Vi piaccia dir?
vi pjat:ʃa dir?

Puccini   E lucevan le stelle, from "La Tosca"
put:ʃini   e lutʃevan le stɛl:le   la tɔska

E lucevan le stelle ed olezzava la terra
e lutʃevan le stɛl:le ed oled:zava la tɛr:ra

e stridea l'uscio dell'orto
e stridɛa luʃo del:lɔrto

49

e un passo sfiorava la rena.
e un pas:so sfjorava la rena.

Entrava ella, fragrante,
entrava el:la, fragrante,

mi cadea fra le braccia.
mi kadea fra le brat:ʃa.

Oh! dolci baci, o languide carezze,
o! doltʃi batʃi, o langwide karet:se,

mentr' io fremente
mentrio fremente

le belle forme disciogliea dai veli!
le bel:le forme diʃoʎea dai veli!

Svanì per sempre il sogno mio d'amore...
zvani per sempre il soɲo mio damore...

l'ora è fuggita e muoio disperato!...
lora ɛ fud:ʒita e mwojo disperato!...

E non ho amato mai tanto la vita!
e non o amato mai tanto la vita!

Puccini   In quelle trine morbide, from ''Manon Lescaut''
put:ʃini   in kwel:le trine morbide   manon lesko

In quelle trine morbide nell' alcova dorata
in kwel:le trine morbide nel:lalkova dorata

v'è un silenzio, un gelido mortal,
vɛ un silɛntsjo, un dʒelido mortal,

v'è un silenzio, un freddo che m' agghiaccia!
vɛ un silɛntsjo, un fred:do ke mag:gjat:ʃa!

Ed io che m' ero avvezza
ed io ke mero av:vetsa

a una carezza voluttuosa
a una karet:sa volut:twoza

di labbra ardenti e d' infuocate braccia
di lab:brardɛnti e dinfwokate brat:ʃa

or ho tutt' altra cosa!
or o tut:taltra koza!

50

O mia dimora umile, tu mi ritorni innanzi
o mia dimora umile, tu mi ritornin:nantsi

gaia, isolata, bianca come un sogno gentile
gaja, izolata, bjaŋka kome un soɲo dʒentile

e di pace e d' amor!
e di patʃe damor!

Puccini   O mio babbino caro, from "Gianni Schicchi"
put:ʃini   o mio bab:bino karo   dʒan:ni skik:ki

O mio babbino caro, mi piace, è bello;
o mio bab:bino karo, mi pjatʃe ɛ bɛl:lo;

vo' andare in Porta Rossa
vo andare in pɔrta rɔs:sa

a comperar l' anello! Sì, ci voglio andare!
a komperar lanɛl:lo! si, tʃi vɔʎo andare!

e se l' amassi indarno, andrei sul Ponte Vecchio,
e se lamas:si indarno, andrɛi sul pɔnte vɛk:kjo,

ma per buttarmi in Arno!
ma per but:tar min arno!

Mi struggo e mi tormento! O Dio, vorrei morir
mi strug:go e mi tormɛnto! o dio vor:rɛi morir

Babbo, pietà, pietà!
bab:bo, pjeta, pjeta!

Puccini   Quando me' n vo' , from "La Bohême"
put:ʃini   kwando men vɔ   la boɛm

Quando me' n vo' soletta per la via la gente sosta e mira
kwando men vɔ solet:ta per la via la dʒɛnte sɔsta e mira

e la bellezza mia tutta ricerca in me da capo a piè;
e la bel:let:sa mia tut:ta ritʃerka in me da kapo a pje;

ed assaporo allor la bramosìa sottil,
ed as:saporo al:lor la bramozia sot:til,

che da gl'occhi traspira e dai palesi vezzi intender sa
ke da ʎok:ki traspira e dai palezi vet:sintɛnder sa

alle occulte beltà.
al:le ok:kulte bɛlta.

Cosí l'effluvio del desío tutta m'aggira
kozi lef:fluvjo dɛl dezio tut:ta mad:ʒira

felice mi fa, felice mi fa.
felitʃe mi fa, felitʃe mi fa.

E tu che sai che memori e ti struggi,
e tu ke sai ke memori e ti strud:ʒi,

da me tanto rifuggi?
da me tanto rifud:ʒi?

So ben: le angoscie tue non le vuoi dir,
so bɛn, le aŋgoʃe tue non le vwoi dir,

so ben ma ti senti morir!
so bɛn ma ti sɛnti morir!

Puccini   Recondita armonia, from "La Tosca"
put:ʃini   rekonditarmonia   la toska

Recondita armonia di bellezze diverse!...
rekonditarmonia di bel:let:se divɛrse!...

È bruna Floria, l'ardente amante mia,
ɛ bruna floria, lardɛnte amante mia,

e te, beltade ignota
e te, bɛltade iɲota

cinta di chiome bionde!
tʃinta di kjome bjonde!

Tu azzurro hai l'occhio Tosca ha l'occhio nero!
tu ad:zur:ro ai lok:kjo toska a lok:kjo nero!

L'arte nel suo mistero
larte nɛl suo mistɛro

le diverse bellezze insiem confonde:
le divɛrse bel:let:se insjɛm konfonde,

ma nel ritrar costei
ma nɛl ritrạr kostẹi

il mio solo pensiero,
il mịo sọlo pɛnsjẹro,

ah! il mio sol pensier sei tu!
a! il mịo sol pɛnsjẹr sẹi tu!

Tosca sei tu!
tọska sẹi tu!

Puccini   Si, mi chiamano Mimì, from "La Bohême"
put:ʃini   si, mi kjạmano mimị   la boɛm

Si, mi chiamano Mimì ma il mio nome è Lucia.
si, mi kjạmano mimị ma il mịo nọmɛ lutʃịa.

La storia mia è breve: A tela o a seta
la stọrja mịa ɛ brẹve, a tẹla o a sẹta

ricamo in casa e fuori......
rikạmo in kạza e fwọri......

Son tranquilla e lieta ed è mio svago far gigli e rose.
son traŋkwil:la e ljẹta ed ɛ mio zvạgo far dʒiʎe rọze.

Mi piaccion quelle cose che han sì dolce malìa,
mi pjatʃon kwẹl:le kọze ke ạn si dọltʃe malịa,

che parlano d'amor, di primavere,
ke pạrlano damọr, di primavẹre,

che parlano di sogni e di chimere,
ki pạrlano di sọɲe di kimɛre,

quelle cose che han nome poesia, Lei m'intende?
kwẹl:le kọze ke ạn nọme poezịa, lẹi mintɛnde?

Mi chiamano Mimì, il perchè non so.
mi kjạmano mimị, il pɛrkẹ non sɔ.

Sola, mi fo il pranzo da me stessa.
sọla, mi fo il prạntso da me stẹs:sa.

Non vado sempre a messa ma prego assai il Signor.
non vạdo sɛmpre a mɛs:sa ma prɛgo as:sail siɲor.

Vivo sola, soletta, Là in una bianca cameretta:
vịvo sọla, solẹt:ta, la in ụna bjạŋka kamerẹt:ta,

53

guardo sui tetti e in cielo,
gwardo sui tet:ti e in tʃɛlo,

ma quando vien lo sgelo il primo sole è mio,
ma kwando vjɛn lo zdʒelo il primo sole mio,

il primo bacio dell' aprile è mio!
il primo batʃo del:laprile ɛ mio!

Il primo sole è mio!
il primo sole ɛ mio!

Germoglia in un vaso una rosa.
dʒermoʎa in un vazo una roza.

Foglia a foglia la spio! Così gentil
foʎa foʎa la spio!   kozi dʒɛntil

il profumo d' un fior! Ma i fior ch' io faccio,
il profumo dun fjor! ma i fjor kio fat:ʃo,

ahimè! non hanno odore!
aimɛ!   non an:nodore!

Altro di me non le saprei narrare:
altro di me non le saprɛi nar:rare.

sono la sua vicina che la vien fuori d' ora a importunare.
sono la sua vitʃina ke la vjɛn fwori dora importunare.

Puccini   Un bel dì, from "Madama Butterfly"
put:ʃini   un bɛl di   madama botɛrflai

Un bel dì, vedremo levarsi un fil di fumo
un bɛl di, vedremo levarsi un fil di fumo

sull' estremo confin del mare.
sul:lestrɛmo konfin dɛl mare.

E poi la nave appare
e poi la nave ap:pare

Poi la nave bianca entra nel porto,
poi la nave bjaŋka entra nɛl porto,

romba il suo saluto. Vedi?
romba il suo saluto. vedi?

È venuto! Io non gli scendo incontro.
ɛ venuto! io non ʎi ʃendo iŋkontro.

54

Io no. Mi metto là sul ciglio del colle
io nɔ. mi met:to la sul tʃiʎo dɛl kɔl:le

e aspetto gran tempo e non mi pesa, la lunga attesa.
e aspɛt:to gran tɛmpo e·non mi peza, la luŋgat:teza.

È uscito dalla folla cittadina
ɛ uʃito dal:la fɔl:la tʃit:tadina

un uomo, un picciol punto s'avvia per la collina.
un wɔmo, un pitʃɔl punto sav:via per la kɔl:lina.

Chi sarà? E come sarà giunto che dirà?
ki sara? e kome sara dʒunto ke dira?

Chiamerà Butterfly dalla lontana.
kjamera bɔtɛrflai dal:la lontana.

Io senza dar risposta me ne starò nascosta
io sɛntsa dar risposta me ne starɔ naskɔsta

un po' per celia
un pɔ per tʃɛlja

e un po' per non morire al primo incontro,
e un pɔ per non morire al primo iŋkontro,

ed egli alquanto in pena chiamerà,
ed e ʎalkwanto in pena kjamera,

Piccina mogliettina olezzo di verbena,
pitʃina moʎetina oled:zo di vɛrbena,

i nomi che mi dava al suo venire
i nomi ke mi daval suo venire

Tutto questo avverrà, te lo prometto.
tut:to kwesto av:ver:ra, te lo promet:to.

Tienti la tua paura,
tjɛnti la tua paura,

io con sicura fede l'aspetto.
io kon sikura fede laspɛt:to.

Puccini   Vissi d'arte from "La Tosca"
put:ʃini   vis:si darte   la tɔska

Vissi d'arte, vissi d'amore,
vis:si darte, vis:si damore,

non feci mai male ad anima viva!
non fetʃi mai male ad anima viva! ·

Con man furtiva quante miserie conobbi, aiutai.
kon man furtiva kwante mizɛrje konɔb:bi, ajutai.

Sempre con fè sincera
sɛmpre kon fe sintʃɛra

la mia preghiera ai santi tabernacoli salì.
la mia pregjera ai santi tabɛrnakoli sali.

Sempre con fè sincera diedi fiori agli altar.
sɛmpre kon fe sintʃɛra djedi fjori aʎaltar.

Nell'ora del dolore perchè, perchè,
nel:lora dɛl dolore pɛrke, pɛrke,

Signore, perchè me ne rimuneri così?
siɲore, pɛrke me ne rimuneri kozi?

Diedi gioielli della Madonna al manto, e diedi il canto
djedi dʒojɛl:li del:la madɔn:nal manto, e djɛdil kanto

agli astri, al ciel, che ne ridean più belli.
aʎastri, al tʃɛl, ke ne ridɛan pju bɛl:li.

Nell'ora del dolor perchè, perchè,
nel:lora dɛl dolor pɛrke, pɛrke,

Signor, ah, perchè me ne rimuneri così?
siɲor, a, pɛrke me ne rimuneri kozi?

Respighi   Nebbie
respigi   neb:bje

Soffro Lontan lontano Le nebbie sonnolente
sɔf:fro lontan lontano le neb:bje son:nolɛnte

Salgono dal tacente Piano.
salgono dal tatʃɛnte pjano.

Alto gracchiando, i corvi, Fidati all'ali nere,
alto grak:kjando, i kɔrvi, fidati al:lali nere,

Traversan le brughiere torvi.
travɛrsan le brugjere tɔrvi.

Dell'aere ai morsi crudi Gli addolorati tronchi
del:laɛre ai mɔrsi krudi ʎad:dolorati troŋki

56

Offron, pregando, i bronchi nudi.
ọf:fron, pregandọ, ị brọŋki nụdi.

Come ho freddo!   Son sola;
kọme ọ frẹd:do!   son sọla;

Pel grigio ciel sospinto Un gemito d'estinto vola;
pel gridʒo tʃɛl sospịnto un dʒɛmito destịnto vọla;

E mi ripete: Vieni; È buia la vallata.
e mi ripẹte: vjɛni; ɛ bụja la val:lạta.

O triste, o disamata vieni!   Vieni!
O trịste, ọ dizamạta vjɛni!   vjɛni!

Rosa	Star vicino
rọza	star vitʃịno

Star vicino al bel idol che s'ama,
star vitʃịno ạl bɛl idọl ke sạma,

è il più vago diletto d'amor!
ɛ il pju vạgo dilẹt:to damọr!

Star lontan da colei che si brama,
star lọntan da kolẹi ke si brạma,

è d'amor il più mesto dolor!
ɛ damọr il pju mẹsto dolọr!

Rossini	Ecco ridente in cielo, from "Il Barbiere di Siviglia"
ros:sịni	ẹk:ko ridẹnte in tʃɛlo il barbjɛre di sivịʎa

Ecco ridente in cielo, Spunta la bella aurora,
ẹk:ko ridẹnte in tʃɛlo, spụnta la bɛl:la aurọra,

E tu non sorgi ancora E puoi dormir così? Ah!
e tu non sọrdʒi ạŋkọra e pwọi dormịr kozị? a!

Sòrgi mia dolce speme, Vieni bell'Idol mio,
sọrdʒi mịa dọltʃe spẹme, vjɛni bel:lịdol mịo,

Rendi men crudo, oh Dio! Lo stral che mi ferì;
rɛndi men krudo dio!   lo stral ke mi feri;

Oh, sorte! già veggo? Quel caro sembiante;
o, sɔrte! dʒa veg:go? kwɛl karo sembjante;

Quest' anima amante ottenne pietà?
kwestanima amante ot:tɛn:ne pjeta?

Rossini   La calunnia è un venticello, from "Il Barbiere di Siviglia"
ros:sini   la kalun:nja ɛ un vɛntitʃɛl:lo   il barbjɛre di siviʎa

La calunnia è un venticello, un' auretta assai gentile,
la kalun:nja ɛ un vɛntitʃɛl:lo, un aurɛt:ta as:sai dʒentile,

che insensibile e sottile, leggermente, dolcemente,
ke insɛnsibile sot:tile, led:ʒɛrmente, doltʃemente,

incomincia a sussurrar. Piano piano, terra terra,
iŋkomintʃa sus:sur:rar. pjano pjano, tɛr:ra tɛr:ra,

sotto voce, sibilando, va scorrendo, va ronzando,
sɔt:to vɔtʃe, sibilando, va skor:rɛndo, va rondzando,

nelle orecchie della gente s' introduce destramente,
nɛl:le orɛk:kje dɛl:la dʒente sintrodutʃe destramente,

alle teste ed i cervelli, fa stordire e fa gonfiar.
al:le tɛste di tʃɛrvɛl:li, fa stordire fa gonfjar.

Dalla bocca fuori uscendo, lo schiamazzo va crescendo;
dal:la bɔk:ka fwɔri uʃɛndo, lo skjamat:so va kreʃɛndo;

prende forza a poco a poco, vola già di loco in loco
prɛnde fɔrtsa pɔko a pɔko, vola dʒa di lɔko in lɔko

sembra il tuono, la tempesta, che nel sen della foresta
sɛmbra il twɔno, la tempɛsta, ke nɛl sen dɛl:la forɛsta

va fischiando, brontolando, e ti fa d' orror gelar.
va fiskjando, brontolando, e ti fa dor:ror dʒelar.

Alla fin trabocca e scoppia, si propaga, si raddoppia
al:la fin trabɔk:ka e skɔp:pja, si propaga, si rad:dɔp:pja

e produce un' esplosione come un colpo di cannone
e produtʃe un esplozjone kome un kɔlpo di kan:none

un tremuoto, un temporale che fa l' aria rimbombar;
un tremwɔto, un tɛmporale ke fa larja rimbombar;

58

E il meschino calunniato, avvilito, calpestato,
e il meskino kalun:njato, av:vilito, kalpestato,

sotto il pubblico flagello per gran sorte va a crepar!
sot:to il pub:bliko fladʒɛl:lo per gran sɔrte va krepar!

Rossini   La Danza
ros:sini   la dantsa

Già la luna è in mezzo al mare, mamma mia, si salterà!
dʒa la luna ɛ in mɛd:ʒo al mare, mam:ma mia, si saltera!

L'ora è bella per danzare, chi è in amor non mancherà.
lɔra ɛ bɛl:la per dantsare, kjɛ in amɔr non maŋkera.

Già la luna è in mezzo al mare, mamma mia, si salterà!
dʒa la luna ɛ in mɛd:ʒo al mare, mam:ma mia, si saltera!

Presto in danza a tondo, a tondo, donne mie venite qua,
prɛsto in dantsa tondo, a tondo, don:ne mie venite kwa,

un garzon bello e giocondo a ciascuna toccherà,
un gardzon bɛl:lo e dʒokondo a tʃaskuna tok:kera,

finchè in ciel brilla una stella e la luna splenderà.
fiŋke in tʃɛl bril:la una stɛl:la e la luna splɛndera.

Il più bel con la più bella tutta notte danzerà.
il pju bɛl kon la pju bɛl:la tut:ta nɔt:te dantsera.

Mamma mia, già la luna è in mezzo al mare,
mam:ma mia, dʒa la luna ɛ in mɛd:ʒo al mare,

mamma mia, si salterà. Frinche, mamma mià, si salterà
mam:ma mia, si saltera. friŋke, mam:ma mia, si saltera!

Salta, salta, gira, gira, ogni coppia a cerchio va,
salta, salta, dʒira, dʒira, ɔɲi kɔp:pja tʃɛrkjo va,

già s'avanza, si ritira e all' assalto tornerà.
dʒa savantsa, si ritira e al:las:salto tornera.

Serra, serra, colla bionda, colla bruna va qua e là
sɛr:ra, sɛr:ra, kɔl:la bjonda, kɔl:la bruna va kwa e la

colla rosa va a seconda, colla smorta fermo sta.
kɔl:la rɔza va a sekonda, kɔl:la smɔrta fɛrmo sta.

Viva il ballo a tondo a tondo, sono un Re, sono un Pascià,
viva il bal:lo a tondo a tondo, sono un re, sono un paʃa,

e il più bel piacer del mondo la più cara voluttà.
e̬ i̬l pju bɛl pjatʃe̱r dɛl mo̱ndo la pju ka̱ra volut:ta̱...

Rossini   Largo al factotum della città, from "Il Barbiere di Siviglia"
ros:si̱ni   la̱rgo al faktȯtum dɛl:la tʃit:ta̱   il barbjɛ̱re di sivi̱ʎa

Largo al factotum della città, largo! la!
la̱rgo a̱l faktȯtum dɛl:la tʃit:ta̱, la̱rgo! la.

Presto a bottega, che l'alba è già, presto! la!
prɛ̱sto a̱ bot:te̱ga, ke la̱lba ɛ̬ dʒa, prɛ̱sto! la.

Ah, che bel vivere, che bel piacere,
a, ke bɛl vi̱vere, ke bɛl pjatʃe̱re,

per un barbiere di qualità,
per un barbjɛ̱re di kwalita̱,

Ah bravo, Figaro, bravo bravissimo, bravo
a bra̱vo, fi̱garo, bra̱vo bravi̱s:simo, bra̱vo.

Fortunatissimo per verità; bravo! la!
fortunati̱s:simo per verita̱; bra̱vo! la!

Pronto a far tutto la notte e il giorno,
pro̱nto a̱ far tu̱t:to la no̱t:te̬ il dʒo̱rno,

sempre d'intorno in giro sta.
sɛ̱mpre dinto̱rno in dʒi̱ro sta.

Miglior cuccagna per un barbiere,
miʎo̱r kuk:ka̱ɲa per un barbjɛ̱re,

vita più nobile, nò, non si dà!
vi̱ta pju nȯbile, nɔ, non si da!

Rasori, pettini, lancette e forbici
ra̱zori, pɛ̱t:tini, la̱ntʃet:te fȯrbitʃi

al mio comando tutto qui sta.
al mi̱o koma̱ndo tu̱t:to kwi sta.

V'è la risorsa poi del mestiere
vɛ la rizo̱rsa po̱i dɛl mestjɛre

colla donnetta, col cavaliere, la ran larala.
ko̱l:la don:nɛ̱t:ta, kol kavaljɛre, la ran larala.

Tutti mi chiedono, tutti mi vogliono,
tu̱t:ti mi kjɛ̱dono, tu̱t:ti mi vȯʎono,

60

donne, ragazzi, vecchie, fanciulle.
dǫn:ne, ragat:si, vɛk:kje, fantʃul:le.

Qua la parrucca! presto la barba!
kwa la par:ruk:ka! prɛsto la bạrba!

qua la sanguigna! presto il biglietto!
kwa la saŋgwiɲa! prɛstǫ il biʎet:to!

Figaro! ohimè! che furia, ohimè!
fịgaro! ɔimɛ! ke fụrja, ɔimɛ!

che folla! un' alla volta per carità,
ke fǫl:la! un ạl:la vǫlta per karitạ,

Figaro! Son qua. Figaro qua, Figaro là,
fịgaro! son kwa. fịgaro kwa, fịgaro la,

Figaro sù, Figaro giù!
fịgaro su, fịgaro dʒu!

Pronto prontissimo son come un fulmine,
prǫnto prontịs:simo son kǫme un fụlmine,

sono il factotum della città!
sǫnǫ il faktǫtum dɛl:la tʃit:tạ!

Ah, bravo Figaro, bravo bravissimo!
a, brạvo, fịgaro, brạvo bravịs:simo!

Rossini   Una voce poco fa, from "Il Barbiere di Siviglia"
ros:sịni   ụna vǫtʃe pǫko fa   il barbjɛre di sivịʎa

Una voce poco fa: Qui nel cor mi risuonò!
ụna vǫtʃe pǫko fa, kwi nɛl kɔr mi riswonǫ!

Il mio cor ferito è già; E Lindor fu che il piagò.
il mịo kɔr ferịtǫ ɛ dʒa; e lindǫr fu ke ịl pjagǫ.

Sì, Lindoro mio sarà! Lo giurai, la vincerò.
si, lindǫro mịo sarạ! lo dʒurại, la vintʃerǫ.

Il tutor ricuserà; Io l'ingegno aguzzerò:
il tutǫr rikuzerạ; ịo lindʒeɲo ạgut:serǫ,

Alla fin s'acchetterà, E contenta io resterò,
ạl:la fin sak:ket:terạ, e kontɛnta ịo resterǫ,

Si, Lindoro mia sarà! Lo giurai – la vincerò.
si, lindoro mio sara! lo dʒurai – la vintʃero.

Io sono docile, Son rispettosa, Sono obbediente
io sono dotʃile, son rispet:toza, sono ob:bedjɛnte

Dolce amorosa; Mi lascio reggere, Mi fo guidar,
doltʃe amoroza; mi laʃo rɛd:ʒere, mi fo gwidar,

Ma se mi toccano dov' è il mio debole, Sarò una
ma se mi tok:kano dove il mio debole, saro una

vipera, sarò, E cento trappole prima di cedere,
vipera, saro, e tʃɛnto trap:pole prima di tʃɛdere,

farò giocar.
faro dʒokar.

Sarti|sarti| Lungi dal caro bene
Secchi|sɛk:ki| lundʒi dal karo bɛne

Lungi dal caro bene vivere non poss'io!
lundʒi dal karo bɛne vivere non pos:sio!

Sono in un mar di pene, Lungi dal caro bene,
sono in un mar di pene, lundʒi dal karo bɛne,

sento mancarmi il cor! Un dolce estremo sonno
sɛnto maŋkarmil kor! un doltʃestrɛmo son:no

se lei mirar non ponno, mi chiuda i lumi ancor.
se lɛi mirar non pon:no, mi kjuda i lumi aŋkor.

Scarlatti   Chi vuole innamorarsi
skarlat:ti   ki vwole in:namorarsi

Chi vuole innamorarsi, Ci deve ben pensar!
ki vwole in:namorarsi, tʃi deve bɛn pensar!

Amore è un certo foco, Che, se s' accende un poco,
amore un tʃɛrto foko, ke, se sat:ʃɛnde un poko,

Eterno suol durar, eterno suol durare, suol durar.
etɛrno swɔl durar, etɛrno swɔl durare, swɔl durar.

Non è lieve tormento, Aver piagato il cor!
non ɛ ljeve tɔrmento, avɛr pjagato il kɔr!

Soggetta ogni volere A due pupille arciere,
sodʒɛt:ta oɲi volere a due pupil:le artʃere,

Chi serve al Dio d'amor.
ki sɛrve al dio damɔr.

Scarlatti   Già il sole dal Gange
skarlat:ti   dʒa il sole dal gandʒe

Già il sole dal Gange più chiaro sfavilla
dʒa il sole dal gandʒe pju kjaro sfavil:la

e terge ogni stilla dell'alba che piange.
e tɛrdʒe oɲi stil:la del:lalba ke pjandʒe.

Col raggio dorato ingemma ogni stelo,
kol rad:ʒo dorato indʒɛm:ma oɲi stɛlo,

e gli astri del cielo dipinge nel prato.
e   ʎastri dɛl tʃɛlo dipindʒe nɛl prato.

Scarlatti   O cessate di piagarmi
skarlat:ti   o tʃes:sate di pjagarmi

O cessate di piagarmi, o lasciatemi morir!
o tʃes:sate di pjagarmi, o laʃatemi morir!

Luc'ingrate dispietate più del gelo e più dei marmi
lutʃiŋgrate dispjetate pju dɛl dʒelo e pju dei marmi

fredde e sorde ai miei martir!
frɛd:de sɔrde ai mjɛi martir!

Più d'un angue, più d'un aspe
pju dun aŋgwe, pju dun aspe

crude e sorde ai miei sospir!
krude sɔrde ai mjɛi sospir!

Occhi alteri, voi petete,
ǫk:ki altɛri vǫi potęte,

Voi potete risanarmi,
vǫi potęte risanarmi,

e godete al mio languir!
e godęte al mio laŋgwir!

Scarlatti   Rugiadose, odorose
skarlat:ti   rudʒadǫze, odorǫze

Rugiadose, odorose, Violette graziose,
rudʒadǫze, odorǫze, violet:te gratsiǫze,

Voi vi state vergognose, mezzo ascose
vǫi vi state vergoɲǫze, mɛd:zo askǫze

tra le foglie, e sgridate le mie voglie
tra le fǫʎe,   e zgridate le mie vǫʎe

che son troppo ambiziose.
ke son trǫp:po ambitsjǫze.

Scarlatti   Se Florindo è fedele
skarlat:ti   se florindo ɛ fedęle

Se Florindo è fedele io m' innamorerò,
se florindo ɛ fedęle io min:namorerǫ,

s' è fedele Florindo m' innamorerò.
sɛ fedęle florindo min:namorerǫ.

Potrà ben l' arco tendere il faretrato arcier,
potra bɛn larko tɛndere il faretrato artʃɛr.

ch' io mi saprò difendere d' un guardo lusinghier.
kio mi saprǫ difɛndere dun gwardo luziŋgjɛr.

Preghi, pianti e querele, io non ascolterò,
prɛgi, pjanti e kwerɛle, io non askolterǫ,

ma se sarà fedele io m' innamorerò
ma se sara fedęle io min:namorerǫ.

Scarlatti   Sento nel core
skarlat:ti   sɛnto nɛl kɔre

Sento nel core certo dolore,
sɛnto nɛl kɔre tʃɛrto dolɔre,

che la mia pace turbando va: nel core.
ke la mia patʃe turbando va, nɛl kɔre.

Splende una face che l' alma accende,
splɛnde una fatʃe ke lal mat:ʃɛnde,

se non è amore, amor sarà.
se non ɛ amɔre, amor sara.

Stradella   Per Pietà
stradɛl:la   per pjeta

Per pietà, deh, torna a me!   Amor mio e dove sei?
per pjeta, dɛ, torna a me!   amor mio e dɔve sɛi?

Son dolenti i lumi miei Non san viver senza te.
son dolɛnti lumi mjɛi non   san viver sɛntsa te.

Torelli   Tu lo sai
torɛl:li   tu lo sai

Tu lo sai quanto t' amai
tu lo sai kwanto tamai

tu lo sai, lo sai crudel!
tu lo sai, lo sai krudɛl!

Io non bramo altra mercé,
io non bramo altra mɛrtʃe,

Ma ricordati di me
ma rikɔrdati di me,

E poi sprezza un infedel!
e poi sprɛt:sa un infedɛl!

Verdi   Addio del passato, from "La Traviata"
verdi   ad:dio del pas:sato   la travjata

Attendo, attendo, nè a me giungon mai!
at:tɛndo, at:tɛndo, ne a me dʒuŋgon mai!

Oh come son mutata! Ma il Dottore
o kome son mutata!   ma il dot:tore

a sperar pure m'esorta! Ah, con tal morbo
a sperar pure mezorta!   a, kon tal morbo

ogni speranza è morta!
oɲi sperantsa ɛ morta!

Addio del passato, bei sogni ridenti,
ad:dio del pas:sato, bɛi soɲi ridɛnti,

le rose del volto già sono pallenti;
le roze del volto dʒa sono pal:lɛnti;

l'amore d'Alfredo perfino mi manca,
lamore dalfredo perfino mi maŋka,

conforto, sostegno dell'anima stanca,
konforto, sosteɲo del:lanima staŋka,

conforto, sostegno. Ah! della Traviata
konforto, sosteɲo. a! del:la travjata

sorridi al desío, a lei deh perdona,
sor:ridi al dezio, a lɛi dɛ perdona,

tu accoglila, o Dio! Ah! tutto finì, or tutto finì!
tu ak:koʎila, o dio! a! tut:to fini, or tut:to fini!

Le gioje, i dolori tra poco avran fine;
le dʒoje, i dolori tra poko avran fine;

la tomba ai mortali di tutto è confine!
la tomba ai mortali di tut:to ɛ konfine!

Non lagrima o fiore avrà la mia fossa!
non lagrima o fjore avra la mia fos:sa!

non croce col nome che copra quest'ossa!
non krotʃe kol nome ke kopra kwestos:sa!

Non croce, non fior! Ah! della Traviata.....
non krotʃe, non fjor! a! del:la travjata.....

Verdi   Ah, fors' è lui, from "La Traviata"
vɛrdi   a, fɔrsɛ lui   la travjata

È strano! è strano!
ɛ strano! ɛ strano!

in core scolpiti ho quegli accenti!
in kɔre skolpiti o kweʎat:ʃɛnti!

Saria per me sventura un serio amore?
saria per me zvɛntura un sɛrjo amore?

Che risolvi, o turbata anima mia?
ke rizɔlvi, o turbatanima mia?

Null' uomo ancora l' accendeva.
nul:lwɔmo aŋkora lat:ʃɛndeva.

Oh gioja ch' io non conobbi, esser amato amando!
o dʒɔja kio non konɔb:bi, ɛs:ser amato amando!

E sdegnarla poss' io per l' aride follie del viver mio?
e zdeɲarla pɔs:sio per laride fol:lie dɛl vivɛr mio?

Ah, fors' è lui che l' anima solinga ne' tumulti,
a, fɔrsɛ lui ke lanima soliŋga ne tumulti,

godea sovente pingere de suoi colori occulti!
godɛa sovɛnte pindʒere de swɔi kolɔrjok:kulti!

Lui, che modesto e vigile all' egre soglie ascese,
lui, ke modɛsto e vidʒile al:legre soʎe aʃeze,

e nuova febbre accese, destandomi all' amor!
e nwɔva fɛb:bre at:ʃeze, destandomi al:lamor!

A quell' amor, ch' e palpito
a kwɛl:lamor, ke palpito

dell' universo intero, misterioso, altero,
del:luniversɔ interɔ, misteriozo, altɛro,

croce e delizia, delizia al cor.
krotʃe delitsja, delitsjal kor.

Follie! follie! delirio vano è questo!
fol:lie! fol:lie! delirjo vano ɛ kwesto!

Povera donna, sola, abbandonata
povera dɔn:na, sɔla, ab:bandonata

in questo popoloso deserto che appellano Parigi,
in kwesto popoloso dezɛrto ke ap:pɛl:lano paridʒi,

che spero or più' che far degg' io? gioire!
ke spɛror pju? ke far ded:ʒio? dʒoire!

di voluttà ne' vortici, di voluttà perir! Gioir!
di volut:ta̱ ne vo̱rtitʃi, di volut:ta̱ perir! dʒoi̱r!

Sempre libera degg'io folleggiare di gioja in gioja,
se̱mpre li̱bera ded:ʒio fol:led:ʒare di dʒo̱ja̱ in dʒo̱ja,

vo' che scorra il viver mio pei sentieri del piacer.
vo ke sko̱r:ra̱ il vi̱ver mi̱o pe̱i sentje̱ri del pjatʃe̱r.

Nasca il giorno, o il giorno muoja,
na̱ska̱ il dʒo̱rno, o̱ il dʒo̱rno mwo̱ja,

sempre lieta ne' ritrovi,
se̱mpre lje̱ta ne ritro̱vi,

a diletti sempre nuovi dee volare il mio pensier.
a dile̱t:ti se̱mpre nwo̱vi de vola̱re il mi̱o pensje̱r.

Verdi   Ave Maria, from "Otello"
ve̱rdi   a̱ve mari̱a   ote̱l:lo

Ave Maria, piena di grazia,
a̱ve mari̱a, pje̱na di gra̱tsja,

eletta Fra le spose e le vergini sei tu,
ele̱t:ta fra le spo̱ze le ve̱rdʒini se̱i tu,

Sia benedetto il frutto,
si̱a benede̱t:to̱ il fru̱t:to,

Di tue materne viscere: Gesù!
di tu̱e mate̱rne viʃere, dʒezu̱!

Prega per chi adorando a te si prostra,
pre̱ga per kjadora̱ndo a̱ te si pro̱stra,

Prega pel peccator, per l'innocente,
pre̱ga pel pek:kato̱r, per lin:notʃe̱nte,

E pel debole oppresso e pel possente,
e pel de̱bole op:pre̱s:so̱ e pel pos:se̱nte,

Misero anch'esso, tua pietà dimostra.
mi̱zero a̱ŋke̱s:so, tu̱a pjeta̱ dimo̱stra.

Prega per chi sotto l'oltraggio piega la fronte
pre̱ga per ki so̱t:to loltra̱d:ʒo pje̱ga la fro̱nte

e sotto la malvagia sorte;
so̱t:to la malva̱dʒa so̱rte;

Per noi, per noi, tu prega, prega sempre
per nọi, per nọi, tu prẹga, prẹga sẹmpre

e nell'ora della morte nostra, Prega per noi,
e nel:lọra dẹl:la mọrte nọstra, prẹga per nọi,

Ave Maria Ave! Amen!
ạve marịa ạve   amɛn!

Verdi   Caro nome, from "Rigoletto"
vẹrdi   kạro nọme   rigolẹt:to

Gualtier Maldè! nome di lui si amato,
gwaltjẹr maldẹ! nọme di lụi si ‿amạto,

ti scolpisci nel core innamorato!
ti skolpiʃi nɛl kọre in:namorạto!

Caro nome che il mio cor festi primo palpitar,
kạro nọme kẹ‿il mịo kor fẹsti prịmo palpitạr,

le delizie dell'amor mi déi sempre rammentar!
le delịtsje dẹl:lamọr mi dẹi sẹmpre ram:mentạr!

Col pensier il mio desir a te sempre volerà,
kol pɛnsjẹr il mịo dezịr a te sẹmpre volerạ,

e fin l'ultimo sospir, caro nome, tuo sarà.
e fin lụltimo sospịr, kạro nọme, tụo sarạ.

...tuo sarà, il mio desir a te ognora volerà,
   tụo sarạ, il mịo dezịr a te oɲora volerạ,

fin l'ultimo sospiro tuo sarà!
fin lụltimo sospịro tụo sarạ!

Verdi   Celeste Aïda, from "Aïda"
vẹrdi   tʃelɛste aịda

Se quel guerrier io fossi!
se kwɛl gwer:rjẹr ịo fọs:si!

se il mio sogno si avverasse!
sẹ‿il mịo sọɲo si ‿av:verạs:se!

Un esercito di prodi da me guidato,
un ezɛrtʃito di prɔdi da me gwidato,

e la vittoria e il plauso di Menfi tutta!
e la vit:tɔrja e il plauzo di mɛnfi tut:ta!

E a te, mia dolce Aïda,
e a te, mia dɔltʃe aida,

tornar di lauri cinto dirti:
tornar di lauri tʃinto dirti,

per te ho pugnato, per te ho vinto!
per te ɔ puɲato, per te ɔ vinto!

Celeste Aïda, forma divina,
tʃelɛste aida, fɔrma divina,

mistico serto di luce e fior,
mistiko sɛrto di lutʃe fjor,

del mio pensiero tu sei regina,
dɛl mio pɛnsjero tu sɛi redʒina,

tu di mia vita sei lo splendor.
tu di mia vita sɛi lo splɛndɔr.

Il tuo bel cielo vorrei ridarti,
il tuo bɛl tʃɛlo vor:rɛi ridarti,

le dolci brezze del patrio suol;
le dɔltʃe brɛd:ze dɛl patrjo swɔl;

un regal serto sul crin posarti,
un regal sɛrto sul krin pozarti,

ergerti un trono vicino al sol, ah!
erdʒɛrti un trɔno vitʃino al sol, a!

Celeste Aïda, forma divina,
tʃelɛste aida, fɔrma divina,

mistico raggio di luce e fior.....
mistiko rad:ʒo di lutʃe fjor.....

Verdi   Credo, from "Otello"
vɛrdi   krɛdo   otɛl:lo

Vanne; la tua meta già vedo.
van:ne; la tua mɛta dʒa vedo.

70

Ti spinge il tuo dimone e il tuo dimon son io,
ti spindʒe il tuo dimone e il tuo dimon son io,

e me trascina il mio,
e me traʃina il mio,

nel quale io credo inesorato Iddio:
nɛl kwale io kredo inezorato id:dio

Credo in un Dio crudel che m'ha creato simile a sè,
kredo in un dio krudɛl ke ma   kreato simile a se,

e che nell'ira io nomo.
e ke nel:lira io nomo.

Dalla viltà d'un germe o d'un atòmo vile son nato.
dal:la vilta dun dʒɛrme o dun atomo vile son nato.

Son scellerato perchè son uomo, e sento il fango
son ʃel:lerato pɛrke son womo, e sɛnto il faŋgo

originario in me. Sì! quest'è la mia fè!
oridʒinarjo in me. si, kwɛst ɛ la mia fe!

Credo con fermo cuor,
kredo kon fermo kwor,

siccome crede la vedovella al tempio,
sik:kome krede la vedovɛl:lal tɛmpjo,

che il mal ch'io penso e che da me procede
ke il mal kio pɛnso e ke da me protʃɛde

per mio destino adempio.
per mio destino adɛmpjo.

Credo che il giusto è un istrion beffardo
kredo ke il dʒusto ɛ un istrjon bef:fardo

e nel viso e nel cuor,
e nɛl vizo e nɛl kwor,

che tutto è in lui bugiardo, lagrima, bacio,
ke tut:to ɛ in lui budʒardo, lagrima, batʃo,

sguardo, sacrificio ed onor.
zgwardo, sakrifitʃo ed onor.

E credo l'uom gioco d'iniqua sorte
e kredo lwom dʒoko dinikwa sorte

dal germe della culla al verme dell'avel.
dal dʒɛrme del:la kul:la al vɛrme del:lavɛl.

Vien dopo tanta irrision la Morte. E poi?
vjɛn dopo tɑnta ir:rizjon la mɔrte. e pọi?

La Morte è il Nulla è vecchia fola il Ciel.
la mɔrte ɛ il nul:la ɛ vɛk:kja fola il tʃɛl.

Verdi   Di Provenza il mar, from "La Traviata"
verdi   di provɛntsa il mar   la travjɑta

Di Provenza il mar, il suol chi dal cor ti cancellò?
di provɛntsa il mar, il swɔl ke dal kɔr ti kantʃel:lọ

Al natío fulgente sol qual destino ti furò?
al natịo fuldʒɛnte sol kwal destịno ti furọ?

Oh rammenta pur nel duol ch'ivi gioia a te brillò,
o ram:mɛnta pur nɛl dwɔl kịvi dʒọja te bril:lọ,

e che pace colà sol su te splendere ancor può,
e ke pɑtʃe kolɑ sol su te splɛndere ɑŋkọr pwɔ,

Dio mi guidò!
dịo mi gwidọ!

Ah il tuo vecchio genitor tu non sai quanto soffrì!
ɑ il tụo vɛk:kjo dʒenitọr tu non sɑi kwɑnto sof:frị

Te lontano di squallor il suo tetto si coprì.
te lontɑno di skwal:lọr il sụo tẹt:to si koprị.

Ma se alfin ti trovo ancor, se in me speme non fallì,
ma se ɑlfịn ti trọvo ɑŋkọr, se in me spẹme non fal:lị,

se la voce dell'onor in te appien non ammutì
se la vọtʃe del:lonọr in te ɑp:pjẹn non am:mutị

ma se il fin ti trovo ancor,
ma sẹ il fin ti trọvo ɑŋkọr,

se in me speme non fallì, Dio m'esaudì!
se in me spẹme non fal:lị, dịo mezaudị!

Verdi   Ella giammai m'amò, from "Don Carlo"
verdi   ẹl:la dʒam:mɑi mamọ   dɔn kɑrlo

Ella giammai m'amò! no! quel cor chiuso è a me,
ẹl:la dʒam:mɑi mamọ! nɔ! kwɛl kɔr kjụzo ɛ a me,

72

amor per me non ha!   Io la rivedo ancor
amor per me non a!   io la rivedo aŋkɔr

contemplar trista in volto
kontɛmplar trista in vɔlto

il mio crin bianco il dì che qui di Francia venne.
il mio krin bjaŋko il di ke kwi di frantʃa vɛn:ne.

No, amor per me non ha!
nɔ, amɔr per me non a!

Ove son?   Quei doppier presso a finir!
ɔve son?   kwei dop:pjɛr prɛs:so a finir,

L'aurora imbianca il mio veron già spunta il dì!
laurɔra imbjaŋka il mio verɔn dʒa spunta il di!

Passar veggo i miei giorni lenti!
pas:sar veg:go i mjɛi dʒorni lɛnti!

il sonno o Dio, sparì da' miei occhi languenti.
il sɔn:no dio, spari da mjɛi ɔk:ki laŋgwɛnti.

Dormirò sol nel manto mio regal,
dɔrmirɔ sol nɛl manto mio regal,

quando la mia giornata è giunta a sera,
kwando la mia dʒornata ɛ dʒunta sera,

dormirò sol sotto la volta nera, avel dell'Escurial.
dɔrmirɔ sol sɔt:to la vɔlta nera, avɛl del:leskurial.

Se il serto regal a me desse il poter
se il sɛrto regal a me dɛs:se il potɛr

di leggere nei cor,   che Dio può sol può sol veder!
di lɛd:ʒere nei kor,   ke dio pwɔ sol pwɔ sol vedɛr!

Se dorme il prence, veglia il traditore;
se dɔrme il prɛntʃe, veʎa il traditore;

il serto perde il re, il consorte l'onore!
il sɛrto pɛrde il re, il konsɔrte lonore!

Verdi   Eri tu, from "Un Ballo in Maschera"
verdi   ɛri tu   un bal:lo in maskera

Alzati!   là tuo figlio a te concedo riveder.
altsati!   la tuo fiʎo a te kontʃedo rivedɛr.

73

Nell'ombra e nel silenzio,
nel:lombra e nɛl silɛntzjo,

là il tuo rossore e l'onta mia nascondi!
la il tu̯o ros:sore lonta mi̯a naskondi!

Non è su lei, nel suo fragile petto
non ɛ su lɛi, nɛl su̯o fradʒile pɛt:to

che colpir degg'io. Altro,
ke kolpir ded:ʒio. altro,

ben altro sangue a terger dessi l'offesa.
bɛn altro saŋgwe a tɛrdʒɛr des:si lof:feza.

Il sangue tuo!
il saŋgwe tu̯o!

E lo trarrà il pugnale dallo sleal tuo core:
e lo trar:ra il puɲale dal:lo zleal tu̯o kɔre,

delle lacrime mie vendicator!
del:le lakrime mi̯e vɛndikatɔr!

Eri tu che macchiavi quell'anima,
ɛri tu ke mak:kjavi kwel:lanima,

la delizia dell'anima mia...
la delitsja del:lanima mi̯a...

che m'affidi e d'un tratto esecrabile
ke maf:fidi e dun trat:to ezekrabile

l'universo avveleni per me!
lunivɛrso av:velɛni per me!

Traditor!   che compensi in tal guisa
traditɔr!   ke kompɛnsin tal gwiza

dell'amico tuo primo,...la fè!
del:lamiko tu̯o primo ...la fe!

O dolcezze perdute! o memorie
o doltʃet:se pɛrdute! o memɔrje

d'un amplesso che l'essere india!
dun amplɛs:so ke lɛs:sere india!

quando Amelia, sì bella, si candida
kwando amelja, si bɛl:la, si kandida

sul mio seno brillava d'amor!
sul mi̯o seno bril:lava damɔr!

74

È finita: non siede che l'odio,
ɛ finita, non sjede ke lodjo,

e la morte nel vedovo cor!
e la morte nel vedovo kor!

O dolcezze perdute!
o doltʃet:se pɛrdute!

o speranze d'amor!
o sperantse damor!

Verdi   Il lacerato spirito, from "Simon Boccanegra"
verdi   il latʃerato spirito   simon bok:kanegra

A te l'estremo addio palagio altero,
a te lestremo ad:dio paladʒo altɛro,

freddo sepolcro dell'angiolo mio!
fred:do sepolkro del:landʒolo mio!

Nè a proteggerti valsi! . . .
ne a protɛd:dʒerti valsi!

Oh maledetto! . . . oh vile seduttore! . . .
o maledet:to!   o vile sedut:tore!

E tu, Vergin, soffristi
e tu, verdʒin, sof:fristi

rapita lei la verginal corona?
rapita lɛi la vɛrdʒinal korona?

Ah! che dissi? . . . deliro! . . . ah, mi perdona!
a! ke dis:si?   deliro!   a, mi pɛrdona!

Il lacerato spirito del mesto genitore
il latʃerato spirito dɛl mɛsto dʒenitore

era serbato a strazio d'infamia e di dolore.
ɛra sɛrbato a stratsjo dinfamja e di dolore.

Il serto a lei de'martiri pietoso il cielo diè
il sɛrto a lɛi de martiri pjetozo il tʃɛlo dje

Resa al fulgor degli angeli, prega, Maria per me.
rezal fulgor de ʎandʒeli, prɛga, maria per me.

75

Verdi   Infelice, from "Ernani"
vˌerdi   infelˌitʃe   ernˌani

Che mai vegg'io
ke mˌai vedːʒio

nel penetral più sacro di mia magione,
nɛl penetrˌal pju sˌakro di mˌia madʒˌone,

presso a lei che sposa, esser dovrà d'un Silva,
prˌɛsːso a lˌɛi ke spˌoza, ɛsːser dovrˌa dun sˌilva,

due seduttori io scorgo!
dˌue sedutːtˌori ˌio skˌorgo!

Entrate, olà miei fidi cavalieri!
ɛntrˌate, olˌa, mjˌɛi fˌidi kavaljˌeri!

Sia ognun testimon del disonore
sˌia oɲˌun testimˌon dɛl dizonˌore

Dell' onta che si reca al suo signore.
delːlˌonta ke si rˌɛkal sˌuo siɲˌore.

Infelice! e tu credevi Si bel giglio immaculato!
infelˌitʃe e tu krˌedevi si bɛl gˌiʎo imːmakulˌato

Del tuo crine fra le nevi
dɛl tˌuo krˌine fra le nˌevi

piomba invece il disonor.
pjˌomba invˌetʃe il dizonˌor.

Ah perchè perchè l'etade in seno
a pɛrkˌe pɛrkˌe letˌade in sˌeno

Giovin core m'ha serbato!
dʒˌovin kˌore ma sɛrbˌato!

Mi dovevan gli anni almeno
mi dovˌevan ʎi ˌanːni almˌeno

Far di gelo, far di gelo ancora il cor!
far di dʒˌɛlo, far di dʒˌɛlo aŋkˌora il kˌor!

Verdi   La donna è mobile, from "Rigoletto"
vˌerdi   la dˌonːna ɛ mˌobile   rigolˌetːto

La donna è mobile qual piuma al vento,
la dˌonːna ɛ mˌobile kwal pjˌumal vˌɛnto,

muta d'accento e di pensiero.
muta dat:ʃɛnto e di pɛnsjɛro.

Sempre un amabile leggiadro viso,
sɛmprɛ un amabile led:ʒadro vizo,

in pianto o in riso, è menzognero.
in pjantọ in riso, ɛ mɛntsoɲɛro.

La donna è mobil qual piuma al vento
la don:na ɛ mọbil kwal pjumal vɛnto

muta d'accento e di pensier.
muta dat:ʃɛnto e di pɛnsjɛr.

È sempre misero chi a lei s'affida,
ɛ sɛmpre mizero ki a lɛi saf:fida,

chi le confida mal cauto il core!
ki le konfida mal kautọ il kọre!

Pur mai non sentesi felice appieno
pur mai non sɛntesi felitʃe ap:pjeno

chi su quel seno non liba amore!
ki su kwɛl sɛno non libamọre!

Verdi   O don fatale, from ''Don Carlo''
vɛrdi   o dɔn fatale   dɔn karlo

O don fatale, o don crudel,
o dɔn fatale, o dɔn krudɛl,

che in suo furor mi fece il cielo!
kẹ in suo furọr mi fɛtʃe il tʃɛlo!

Tu che ci fai Si vane altere,
tu ke tʃi fai si vane altɛre,

ti maledico, o mia beltà!
ti malediko, o mịa bɛltạ!

Versar, sol posso il pianto,
vɛrsar, sol pɔs:sọ il pjanto,

Speme non ho, soffrir dovrò,
spɛme non ɔ, sof:frir dovrọ,

Il mio delitto è orribil tanto,
il mịo delit:to ɛ ɔr:ribil tanto,

Che cancellar mai nol potrò.
ki kantʃelːar mai nol potrǫ.

O mia regina, io t'immolai
o mịa redʒina, ịo timːmolại

Al folle error di questo cor!
al fǫlːle erːrǫr di kwẹsto kɔr!

Solo in un chiostro al mondo omai
sǫlǫ ịn un kjǫstro al mǫndomại

Potrò celar il mio dolor.
potrǫ tʃelạr il mịo dolǫr.

Ohimè! O mia regina, solo in un chiostro
ɔimẹ! o mịa redʒina, sǫlǫ ịn un kjǫstro

al mondo omai Potrò celar il mio dolore.
al mǫndomại potrǫ tʃelạr il mịo dolǫre.

Oh ciel! e Carlo a morte domani gran Dio,
o tʃɛl! e kạrlo a mǫrte domạni gran dịo,

forse andrà! Ah!
fǫrse ạndrạ! a!

un dì mi resta, la speme m'arride!
un di mi rẹsta, la spẹme marːrịde!

Sia benedetto il ciel, lo salverò!
sịa benedẹtːtǫ il tʃɛl, lo salverǫ!

Verdi   O tu, Palermo, from " I Vespri Siciliani"
verdi   o tu, palẹrmo   i vẹspri sitʃiljạni

O patria, o cara patria, alfin ti veggo,
o pạtria, o kạra pạtria, alfịn ti vẹgːgo,

l'esule ti saluta dopo sì lunga assenza.
lẹzule ti salụta dǫpo si lụŋga asːsẹntsa.

Il fiorente tuo suolo repien d'amore io bacio,
il fjorẹnte tụo swǫlo ripjẹn damǫre ịo batʃo,

reco il mio voto a te col braccio e il core!
rẹko il mịo vǫto ạ te kol bratːʃo e il kǫre!

O tu, Palermo, terra adorata,
o tu palẹrmo, tɛrːra adorạta,

a me sì caro riso d'amor, ah,
a me si k**a**ro r**i**so damor, a,

alza la fronte tanto oltraggiata,
altsa la fr**o**nte t**a**nto oltrad:ʒata,

il tuo ripiglia primier splendor!
il t**u**o ripiʎa primj**e**r splend**o**r!

Chiesi aïta a straniere nazioni,
kj**ɛ**zi a**i**ta stranj**e**re natsj**o**ni,

ramingai per castella città;
ramiŋg**a**i per kast**ɛ**l:l**a** e tʃit:t**a**;

ma insensibil al fervido sprone dicea ciascun:
ma ins**ɛ**ns**i**bil al f**ɛ**rvido spr**o**ne d**i**tʃea tʃask**u**n,

Siciliani, ov' è il prisco valor?
sitʃilj**a**ni, **o**v **ɛ** il pr**i**sko val**o**r?

Su, sorgete a vittoria all' onor!
su, sordʒ**e**te a vit:t**o**rja **a**l:lon**o**r!

....il tuo ripiglia almo splendor,
   il t**u**o rip**i**ʎalmo splend**o**r,

ah, torna al primiero, almo splendor!
a, t**o**rnal primj**e**ro, **a**lmo splend**o**r!

Verdi	Pace, pace, mio Dio, from "La Forza del Destino"
v**ɛ**rdi	p**a**tʃe, p**a**tʃe mio dio	la f**o**rtsa dɛl destino

Pace, mio Dio!
p**a**tʃe, mio d**i**o!

Cruda sventura M'astringe, ahimè a languir;
kr**u**da zvent**u**ra mastr**i**ndʒe, **a**im**ɛ** a l**a**ŋgwir;

Come il dì primo da tant' anni dura
k**o**me il di pr**i**mo da tant**a**n:ni d**u**ra

Profonde il mio soffrir. Pace, mio Dio!
prof**o**nde il m**i**o sof:fr**i**r. p**a**tʃe, mio d**i**o!

L'amai, gli è ver! ma di beltà e valore
lam**a**i, ʎɛ ver! ma di bɛlt**a** e val**o**re

Cotanto Iddio l'ornò, Che l'amo ancor,
kot**a**nt**o** id:dio lorn**o**, ke l**a**mo aŋk**o**r,

nè togliermi dal core L' immagin sua saprò.
ne toʎɛrmi   dal kɔre lim:madʒin sua saprɔ.

Fatalità! un delitto Disgiunti n'ha quaggiù!
fatalita! un delit:to dizdʒunti na kwad:ʒu!

Alvaro, io t'amo, e su nel cielo è scritto:
alvaro, io tamo, e su nɛl tʃɛlo ɛ skrit:to,

Non ti vedrò mai più! Oh Dio, Dio, fa ch'io muoja;
non ti vedrɔ mai pju! o dio, dio, fa kio mwɔja;

chè la calma può darmi morte sol.
ke la kalma pwɔ darmi mɔrte sol.

Invan la pace qui sperò quest' alma
invan la patʃe kwi sperɔ kwest alma

In preda a tanto, a tanto duol,
in prɛda tanto, a tanto dwɔl,

in mezzo a tanto, a tanto duol.
in mɛd:ʒo a tanto, a tanto dwɔl.

Invan la pace quest' alma,
invan la patʃe kwestalma,

invan la pace quest' alma invan sperò.
invan la patʃe kwestalma invan sperɔ.

Misero pane a prolungar mi vieni la sconsolata vita.
mizɛro pane a proluŋgar mi vjɛni la skonsolata vita.

Ma chi giunge? Chi profanare ardisce il sacro loco?
ma ki dʃundʒe? ki profanare ardiʃe il sakro lɔko?

Maledizione!
maleditsjɔne!

Verdi   Questa o quella, from "Rigoletto"
verdi   kwesta o kwel:la   rigolet:to

Questa o quella per me pari sono
kwesta o kwel:la per me pari sono

a quant'altre d'intorno,
a kwantaltre dintorno,

d'intorno mi vedo, del mio core l'impero non cedo
dintorno mi vedo, dɛl mio kɔre limpɛro non tʃɛdo

80

meglio ad una, che ad altra beltà.
mɛʎo ad una, ke ad altra bɛltą.

La costoro avvenenza è qual dono
la kostǫro av:venɛntsa ɛ kwal dǫno

di che il fato ne infiora la vita; s'oggi questa
di ke il fato nɛ infjǫra la vįta; sǫd:ʒi kwęsta

mi torna gradita, forse un' altra doman lo sarà,
mi tǫrna gradįta, fǫrsę un ạltra domạn lo sarạ,

La costanza, tiranna del core, detestiamo qual morbo,
la kostạntsa, tirạn:na dɛl kǫre, detestjạmo kwal mǫrbo,

qual morbo crudele, sol chi vuole si serbi fedele;
kwal mǫrbo krudęle, sol ki vwǫle si sɛrbi fedęle;

Non v'ha amor se non v'è libertà.
non va amǫr se non vɛ libɛrtạ.

De' mariti il geloso furore,
de marįtil dʒelǫzo furǫre,

degli amanti le smanie derido,
deʎamạnti le zmạnje derįdo,

anco d'Argo i cent'occhi disfido se mi punge,
aŋko dạrgo i tʃɛntǫk:ki disfįdo se mi pųndʒe,

se mi punge una qualche beltà.
se mi pųndʒe ųna kwạlke bɛltą.

Verdi   Ritorna vincitor, from "Aida"
vęrdi   ritǫrna vintʃitǫr   aįda

Ritorna vincitor! E dal mio labbro uscì l'empia parola!
ritǫrna vintʃitǫr! e dal mįo lab:bro ųʃi lɛmpja parǫla!

Vincitor del padre mio, di lui che impugna l'armi per me
vintʃitǫr dɛl pạdre mįo, di lųi kę impuɲa lạrmi per me

per ridonarmi una patria, una reggia e il nome illustre
per ridonạrmi ųna pạtria, ųna rɛd:ʒa ę il nǫmę il:lųstre

che qui celar m'è forza! Vincitor de' miei fratelli
ke kwi tʃelạr mɛ fǫrtsa! vintʃitǫr de mjęi fratęl:li

ond'io lo vegga, tinto del sangue amato,
ondįo lo vęg:ga, tįnto dɛl saŋgwe ạmato,

trionfar nel plauso dell' Egizie coorti!
trionfar nɛl plauzo del:ledʒitsje koorti!

E dietro il carro, un Re mio padre di catene avvinto!
e djɛtro il kar:ro, un re mio padre di katene av:vinto!

L' insana parola, o Numi, sperdete!
linsana parola, o numi, spɛrdete!

Al seno d'un padre la figlia rendete;
al seno dun padre la fiʎa rɛndete;

Struggete le squadre dei nostri oppressor! Ah!
strud:ʒete le skwadre dei nɔstri op:pres:sor! a!

sventurata! che dissi? e l'amor mio?
zvɛnturata! ke dis:si? e lamor mio?

Dunque scordar poss'io
dunkwe skordar pos:sio

Questo fervido amore che, oppressa e schiava,
kwɛsto fɛrvido amore ke, op:prɛs:sa e skjava,

Come raggio di sol qui mi beava?
kome rad:ʒo di sol kwi mi beava?

Imprecherò la morte a Radamès, a lui ch'amo pur tanto?
imprekero la mɔrte a radamɛs, a lui kamo pur tanto?

Ah! non fu in terra mai da più crudeli
a, non fu in tɛr:ra mai da pju krudɛli

angoscie un core affranto!
aŋgoʃe un kɔre af:franto!

I sacri nomi di padre, d'amante,
i sakri nomi di padre, damante,

Nè profferir poss'io, nè ricordar,
ne prof:ferir pɔs:sio, ne rikordar,

Per l'un per l'altro confusa,
per lun per laltro konfuza,

tremante Io piangere vorrei pregar.
tremante io pjandʒere vor:rei pregar.

Ma la mia prece in bestemmia si muta.
ma la mia prɛtʃe in bestem:mja si muta.

Delitto è il pianto a me, colpa il sospir,
delit:to ɛ il pjanto a me kolpa il sospir,

In notte cupa la mente è perduta,
in nɔt:te kupa la mente ɛ perduta,

E nell'ansia crudel vorrei morir!
e nel:lansja krudɛl vor:rɛi morir!

Numi, pietà del mio soffrir!
numi, pjeta dɛl mio sof:frir!

Speme non v'ha pel mio dolor;
spɛme non va pel mio dolor;

Amor fatal, tremendo amor spezzami il cor, fammi morir!
amor fatal, tremɛndo amor spɛt:samil kɔr, fam:mi morir!

Numi, pietà del mio soffrir.
numi, pjeta dɛl mio sof:frir.

Verdi   Stride la vampa, from "Il Trovatore"
verdi   stride la vampa   il trovatore

Stride la vampa, la folla indomita corre a quel foco,
stride la vampa, la fɔl:la indomita kɔr:re a kwɛl fɔko,

lieta in sembianza, urli di gioja intorno echeggiano,
ljeta in sembjantsa, urli di dʒɔja intorno ekɛd:ʒano,

cinta di sgherri donna s'avanza;
tʃinta di zgɛr:ri dɔn:na savantsa;

sinistra splende sui volti orribile
sinistra splɛnde sui vɔlti or:ribile

La tetra fiamma che s'alza,
la tɛtra fjam:ma ke saltsa,

che s'alza al ciel, che s'alza al ciel.
ke saltsa al tʃɛl, ke sal tsal tʃɛl.

Stride la vampa, giunge la vittima nero vestita,
stride la vampa, dʒundʒe la vit:tima nɛro vestita,

discinta e scalza; grido feroce di morte levasi,
diʃinta e skaltsa; grido ferotʃe di mɔrte lɛvasi,

l'eco il ripete di balza in balza;
lɛko il ripɛte di baltsa in baltsa;

sinistra splende sui volti orribili
sinistra splɛnde sui vɔlti or:ribili

la tetra fiamma che s'alza al ciel.
la tɛtra fjam:ma ke saltsal tʃɛl.

Verdi   Volta la terrea, from "Un Ballo in Maschera"
v̯erdi   v̯olta la ter:rɛa   un bal:lo in maskera

Volta la terrea fronte alle stelle!
v̯olta la ter:rɛa fronte al:le stel:le!

come sfavilla la sua pupilla,
kome sfavil:la la sụa pupil:la,

quando alle belle il fin predice
kwando al:le bɛl:le il fin preditʃe

mesto o felice dei loro amor!
mesto o felitʃe dei loro amor!

Ah, e con Lucifero d'accordo ognor!
a, e kon lutʃifero dak:kor doɲor!

Chi la profetica sua gemma afferra,
ki la profɛtika sụa dʒem:ma af:fɛr:ra,

o passi'l mare voli alla guerra,
o pas:sil mare voli al:la gwɛr:ra,

le sue vicende soavi, amare,
le sụe vitʃɛnde soavi, amare,

da questa apprende nel dubbio cor.
da kwɛsta ap:prɛnde nɛl dub:bjo kor.

Vivaldi   Un certo non so che
vivaldi   un tʃɛrto non sɔ ke

Un certo non so che Mi giunge e passa il cor,
un tʃɛrto non sɔ ke mi dʒundʒe pas:sa il kor,

Eppur dolor non è,   Se questo fosse amor?
ep:pur dolor non ɛ,   se kwɛsto fos:se amor?

Nel suo vorace ardor, Già posi incauta, posi il piè?
nel sụo voratʃe ardor, dʒa posiŋkauta, posil pje?

PHONETIC TRANSCRIPTION OF GERMAN SONGS AND ARIAS

Werner Singer and Berton Coffin

The German songs have been transcribed phonetically
according to the indicated bibliography with the following
indicated exceptions. These exceptions are due to the fact
that this book is written primarily for singers, that this is
a transcription of phonetic principles used in the singing of
the German language, as used by German singers, and that the
transcription is written for a fluent reading of the phonetic
sounds and accents.

Punctuation

Punctuation is placed in the phonetic transcription to
enable the singer to read the phonetics with the phrasing of
the text.

Indication of Accent

It is felt that the underlined accent (fɛrge:blɪçəs
ʃtɛntçɛn) will read more fluently than (fɛr'ge:blɪçəs
'ʃtɛntçən) the usual accent indication.

Double Liquid Consonants

In this text the double liquid consonants mm, nn, ll and
rr will be written as two consonants as in the following words:
Himmel, Wellen, Sonne and Herren. While it may be correct to
call such combinations long consonants, it is not necessary
that they be long but that they be split in the middle. The
split being accompanied by a variation of breath pressure or
a wave in which a slight decrease of pressure is followed by
an increase of pressure. This applies only to singing
(according to Wilcke), not to the speech of the stage German
(according to Siebs). It is necessary because singing is
usually more prolonged than speech.

Wilcke in German Diction in Singing (translated from the
German) states, "in singing, the student should accustom him-
self to lightly strike the first consonant at the utmost end
of the syllable, as for instance in the Himmel, alle, Nonne....,
then to clearly articulate the following consonant."

Do not sing:	a-lle	Wo-nnen
not	all-e	Wonn-en
but sing:	al le	Won nen

Diphthongs

Foreign singers, besides having difficulty with the German
/r/, which inclines towards the schwa [ə], have great difficulty with the German diphthongs because they make the van-
ishes too close. Also, Wilcke in German Diction in Singing

85

points out that the /a/ sound in nein is "a fairly light /a/."
I have transcribed this diphthong as [ae] whereas the /a/
sound in Haus "is generally conceded to be a not too lightly
colored /a/." I have transcribed this diphthong as [ao].
The diphthong of the word Leute has been transcribed as [ɔø]
according to Siebs. These transcriptions give the best
continuation of vibrations known as cantilena or singing
line. For more information see Overtones of Bel Canto (the
Phonetic Basis of Artistic Singing), Coffin, 1980.

The combination of d and t between two words

In words ending in d or t followed by words beginning with
d or t, a strong t is used to give the articulation. However,
in this transcription it is indicated by a tie in the four
possible combinations, i.e., und Treu, bist du, nicht treu, and
und das. The tie is also used when the same sounds occur phonetically, i.e., bist zu.....bɪst tsuː. This is true of other
consonants which have the same place of articulatory contact.
This is so the vocal line will be less interrupted.

Symbol for glottal attack, | rather than ?

The | symbol for glottal attack has been used instead of
the ? symbol frequently used. Siebs 1958. The glottal attack,
long feared by singers and teachers of singing, has been
transcribed only during the flow of a phrase, not at the
beginning. Artistic use of this interruption of vocal line is
necessary for intelligibility of the German language.

Long and Short Vowels

The singer should at all times note the difference between
the long and short vowels which are characteristic of the German language. The vowels eː, iː, yː, etc., should be held as
long as possible in the time value allotted by the music and, in
contrast, the short vowels ɛ, ɪ, ʏ, etc., should be shortened by
the slight anticipation of the closing consonant of the syllable. The symbol ː indicates a vowel is long. Absence of the
symbol indicates a short vowel.

ig Endings

All ig endings have been transcribed as ɪç with the following exception. When the ig ending is followed in a word by
ich suffix the ig is transcribed as ɪk, i.e., königlich would
sound better to the ear pronounced køːnɪklɪç rather than
køːnɪçlɪç according to authorities, see Bithell. Apparently
the double fricative is of questionable taste.

Value of the phonetic symbols used in the transcription of German

Phonetic Symbol	Sounds as derived from English sounds	As found in German words
	VOWELS	
long ɑː	like /a/ in Father (pronounced long)	Kahn......kɑːn
short a	father (pronounced short)	Mann......man
long ɛː	men, set, (pronounced long)	währen....vɛːrən
short ɛ	men, set, (pronounced short)	weg.......vɛk
long eː	as in grey (without the diphthong vanish to i.)	Teer......teːr
short e	as above but short duration	der.......der
ə	like e in quicken	baden.....bɑːdən
long iː	believe	Sieb......ziːp
short ɪ	in, is	in........ɪn
long oː	Rose, loan (without diphthong vanish to u.)	Rose......roːzə
short ɔ	got, with lips more rounded	Gott......gɔt
long uː	food, loom	Kuh.......kuː
short ʊ	put, book	Unter.....ʊntər
long øː	gate pronounced with kiss formation (tongue position of e, lip position of u)	Löhne.....løːnə
short œ	met pronounced with rounded lips	Götter....gœtər
long yː	meat with rounded lips	Lüge......lyːgə
short ʏ	it with rounded lips	Müller....mʏlər
	DIPHTHONGS	
ae	mine, thy	Mein......maen
ɑo	house, mount	Haus......hɑos
ɔø	boy	treu......trɔø
	CONSONANTS	
b	bad, both	Bote......boːtə
ç	human |çuman|, frictional and whispered	Licht.....lɪçt

87

d	dine, tongue almost touching upper teeth	dein......daen	
f	fine	fein......faen	
g	give, God	geben.....geːbən	
h	His, house	Herr......hɛr	
x	very slowly whisper the word hock so that the back of the tongue rises slowly towards the |k| without the tongue contacting the velum	Bach......bax	
j	yes	ja........jɑː	
k	key	Kopf......kɔpf	
l	clear l, even after vowels more fronted and dental than in English. May be obtained by taking position and tongue tension of th in English and pronouncing it l	Welle.....vɛllə	
m	mine	Mein......maen	
n	nine	Nein......naen	
ŋ	Ring	Ring......rɪŋ	
p	past	Post......pɔst	
r	roll, but with rolled r	reden.....reːdən (little heard on endings)	
s	less, best	es........ɛs	
ʃ	shine	Schein....ʃaen	
t	tall, tongue touching upper teeth	Tahl......tɑːl	
v	voice, vine	Wein......vaen	
z	zoo	so........zoː	
|	glottal stop produced by sudden release of breath after it has been banked up behind the vocal chords. The variation of intensity in the glottal stop is of a high artistic importance. When overdone, it can be injurious to the voice.	nur |alleine |ist's	

Bach   Bist du bei mir
          bɪst duː b͜ae miːr

Bist du bei mir, geh ich mit Freuden
bɪst duː b͜ae miːr, geː |ɪç mɪt frɔ͜ødən

zum Sterben und zu meiner Ruh!
tsum ʃtɛrbən |ʊnt tsuː m͜aenər ruː

Ach, wie vergnügt wär so mein Ende,
ax, viː fɛrgny͜ːkt vɛːr zoː m͜aen |ɛndə

es drückten deine lieben Hände
ɛs dry͜ktən d͜aenə liːbən hɛndə

mir die getreuen Augen zu!
miːr di gətrɔ͜øn |͜aogən tsuː

Bach   Es ist vollbracht
          ɛs |ɪst fɔlbra͜xt

Es ist vollbracht!
ɛs |ɪst fɔlbra͜xt

Vergiss ja nicht dies Wort,
fɛrgɪs jaː nɪçt diːs vɔrt,

mein Herz, das Jesus spricht,
m͜aen hɛrts, das jeːzʊs ʃprɪçt

da er am Kreuze für dich stirbet
daː |eːr |am krɔ͜øtsə fyːr dɪç ʃtɪrbət

und dir die Seligkeit erwirbet,
|ʊnt diːr di zeːlɪçk͜aet |ɛrvɪrbət,

da er, der Alles, Alles wohl gemacht
daː |eːr der |alləs, |alləs voːl gəma͜xt

nunmehro spricht: es ist vollbracht!
nu͜ːnmero ʃprɪçt, ɛs |ɪst fɔlbra͜xt

Bach   Komm, süsser Tod
            kɔm, zyːsər toːt

Komm, süsser Tod, komm, sel'ge Ruh'!
kɔm, zyːsər toːt, kɔm, zeːlgə ruː,

Komm, führe mich in Friede,
kɔm, fyːrə mɪç |ɪn friːdə,

weil ich der Welt bin müde.
vael |ɪç der vɛlt bɪn myːdə.

Ach komm, ich wart' auf dich,
ax kɔm, ɪç vart |aof dɪç,

komm bald und führe mich,
kɔm balt |unt fyːrə mɪç,

drück' mir die Augen zu.
drʏk miːr di |aogən tsuː.

Komm, sel'ge Ruh'!
kɔm, zeːlgə ruː

Beethoven   Abscheulicher! wo eilst du hin?
                 apʃɔølɪçer   voː |aelst duː hɪn

                 "Fidelio"
                 fideːlio

Abscheulicher! wo eilst du hin?
apʃɔølɪçer   voː aelst duː hɪn

was hast du vor in wildem Grimme?
vas hast duː foːr |ɪn vɪldəm grɪmmə

Des Mitleids Ruf,
dɛs mɪtlaets ruːf,

der Menschheit Stimme
der mɛnʃhaet ʃtɪmmə

rührt nichts mehr deinen Tigersinn.
ryːrt nɪçtss meːr daenən tiːgərzɪn.

Doch toben auch wie Meereswogen
dɔx toːbən |aox viː meːrəsvoːgən

90

dir in der Seele Zorn und Wuth,
diːr |ɪn der zeːlə tsɔrn ʊnt vuːt,

so leuchte mir ein Farbenbogen,
zoː lɔøçtə miːr |aen farbənboːgən,

der hell auf dunklen Wolken ruht.
der hɛl |aof dʊŋklən vɔlkən ruːt.

Der blickt so still', so friedlich nieder,
der blɪkt zoː ʃtɪl, zoː friːtlɪç niːdər,

der spiegelt alte Zeiten wieder,
der ʃpiːgəlt |altə tsaetən viːdər,

und neu besänftigt wallt mein Blut.
|ʊnt nɔø bəzɛnftɪçt valt maen bluːt.

Komm Hoffnung, lass den letzten Stern
kɔm hɔfnʊŋ, las den lɛtstən ʃtɛrn

der Müden nicht erbleichen,
der myːdən nɪçt |ɛrblaeçən,

o komm, erhell' mein Ziel, sei's noch so fern,
oː kɔm, |ɛrhɛl maen tsiːl, zaes nɔx zoː fɛrn,

die Liebe, sie wird's erreichen,
di liːbə, ziː vɪrts |ɛrraeçən,

ja, ja, sie wird's erreichen.
jɑː, jɑː, ziː vɪrts |ɛrraeçən.

Komm, o komm, komm, o Hoffnung!
kɔm, oː kɔm, kɔm, oː hɔfnʊŋ

Lass den letzten Stern
las den lɛtstən ʃtɛrn

der Müden nicht erbleichen!
der myːdən nɪçt |ɛrblaeçən

Erhell' ihr Ziel, sei's noch so fern,
ɛrhɛl |iːr tsiːl, zaes nɔx zoː fɛrn,

die Liebe wird's erreichen.
di liːbə vɪrts |ɛrraeçən.

Ich folg' dem innern Triebe,
ıç fɔlk dem |ınnərn triːbə,

ich wanke nicht,
ıç vaŋkə nıçt,

mich stärkt die Pflicht der treuen Gattenliebe.
mıç ʃtɛrkt di pflıçt der trɔ͜øən ga͟tənliːbə.

O du, für den ich alles trug,
oː duː, fyːr den |ıç |alləs truːk,

könnt' ich zur Stelle dringen,
kœnt |ıç tsuːr ʃtɛllə drı͟ŋən,

wo Bosheit dich in Fesseln schlug,
voː bo͟ːshaet dıç |ın fɛsəln ʃluːk,

und süssen Trost dir bringen!
ʊnt sy͟ːsən troːst diːr brı͟ŋən

Beethoven   Adelaide
               adəlai͟ːdə

Einsam wandelt dein Freund im Frühlingsgarten,
a͟enzam va͟ndəlt da͟en frɔ͜ønt |ım fryːlıŋsgartən,

mild vom lieblichen Zauberlicht umflossen,
mılt vɔm li͟ːplıçən tsɑobərlıçt |umflɔ͟sən,

das durch wankende Blüthenzweige zittert,
das dʊrç vaŋkəndə bly͟ːtəntsvaegə tsı͟tərt,

Adelaide!
adəlai͟ːdə

In der spiegelnden Fluth, im Schnee der Alpen,
ın der ʃpi͟ːgəlndən fluːt, ım ʃneː der |a͟lpən,

in des sinkenden Tages Goldgewölke,
ın dɛs zı͟ŋkəndən tɑ͟ːgəs gɔ͟ltgvœlkə,

im Gefilde der Sterne strahlt dein Bildnis,
ım gəfı͟ldə der ʃtɛrnə ʃtrɑ͟ːlt da͟en bı͟ltnıs,

Adelaide!
adəlai͟ːdə

92

Abendlüftchen im zarten Laube flüstern,
aːbəntlʏftçən |ɪm tsɑːrtən lɑobə flʏstərn,

Silberglöckchen des Mai's im Grase säuseln,
zɪlbərglœkçən dɛs maes |ɪm grɑːzə zɔøzəln,

Wellen rauschen und Nachtigallen flöten:
vɛllən rɑoʃən |ʊnt naxtigallən fløːtən,

Adelaide!
adəlaiːdə

Einst, o Wunder! entblüht auf meinem Grabe
aenst, oː vʊndər ɛntblyːt |ɑof maenəm grɑːbə

eine Blume der Asche meines Herzens,
|aenə bluːmə der |aʃə maenəs hɛrtsəns,

deutlich schimmert, auf jedem Purpurblättchen:
dɔøtlɪç ʃɪmmərt, ɑof jeːdəm pʊrpurblɛtçən,

Adelaide!
adəlaiːdə

Beethoven   Die Ehre Gottes aus der Natur
                 di |eːrə gɔtəs |ɑos der natuːr

Die Himmel rühmen des Ewigen Ehre,
di hɪmməl ryːmən dɛs |eːvɪgən |eːrə,

ihr Schall pflanzt seinen Namen fort.
iːr ʃal pflantst zaenən nɑːmən fɔrt.

Ihn rühmt der Erdkreis,
iːn ryːmt der |eːrtkraes,

ihn preisen die Meere, vernimm, o Mensch,
iːn praezən di meːrə, fɛrnɪm, oː mɛnʃ,

ihr göttlich Wort!
iːr gœtlɪç vɔrt

Wer trägt der Himmel unzählbare Sterne?
veːr trɛːkt der hɪmməl |ʊntsɛːlbarə ʃtɛrnə

Wer führt die Sonn' aus ihrem Zelt?
veːr fyːrt di zɔn |ɑos |iːrəm tsɛlt

93

Sie kommt und leuchtet und lacht uns von ferne
zi kɔmt |ʊnt lɔøçtət |ʊnt laxt |ʊns fɔn fɛrnə

und läuft den Weg gleich als ein Held.
|ʊnt lɔøft den veːk glaeç |als |aen hɛlt.

Beethoven   Die Trommel gerühret
               di trɔmməl gəryːrət

Die Trommel gerühret, das Pfeifchen gespielt!
di trɔmməl gəryːrət, das pfaefçən gəʃpiːlt

Mein Liebster gewaffnet dem Haufen befiehlt,
maen liːpstər gəvafnət dem haofən bəfiːlt,

die Lanze hoch führet, die Leute regieret.
di lantsə hoːx fyːrət, di lɔøtə rəgiːrət

Wie klopft mir das Herz!
viː klɔpft miːr das hɛrts

Wie wallt mir das Blut!
viː valt miːr das bluːt

O hätt ich ein Wämslein und Hosen und Hut!
oː hɛt |ɪç |aen vɛmslaen |ʊnt hoːzən |ʊnt huːt

Ich folgt' ihm zum Thor 'naus
ɪç fɔlkt |iːm tsum toːr naos

mit muthigem Schritt,
mɪt muːtɪgəm ʃrɪt,

ging' durch die Provinzen, ging' überall mit.
giŋ dʊrç di provɪntsən, giŋ |yːbər |al mit.

Die Feinde schon weichen, wir schiessen da drein;
di faendə ʃoːn vaeçən, viːr ʃiːsən daː draen

Welch' Gluck sondergleichen,
velç glʏk zɔndərglaeçən,

ein Mannsbild zu sein!
|aen mansbɪlt tsuː zaen

Beethoven   Freudvoll und leidvoll
              frɔøtfɔl |ʊnt laetfɔl

Freudvoll und leidvoll, gedankenvoll sein;
frɔøtfɔl |ʊnt laetfɔl, gədaŋkənfɔl zaen

Langen und bangen in schwebender Pein;
laŋən |ʊnt baŋən |ɪn ʃveːbəndər paen

himmelhoch jauchzend, zum Tode betrübt;
hɪmməlhoːx jaoxtsənt, tsʊm toːdə bətryːpt

glücklich allein ist die Seele, die liebt!
glʏklɪç |allaen |ɪst di zeːlə, di liːpt

Beethoven   Ich liebe dich
              ɪç liːbə dɪç

Ich liebe dich, so wie du mich,
ɪç liːbə dɪç, zoː viː duː mɪç,

am Abend und am Morgen,
am aːbənt |ʊnt |am mɔrgən,

noch war kein Tag, wo du und ich
nɔx vaːr kaen taːk, voː duː |ʊnt |ɪç

nicht theilten uns're Sorgen.
nɪçt taeltən |ʊnzrə zɔrgən.

Auch waren sie für dich und mich
aox vaːrən ziː fyːr dɪç |ʊnt mɪç

getheilt leicht zu ertragen;
gətaelt laeçt tsuː |ɛrtraːgən,

du tröstetest im Kummer mich,
duː trøːstətəst |ɪm kʊmmər mɪç,

ich weint' in deine Klagen,
ɪç vaent |ɪn daenə klaːgən,

D'rum Gottes Segen über dir,
drʊm gɔtəs zeːgən |yːbər diːr,

du meines Lebens Freude,
duː maenəs leːbəns frɔødə,

95

Gott schütze dich, erhalt' dich mir,
gɔt ʃʏtsə dɪç, ɛrhalt dɪç miːr,

schütz' und erhalt' uns beide!
ʃʏts |ʊnt |ɛrhalt |ʊns baedə

Beethoven   Mailied
              maeliːt

Wie herrlich leuchtet mir die Natur,
viː hɛrlɪç lɔøçtət miːr di natuːr,

wie glänzt die Sonne, wie lacht die Flur!
viː glɛntst di zɔnnə, viː laxt di fluːr

Es dringen Blüthen aus jedem Zweig
ɛs drɪŋən blyːtən |aos jeːdəm tsvaek

und tausend Stimmen
|ʊnt taozənt ʃtɪmmən

aus dem Gesträuch,
|aos dem gəʃtrɔøç,

und Freud' und Wonne aus jeder Brust:
|ʊnt frɔøt |ʊnt vɔnnə |aos jeːdər brʊst,

O Erd' o Sonne, o Glück, o Lust!
oː |eːrt, oː zɔnnə, oː glʏk, oː lʊst

O Lieb', o Liebe, so golden schön,
oː liːp, oː liːbə, zoː gɔldən ʃøːn,

wie Morgenwolken auf jenen Höh'n!
viː mɔrgənvɔlkən |aof jeːnən høːn

Du segnest herrlich das frische Feld,
duː zeːgnəst hɛrlɪç das frɪʃə fɛlt,

Im Blüthendampfe die volle Welt.
ɪm blyːtəndampfə di fɔllə vɛlt.

O Mädchen, Mädchen, wie lieb' ich dich!
oː mɛːtçən, mɛːtçən, viː liːp |ɪç dɪç

wie blickt dein Auge, wie liebst du mich!
viː blɪkt daen |aogə, viː liːpst duː mɪç

96

So liebt die Lerche Gesang und Luft,
zoː liːpt di lɛrçə gəzaŋ |unt luft,

und Morgenblumen den Himmelsduft,
unt mɔrgənbluːmən den hɪmməlsduft,

wie ich dich liebe mit warmem Blut,
viː |ɪç dɪç liːbə mɪt varməm bluːt,

die du mir Jugend und Freud' und Muth
di duː miːr juːgənt |unt frɔøt |unt muːt

zu neuen Liedern und Tänzen gibst.
tsuː nɔøən liːdərn |unt tɛntsən giːpst.

Sei ewig glücklich, wie du mich liebst!
zae |eːvɪç glʏklɪç, viː duː mɪç liːpst

Beethoven   Mit einem gemalten Band
                 mɪt |aenəm gəmaltən bant

Kleine Blumen, kleine Blätter
klaenə bluːmən, klaenə blɛtər

streuen mir mit leichter Hand
ʃtrɔøən miːr mɪt laeçtər hant

gute junge Frühlingsgötter
guːtə juŋə fryːliŋsgœttər

tändelnd auf ein luftig Band
tɛndəlnt |aof |aen luftɪç bant.

Zephyr, nimm's auf deine Flügel,
tseːfɪr, nɪms |aof daenə flyːgəl,

schling's um meiner Liebsten Kleid;
ʃlɪŋs |um maenər liːpstən klaet

und so tritt sie vor den Spigel
unt zoː trɪt ziː foːr den ʃpiːgəl

all' in ihrer Munterkeit.
|al |ɪn |iːrər muntərkaet.

Sieht mit Rosen sich umgeben,
ziːt mɪt roːzən zɪç |umgeːbən,

selbst wie eine Rose jung.
zelpst viː ˈaenə roːzə juŋ.

Einen Blick, geliebtes Leben!
aenən blɪk, gəliːptəs leːbən

und ich bin belohnt genung.
ʊnt ˈɪç bɪn bəloːnt gənuŋ.

Fühle, fühle, was dies Herz empfindet,
fyːlə, fyːlə, vas diːs hɛrts ˈɛmpfɪndət,

reiche frei mir deine Hand,
raeçə frae miːr daenə hant,

und das Band, das uns verbindet,
ʊnt das bant, das ˈʊns fɛrbɪndət,

sei kein schwaches Rosenband.
zae kaen ʃvaxəs roːzənbant.

Beethoven   Wonne der Wehmuth
               vɔnnə der veːmuːt

Trocknet nicht, Thränen der ewigen Liebe!
trɔknət nɪçt, trɛːnən der ˈeːvɪgən liːbə

Ach, nur dem halb getrockneten Auge wie öde,
ax, nuːr dem halp gətrɔknətən ˈaogə viː ˈøːdə,

wie todt die Welt ihm erscheint!
viː toːt di vɛlt ˈiːm ˈɛrʃaent

Trocknet nicht, Thränen unglücklicher Liebe.
trɔknət nɪçt, trɛːnən ˈʊnglʏlɪçər liːbə,

Bohm   Still wie die Nacht
          ʃtɪl viː di naxt

Still wie die Nacht, tief wie das Meer,
ʃtɪl viː di naxt, tiːf viː das meːr,

soll deine Liebe sein!
zɔl daenə liːbə zaen

Wenn du mich liebst so wie ich dich,
vɛn duː mɪç liːpst zoː viː ˈɪç dɪç,

will ich dein eigen sein.
vɪl |ɪç daen |aegən zaen.

Heiss wie der Stahl und fest wie der Stein
haes viː der ʃtaːl |unt fɛst viː der ʃtaen

soll deine Liebe sein!
zɔl daenə liːbə zaen

Brahms   An die Nachtigall
          an di naxtigal

Geuss' nicht so laut der liebentflamten Lieder
gɔøs nɪçt zoː laot der liːp|ɛntflamtən liːdər

tonreichen Schall
toːnraeçən ʃal

vom Blütenast des Apfelbaums hernieder,
fɔm blyːtən|ast dɛs |apfəlbɑoms hɛrniːdər

O Nachtigall!
oː naxtigal

Du tönest mir mit deiner süssen Kehle
duː tøːnəst miːr mɪt daenər zyːsən keːlə

die Liebe wach;
di liːbə vax,

denn schon durchbebt die Tiefen meiner Seele
dɛn ʃoːn durçbeːpt di tiːfən maenər zeːlə

dein schmelzend "Ach."
daen ʃmɛltsənt |ax.

Dann flieht der Schlaf von neuem dieses Lager,
dan fliːt der ʃlaːf fɔn nɔøəm diːzəs laːgər,

ich starre dann
ɪç ʃtarrə dan

mit nassem Blick und todtenbleich und hager
mɪt nasəm blɪk |unt toːtənblaeç |unt hɑːgər

den Himmel an
den hɪmməl |an.

Fleuch, Nachtigall, in grüne Finsternisse,
flɔøç, naxtigal, ɪn gryːnə fɪnstərnɪsə,

ins Haingesträuch,
ɪns haengəʃtrɔøç,

und spend' im Nest der treuen Gattin Küsse,
ʊnt ʃpɛnt |ɪm nɛst der trɔøən gatɪn kʏsə,

entfleuch!
ɛntflɔøç

Brahms   An eine Aeolsharfe
Wolf   an |aenə |ɛːɔlsharfə

Angelehnt an die Efeuwand dieser alten
angəleːnt |an di |eːfɔøvant diːzər |altən

Terrasse,
tɛrrasə,

du, einer luftgebornen Muse
duː, aenər lʊftgəbɔrnən muːzə

geheimnisvolles Saitenspiel,
gəhaemnɪsfɔlləs zaetənʃpiːl,

fang' an, fange wieder an deine melodische Klage.
faŋ |an, faŋə viːdər |an daenə meloːdɪʃe klɑːgə.

Ihr kommet, Winde, fern herüber,
iːr kɔmmət, vɪndə, fɛrn hɛryːbər,

ach! von des Knaben, der mir so lieb war,
ax fɔn dɛs knɑːbən der miːr zoː liːp vɑːr,

frisch grünendem Hügel.
frɪʃ gryːnəndəm hyːgəl.

Und Frühlingsblüten unterweges streifend,
ʊnt fryːlɪŋsblyːtən |untərveːgəs ʃtraefənt,

übersättigt mit Wohlgerüchen,
yːbərzɛtɪçt mɪt voːlgərʏçən,

wie süss bedrängt ihr dies Herz!
viː zyːs bədrɛŋt |iːr diːs hɛrts

Und säuselt her in die Saiten,
unt zɔøzəlt heːr |ɪn di zaetən,

angezogen von wohllautender Wehmut,
angətsoːgən fɔn voːllaotəndər veːmuːt,

wachsend im Zug meiner Sehnsucht
vaksənt |ɪm tsuːk maenər zeːnzuxt

und hinsterbend wieder.
|unt hɪnʃtɛrbənt viːdər.

Aber auf einmal, wie der Wind heftiger
aːbər |aof |aenmaːl, viː der vɪnt hɛftɪgər

herstösst,
hɛrʃtøːst,

ein holder Schrei der Harfe
aen hɔldər ʃrae der harfə

wiederholt mir zu süssem Erschrecken
viːdərhoːlt miːr tsuː zyːsəm |ɛrʃrɛkən

meiner Seele plötzliche Regung,
maenər zeːlə plœtslɪçə reːguŋ,

und hier, die volle Rose streut geschüttelt
unt hiːr, di fɔllə roːzə ʃtrøøt gəʃʏtəlt

all' ihre Blätter vor meine Füsse!
|al |iːrə blɛtər foːr maenə fyːsə

Brahms   Auf dem Kirchhofe
          aof dem kɪrçhoːfə

Der Tag ging regenschwer und sturmbewegt,
der taːk gɪŋ reːgənʃveːr |unt ʃturmbəveːkt,

ich war an manch' vergess'nem Grab' gewesen,
ɪç vaːr |an manç fɛrgɛsnəm graːp gəveːzən,

verwittert Stein und Kreuz, die Kränze alt,
fɛrvɪtərt ʃtaen |unt krøøts, di krɛntsə |alt,

die Namen überwachken, kaum zu lesen.
di naːmən |yːbərvaksən, kaom tsuː leːzən

101

Der Tag ging sturmbewegt und regenschwer,
der tɑːk gɪŋ ʃtʊrmbəveːkt │ʊnt reːgənʃveːr,

auf allen Gräbern fror das Wort: Gewesen.
│ɑof │allən grɛːbərn froːr das vɔrt, gəveːzən.

Wie sturmestot die Särge schlummerten,
viː ʃtʊrməstoːt di zɛrgə ʃlʊmmərtən,

auf allen Gräbern taute still: Genesen.
ɑof │allən grɛːbərn tɑotə ʃtɪl, gəneːzən.

Brahms   Botschaft
              boːtʃaft

Wehe, Lüftchen, lind und lieblich
veːə, lʏftçən, lɪnt │ʊnt liːplɪç

um die Wange der Geliebten,
│ʊm di vaŋə der gəliːptən,

spiele zart in ihrer Locke,
ʃpiːlə tsart │ɪn │iːrər lɔkə,

eile nicht, hinweg zu flieh'n.
ɑelə nɪçt, hɪnvɛk tsuː fliːn.

Tut sie dann vielleicht die Frage,
tuːt ziː dan filɑeçt di frɑːgə

wie es um mich Armen stehe,
viː │ɛs │ʊm mɪç │armən ʃteːə,

Sprich, "Unendlich war sein Wehe,
ʃprɪç, │ʊn│ɛntlɪç vɑːr zɑen veːə,

höchst bedenklich seine Lage;
hœçst bədɛŋklɪç zɑenə lɑːgə,

aber jetzo kann er hoffen,
ɑːbər jɛtso kan ˈ│eːr hɔfən,

wieder herrlich aufzuleben,
viːdər hɛrlɪç │ɑoftsuleːbən,

denn du, Holde, denkst an ihn."
dɛn duː, hɔldə, dɛŋkst │an │iːn.

102

Brahms   Das Mädchen spricht
               das mɛːtçən ʃprɪçt

Schwalbe sag' mir an, ist's dein alter Mann
ʃvalbə, zaːk miːr |an, ɪsts daen |altər man,

mit dem du's Nest gebaut?
mɪt dem duːs nɛst gəbaot.

mit dem du's Nest gebaut?
mɪt dem duːs nɛst gəbaot

oder hast du jüngst erst dich ihm vertraut?
oːdər hast duː jʏŋst |ɛrst dɪç |iːm fɛrtraot

Sag', was zwitschert ihr, sag', was flüstert ihr
zaːk, vas tsvɪtʃərt |iːr, zaːk vas flʏstərt |iːr

des Morgens so vertraut, des Morgens so
dɛs mɔrgəns zoː fɛrtraot, dɛs mɔrgəns zoː

vertraut?
fɛrtraot

Gelt, du bist wohl auch noch nicht lange Braut?
gɛlt, duː bɪst voːl |aox nɔx nɪçt laŋə braot

Brahms   Dein blaues Auge
               daen blaoəs |aogə

Dein blaues Auge hält so still,
daen blaoəs |aogə hɛlt zoː ʃtɪl,

ich blicke bis zum Grund.
ɪç blɪkə bɪs tsum grunt.

Du fragst mich, was ich sehen will?
duː fraːkst mɪç, vas |ɪç zeːən vɪl

Ich sehe mich gesund.
ɪç zeːə mɪç gəzunt.

Es brannte mich ein glühend Paar,
ɛs brantə mɪç |aen glyːənt paːr,

noch schmerzt das Nachgefül:
nɔx ʃmɛrtst das naxgəfyːl,

das deine ist wie See so klar
das daenə |ɪst viː zeː zoː klɑːr

und wie ein See so kühl.
|ʊnt viː |aen zeː zoː kyːl.

Brahms   Der Schmied
            der ʃmiːt

Ich hör' meinen Schatz, den Hammer er schwinget,
ɪc høːr maenən ʃats, den hammər |eːr ʃvɪŋət,

das rauschet, das klinget, das dringt
das raoʃət, das klɪŋət, das drɪŋt

in die Weite
|ɪn di vaetə

wie Glockengeläute, durch Gassen und Platz.
viː glɔkəngələøtə, dʊrç gasən |ʊnt plats.

Am schwarzen Kamin, da sitzet mein Lieber,
am ʃvartsən kamiːn, dɑː zɪtsət maen liːbər,

doch, geh' ich vorüber, die Bälge dann sausen,
dɔx, geː |ɪç foryːbər, di bɛlgə dan zaozən,

die Flammen aufbrausen, und lodern um ihn.
di flammən |aofbraozən, ʊnt loːdərn |ʊm |iːn.

Brahms   Der Tod, das ist die kühle Nacht
            der toːt, das |ɪst di kyːlə naxt

Der Tod, das ist die kuhle Nacht,
der toːt, das |ɪst di kyːlə naxt,

das Leben ist der schwule Tag.
das leːbən |ɪst der ʃvyːlə tɑːk.

Es dunkelt schon, mich schläfert,
ɛs dʊŋkəlt ʃoːn, mɪç ʃlɛːfərt,

der Tag hat mich müd' gemacht.
der tɑːk hat mɪç myːt gəmaxt.

Über mein Bett erhebt sich ein Baum,
yːbər maen bɛt |ɛrheːpt zɪç |aen baom,

104

d'rin singt die junge Nachtigall;
drɪn zɪŋt di juŋə naxtigal

sie singt von lauter Liebe,
ziː zɪŋt fɔn laotər liːbə,

ich hör' es sogar im Traum.
ɪç høːr |ɛs zogaːr |ɪm traom.

Brahms   Die Mainacht
              di maenaxt

Wann der silberne Mond durch die Gesträuche
van der zɪlbərnə moːnt durç di gəʃtrɔøçə

blinkt,
blɪŋkt,

und sein schlummerndes Licht über den
ʊnt zaen ʃlʊmmərndəs lɪçt |yːbər den

Rasen streut,
raːzən ʃtrɔøt,

und die Nachtigall flötet, wandl' ich
ʊnt di naxtigal fløːtət, vandl |ɪç

traurig von Busch zu Busch.
traorɪç fɔn buʃ tsuː buʃ.

Überhüllet vom Laub girret ein Taubenpaar
yːbərhyllət fɔm laop gɪrrət |aen taobənpaːr

sein Entzücken mir vor; aber ich wende mich,
zaen |ɛnttsykən miːr foːr, aːbər |ɪç vɛndə mɪç,

suche dunklere Schatten,
zuːxə dʊŋklərə ʃatən,

und die einsame Träne rinnt.
ʊnt di |aenzaːmə trɛːnə rɪnt.

Wann, o lächelndes Bild, welches wie Morgenrot
van, oː lɛçəlndəs bɪlt, vɛlçəs viː mɔrgənroːt

durch die Seele mir strahlt,
durç di zeːlə miːr ʃtraːlt,

find ich auf Erden dich?
fɪnt |ɪç |aof |eːrdən dɪç

Und die einsame Träne bebt
ʊnt di |aenzamə trɛːnə beːpt

mir heisser, heisser die Wang herab.
miːr haesər, haesər di vaŋ hɛrap.

Brahms   Feldeinsamkeit
           fɛlt|aenzamkaet

Ich ruhe still im hohen grünen Gras
ɪç ruːə ʃtɪl |ɪm hoːən gryːnən graːs

und sende lange meinen Blick nach oben,
|ʊnt zɛndə laŋə maenən blɪk naːx |oːbən,

von Grillen rings umschwirrt ohn' Unterlass,
fon grɪllən rɪŋs |ʊmʃvɪrt |oːn |ʊntərlas,

von Himmelsbläue wundersam umwoben.
fon hɪmməlsblɔøə vʊndərzam |ʊmvoːbən.

Die schönen weissen Wolken zieh'n dahin
di ʃøːnən vaesən vɔlkən tsiːn dahɪn

durch's tiefe Blau, wie schöne stille Träume,
dʊrçs tiːfə blao, viː ʃøːnə stɪllə trɔømə,

mir ist, als ob ich längst gestorben bin
miːr |ɪst, als |ɔp |ɪç lɛŋst gəʃtɔrbən bɪn

und ziehe selig mit durch ew'ge Räume.
ʊnt tsiːə zeːlɪç mɪt dʊrç |eːvgə rɔømə.

Brahms   Immer leiser wird mein Schlummer
           ɪmmər laezər vɪrt maen ʃlʊmmər

Immer leiser wird mein Schlummer,
ɪmmər laezər vɪrt maen ʃlʊmmər,

nur wie Schleier liegt mein Kummer
nuːr viː ʃlaeər liːkt maen kʊmmər

zitternd über mir.
tsɪtərnt |yːbər miːr.

106

Oft im Traume hör' ich dich
ɔft │ɪm traomə hø:r │ɪç dɪç

rufen draus vor meiner Tür,
ru:fən draos fo:r maenər ty:r,

niemand wacht und öffnet dir,
ni:mant vaxt │unt │œfnət di:r,

ich erwach' und weine bitterlich.
ɪç │ɛrvax │unt vaenə bɪtərlɪç.

Ja, ich werde sterben müssen,
ja:, ɪç ve:rdə ʃtɛrbən mʏsən,

eine Andre wirst du küssen,
aenə │andrə vɪrst du: kʏsən,

wenn ich bleich und kalt;
vɛn │ɪç blaeç │unt kalt,

eh' die Maienlüfte weh'n,
e: di maeənlʏftə ve:n,

eh' die Drossel singt im Wald:
e: di drɔsəl zɪŋkt │ɪm valt,

Willst du mich noch einmal seh'n,
vɪlst du: mɪç mɔx │aenma:l ze:n,

komm', o komme bald, domm' o komme bald!
kɔm, o: kɔmmə balt, kɔm o: kɔmmə balt

Brahms   In der Fremde
Schumann   ɪn der frɛmdə

Aus der Heimat hinter den Blitzen rot,
aos der haemat hɪntər den blɪtsən ro:t,

da dommen die Wolken her.
da: kɔmmən di vɔlkən he:r.

Aber Vater und Mutter sind lange tot,
a:bər fa:tər │unt mutər zɪnt laŋə to:t,

es kennt mich dort keiner mehr.
ɛs kɛnt mɪç dɔrt kaenər me:r.

Wie bald, ach, wie bald kommt die stille Zeit,
viː balt, ax, viː balt kɔmt di ʃtɪllə tsaet,

da ruhe ich auch, und über mir rauscht
daː ruːə |ɪç |aox, unt |yːbər miːr raoʃt

die schöne Waldeinsamkeit,
di ʃøːnə valt|aenzamkaet,

und keiner kennt mich mehr hier.
unt kaenər kɛnt mɪç meːr hiːr.

Brahms   In Waldeseinsamkeit
            ɪn valdəs|aenzamkaet

Ich sass zu deinen Füssen in Waldeseinsamkeit;
ɪç zaːs tsuː daenən fyːsən |ɪn valdəs|aenzamkaet,

Windesatmen, Sehnen ging durch die Wipfel breit.
vɪndəs|aːtmən, zeːnən gɪŋ durç di vɪpfəl braet.

In stummen Ringen senkt' ich
ɪn ʃtummən rɪŋən zɛŋkt |ɪç

das Haupt in deinen Schoss,
das haopt |ɪn daenən ʃoːs,

und meine bebenden Hände um deine Knie
unt maenə beːbəndən hɛndə |um daenə kniː

ich schloss.
|ɪç ʃlɔs.

Die Sonne ging hinunter, der Tag verglühte all,
di zɔnnə gɪŋ hɪnuntər, der taːk fɛrglyːtə |al,

ferne, sang eine Nachtigall.
fɛrnə, zaŋ |aenə naxtigal.

Brahms   Liebestreu
            liːbəstrɔø

"O versenk', o versenk' dein Leid, mein Kind,
oː fɛrzɛŋk, oː fɛrzɛŋk daen laet, maen kɪnt,

in die See, in die Tiefe See!"
ɪn di zeː, ɪn di tiːfə zeː.

Ein Stein wohl bleibt auf des Meeres Grund,
aen ʃtaen voːl blaept |aof dɛs meːrəs grʊnt,

mein Leid kommt stets in die Höh'.
maen laet kɔmt ʃteːts |ɪn di høː.

"Und die Lieb', die du im Herzen trägst,
ʊnt di liːp, di duː |ɪm hɛrtsən trɛːkst,

brich sie ab, brich sie ab, mein Kind!"
brɪç ziː |ap, brɪç ziː |ap, maen kɪnt

Ob die Blum' auch stirbt, wenn man sie bricht,
ɔp di bluːm |aox ʃtɪrpt, vɛn man ziː brɪçt,

treue Lieb' nicht so geschwind.
trɔɶə liːp nɪçt zoː gəʃvɪnt.

"Und die Treu', 's war nur ein Wort,
ʊnt di trɔɶ, svaːr nuːr |aen vɔrt,

in den Wind damit hinaus!"
|ɪn den vɪnt damɪt hɪnaos

O Mutter, und splittert der Fels auch im Wind,
oː mʊtər, ʊnt ʃplɪtərt der fɛls |aox |ɪm vɪnt,

Meine Treue, die hält ihn aus.
maenə trɔɶə, di hɛlt |iːn |aos.

Brahms   Meine Liebe ist grün
           maenə liːbə |ɪst gryːn

Meine Liebe ist grün wie der Fliederbusch,
maenə liːbə |ɪst gryːn viː der fliːdərbʊʃ,

und mein Lieb ist schön wie die Sonne,
|ʊnt maen liːp |ɪst ʃøːn viː di zɔnnə,

die glänzt wohl herab auf den Fliederbusch
di glɛntst voːl hɛrap |aof den fliːdərbʊʃ

und füllt ihn mit Duft und mit Wonne.
|ʊnt fʏlt |iːn mɪt dʊft |ʊnt mɪt vɔnnə.

Meine Seele hat Schwingen der Nachtigall
maenə zeːlə hat ʃvɪŋən der naxtigal

und wiegt sich in blühendem Flieder,
|ʊnt viːkt zɪç |ɪn blyːəndəm fliːdər,

und jauchzet und singet von Duft berauscht
ʊnt jɑoxtsət |ʊnt zɪŋət fɔn dʊft bərɑoʃt

viel liebestrunkene Lieder.
fiːl liːbəstrʊŋkənə liːdər.

Brahms   Minnelied
            mɪnnəliːt

Holder klingt der Vogelsang,
hɔldər klɪŋt der foːgəlzaŋ,

wenn die Engelreine,
vɛn di |ɛŋəlraenə,

die mein Jünglingsherz bezwang,
di maen jyŋlɪŋshɛrts bətsvaŋ,

wandelt durch die Haine.
vandəlt dʊrç di haenə.

Röter blühen Tal und Au,
røːtər blyːən taːl |ʊnt |ɑo,

grüner wird der Wasen,
gryːnər vɪrt der vɑːzən,

wo die Finger meiner Frau Maienblumen lasen.
voː di fɪŋər maenər frɑo maeənbluːmən lɑːzən.

Ohne sie ist alles tot,
oːnə ziː |ɪst |alləs toːt,

welk sind Blüt' und Kräuter:
vɛlk zɪnt blyːt |ʊnt krɔøtər,

und kein Frühlingsabendrot
ʊnt kaen fryːlɪŋs|ɑːbəntroːt

dünkt mir schön und heiter.
dʏŋkt miːr ʃøːn |ʊnt haetər.

Traute, minnigliche Frau wollest nimmer fliehen,
trɑotə, mɪnnɪklɪçə frɑo vɔlləst nɪmmər fliːən,

dass mein Herz, gleich dieser Au,
das maen hɛrts, glaeç diːzər |ɑo,

mög' in Wonne blühen.
møːk |ɪn vɔnnə blyːən.

Brahms   Nachtigall
            naxtigal

O Nachtigall, dein süsser Schall,
oː naxtigal, daen zyːsər ʃal,

er dringet mir durch Mark und Bein.
eːr drɪŋət miːr dʊrç mark |ʊnt baen.

Nein, trauter Vogel, nein!
naen, trɑotər foːgəl, naen

Was in mir schafft so süsse Pein,
vas |ɪn miːr ʃaft zoː zyːsə paen,

das ist nicht dein,
das |ɪst nɪçt daen,

das ist von andern, himmelschönen,
das |ɪst fɔn |andərn, hɪmməlʃøːnən,

nun längst für mich verklungenen Tönen
nuːn lɛŋst fyːr mɪç fɛrkluŋənən tøːnən

in deinem Lied ein leiser Wiederhall!
|ɪn daenəm liːt |aen laezər viːdərhal

Brahms   Nicht mehr zu dir zu gehen
            nɪçt meːr tsuː diːr tsuː geːən

Nicht mehr zu dir zu gehen,
nɪçt meːr tsuː diːr tsuː geːən,

beschloss ich und beschwor ich,
bəʃlɔs |ɪç |ʊnt bəʃvoːr |ɪç,

und gehe jeden Abend,
ʊnt geːə jeːdən |ɑːbənt,

denn jede Kraft, denn jede Kraft
dɛn jeːdə kraft, dɛn jeːdə kraft

111

und jeden Halt verlor ich.
|unt je:dən halt fɛrlo:r |ıç.

Ich möchte nicht mehr leben,
ıç mœçtə nıçt me:r le:bən,

möcht augenblicks verderben,
mœçt |aogənblıks fɛrdɛrbən,

und möchte doch auch leben für dich, mit dir,
unt mœçtə dɔx |aox le:bən fy:r dıç, mıt di:r,

und nimmer sterben.
unt nımmər ʃtɛrbən.

Ach, rede, sprich ein Wort nur,
ax, re:də, ʃprıç |aen vɔrt nu:r,

ein einziges, ein klares;
aen |aentsıgəs, |aen kla:rəs,

gib Leben oder Tod mir,
gi:p le:bən |o:dər to:t mi:r,

nur dein Gefühl enthülle mir, dein wahres!
nu:r daen gəfy:l |ɛnthyllə mi:r, daen va:rəs

Brahms   O kühler Wald
            o: ky:lər valt

O kühler Wald, wo rauschest du,
o: ky:lər valt, vo: raoʃəst du:,

in dem mein Liebchen geht?
ın dem maen li:pçən ge:t

O Wiederhall, wo lauschest du,
o: vi:dərhal, vo: laoʃəst du:,

der gern mein Lied versteht?
der gɛrn maen li:t fɛrʃte:t

Im Herzen tief da rauscht der Wald,
ım hɛrtsən ti:f da: raoʃt der valt,

in dem mein Liebchen geht,
ın dem maen li:pçən ge:t,

in Schmerzen schlief der Wiederhall,
ın ʃmɛrtsən ʃliːf der viːdərhal,

die Lieder sind verweht.
di liːdər zınt fɛrveːt.

Brahms   O liebliche Wangen
         oː liːplıçə vaŋən

O liebliche Wangen, ihr macht mir Verlangen,
oː liːplıçə vaŋən, |iːr maxt miːr fɛrlaŋən,

dies rote, dies weisse zu schauen mit Fleisse.
diːs roːtə, diːs vaesə tsuː ʃaoən mıt flaesə.

Und dies nur alleine ist's nicht, was ich meine;
unt diːs nuːr |allaenə |ısts nıçt, vas |ıç maenə

zu schauen, zu grüssen, zu rühren, zu küssen!
tsuː ʃaoən, tsuː gryːsən, tsuː ryːrən, tsuː kʏsən

ihr macht mir Verlangen, O liebliche Wangen!
iːr maxt miːr fɛrlaŋən, oː liːplıçə vaŋən

O Sonne der Wonne! O Wonne der Sonne!
oː zɔnnə der vɔnnə oː vɔnnə der zɔnnə

O Augen, so saugen das Licht meiner Augen.
oː |aogən, zoː zaogən das lıçt maenər |aogən

O englische Sinnen! O himmlisch Beginnen!
oː |ɛŋlıʃə zınnən oː hımlıʃ bəgınnən

O Himmel auf Erden! magst du mir nicht werden,
oː hımməl |aof |eːrdən makst duː miːr nıçt veːrdən

O Wonne der Sonne, O Sonne der Wonne!
oː vɔnnə der zɔnnə, oː zɔnnə der vɔnne

O Schönste der Schönen! benimm mir dies Sehnen,
oː ʃøːnstə der ʃøːnən bənım miːr diːs zeːnən,

komm eile, komm, komme, du Süsse du Fromme!
kɔm |aelə, kɔm, kɔmmə, duː zyːsə duː frɔmmə

Ach Schwester, ich sterbe, ich sterb',
ax ʃvɛstər, ıç ʃtɛrbə, ıç stɛrp,

ich verderbe,
ıç fɛrdɛrbə,

komm, komme, komm eile, komm, komme, komm eile,
kɔm, kɔmmə, kɔm |aelə, kɔm, kɔmmə, kɔm |aelə,

benimm mir dies Sehnen, O Schönste der Schönen.
bən<u>ım</u> mi:r di:s ze:nən, o: ʃø:nstə der ʃø:nən.

Brahms   O wüsst ich doch den Weg zurück
           o: vy:st |ıç dɔx den ve:k tsurʏk

O wusst' ich doch den Weg züruck,
o: vy:st |ıç dɔx den ve:k tsurʏk,

den lieben Weg zum Kinderland!
den li:bən ve:k tsum kındərlant

O warum sucht' ich nach dem Glück
o: var<u>ʊm</u> zu:xt |ıç nɑ:x dem glʏk

und liess der Mutter Hand?
ʊnt li:s der m<u>ʊ</u>tər hant

O wie mich sehnet auszuruh'n,
o: vi: mıç ze:nət |ɑostsuru:n,

von keinem Streben aufgeweckt,
fɔn kaenəm ʃtre:bən |ɑofgəvɛkt,

die müden Augen zuzutun,
di my:dən |ɑogən tsu:tsutu:n,

von Liebe sanft bedeckt!
fɔn li:bə zanft bədɛkt

Und nichts zu forschen, nichts zu späh'n,
ʊnt nıçts tsu: f<u>ɔ</u>rʃən, nıçts tsu: ʃpɛ:n,

und nur zu träumen leicht und lind,
ʊnt nu:r tsu: tr<u>ɔø</u>mən laeçt |ʊnt lınt,

der Zeiten Wandel nicht zu seh'n,
der ts<u>ae</u>tən vandəl nıçt tsu: ze:n,

zum zweiten Mal ein Kind!
tsum tsv<u>ae</u>tən mɑ:l |aen kınt

O zeigt mir doch den Weg zurück,
o: tsaekt mi:r dɔx den ve:k tsurʏk,

den lieben Weg zum Kinderland!
den li:bən ve:k tsum kɪndərlant

Vergebens such' ich nach dem Glück,
fɛrge:bəns zu:x |ɪç nɑ:x dem glʏk,

ringsum ist öder Strand.
rɪŋs|um |ɪst |ø:dər ʃtrant.

Brahms   Sapphische Ode
              zapfɪʃə |o:də

Rosen brach ich nachts mir am dunklen Hage;
ro:zən brɑ:x |ɪç naxts mi:r |am duŋklən hɑ:gə,

süsser hauchten Duft sie als je am Tage;
zy:sər hɑoxtən dʊft zi: |als je: |am tɑ:gə,

doch verstreuten reich die bewegten Äste
dɔx fɛrʃtrɔøtən raeç di bəve:ktən |ɛstə

Tau, der mich nässte.
tɑo, der mɪç nɛstə.

Auch der Küsse Duft mich wie nie berückte,
ɑox der kʏsə dʊft mɪç vi: ni: bərʏktə,

die ich nachts vom Strauch deiner Lippen pflückte:
di |ɪç naxts fɔm ʃtrɑox daenər lɪpən pflʏktə,

doch auch dir, bewegt im Gemüt gleich jenen,
dɔx |ɑox di:r, bəve:kt |ɪm gəmy:t glaeç je:nən,

tauten die Tränen.
tɑotən di trɛ:nən.

Brahms   Sonntag
              zɔntɑ:k

So hab' ich doch die ganze Woche
zo: hɑ:p |ɪç dɔx di gantsə vɔxə

mein feines Liebchen nicht geseh'n,
maen faenəs li:pçən nɪçt gəze:n,

115

ich sah es an einem Sonntag
ıç zaː |ɛs |an |aenəm zɔntaːk

wohl vor der Türe steh'n:
voːl foːr der tyːrə ʃteːn,

das tausendschöne Jungfraülein,
das taozəntʃøːnə juŋfrɔølaen,

das tausendschöne Herzelein,
das taozəntʃøːnə hɛrtsəlaen,

wollte Gott, wollte Gott,
vɔltə gɔt, vɔltə gɔt,

ich wär' heute bei ihr!
|ıç vɛːr hɔøtə bae |iːr

So will mir doch die ganze Woche
zoː vɪl miːr dɔx di gantsə vɔxə

das Lachen nicht vergeh'n,
das laxən nıçt fɛrgeːn,

ich sah es en einem Sonntag
ıç zaː |ɛs |an |aenəm zɔntaːk

wohl in die Kirche geh'n:
voːl |ın di kırçə geːn,

das tausendschöne Jungfraülein,
das taozəntʃøːnə juŋfrɔølaen,

das tausendschöne Herzelein,
das taozəntʃɔːnə hɛrtsəlaen,

wollte Gott, wollte Gott,
vɔltə gɔt, vɔltə gɔt,

ich wär' heute bei ihr!
|ıç vɛːr hɔøtə bae |iːr

Brahms   Ständchen
          ʃtɛntçən

Der Mond steht über dem Berge,
der moːnt ʃteːt |yːbər dem bɛrgə,

so recht für verliebte Leut;
zoː rɛçt fyːr fɛrliːptə lɔøt,

im Garten rieselt ein Brunnen,
ɪm gartən riːzəlt |aen brʊnnən,

sonst Stille weit und breit.
zɔnst ʃtɪllə vaet |ʊnt braet.

Neben der Mauer im Schatten,
neːbən der maoər |ɪm ʃatən,

da steh'n der Studenten drei
daː ʃteːn der ʃtudɛntən drae

mit Flöt' und Geig' und Zither,
mɪt fløːt |ʊnt gaek |ʊnt tsɪtər,

und singen und spielen dabei.
ʊnt zɪŋən |ʊnt ʃpiːlən dabae.

Die Klänge schleichen der Schönsten
di klɛŋə ʃlaeçən der ʃøːnstən

sacht in den Traum hinein,
zaxt |ɪn den traom hinaen,

sie schaut den blonden Geliebten
ziː ʃaot den blɔndən gəliːptən

und lispelt: "vergiss nicht mein'"
|ʊnt lɪspəlt, fɛrgɪs nɪçt maen.

Brahms   Therese
          tereːzə

Du milchjunger Knabe, wie schaust du mich an?
duː mɪlçjuŋər knaːbə, vi ʃaost duː mɪç |an

Was haben deine Augen für eine Frage getan!
vas haːbən daenə |aogən fyːr |aenə fraːgə gətaːn

117

Alle Ratsherrn in der Stadt und alle
ˈalə ˈrɑːtshɛrn ‖ɪn der ʃtat ‖ʊnt ‖alə

Weisen der Welt
ˈvaezən der vɛlt

bleiben stumm auf die Frage,
ˈblaebən ʃtʊm ‖ɑof di ˈfrɑːgə,

die deine Augen gestellt!
di ˈdaenə ‖ɑogən gəˈʃtɛlt

Eine Meermuschel liegt auf dem Schrank
ˈaenə ˈmeːrmuʃəl liːkt ‖ɑof dem ʃraŋk

meiner Bas': da halte dein Ohr d'ran,
ˈmaenər bɑːs, dɑː ˈhaltə daen ‖oːr dran,

dann hörst du etwas!
dan høːrst duː ‖ɛtvas

Brahms   Vergebliches Ständchen
          fɛrˈgeːblɪçəs ʃtɛntçən

Guten Abend, mein Schatz, guten Abend, mein Kind!
ˈguːtən ‖ɑːbənt maen ʃats, ˈguːtən ‖ɑːbənt, maen kɪnt

Ich komm' aus Lieb' zu dir,
ɪç kɔm ‖ɑos liːp tsuː diːr,

ach, mach' mir auf die Tür.
ax max miːr ‖ɑof di tyːr.

Mein' Tür ist verschlossen,
maen tyːr ‖ɪst fɛrˈʃlɔsən,

ich lass' dich nicht ein;
‖ɪç las dɪç nɪçt ‖aen,

Mutter, die rät mir klug,
ˈmʊtər, di rɛːt miːr kluːk,

wärst du herein mit Fug
vɛrst duː hɛˈraen mɪt fuːk

wär's mit mir vorbei!
vɛːrs mɪt miːr ˈfɔrbae

118

So kalt ist die Nacht, so eisig der Wind,
zoː kalt |ɪst di naxt, zoː |ae̯zɪç der vɪnt,

dass mir das Herz erfriert,
das miːr das hɛrts |ɛrfriːrt,

mein Lieb' erlöschen wird,
mae̯n liːp |ɛrlœʃən vɪrt,

öffne mir, mein Kind, öffne mir, mein Kind!
œfnə miːr, mae̯n kɪnt, œfnə miːr, mae̯n kɪnt

Löschet dein' Lieb', lass' sie löschen nur!
lœʃət dae̯n liːp, las ziː lœʃən nuːr

Löschet sie, immerzu, geh' heim zu Bett, zur Ruh',
lœʃət ziː, ɪmmərtsuː, geː hae̯m tsuː bɛt, tsuːr ruː,

gute Nacht, mein Knab', gute Nacht, mein Knab'!
guːtə naxt, mae̯n knɑːp, guːtə naxt, mae̯n knɑːp

Brahms   Verrat
          fɛrrɑːt

Ich stand in einer lauen Nacht
ɪç ʃtant |ɪn |ae̯nər lao̯ən naxt

an einer grünen Linde,
|an |ae̯nər gryːnən lɪndə,

der Mond schien hell, der Wind ging sacht,
der moːnt ʃiːn hɛl, der vɪnt gɪŋ zaxt,

der Giessbach floss geschwinde.
der giːsbax flɔs gəʃvɪndə.

Die Linde stand vor Liebchens Haus,
di lɪndə ʃtant foːr liːpçəns hao̯s,

die Türe hört ich knarren.
di tyːrə høːrt |ɪç knarrən.

Mein Schatz liess sacht ein Mannsbild 'raus:
mae̯n ʃats liːs zaxt |ae̯n mansbɪlt rao̯s,

"Lass morgen mich nicht harren;
las mɔrgən mɪç nɪçt harrən,

lass mich nicht harren, süsser Mann,
las mɪç nɪçt harrən, zyːsər man,

wie hab ich dich so gerne!
viː haːp |ɪç dɪç zoː gɛrnə.

Ans Fenster klopfe leise an,
ans fɛnstər klɔpfə laezə |an,

mein Schatz ist in der Ferne, ja Ferne!"
maen ʃats |ɪst |ɪn der fɛrnə, jaː fɛrnə.

Lass ab vom Druck und Kuss, Feinslieb,
las |ap fɔm druk |unt kʊs, faensliːp,

du Schöner im Sammetkleide,
duː ʃøːnər |ɪm zammətklaedə,

nun spute dich, du feiner Dieb,
nuːn ʃpuːtə dɪç, duː faenər diːp,

ein Mann harrt auf der Heide, ja Heide.
aen man hart |aof der haedə, jaː haedə.

Der Mond scheint hell, der Rasen grün
der moːnt ʃaent hɛl, der raːzən gryːn

ist gut zu unsrem Begegnen,
|ɪst guːt tsuː |unzrəm bəgeːgnən,

du trägst ein Schwert und nickst so kühn,
duː trɛːkst |aen ʃveːrt |unt nɪkst zoː kyːn,

Dein Liebschaft will ich segnen, ja segnen!
daen liːpʃaft vɪl |ɪc zeːgnən, jaː zeːgnən

Und als erschien der lichte Tag,
unt |als |ɛrʃiːn der lɪçtə taːk,

was fand er auf der Heide?
vas fant |eːr |aof der haedə

Ein Toter in den Blumen lag
aen toːtər |ɪn den bluːmən laːk

zu einer Falschen Leide, ja Leide.
tsuː |aenər falʃən laedə, jaː laedə.

Brahms   Vier Ernste Gesänge
           fiːr |ɛrnstə ɡəzɛŋə

           1. Denn es gehet dem Menschen
               dɛn |ɛs ɡeːət dem mɛnʃən

Denn es gehet dem Menschen, wie dem Vieh,
dɛn |ɛs ɡeːət dem mɛnʃən, viː dem fiː,

wie dies stirbt, so stirbt er auch;
viː diːs ʃtɪrpt, zoː ʃtɪrpt |eːr |ɑox,

und haben alle einerlei Odem;
ʊnt hɑːbən |allə |aenərlae |oːdəm,

und der Mensch hat nichts mehr, denn das Vieh:
ʊnt der mɛnʃ hat nɪçts meːr, dɛn das fiː,

denn es ist alles eitel.
dɛn |ɛs |ɪst |alləs |aetəl.

Es fährt alles an einen Ort;
ɛs fɛːrt |alləs |an |aenən |ɔrt,

es ist alles von Staub gemacht,
ɛs |ɪst |alləs fɔn ʃtɑop ɡəmaxt,

und wird wieder zu Staub.
ʊnt vɪrt viːdər tsuː ʃtɑop.

Wer weiss ob der Geist des Menschen aufwärts fahre,
veːr vaes |ɔp der ɡaest dɛs mɛnʃən |ɑofvɛrts fɑːrə,

und der Odem des Viehes unterwärts
ʊnt der |oːdəm dɛs fiːəs |ʊntərvɛrts

unter die Erde, unterwärts unter die Erde fahre?
|ʊntər di |eːrdə, ʊntərvɛrts ʊntər di |eːrdə fɑːrə

Darum sahe ich, dass nichts bessers ist,
darʊm zaːə |ɪç, das nɪçts bɛsərs |ɪst,

denn dass der Mensch fröhlich sei
dɛn das der mɛnʃ frøːlɪç zae

in seiner Arbeit,
|ɪn zaenər |arbaet,

121

denn das ist sein Teil.
dɛn das |ɪst zaen tael.

Denn wer will ihn dahin bringen,
dɛn veːr vɪl |iːn dahɪn brɪŋən,

dass er sehe, was nach ihm geschehen wird?
das |eːr zeːə, vas nɑːx |iːm gəʃeːən vɪrt

Brahms   Vier Ernste Gesänge
           2. Ich wandte mich
               ɪç vantə mɪç

Ich wandte mich und sahe an alle,
ɪç vantə mɪç |unt zɑːə |an |allə,

die Unrecht leiden unter der Sonne;
di |unrɛçt laedən |untər der zɔnnə,

und siehe, da waren Tränen,
unt ziːə, dɑː vɑːrən trɛːnən,

Tränen derer die Unrecht litten,
trɛːnən deːrər di |unrɛçt lɪtən,

und hatten keinen Tröster;
unt hatən kaenən trøːstər,

und die ihnen Unrecht taten waren zu mächtig,
unt di |iːnən |unrɛçt tɛːtən vɑːrən tsuː mɛçtɪç,

dass sie keinen Tröster haben konnten.
das ziː kaenən trøːstər hɑːbən kɔntən.

Da lobte ich die Toten,
dɑː loːptə |ɪç di toːtən,

die schon gestorben waren,
di ʃoːn gəʃtɔrbən vɑːrən,

mehr als die Lebendigen,
meːr |als di lebɛndɪgən,

die noch das Leben hatten.
di nɔx das leːbən hatən.

Und der noch nicht ist,
unt der nɔx nɪçt |ist,

122

ist besser, als alle beide,
ɪst bɛsər, als |alə baedə,

und des Bösen nicht inne wird,
ʊnt dɛs bøːzən nɪçt |ɪnnə vɪrt,

das unter der Sonne geschieht.
das |ʊntər der zɔnnə gəʃiːt.

Brahms   Vier Ernste Gesänge
             3. O Tod, wie bitter bist du
                 oː toːt, viː bɪtər bɪst duː

O Tod, wie bitter bist du,
oː toːt, viː bɪtər bɪst duː,

wenn an dich gedenket ein Mensch,
vɛn |an dɪç gədɛŋkət |aen mɛnʃ,

der gute Tage und genug hat
der guːtə tɑːgə |ʊnt gənuːk hat

und ohne Sorge lebet;
|ʊnt |oːnə zɔrgə leːbət,

und dem es wohlgeht in allen Dingen
ʊnt dem |ɛs voːlgeːt |ɪn |allən dɪŋən

und noch wohl essen mag!
|ʊnt nɔx voːl |ɛsən mɑːk

O Tod, wie wohl tust du dem Dürftigen,
oː toːt, viː voːl tuːst duː dem dʏrftɪgən,

der da schwach und alt ist,
der dɑː ʃvax |ʊnt |alt |ɪst,

der in allen Sorgen steckt,
der |ɪn |allən zɔrgən ʃtɛkt,

und nichts Bessers zu hoffen,
ʊnt nɪçts bɛsərs tsuː hɔfən,

noch zu erwarten hat!
nɔx tsuː |ɛrvartən hat

O Tod, wie wohl tust du.
oː toːt, viː voːl tuːst du.

123

Brahms   Vier Ernste Gesänge
          4. Wenn ich mit Menschen
              vɛn |ɪç mɪt mɛnʃən

Wenn ich mit Menschen und mit Engelszungen redete,
vɛn |ɪç mɪt mɛnʃən |ʊnt mɪt |ɛŋəlstsʊŋən reːdətə,

und hätte der Liebe nicht,
ʊnt hɛtə der liːbə nɪçt,

so wär ich ein tönend Erz,
zoː vɛːr |ɪç |aen tøːnənt |ɛrts,

oder eine klingende Schelle.
oːdər |aenə klɪŋəndə ʃɛllə.

Und wenn ich weissagen könnte, und wüsste
ʊnt vɛn |ɪç vaeszɑːgən kœntə, |ʊnt vʏstə

alle Geheimnisse und alle Erkenntniss,
|allə gəhaemnɪsə |ʊnt |allə |ɛrkɛntnis,

und hätte allen Glauben, also,
ʊnt hɛtə |allən glɑobən, |alzo,

dass ich Berge versetzte;
das |ɪç bɛrgə fɛrzɛtstə,

und hätte der Liebe nicht, so wäre ich nichts.
ʊnt hɛtə der liːbə nɪçt, zoː vɛːrə |ɪç nɪçts.

Und wenn ich alle meine Habe den Armen gäbe,
ʊnt vɛn |ɪç |allə maenə hɑːbə den |armən gɛːbə,

und liesse meinen Leib brennen;
ʊnt liːsə maenən laep brɛnnən,

und hätte der Liebe nicht,
ʊnt hɛtə der liːbə nɪçt,

so wäre mir's nichts nütze.
zoː vɛːrə miːrs nɪçts nʏtsə.

Wir sehen jetzt durch einen Spiegel
viːr zeːən jɛtst dʊrç |aenən ʃpiːgəl

in einem dunkeln Worte;
|ɪn |aenəm dʊŋkəln vɔrtə,

dann aber von Angesicht zu Angesichte.
dan |aːbər fɔn |angəzɪçt tsuː |angəzɪçtə.

Jetzt erkenne ich's stückweise,
jɛtst |ɛrkɛnnə |ɪçs ʃtʏkvaezə,

dann aber werd' ich's erkennen,
dan |aːbər veːrt |ɪçs |ɛrkɛnnən,

gleich wie ich erkennet bin.
glaeç viː |ɪç |ɛrkɛnnət bɪn.

Nun aber bleibet Glaube, Hoffnung,
nuːn |aːbər blaebət glaobə, hɔfnuŋ,

Liebe, diese drei;
liːbə, diːzə drae,

aber die Liebe ist die grösseste unter ihnen.
aːbər di liːbə |ɪst di grøːsəstə |untər |iːnən.

Brahms   Von ewiger Liebe
            fɔn |eːvɪgər liːbə

Dunkel, wie dunkel in Wald und in Feld.
duŋkəl, viː duŋkəl |ɪn valt |unt |ɪn fɛlt

Abend schon ist es, nun schweiget die Welt.
aːbənt ʃoːn |ɪst |ɛs, nuːn ʃvaegət di vɛlt.

Nirgend noch Licht, und nirgend noch Rauch, ja,
nɪrgənt nɔx lɪçt, unt nɪrgənt nɔx raox, jaː,

und die Lerche sie schweiget nun auch.
unt di lɛrçə ziː ʃvaegət nuːn |aox.

Kommt aus dem Dorfe der Bursche heraus,
kɔmt |aos dem dɔrfə der burʃə hɛraos,

gibt das Geleit der Geliebten nach Haus,
giːpt das gəlaet der gəliːptən nax haos,

führt sie an Weidengebüsche vorbei,
fyːrt ziː |an vaedəngəbʏʃə fɔrbae,

redet so viel und so mancherlei:
reːdət zoː fiːl |unt zoː mançərlae,

"Leidest du Schmach und betrübest du dich,
laedəst duː ʃmaːx | unt bətryːbəst duː dɪç,

leidest du Schmach von andern um mich,
laedəst duː ʃmaːx fɔn |andərn |um mɪç,

werde die Liebe getrennt so geschwind,
veːrdə di liːbə gətrɛnt zoː gəʃvɪnt,

schnell wie wir früher vereiniget sind.
ʃnɛl viː viːr fryːər fɛr|aenɪgət zɪnt.

Scheide mit Regen und scheide mit Wind,
ʃaedə mɪt reːgən |unt ʃaedə mɪt vɪnt,

schnell wie wir früher vereiniget sind."
ʃnɛl viː viːr fryːər fɛr|aenɪgət zɪnt.

Spricht das Mägdelein, Mägdelein spricht:
ʃprɪçt das mɛːkdəlaen, mɛːkdəlaen ʃprɪçt,

"Unsere Liebe, sie trennet sich nicht!
unzərə liːbə, ziː trɛnnət zɪç nɪçt

Fest ist der Stahl und das Eisen gar sehr,
fɛst |ɪst der ʃtaːl |unt das |aezən gaːr zeːr,

unsere Liebe ist fester noch mehr.
unzərə liːbə |ɪst fɛstər nɔx meːr.

Eisen und Stahl, man schmiedet sie um,
aezən |unt ʃtaːl, man ʃmiːdət ziː |um,

unsere Liebe, wer wandelt sie um?
unzərə liːbə, veːr vandəlt ziː |um

Eisen und Stahl, sie können zergehn,
aezən |unt ʃtaːl, ziː kœnnən tsɛrgeːn,

unsere Liebe muss ewig, ewig bestehn."
unzərə liːbə mus |eːvɪç, eːvɪç bəʃteːn.

Brahms　　　Wie bist du meine Königin
　　　　　　viː bɪst duː maenə køːnɪgɪn

Wie bist du meine Königin,
viː bɪst duː maenə køːnɪgɪn,

durch sanfte Güte wonnevoll!　Du lächle nur,
dʊrç zanftə gyːtə vɔnnəfɔl.　duː lɛçlə nuːr,

Lenzdüfte wehn durch mein Gemüte, wonnevoll!
lɛntsdʏftə veːn dʊrç maen gəmyːtə, vɔnnəfɔl.

Frisch aufgeblühter Rosen Glanz,
frɪʃ |aofgəblyːtər roːzən glants,

vergleich ich ihn den deinigen?
fɛrglaeç |ɪç |iːn den daenigən.

Ach, über alles, was da blüht,
ax, yːbər |alləs, vas daː blyːt,

ist deine Blüte, wonnevoll!
ɪst daenə blyːtə, vɔnnəfɔl.

Durch tote Wüsten wandle hin,
dʊrç toːtə vyːstən vandlə hɪn,

und grüne Schatten breiten sich,
ʊnt gryːnə ʃatən braetən zɪç,

ob fürchterliche Schwüle dort
ɔp fʏrçtərlɪçə ʃvyːlə dɔrt

ohn' Ende brüte, wonnevoll.
|oːn |ɛndə bryːtə, vɔnnəfɔl.

Lass mich vergehn in deinem Arm!
las mɪç fɛrgeːn |ɪn daenəm |arm.

Es ist in ihm ja selbst der Tod,
ɛs |ɪst |ɪn |iːm jaː zɛlpst der toːt,

ob auch die herbste Todesqual
ɔp |aoç di hɛrpstə toːdəskvaːl

die Brust durchwüte, wonnevoll, wonnevoll!
di brʊst dʊrçvyːtə, vɔnnəfɔl, vɔnnəfɔl.

127

Brahms   Wiegenlied
             vi͡ːgənliːt

Guten Abend, gut' Nacht,
guːtən |aːbənt, guːt naxt,

mit Rosen bedacht, mit Näg'lein besteckt,
mɪt ro͡ːzən bəda͡xt, mɪt nɛ͡ːglaen bəʃtɛ͡kt,

schlupf' unter die Deck'.
ʃlʊpf |u͡ntər di dɛk.

Morgen früh, wenn Gott will,
mɔ͡rgən fryː, vɛn gɔt vɪl,

wirst du wieder geweckt.
vɪrst duː vi͡ːdər gəvɛ͡kt.

Guten Abend, gut' Nacht,
guːtən |aːbənt, guːt naxt,

von Eng'lein bewacht
fɔn |ɛ͡ŋlaen bəva͡xt,

die zeigen im Traum
di tsa͡egən |ɪm tra͡om

dir Christkindleins Baum:
diːr krɪ͡stkɪntlaens ba͡om,

Schlaf' nun selig und süss,
ʃlaːf nuːn ze͡ːlɪç |ʊnt zyːs,

schau' im Traum's Paradies.
ʃa͡o |ɪm tra͡oms paradi͡ːs.

Brahms   Wie Melodien zieht es
             viː melodi͡ːən tsiːt |ɛs

Wie Melodien zieht es
viː melodi͡ːən tsiːt |ɛs

mir leise durch den Sinn,
miːr la͡ezə dʊrç den zɪn,

wie Frühlingsblumen blüht es,
viː fry͡ːlɪŋsbluːmən blyːt |ɛs,

und schwebt wie Duft dahin.
ʊnt ʃveːpt viː dʊft dahɪn.

Doch kommt das Wort und fasst es
dɔx kɔmt das vɔrt |ʊnt fast |ɛs

und führt es vor das Aug',
|ʊnt fyːrt |ɛs foːr das aok,

wie Nebelgrau erblasst es
viː neːbəlgrao |ɛrblast |ɛs

und schwindet wie ein Hauch.
|ʊnt ʃvɪndət viː |aen haox.

Und dennoch ruht im Reime
ʊnt dɛnnɔx ruːt |ɪm raemə

verborgen wohl ein Duft,
fɛrbɔrgən voːl |aen dʊft,

den mild aus stillem Keime
den mɪlt |aos ʃtɪlləm kaemə

ein feuchtes Auge ruft.
|aen fɔøçtəs |aogə ruːft.

Brahms   Wir wandelten, wir zwei zusammen
           viːr vandəltən, viːr tsvae tsuzammən

Wir wandelten, wir zwei zusammen,
viːr vandəltən, viːr tsvae tsuzammən,

ich war so still und du so stille;
ɪç vaːr zoː ʃtɪl |ʊnt duː zoː ʃtɪllə,

ich gäbe viel, um zu erfahren,
ɪç gɛːbə fiːl, ʊm tsuː |ɛrfaːrən,

was du gedacht in jenem Fall.
vas duː gədaxt |ɪn jeːnəm fal.

Was ich gedacht, unausgesprochen verbleibe das!
vas |ɪç gədaxt, ʊn|aosgəʃprɔxən fɛrblaebə das

Nur Eines sag' ich, Eines sag' ich:
nuːr |aenəs zaːk |ɪç, aenəs zaːk |ɪç,

129

So schön war alles, was ich dachte,
zo: ʃø:n vɑːr |alləs, vas |ıç daxtə,

so himmlisch heiter war es all'.
zo: hımlıʃ haetər vɑːr |es |al.

In meinem Haupte die Gedanken,
ın maenəm hɑoptə di gədaŋkən,

sie läuteten wie gold'ne Glöckchen;
zi: lɔøtətən vi: gɔldnə glœkçən,

so wundersüss, so wunderlieblich
zo: vundərzy:s, zo: vundərli:plıç

ist in der Welt kein and'rer Hall.
|ıst |ın der vɛlt kaen |andrər hal.

Handel   Dank sei Dir, Herr
            daŋk zae di:r, hɛr

Dank sei Dir, Herr,
daŋk zae di:r, hɛr,

Du hast Dein Volk mit Dir geführt,
du: hast daen fɔlk mıt di:r gəfy:rt,

Israel hin durch das Meer.
ısra|e:l hın durç das me:r.

Wie eine Heerde zog es hindurch,
vi: |aenə he:rdə tso:k |es hındurç,

Herr, Deine Hand schützte es
hɛr, daenə hant ʃytstə |es

in Deiner Güte gabst Du ihm Heil.
ın daenər gy:tə gɑ:pst du: |i:m hael.

Dank sei Dir Herr.
daŋk zae di:r hɛr.

Liszt   Es muss ein Wunderbares sein
            ɛs mʊs |aen vʊndərbɑːrəs zaen

Es muss ein Wunderbares sein
ɛs mʊs |aen vʊndərbɑːrəs zaen

ums Lieben zweier Seelen,
|ʊms liːbən tsvaeər zeːlən,

sich schliessen ganz einander ein,
zɪç ʃliːsən gants |aenandər |aen,

sich nie ein Wort verhehlen,
zɪç niː |aen vɔrt fɛrheːlən,

und Freud und Leid und Glück und Noth
ʊnt frɔøt |ʊnt laet |ʊnt glʏk |ʊnt noːt

so mit einander tragen;
zoː mɪt |aenandər trɑːgən,

vom ersten Kuss bis in den Tod
fɔm |eːrstən kʊs bɪs |ɪn den toːt

sich nur von Liebe sagen.
zɪç nuːr fɔn liːbə zɑːgən.

Mahler   Blicke mir nicht in die Lieder
           blɪkə miːr nɪçt |ɪn di liːdər

Blicke mir nicht in die Lieder!
blɪkə miːr nɪçt |ɪn di liːdər

Meine Augen schlag' ich nieder,
maenə |aogən ʃlɑːk |ɪç niːdər,

wie ertappt auf böser Tat.
viː |ɛrtapt |aof bøːzər tɑːt.

Selber darf ich nicht getrauen,
zɛlbər darf |ɪç nɪçt gətraoən,

ihrem Wachsen zuzuschauen.
iːrəm vaksən tsuːtsuʃaoən.

Blicke mir nicht in die Lieder!
blɪkə miːr nɪçt |ɪn di liːdər

Deine Neugier ist Verrat!
daenə nɔ͜øgiːr │ɪst fɛrraːt

Bienen, wenn sie Zellen bauen,
biːnən, vɛn ziː tsɛllən ba͜oən,

lassen auch nicht zu sich schauen,
la͜sən │a͜ox nɪçt tsuː zɪç ʃa͜oən,

schauen selbst auch nicht zu.
ʃa͜oən zɛlpst │a͜ox nɪçt tsuː.

Wenn die reichen Honigwaben
vɛn di ra͜eçən ho͜ːnɪçvaːbən

sie zu Tag gefördert haben,
ziː tsuː taːk gəfœrdərt haːbən,

dann vor allen nasche du.
dan fɔr │a͜llən na͜ʃə duː.

Mahler   Der Tamboursg'sell
              der ta͜mbuːrsgzɛl

Ich armer Tamboursg'sell!
ɪç │armər ta͜mbuːrsgzɛl

Man führt mich aus dem G'wölb,
man fyːrt mɪç │a͜os dem gvœlp,

Wär' ich ein Tambour blieben,
vɛːr │ɪç │a͜en ta͜mbuːr bliːbən,

dürft' ich nicht gefangen liegen!
dʏrft │ɪç nɪçt gəfa͜ŋən liːgən

O Galgen, du hohes Haus,
oː ga͜lgən, duː ho͜ːəs ha͜os,

du siehst so furchtbar aus!
duː ziːst zoː fu͜rçtbaːr │a͜os

Ich schau' dich nicht mehr an!
ɪç ʃa͜o dɪç nɪçt meːr │an

weil i weiss, dass i g'hör d'ran!
va͜el │iː va͜es, das │iː ghøːr dran

132

Wenn Soldaten vorbei marschier'n,
vɛn zɔldatən fɔrbae marʃiːrn,

bei mir nit einquartier'n,
bae miːr nɪt |aenkvartiːrn,

wenn sie fragen, wer i g'wesen bin:
vɛn ziː fraːgən, veːr |iː gveːzən bɪn,

Tambour von der Leibkompanie!
tambuːr fɔn der laepkɔmpaniː.

Gute Nacht, ihr Marmelstein',
guːtə naxt, |iːr marməlʃtaen,

ihr Berg' und Hugelein!
iːr bɛrk |ʊnt hyːgəlaen

Gute Nacht, ihr Offizier, Korporal
guːtə naxt, iːr |ɔfitsiːr, kɔrporaːl

und Musketier!
|ʊnt mʊskətiːr

Ich schrei' mit heller Stimm':
ɪç ʃrae mɪt hɛllər ʃtɪm,

von Euch ich Urlaub nimm! Gute Nacht!
fɔn |ɔøç |ɪç |uːrlaop nɪm guːtə naxt

Mahler   Ich atmet' einen linden Duft
            ɪç |atmət |aenən lɪndən dʊft

Ich atmet' einen linden Duft.
ɪç |atmət |aenən lɪndən dʊft.

Im Zimmer stand ein Zweig der Linde,
ɪm tsɪmmər ʃtant |aen tsvaek der lɪndə,

ein Angebinde von lieber Hand.
aen |angəbɪndə fɔn liːbər hant.

Wie lieblich war der Lindenduft.
viː liːplɪç vaːr der lɪndəndʊft.

Wie lieblich ist der Lindenduft.
viː liːplɪç |ɪst der lɪndəndʊft.

das Lindenreis brachst du gelinde!
das lɪndənraes braːxst duː gəlɪndə

Ich atme leis im Duft der Linde,
ɪç |atmə laes |ɪm dʊft der lɪndə,

der Liebe linden Duft.
der liːbə lɪndən dʊft.

Mahler Ich bin der Welt abhanden gekommen
     ɪç bɪn der vɛlt |aphandən gəkɔmmən

Ich bin der Welt abhanden gekommen,
ɪç bɪn der vɛlt |aphandən gəkɔmmən,

mit der ich sonst viele Zeit verdorben;
mɪt der |ɪç zɔnst fiːlə tsaet fɛrdɔrbən,

sie hat so lange nichts von mir vernommen
ziː hat zoː laŋə nɪçts fɔn miːr fɛrnɔmmən

sie mag wohl glauben, ich sei gestorben!
ziː maːk voːl glaobən, ɪç zae gəʃtɔrbən

Es ist mir auch gar nichts daran gelegen,
ɛs |ɪst miːr |aox gaːr nɪçts daran gəleːgən,

ob sie mich für gestorben hält.
ɔp ziː mɪç fyːr gəʃtɔrbən hɛːlt.

Ich kann auch gar nichts sagen dagegen,
ɪç kan |aox gaːr nɪçts zaːgən dageːgən,

denn wirklich bin ich gestorben der Welt.
dɛn vɪrklɪç bɪn |ɪç gəʃtɔrbən der vɛlt.

Ich bin gestorben dem Weltgetümmel
ɪç bɪn gəʃtɔrbən dem vɛltgətʏmməl.

und ruh' in einem stillen Gebiet.
|ʊnt ruː |ɪn |aenəm ʃtɪllən gəbiːt.

Ich leb allein in meinem Himmel,
ɪç leːp |allaen |ɪn maenəm hɪmməl,

in meinem Lieben, in meinem Lied.
ɪn maenəm liːbən, ɪn maenəm liːt.

Mahler   Liebst du um Schönheit
             liːpst duː |ʊm ʃøːnhaet

Liebst du em Schönheit, o nicht mich liebe!
liːpst duː |ʊm ʃøːnhaet, oː nɪçt mɪç li͡ːbə

Liebe die Sonne, sie trägt ein goldnes Haar!
li͡ːbə di zɔnnə, ziː trɛːkt |aen gɔldnəs haːr

Liebst du um Jugend, o nicht mich liebe!
liːpst du ʊm ju͡ːgənt, oː nɪçt mɪç li͡ːbə

Liebe den Frühling, der jung ist jedes Jahr!
li͡ːbə den fry͡ːlɪŋ, der jʊŋ |ɪst je͡ːdəs jaːr

Liebst du um Schätze, o nicht mich liebe!
liːpst du |ʊm ʃɛtsə, oː nɪçt mɪç li͡ːbə

Liebe die Meerfrau, sie hat viel Perlen klar!
li͡ːbə di me͡ːrfrɑo, ziː hat fiːl pɛrlən klɑːr

Liebst du um Liebe, o ja, mich liebe!
liːpst duː |ʊm li͡ːbə, ɔː jaː, mɪç li͡ːbə

Liebe mich immer, dich liep' ich immer, immerdar!
li͡ːbə mɪç |ɪmmər, dɪç liːp |ɪç |ɪmmər, ɪmmərdaːr.

Mahler   Um Mitternacht
             ʊm mɪ͡tərnaxt

Um Mitternacht hab' ich gewacht
ʊm mɪ͡tərnaxt hɑːp |ɪç gəvaxt

und aufgeblickt zum Himmel;
|ʊnt |ɑofgəblɪkt tsʊm hɪmməl,

kein Stern vom Sterngewimmel
kaen ʃtɛrn fɔm ʃtɛ͡rngəvɪmməl

hat mir gelacht um Mitternacht.
hat miːr gəla͡xt |ʊm mɪ͡tərnaxt.

Um Mitternacht hab' ich gedacht
ʊm mɪ͡tərnaxt hɑːp |ɪç gəda͡xt

hinaus in dunkle Schranken.
hinɑos |ɪn dʊ͡ŋklə ʃraŋkən.

Es hat kein Lichtgedanken
ɛs hat kaen lɪçtgədaŋkən

mir Trost gebracht um Mitternacht.
miːr troːst gəbraxt |um mɪtərnaxt.

Um Mitternacht nahm ich in acht
ʊm mɪtərnaxt naːm |ɪç |ɪn |axt

die Schläge meines Herzens;
di ʃlɛːgə maenəs hɛrtsəns,

ein einz'ger Puls des Schmerzens
aen |aentsgər pʊls dɛs ʃmɛrtsəns

war angefacht um Mitternacht.
vaːr |angəfaxt |ʊm mɪtərnaxt.

Um Mitternacht kämpft' ich die Schlacht,
ʊm mɪtərnaxt kɛmpft |ɪç di ʃlaxt,

O Menschheit, deiner Leiden;
oː mɛnʃhaet, daenər laedən,

nicht konnt' ich sie entscheiden
nɪçt kɔnt |ɪç ziː |ɛntʃaedən

mit meiner Macht um Mitternacht.
mɪt maenər maxt |ʊm mɪtərnaxt.

Um Mitternacht hab' ich die Macht
ʊm mɪtərnaxt haːp |ɪç di maxt

in Deine Hand gegeben; Herr!
|ɪn daenə hant gəgeːbən, hɛr

Herr über Tod und Leben,
hɛr |yːbər toːt |ʊnt leːbən,

Du hälst die Wacht, um Mitternacht!
duː hɛlst di vaxt, ʊm mɪtərnaxt

Mozart   Abendempfindung
           ɑːbənt|ɛmpfɪnduŋ

Abend ist's, die Sonne ist verschwunden,
ɑːbənt |ɪsts, di zɔnnə |ɪst fɛrʃvʊndən,

und der Mond strahlt Silberglanz;
ʊnt der moːnt ʃtrɑːlt zɪlbərglants,

so entflieh'n des Lebens schönste Stunden,
zoː |ɛntfliːn dɛs leːbəns ʃøːnstə stʊndən,

flieh'n vorüber wie im Tanz.
fliːn fɔryːbər viː |ɪm tants.

Bald entflieht des Lebens bunte Szene,
balt |ɛntfliːt dɛs leːbəns bʊntə stseːnə,

und der Vorhang rollt herab; aus ist unser Spiel,
ʊnt der foːrhaŋ rɔlt hɛrap, ɑos |ɪst |ʊnzər spiːl,

des Freundes Träne fliesset schon auf unser Grab.
dɛs frɔøndəs trɛːnə fliːsət ʃoːn |ɑof |ʊnzər grɑːp.

Bald vielleicht mir weht,
balt filaeçt miːr veːt,

wie Westwind leise, eine stille Ahnung zu,
viː vɛstvɪnt laezə, aenə stɪllə |ɑːnuŋ tsu ,

schliess ich dieses Lebens Pilgerreise,
ʃliːs |ɪç diːzəs leːbəns pɪlgərraezə,

fliege in das Land der Ruh!
fliːgə |ɪn das lant der ruː.

Werd't ihr dann an meinem Grabe weinen,
veːrt |iːr dan |an maenəm grɑːbə vaenən,

trauernd meine Asche sehn,
trɑoərnt maenə |aʃə zeːn,

dann, O Freunde, will ich euch erscheinen
dan, oː frɔøndə, vil |ɪç |ɔeç |ɛrʃaenən

und will Himmel auf euch wehn.
|ʊnt vɪl hɪmməl ɑof |ɔøç veːn.

137

Schenk' auch du ein Tränchen mir
ʃɛŋk |ɑox du |aen trɛːnçən miːr

und pfücke mir ein Veilchen auf mein Grab,
ʊnt pflʏkə miːr |aen faelçən |ɑof maen grɑːp,

und mit deinem seelenvollen Blicke
ʊnt mɪt daenəm zeːlənfɔllən blɪkə

sieh' dann sanft auf mich herab.
ziː dan zanft |ɑof mɪç herap.

Weih' mir eine Träne, und ach!
vae miːr |aenə trɛːnə, ʊnt ax

schäme dich nur nicht, sie mir zu weih'n,
ʃɛːmə dɪç nuːr nɪçt, ziː miːr tsu vaen,

O sie wird in meinem Diademe
oː ziː vɪrt |ɪn maenəm diadeːmə

dann die schönste Perle sein.
dan di ʃøːnstə pɛrlə zaen.

Mozart   Ach, ich fühl's, "Die Zauberflöte"
            ax, ɪç fyːls   di tsɑobərfløːtə

Ach, ich fühl's, es ist verschwunden,
ax, ɪç fyːls, ɛs |ɪst fɛrʃvʊndən,

ewig hin der Liebe Glück!
eːvɪç hɪn der liːbə glʏk

Nimmer kommt ihr, Wonnestunden,
nɪmmər kɔmt |iːr, vɔnnəʃtʊndən,

meinem Herzen mehr zurück.
maenəm hɛrtsən meːr tsurʏk.

Sieh', Tamino, diese Tränen fliessen,
ziː, tamino, diːzə trɛːnən fliːsən,

Trauter, dir allein.
trɑotər, diːr |allaen.

Fühlst du nicht der Liebe Sehnen,
fyːlst duː nɪçt der liːbə zeːnən,

so wird Ruh' im Tode sein.
zoː vɪrt ruː |ɪm toːdə zaen.

Mozart   Als Luise die Briefe
             als luiːzə di briːfə

Erzeugt von heisser Phantasie,
ɛrtsɔøkt fɔn haesər fantaziː,

in einer schwärmerischen Stunde
ɪn |aenər ʃvɛrmərɪʃən ʃtʊndə

zur Welt gebrachte,
tsuːr vɛlt gəbraxtə,

geht zu Grunde, ihr Kinder der Melancholie!
geːt tsuː grʊndə, iːr kɪndər der melaŋkoliː

Ihr danket Flammen euer Sein,
iːr daŋkət flammən |ɔøər zaen,

ich geb euch nun den Flammen wieder,
ɪç geːp |ɔøç nuːn den flammən viːdər,

und all' die schwärmerischen Lieder, denn ach!
ʊnt |al di ʃvɛrmərɪʃən liːdər, dɛn |ax

er sang nicht mir allein.
eːr zaŋ nɪçt miːr |allaen.

Ihr brennet nun, und bald, ihr Lieben,
iːr brɛnnət nuːn, |ʊnt balt, |iːr liːbən,

ist keine Spur von euch mehr hier.
ɪst kaenə ʃpuːr fɔn |ɔøç meːr hiːr.

Doch ach! der Mann, der euch geschrieben,
dɔx |ax. der man, der |ɔøç gəʃriːbən,

brennt lange noch vielleicht in mir.
brɛnt laŋə nɔx filaeçt |ɪn miːr.

Mozart   An Chloe
            an klo:‖e

Wenn die Lieb' aus deinen blauen,
vɛn di li:p ‖a͜os da͜enən bla͜oən,

hellen, offnen Augen sieht,
hɛllən, ɔfnən ‖a͜ogən zi:t,

und vor Lust hinein zu schauen
ʊnt fɔr lʊst hɪna͜en tsu ʃa͜oən

mir's im Herzen klopft und glüht;
mi:rs ‖ɪm hɛrtsən klɔpft ‖ʊnt gly:t,

und ich halte dich und küsse
ʊnt ‖ɪç haltə dɪç ‖ʊnt kʏsə

deine Rosenwangen warm,
da͜enə ro:zənvaŋən varm,

liebes Mädchen,
li:bəs mɛ:tçən,

und ich schliesse zitternd dich in mainen Arm!
ʊnt ‖ɪç ʃli:sə tsɪtərnt dɪç ‖ɪn ma͜enən ‖a:rm

Mädchen, und ich drücke dich an meinen Busen fest,
mɛ:tçən, ʊnt ‖ɪç drʏkə dɪç ‖an ma͜enən bu:zən fɛst,

der im letzten Augenblicke sterbend,
der ‖ɪm lɛtstən ‖a͜ogənblɪkə ʃtɛrbənt,

sterbend nur dich von sich lässt;
ʃtɛrbənt nu:r dɪç fɔn zɪç lɛst,

den berauschten Blick umschattet
den bəra͜oʃtən blɪk ‖ʊmʃatət

eine düstre Wolke mir,
‖a͜enə dy:strə vɔlkə mi:r,

und ich sitze dann ermattet, ermattet,
ʊnt ‖ɪç zɪtsə dan ‖ɛrmatət, ɛrmatət,

aber selig neben dir.
a:bər ze:lɪç ne:bən di:r.

140

Mozart   Das Veilchen
            das fa͜elçən

Ein Veilchen auf der Wiese stand,
a͜en fa͜elçən |ɑof der vi͜ːzə ʃtant,

gebückt in sich und unbekannt:
gəby͜kt |ɪn zɪç |ʊnt |ʊnbəkant,

es war ein herzig's Veilchen.
ɛs vɑːr |a͜en hɛ͜rtsɪçs fa͜elçən.

Da kam ein' junge Schäferin mit leichtem Schritt
dɑː kɑːm |a͜en jʊŋə ʃɛːfərɪn mɪt la͜eçtəm ʃrɪt

und munterm Sinn daher,
|ʊnt mʊntərm zɪn dahe͜ːr,

daher, die Wiese her und sang.
dahe͜ːr, di vi͜ːzə heːr |ʊnt zaŋ.

Ach! denkt das Veilchen,
ax   dɛŋkt das fa͜elçən

wär' ich nur die schönste Blume der Natur,
vɛːr |ɪç nuːr di ʃø͜ːnstə blu͜ːmə der natu͜ːr,

ach, nur ein kleines Weilchen,
ax, nuːr |a͜en kla͜enəs va͜elçən,

bis mich das Liebchen abgepflückt
bɪs mɪç das li͜ːpçən |apgəpflʏkt

und an dem Busen matt gedrückt,
|ʊnt |an dem bu͜ːzən mat gədrʏkt,

ach nur ein Viertelstündchen lang.
ax nuːr |a͜en fi͜ːrtəlʃtʏntçən laŋ.

Ach, aber ach! das Mädchen kam
ax, ɑːbər |ax   das mɛ͜ːtçən kɑːm

und nicht in Acht das Veilchen nahm,
|ʊnt nɪçt |ɪn |axt das fa͜elçən nɑːm,

zertrat das arme Veilchen.
tsɛrtrɑ͜ːt das |armə fa͜elçən.

Es sank und starb und freut' sich noch:
ɛs zaŋk |ʊnt ʃtarp |ʊnt frɔøt zɪç nɔx,

und sterb' ich denn, so sterb' ich doch
ʊnt ʃtɛrp |ɪç dɛn, zoː ʃtɛrp |ɪç dɔx

durch sie, zu ihren Füssen doch.
dʊrç ziː, tsuː |iːrən fyːsən dɔx.

Das arme Veilchen! es war ein herzig's Veilchen.
das |armə faelçən ɛs vaːr |aen hɛrtsɪçs faelcən.

Mozart   Der Hölle Rache, "Die Zauberflöte"
            der hœllə raxə   di tsaobərfløːtə

Der Hölle Rache kocht in meinem Herzen,
der hœllə raxə kɔxt |ɪn maenəm hɛrtsən,

Tod und Verzweiflung flammen um mich her!
toːt |ʊnt fɛrtsvaeflʊŋ flammən |ʊm mɪç heːr

Fühlt nicht durch dich Sarastro Todesschmerzen,
fyːlt nɪçt dʊrç dɪç sarastro toːdəsʃmɛrtsən,

so bist du meine Tochter nimmermehr.
zoː bɪst duː maenə tɔxtər nɪmmərmeːr.

Verstossen sei auf ewig, verlassen sei auf ewig,
fɛrʃtoːsən zae |aof |eːvɪç, vɛrlasən zae |aof |eːvɪç,

zertrümmert sein auf ewig alle Bande der Natur,
tsɛrtrʊmmərt zaen |aof |eːvɪç |allə bandə der natuːr,

wenn nicht durch dich Sarastro wird erblassen!
vɛn nɪçt dʊrç dɪç sarastro vɪrt |ɛrblasən

Hört Rachegötter! hört der Mutter Schwur!
høːrt raxəgœtər   høːrt der mʊtər ʃvuːr.

Mozart   Dies Bildnis ist bezaubernd schön,
             di:s bɪltnɪs |ɪst bətsɑobərnt ʃø:n,

             "Die Zauberflöte"
             di tsɑobərflø:tə

Dies Bildnis ist bezaubernd schön,
di:s bɪltnɪs |ɪst bətsɑobərnt ʃø:n,

wie noch kein Auge je geseh'n!
vi: nɔx kaen |ɑogə je: gəze:n

Ich fühl' es, wie dies Götterbild
ɪç fy:l |es, vi: di:s gœtərbɪlt

main Herz mit neuer Regung füllt.
maen herts mit nɔøər re:guŋ fʏlt.

Dies Etwas kann ich zwar nicht nennen,
di:s |etvas kan |ɪç tsvɑ:r nɪçt nennən,

doch fühl' ich's hier wie Feuer brennen.
dɔx fy:l |ɪçs hi:r vi: fɔøər brennən.

Solldie Empfindung Liebe sein?
zɔl di |empfɪnduŋ li:bə zaen

Ja, ja, die Liebe ist's allein.
jɑ:, jɑ:, di li:bə |ɪsts |allaen.

O, wenn ich sie nur finden könnte!
o:, ven |ɪç zi: nu:r fɪndən kœnte

O, wenn sie doch schon vor mir stände!
o:, ven zi: dɔx ʃo:n fo:r mi:r ʃtendə

Ich würde, warm und rein, was würde ich?
ɪç vʏrdə, varm |unt raen, vas vʏrdə |ɪç

Ich würde sie voll Entzücken
ɪç vʏrdə zi: fɔl enttsʏkən

an diesen heissen Busen drücken,
|an di:zən haesən bu:zən drʏkən,

und ewig wäre sie dann mein!
unt |e:vɪç vɛ:rə zi: dan maen.

143

Mozart   In diesen heil'gen Hallen,
           ɪn diːzən haelgən hallən,

           "Die Zauberflöte"
           di tsɑobərfløːtə

In diesen heil'gen Hallen
ɪn diːzən haelgən hallən

kennt man die Rache nicht,
kɛnt man di raxə nɪçt,

und ist der Mensch gefallen,
ʊnt |ɪst der mɛnʃ gəfallən,

führt Liebe ihn zur Pflicht.
fyːrt liːbə |iːn tsur pflɪçt.

Dann wandelt er an Freundes Hand
dan vandəlt |eːr |an frøndəs hant

vergnügt und froh in's bess're Land!
fɛrgnyːkt |ʊnt froː |ɪns bɛsrə lant.

In diesen heil'gen Mauern,
ɪn diːzən haelgən mɑoərn,

wo Mensch den Menschen liebt,
voː mɛnʃ den mɛnʃən liːpt.

kann kein Verräther lauern,
kan kaen fɛrrɛːtər lɑoərn,

weil man dem Feind vergiebt.
vael man dem faent fɛrgiːpt.

Wen solche Lehren nicht erfreu'n,
veːn zɔlçə leːrən nɪçt |ɛrfrøn,

verdienet nicht ein Mensch zu sein.
fɛrdiːnət nɪçt |aen mɛnʃ tsuː zaen.

Mozart   O Isis und Osiris, "Die Zauberflöte"
            oː |iːzɪs |unt |oziːrɪs,

O Isis und Osiris, schenket der
oː |iːzɪs |unt |oziːrɪs, ʃɛŋkət

Weisheit Geist dem neuen Paar!
der vaeshaet gaest dem nɔøən paːr

Die ihr der Wandrer Schritte lenket,
di |iːr der vandrər frɪtə lɛŋkət,

stärkt mit Geduld sie in Gefahr.
ʃtɛrkt mɪt gədult ziː |ɪn gəfaːr.

Lasst sie der Prüfung Früchte sehen;
last ziː der pryːfuŋ fryçtə zeːən,

doch sollten sie zu Grabe gehen,
dɔx zɔltən ziː tsuː graːbə geːən,

so lohnt der Tugend kühnen Lauf,
zoː loːnt der tuːgənt kyːnən laof,

nehmt sie in euren Wohnsitz auf.
neːmt ziː |ɪn |ɔørən voːnzɪts |aof.

Mozart   Warnung
            varnuŋ

Männer suchen stets zu naschen,
mɛnnər zuxən ʃteːts tsuː naʃən,

lässt man sie allein,
lɛst man ziː |allaen,

leicht sind Mädchen zu erhaschen,
laeçt zɪnt mɛːtçən tsuː ɛrhaʃən,

weiss man sie zu überraschen.
vaes man ziː tsuː |yːbərraʃən.

Soll das zu verwundern sein?
zɔl das tsuː fɛrvundərn zaen

Mädchen haben frisches Blut,
mɛːtçən haːbən frɪʃəs bluːt,

145

und das Naschen schmeckt so gut.
ʊnt das naʃən ʃmɛkt zoː guːt.

Doch das Naschen vor dem Essen
dɔx das naʃən foːr dem |ɛsən

nimmt den Appetit.
nɪmt den |apətiːt.

Manche kam, die das vergessen,
mançə kɑːm, di das fergɛsən,

um den Schatz, den sie besessen,
ʊm den ʃats, den ziː bəzɛsən,

und um ihren Liebsten mit.
ʊnt |ʊm |iːrən liːpstən mɪt.

Väter, lasst euch's Warnung sein,
fɛːtər, last |ɔøçs varnʊŋ zaen

sperrt die Zuckerplätzchen ein!
ʃpɛrt di tsʊkərplɛtsçən |aen

sperrt die jungen Mädchen ein!
ʃpɛrt di jʊŋən mɛːtçən |aen

Reger   Maria Wiegenlied
           maria viːgənliːt

Maria sitzt am Rosenhag
maria zɪtst |am roːzənhɑːk

und wiegt ihr Jesuskind,
|ʊnt viːkt |iːr jeːsuskɪnt,

durch die Blätter leise weht der warme Sommerwind.
dʊrç di blɛtər laezə veːt der varmə zɔmərvɪnt.

Zu ihren Füssen singt ein buntes Vögelein:
tsuː |iːrən fyːsən zɪŋt |aen bʊntəs føːgəlaen,

Schlaf', Kindlein, süsses, schlaf' nun ein!
ʃlɑːf, kɪntlaen, zyːsəs, ʃlɑːf nuːn |aen

Hold ist dein Lächeln,
hɔlt |ɪst daen lɛçəln,

146

holder deines Schlummers Lust,
hɔldər daenəs ʃlʊmmərs lʊst,

leg dein müdes Köpfchen fest
leːk daen myːdəs kœpfçən fɛst

an deiner Mutter Brust!
|an daenər mʊtər brʊst

Schlaf', Kindlein, süsses, schlaf' nun ein.
ʃlɑːf, kɪntlaen, zyːsəs, ʃlɑːf nuːn |aen.

Schubert   Am Grabe Anselmo's
             am grɑːbə |ansɛlmos

Dass ich dich verloren habe,
das |ɪç dɪç fɛrloːrən hɑːbə,

dass du nicht mehr bist,
das duː nɪçt meːr bɪst,

ach, dass hier in diesem Grabe
ax, das hiːr |ɪn diːzəm grɑːbə

mein Anselmo ist, das ist mein Schmerz!
maen |ansɛlmo |ɪst, das |ɪst maen ʃmɛrts

Seht, wie liebten wir uns beide,
zeːt, viː liːptən viːr |uns baedə,

und, so lang' ich bin,
unt, zoː laŋ |ɪç bɪn,

kommt Freude niemals wieder in mein Herz.
kɔmt frɔødə niːmals viːdər |ɪn maen hɛrts.

Schubert   Am Meer
             am meːr

Das Meer erglänzte weit hinaus
das meːr |ɛrglɛntstə vaet hɪnɑos

im letzten Abendscheine;
|ɪm lɛtstən |ɑːbəntʃaenə,

147

wir sassen am einsamen Fischerhaus,
viːr zasən |am |aenzaːmən fɪʃərhaos,

wir sassen stumm und alleine.
viːr zasən ʃtʊm |ʊnt |allaenə.

Der Nebel stieg, das Wasser schwoll,
der neːbəl ʃtiːk, das vasər ʃvɔl,

die Möve flog hin und wieder;
di møːvə floːk hɪn |ʊnt viːdər,

aus deinen Augen liebevoll
aos daenən |aogən liːbəfɔl

fielen die Thränen nieder.
fiːlən di trɛːnən niːdər.

Ich sah sie fallen auf deine Hand
ɪç zaː ziː fallən |aof daenə hant

und bin aufs Knie gesunken;
ʊnt bɪn |aofs kniː gəzʊŋkən,

ich hab von deiner weissen Hand
ɪç haːp fɔn daenər vaesən hant

die Thränen fortgetrunken.
di trɛːnən fɔrtgətrʊŋkən.

Seit jener Stunde
zaet jeːnər ʃtʊndə

verzehrt sich mein Leib,
fɛrtseːrt zɪç maen laep,

die Seele stirbt vor Sehnen;
di zeːlə ʃtɪrpt foːr zeːnən,

mich hat das unglücksel'ge Weib
mɪç hat das |ʊnglʏkzeːlgə vaep

vergiftet mit ihren Thränen.
fɛrgɪftət mɪt |iːrən trɛːnən.

Schubert   An die Leier
             an di laeər

Ich will von Atreus' Söhnen,
ɪç vɪl fɔn |aːtrɔøs zøːnən,

von Kadmus will ich singen!
fɔn katmʊs vɪl |ɪç zɪŋən

Doch meine Saiten tönen nur Liebe im Erklingen.
dɔx maenə zaetən tøːnən nuːr liːbə |ɪm |ɛrklɪŋən.

Ich tauschte um die Saiten,
ɪç taoʃtə |ʊm di zaetən,

die Leier möcht ich tauschen!
di laeər mœçt |ɪç taoʃən

Alcidens Siegesschreiten
altʃiːdəns ziːgəsʃraetən

sollt' ihrer Macht entrauschen!
zɔlt |iːrər maxt |ɛntraoʃən

Doch auch die Saiten tönen
dɔx |aox di zaetən tøːnən

nur Liebe im Erklingen.
nuːr liːbə |ɪm |ɛrklɪŋən.

So lebt denn wohl,
zoː leːpt dɛn voːl,

Heroen!   denn meine Saiten tönen,
heroːən   dɛn maenə zaetən tøːnən,

statt Heldensang zu drohen,
ʃtat hɛldənzaŋ tsuː droːən,

nur Liebe im Erklingen.
nuːr liːbə |ɪm |ɛrklɪŋən.

Schubert   An die Musik
             an di muzi:k

Du holde Kunst, in wie viel grauen Stunden,
du: hɔldə kunst, |ɪn vi: fi:l graoən ʃtundən,

wo mich des Lebens wilder Kreis umstrickt,
vo: mɪç dɛs le:bəns vɪldər kraes |umʃtrɪkt,

hast du mein Herz zu warmer Lieb entzunden,
hast du: maen hɛrts tsu: varmər li:p |ɛntsundən,

hast mich in eine bessre Welt entrückt!
hast mɪç |ɪn |aenə bɛsrə vɛlt |ɛntrʏkt

Oft hat ein Seufzer, deiner Harf entflossen,
ɔft hat |aen zɔʏftsər, daenər harf |ɛntflɔsən,

ein süsser, heiliger Akkord von dir
aen zy:sər, haelɪgər |akɔrt fɔn di:r

den Himmel bessrer Zeiten mir erschlossen,
den hɪmməl bɛsrər tsaetən mi:r |ɛrflɔsən,

du holde Kunst, ich danke dir dafür.
du: hɔldə kunst, |ɪç daŋkə di:r dafy:r.

Schubert   An Silvia
             an zɪ:lvja

Wast ist Silvia, saget an,
vas |ɪst zɪ:lvja za:gət |an,

dass sie die weite Flur preist?
das zi: di vaetə flu:r praest

Schön und zart seh ich sie nahn,
ʃø:n |unt tsa:rt ze: |ɪç zi: na:n,

auf Himmels Gunst und Spur weist,
aof hɪmməls gunst |unt ʃpu:r vaest,

dass ihr alles untertan.
das |i:r |alləs |untərta:n.

Ist sie schön und gut dazu?
ɪst zi: ʃø:n |unt gu:t datsu:

150

Reiz labt wie milde Kindheit;
raets lɑːpt viː mɪldə kɪnthaet,

ihrem Aug eilt Amor zu,
iːrəm |ɑok |aelt |ɑːmɔr tsuː,

dort heilt er seine Blindheit,
dɔrt haelt |eːr zaenə blɪnthaet,

und verweilt in süsser Ruh.
unt fɛrvaelt |ɪn zyːsər ruː.

Darum Silvia tön, o Sang,
darum zɪːlvja tøːn, oː zaŋ,

der holden Silvia Ehren;
der hɔldən zɪːlvja |eːrən,

jeden Reiz besiegt sie lang,
jeːdən raets bəziːkt ziː laŋ,

den Erde kann gewähren:
den |eːrdə kan gəvɛːrən,

Kränze ihr und Saitenklang!
krɛntsə |iːr |unt zaetənklaŋ

Schubert   Auf dem Wasser zu singen
                ɑof dem vasər tsuː zɪŋən

Mitten im Schimmer der spiegelnden Wellen
mɪtən |ɪm ʃɪmmər der ʃpiːgəlndən vɛllən

gleitet, wie Schwäne, der wankende Kahn;
glaetət, viː ʃvɛːnə, der vaŋkəndə kɑːn,

ach, auf der Freude sanft schimmernden Wellen
ax, ɑof der frɔødə zanft ʃɪmmərndən vɛllən

gleitet die Seele dahin wie der Kahn;
glaetət di zeːlə dahɪn viː der kɑːn,

denn von dem Himmel herab auf die Wellen
dɛn fɔn dem hɪmməl hɛrap |ɑof di vɛllən

tanzet das Abendroth rund um den Kahn.
tantsət das |ɑːbəntroːt runt |um den kɑːn.

151

Über den Wipfeln des westlichen Haines
y:bər den vɪpfəln dɛs vɛstlɪçən haenəs

winket uns freundlich der rötliche Schein,
vɪŋkət |uns frɔøntlɪç der rø:tlɪçə ʃaen,

unter den Zweigen des östlichen Haines
untər den tsvaegən dɛs |œstlɪçən haenəs

säuselt der Kalmus im rötlichen Schein;
zɔøzəlt der kalmus |ɪm rø:tlɪçən ʃaen,

Freude des Himmels und Ruhe des Haines
frɔødə dɛs hɪmməls |unt ru:ə dɛs haenəs

atmet die Seel im errötenden Schein.
a:tmət di ze:l |ɪm |errø:təndən ʃaen.

Ach, es entschwindet mit tauigem Flügel
ax, ɛs |ɛntʃvɪndət mɪt taoɪgəm fly:gəl

mir auf den wiegenden Wellen die Zeit.
mi:r |aof den vi:gəndən vɛllən di tsaet.

Morgen entschwinde mit schimmerndem Flügel
mɔrgən |ɛntʃvɪndə mɪt ʃɪmmərndəm fly:gəl

wieder wie gestern und heute die Zeit,
vi:dər vi: gɛstərn |unt hɔøtə di tsaet,

bis ich auf höherem strahlenden Flügel
bɪs |ɪç |aof hø:ərəm ʃtra:ləndən fly:gəl

selber entschwinde der wechselnden Zeit.
zɛlbər |ɛntʃvɪndə der vɛksəlndən tsaet.

Schubert   Aufenthalt
              aofəntalt

Rauschender Strom, brausender Wald,
raoʃəndər ʃtro:m, braozəndər valt,

starrender Fels mein Aufenthalt.
starrəndər fɛls maen aofəntalt.

Wie sich die Welle an Welle reiht,
vi: zɪç di vɛllə |an vɛllə raet,

fliessen die Tränen mir ewig erneut.
fliːsən di trɛːnən miːr |eːvɪç |ɛrnɔøt.

Hoch in den Kronen wogend sich's regt,
hoːx |ɪn den kroːnən voːgənt zɪçs reːkt,

so unaufhörlich mein Herze schlägt.
zoː |unɑofhøːrlɪç maen hɛrtsə ʃlɛːkt.

Und wie des Felsen uraltes Erz,
ʊnt viː dɛs fɛlzən |uːr|altəs |ɛrts,

ewig derselbe bleibet mein Schmerz.
eːvɪç deːrzɛlbə blaebət maen ʃmɛrts.

Schubert   Ave Maria
               ɑːvɛ mariːa

Ave Maria! Jungfrau mild,
ɑːvɛ mariːa juŋfrɑo mɪlt,

erhöre einer Jungfrau Flehen,
ɛrhøːrə |aenər juŋfrɑo fleːən,

aus diesem Felsen starr und wild
ɑos diːzəm fɛlzən ʃtar |ʊnt vɪlt

soll mein Gebet zu dir hin wehen.
zɔl maen gəbeːt tsuː diːr hɪn veːən.

Wir schlafen sicher bis zum Morgen,
viːr ʃlɑːfən zɪçər bɪs tsum mɔrgən,

ob Menschen noch so grausam sind.
ɔp mɛnʃən nɔx zoː grɑozam zɪnt.

O Jungfrau, sieh der Jungfrau Sorgen,
oː juŋfrɑo, ziː der juŋfrɑo zɔrgən,

o Mutter, hör ein bittend Kind!
oː mʊtər, høːr |aen bɪtənt kɪnt

Ave Maria!
ɑːvɛ mariːa

Ave Maria! Unbefleckt!
ɑːvɛ mariːa ʊnbəflɛkt

153

Wenn wir auf diesen Fels hinsinken zum Schlaf,
vɛn viːr |aof diːzən fɛls hɪnzɪŋkən tsum ʃlaːf,

und uns dein Schutz bedeckt,
unt |uns daen ʃuts bədɛkt,

wird weich der harte Fels uns dünken.
vɪrt vaeç der hartə fɛls |uns dʏŋkən.

Du lachelst, Rosendüfte wehen
duː lɛçəlst, roːzəndʏftə veːən

in dieser dumpfen Felsenkluft.
|ɪn diːzər dumpfən fɛlzənkluft.

O Mutter, höre Kindes Flehen,
oː mutər, høːrə kɪndəs fleːən,

o Jungfrau, eine Jungfrau ruft!
oː juŋfrao, aenə juŋfrao ruːft

Ave Maria!   Reine Magd!
aːvɛ mariːa raenə maːkt

Der Erde und der Luft Dämonen,
der |eːrdə |unt der luft dɛmoːnən,

von deines Auges Huld verjagt,
fɔn daenəs |aogəs hult fɛrjaːkt,

sie können hier nicht bei uns wohnen.
ziː kœnnən hiːr nɪçt bae |uns voːnən.

Wir wolln uns still dem Schicksal beugen,
viːr vɔln |uns ʃtɪl dem ʃɪkzaːl bøɡən,

da uns dein heilger Trost anweht;
daː |uns daen haelgər troːst |anveːt,

der Jungfrau wolle hold dich neigen,
der juŋfrao vɔllə hɔlt dɪç naegən,

dem Kind, das für den Vater fleht!   Ave Maria!
dem kɪnt, das fyːr den faːtər fleːt aːvɛ mariːa.

Schubert   Das Wandern
             das vandərn

Das Wandern ist des Müllers Lust, das Wandern!
das vandərn |ɪst dɛs mʏllərs lʊst, das vandərn

Das muss ein schlechter Müller sein,
das mʊs |aen ʃlɛçtər mʏllər zaen,

dem niemals fiel das Wandern ein,
dem niːmaːls fiːl das vandərn |aen,

das Wandern, das Wandern.
das vandərn, das vandərn.

Vom Wasser haben wir's gelernt, vom Wasser!
fɔm vasər haːbən viːrs gəlɛrnt, fɔm vasər

Das hat nicht Rast bei Tag und Nacht,
das hat nɪçt rast bae taːk |ʊnt naxt,

ist stets auf Wanderschaft bedacht,
ɪst ʃteːts |aof vandərʃaft bədaxt,

das Wasser, das Wasser.
das vasər, das vasər.

Das sehn wir auch den Rädern ab, den Rädern!
das zeːn viːr |aox den rɛːdərn |ap, den rɛːdərn

Die gar nicht gerne stille stehn,
di gaːr nɪçt gɛrnə ʃtɪllə ʃteːn,

die sich main Tag nicht müde drehn, die Räder.
di zɪç maen taːk nɪçt myːdə dreːn, di rɛːdər.

Die Steine selbst, so schwer sie sind, die Steine!
di ʃtaenə zɛlpst, zoː ʃveːr ziː zɪnt, di ʃtaenə

Sie tanzen mit den muntern Reih'n
ziː tantsən mɪt den mʊntərn raen

und wollen gar noch schneller sein,
|ʊnt vɔllən gaːr nɔx ʃnɛllər zaen,

die Steine, die Steine.
di ʃtaenə, di ʃtaenə.

O Wandern, Wandern, meine Lust, o Wandern!
oː vandərn, vandərn, maenə lʊst, oː vandərn.

Herr Meister und Frau Meisterin,
hɛr maestər |ʊnt frɑo maestərɪn,

lasst mich in Frieden weiterzieh'n
last mɪç |ɪn friːdən vaetərtsiːn

und wandern, und wandern.
|ʊnt vandərn, ʊnt vandərn.

Schubert   Das Wirtshaus
              das vɪrtshɑos

Auf einen Totenacker hat mich mein Weg gebracht.
ɑof |aenən toːtən|akər hat mɪç maen veːk gəbraxt.

Allhier will ich einkehren,
alhiːr vɪl |ɪç |aenkeːrən,

hab ich bei mir gedacht.
hɑːp |ɪç bae miːr gədaxt.

Ihr grünen Totenkränze könnt wohl
iːr gryːnən toːtənkrɛntsə kœnt voːl

die Zeichen sein,
di tsaeçən zaen,

die müde Wandrer laden ins kühle Wirtshaus ein.
di myːdə vandrər lɑːdən |ɪns kyːlə vɪrtshɑos |aen.

Sind denn in diesem Hause die Kammern
zɪnt dɛn |ɪn diːzəm hɑozə di kammərn

all besetzt?
|al bəzɛtst.

bin matt zum Niedersinken,
bɪn mat tsum niːdərzɪŋkən,

bin tödlich schwer verletzt.
bɪn tøːtlɪç ʃveːr fɛrlɛtst.

O unbarmherzge Schenke,
oː |ʊnbarmhɛrtsgə ʃɛŋkə,

156

doch weisest du mich ab?
dɔx v̬ae̯zəst duː mɪç ˌap

Nun weiter denn, nur weiter,
nuːn v̬ae̯tər dɛn, nuːr v̬ae̯tər,

mein treuer Wanderstab!
mae̯n trɔ̯ø̯ər v̬andərʃtaːp

Schubert   Dem Unendlichen
            dem ˌʊnˌɛntlɪçən

Wie erhebt sich das Herz,
viː ˌɛrhe̯ːpt zɪç das hɛrts,

wenn es dich, Unendlicher, denkt!
v̬ɛn ˌɛs dɪç, ˌʊnˌɛntlɪçər, dɛnkt

Wie sinkt es, wenn es auf sich herunterschaut!
viː zɪŋkt ˌɛs, v̬ɛn ˌɛs ˌao̯f zɪç herʊntərʃao̯t

Elend schauts wehklagend dann und Nacht und Tod!
e̯ːlənt ʃao̯ts v̬e̯ːklaːgənt dan ʊnt naxt ˌʊnt toːt

Allein du rufst mich aus meiner Nacht,
allae̯n duː ruːfst mɪç ˌao̯s mae̯nər naxt,

der im Elend, der im Tode hilft!
der ˌɪm ˌe̯ːlənt, der ˌɪm toːdə hɪlft

Dann denk' ich es ganz,
dan dɛŋk ˌɪç ˌɛs gants,

dass du ewig mich schufst,
das duː ˌe̯ːvɪç mɪç ʃuːfst,

Herrlicher, den kein Preis, unten am Grab,
hɛrlɪçər, den k̬ae̯n prae̯s, ˌʊntən ˌam graːp,

oben am Thron, Herr, Gott, den, dankend entflammt,
o̯ːbən ˌam troːn, hɛr, gɔt, den, daŋkənt ˌɛntflam̯t,

kein Jubel genug besingt!
k̬ae̯n juːbəl gənuːk bəzɪŋkt

Weht, Bäume des Lebens, in's Harfengetön!
ve̯ːt, bɔ̯ø̯mə dɛs le̯ːbəns, ɪns harfəngət̬ø̯ːn.

157

Rausche mit ihnen in's Harfengetön,
raʊʃə mɪt |iːnən |ɪns harfəngətøːn,

krystallner Strom!
krɪstalnər ʃtroːm

Ihr lispelt und rauscht,
iːr lɪspəlt |ʊnt raʊʃt,

und, Harfen, ihr tönt nie es ganz!
ʊnt, harfən, iːr tøːnt niː |ɛs gants

Gott ist es, den ihr preist.
gɔt |ɪst |ɛs, den |iːr praest.

Welten, donnert im feierlichen Gang!
vɛltən, dɔnnərt |ɪm faeərlɪçən gaŋ

Welten, donnert in der Posaunen Chor!
vɛltən, dɔnnərt |ɪn der pozaʊnən kɔr

Tönt, all' ihr Sonnen auf der Strasse voll Glanz,
tøːnt, al |iːr zɔnnən aʊf der ʃtrasə fɔl glants,

in der Posaunen Chor!
ɪn der pozaʊnən kɔr

Ihr Welten, ihr donnert, du, der Posaunen Chor,
iːr vɛltən, iːr dɔnnərt, duː, der pozaʊnən kɔr,

hallest nie es ganz! Gott, nie es ganz!
halləst niː |ɛs gants gɔt, niː |ɛs gants

Gott ist es, den ihr preist!
gɔt |ɪst |ɛs, den |iːr praest

Schubert   Der Atlas
             der |atlas

Ich unglückselger Atlas!
ɪç |ʊnglʏkzeːlgər |atlas

Eine Welt, die ganze Welt der Schmerzen,
aenə vɛlt, di gantsə vɛlt der ʃmɛrtsən,

muss ich tragen,
mʊs |ɪç traːgən,

158

ich trage Unerträgliches,
ɪç trɑːɡə |ʊn|ɛrtrɛːklɪçəs,

und brechen will mir das Herz im Leibe.
ʊnt brɛçən vɪl miːr das hɛrts |ɪm laebə.

Du stolzes Herz, du hast es ja gewollt!
duː ʃtɔltsəs hɛrts, duː hast |ɛs jɑː ɡəvɔlt

Du wolltest glücklich sein,
duː vɔltəst ɡlʏklɪç zaen,

unendlich glücklich, oder unendlich elend,
ʊn|ɛntlɪç ɡlʏklɪç, oːdər |ʊn|ɛntlɪç |eːlənt,

stolzes Herz, und jetzo bist du elend.
ʃtɔltsəs hɛrts, ʊnt jɛtso bɪst duː |eːlənt.

Ich unglücksel'ger Atlas!
ɪç |ʊnɡlʏkzeːlɡər |atlas

Die ganze Welt der Schmerzen muss ich tragen!
di ɡantsə vɛlt der ʃmɛrtsən mʊs |ɪç trɑːɡən

Schubert   Der Doppelgänger
              der dɔpəlɡɛŋər

Still ist die Nacht, es ruhen die Gassen,
ʃtɪl |ɪst di naxt, ɛs ruːən di ɡasən,

in diesem Hause wohnte mein Schatz;
ɪn diːzəm haozə voːntə maen ʃats,

sie hat schon längst die Stadt verlassen,
ziː hat ʃoːn lɛŋst di ʃtat fɛrlasən,

doch steht noch das Haus auf demselben Platz.
dɔx ʃteːt nɔx das haos |aof demzɛlbən plats.

Da steht auch ein Mensch und starrt in die Höhe,
dɑː ʃteːt |aoç |aen mɛnʃ ʊnt ʃtart |ɪn di høːə,

und ringt die Hände vor Schmerzensgewalt;
ʊnt rɪŋt di hɛndə foːr ʃmɛrtsənsɡəvalt,

mir graust es, wenn ich sein Antlitz sehe,
miːr graost |ɛs, vɛn |ɪç zaen |antlɪts zeːə,

159

der Mond zeigt mir meine eigne Gestalt.
der moːnt tsaekt miːr maenə |aegnə gəʃtalt.

Du Doppelgänger, du bleicher Geselle!
duː dopəlgɛŋər, duː blaeçər gəzɛllə

Was äffst du nach mein Liebesleid
vas |ɛfst duː nax maen liːbəslaet

das mich gequält auf dieser Stelle
das mɪç gəkvɛːlt |aof diːzər ʃtɛllə

so manche Nacht, in alter Zeit?
zoː mançə naxt, ɪn |altər tsaet

Schubert   Der Erlkönig
            der |ɛrlkøːnɪç

Wer reitet so spät durch Nacht und Wind?
veːr vaetət zoː spɛːt durç naçt |unt vɪnt

Es ist der Vater mit seinem Kind;
ɛs |ɪst der faːtər mɪt zaenəm kɪnt,

er hat den Knaben wohl in dem Arm,
eːr hat den knaːbən voːl |ɪn dem |arm,

er fasst ihn sicher, er hält ihn warm.
eːr fast |iːn zɪçər, eːr hɛːlt |iːn varm.

Mein Sohn, was birgst du so bang dein Gesicht?
maen zoːn, vas bɪrkst duː zoː baŋ daen gəzɪçt

Siehst, Vater, du den Erlkönig nicht?
ziːst, faːtər, duː den |ɛrlkøːnɪç nɪçt

Den Erlenkönig mit Kron und Schweif?
den |ɛrlənkøːnɪç mɪt kroːn |unt ʃvaef

Mein Sohn, es ist ein Nebelstreif.
maen zoːn, ɛs ɪst |aen neːbəlʃtraef.

"Du liebes Kind, komm, geh mit mir!
duː liːbəs kɪnt, kom, geː mɪt miːr

gar schöne Spiele spiel ich mit dir;
gaːr ʃøːnə ʃpiːlə ʃpiːl |ɪç mɪt diːr,

160

manch bunte Blumen sind an dem Strand,
manç bʊntə bluːmən zɪnt |an dem ʃtrant,

meine Mutter hat manch gülden Gewand."
maenə mʊtər hat manç gʏldən gəvant.

Mein Vater, mein Vater, und hörest du nicht,
maen faːtər, maen faːtər, ʊnt høːrəst duː nɪçt,

was Erlenkönig mir leise verspricht?
vas |ɛrlənkøːnɪç miːr laezə fɛrʃprɪçt

Sei ruhig, bleibe ruhig, mein Kind:
zae ruːɪç, blaebə ruːɪç, maen kɪnt,

in dürren Blättern säuselt der Wind.
ɪn dʏrrən blɛtərn zɔøzəlt der vɪnt.

"Willst, feiner Knabe, du mit mir gehn?
vɪlst, faenər knaːbə, duː mɪt miːr geːn

meine Töchter sollen dich warten schön;
maenə tœçtər zɔllən dɪç vartən ʃøːn,

meine Töchter führen den nächtlichen Reihn
maenə tœçtər fyːrən den nɛçtlɪçən raen

und wiegen und tanzen und singen dich ein,
|ʊnt viːgən |ʊnt tantsən |ʊnt zɪŋən dɪç |aen,

sie wiegen und tanzen und singen dich ein."
ziː viːgən |ʊnt tantsən |ʊnt zɪŋən dɪç |aen.

Mein Vater, mein Vater, und siehst du nicht dort
maen faːtər, maen faːtər, ʊnt ziːst duː nɪçt dɔrt

Erlkönigs Töchter am düstern Ort?
ɛrlkøːnɪçs tœçtər |am dyːstərn |ɔrt

Mein Sohn, mein Sohn, ich seh es genau,
maen zoːn, maen zoːn, ɪç zeː |es gənao,

es scheinen die alten Weiden so grau.
ɛs ʃaenən di |altən vaedən zoː grao.

"Ich liebe dich, mich reizt deine schöne Gestalt,
ɪç liːbə dɪç, mɪç raetst daenə ʃøːnə gəʃtalt.

und bist du nicht willig, so brauch ich Gewalt."
ʊnt bɪst duː nɪçt vɪllɪç, zoː braox |ɪç gəvalt.

"Main Vater, mein Vater, jetzt fasst er mich an!
maen faːtər, maen faːter, jɛtst fast |eːr mɪç |an.

Erlkönig hat mir ein Leids getan!"
ɛrlkøːnɪç hat miːr |aen laets gətaːn.

Dem Vater grauset's, er reitet geschwind,
dem faːtər graozəts, eːr raetət gəʃvɪnt,

er hält in Armen das ächzende Kind,
eːr hɛːlt |ɪn |armən das |ɛçtsəndə kɪnt,

erreicht den Hof mit Müh und Not;
ɛrraeçt den hoːf mɪt myː |ʊnt noːt,

in seinen Armen das Kind war tot.
ɪn zaenən |armən das kɪnt vaːr toːt.

Schubert   Der Leiermann
             der laeərman

Drüben hinterm Dorfe steht ein Leiermann,
dryːbən hɪntərm dɔrfə ʃteːt |aen laeərman,

und mit starren Fingern dreht er, was er kann.
ʊnt mɪt ʃtarrən fɪŋərn dreːt |eːr, vas |eːr kan.

Barfuss auf dem Eise wankt er hin und her,
barfuːs aof dem |aezə vaŋkt |eːr hɪn |ʊnt heːr,

und sein kleiner Teller bleibt ihm immer leer.
ʊnt zaen klaenər tɛllər blaept |iːm |ɪmmər leːr.

Keiner mag ihn hören, keiner sieht ihn an,
kaenər maːk |iːn høːrən, kaenər ziːt |iːn |an,

und die Hunde knurren um den alten Mann.
ʊnt di hʊndə knʊrrən |ʊm den |altən man.

Und er lässt es gehen alles, wie es will,
ʊnt |eːr lɛst |ɛs geːən |alləs, viː |ɛs vɪl,

dreht, und seine Leier steht ihm nimmer still.
dreːt, ʊnt zaenə laeər ʃteːt |iːm nɪmmər ʃtɪl.

162

Wunderlicher Alter, soll ich mit dir gehn?
vʊndərlɪçər |altər, zɔl |ɪç mɪt diːr geːn.

Willst zu meinen Liedern deine Leier drehn?
vɪlst tsuː maenən liːdərn daenə laeər dreːn.

Schubert   Der Lindenbaum
             der lɪndənbɑom

Am Brunnen vor dem Tore da steht ein Lindenbaum;
am brʊnnən foːr dem toːrə dɑː ʃteːt |aen lɪndənbɑom

ich träumt' in seinem Schatten
ɪç trɔømt |ɪn zaenəm ʃatən

so manchen süssen Traum.
zoː mançən zyːsən trɑom.

Ich schnitt in seine Rinde
ɪç ʃnɪt |ɪn zaenə rɪndə

so manches liebe Wort;
zoː mançəs liːbə vɔrt,

es zog in Freud und Leide
ɛs tsoːk |ɪn frɔøt |ʊnt laedə

zu ihm mich immerfort.
tsuː |iːm mɪç |ɪmmərfɔrt.

Ich musst auch heute wandern
ɪç mʊst |ɑox hɔøtə vandərn

vorbei in tiefer Nacht,
fɔrbae |ɪn tiːfər naxt,

da hab ich noch im Dunkel die Augen zugemacht.
dɑː hɑːp |ɪç nɔx |ɪm dʊŋkəl di |ɑogən tsuɡəmaxt.

Und seine Zweige rauschten,
ʊnt zaenə tsvaegə rɑoʃtən,

als riefen sie mir zu:
als riːfən ziː miːr tsuː,

komm her zu mir, Geselle,
kɔm heːr tsuː miːr, ɡəzɛllə,

hier findst du deine Ruh!
hiːr fɪndst duː daenə ruː.

Die kalten Winde bliesen
di kaltən vɪndə bliːzən

mir grad ins Angesicht,
miːr graːt |ɪns |angəzɪçt

der Hut flog mir vom Kopfe,
der huːt floːk miːr fɔm kɔpfə,

ich wendete mich nicht.
ɪç vɛndətə mɪç nɪçt.

Nun bin ich manche Stunde entfernt
nuːn bɪn |ɪç mançə ʃtʊndə |ɛntfɛrnt

von jenem Ort,
fɔn jeːnəm |ɔrt,

und immer hör ich's rauschen:
ʊnt |ɪmmər høːr |ɪçs raoʃən,

du fändest Ruhe dort!
duː fɛndəst ruːə dɔrt.

Schubert   Der Musensohn
              der muːzənzoːn

Durch Feld und Wald zu schweifen,
dʊrç fɛlt |ʊnt valt tsuː ʃvaefən,

mein Liedchen weg zu pfeifen,
maen liːtçən vɛk tsuː pfaefən,

so geht's von Ort zu Ort!
zoː geːts fɔn |ɔrt tsuː |ɔrt

Und nach dem takte reget
ʊnt nax dem taktə reːgət

und nach dem Mass beweget
ʊnt nax dem maːs bəveːgət

sich alles an mir fort.
zɪç |alləs |an miːr fɔrt.

164

Ich kann sie kaum erwarten,
ıç kan ziː kɑom |ɛrvartən,

die erste Blum im Garten,
di |ɛrstə bluːm |ım gartən,

die erste Blüt am Baum.
di |ɛrstə blyːt |am bɑom.

Sie grüssen meine Lieder,
ziː gryːsən maenə liːdər,

und kommt der Winter wieder,
unt kɔmt der vıntər viːdər,

sing ich noch jenen Traum.
zıŋ |ıç nɔx jeːnən trɑom.

Ich sing ihn in der Weite,
ıç zıŋ |iːn |ın der vaetə,

auf Eises Läng und Breite,
ɑof |aezəs lɛŋ |unt braetə,

da blüht der Winter schön!
dɑː blyːt der vıntər ʃøːn.

Auch diese Blüte schwindet,
ɑox diːzə blyːtə ʃvındət,

und neue Freude findet sich auf bebauten Höhn.
unt nɔøə frɔødə fındət zıç |ɑof bəbɑotən høːn.

Denn wie ich bei der Linde
dɛn viː |ıç bae der lındə

das junge Völkchen finde,
das juŋə fœlkçən fındə,

sogleich erreg ich sie.
zoːglɑeç |ɛrreːk |ıç ziː.

Der stumpfe Bursche bläht sich,
der ʃtumpfə burʃə blɛːt zıç,

das steife Mädchen dreht sich nach meiner Melodie.
das ʃtaefə mɛːtçən dreːt zıç nax maenər melodiː.

Ihr gebt den Sohlen Flügel
iːr geːpt den zoːlən flyːgəl

und treibt durch Tal und Hügel
|ʊnt traept dʊrç taːl |ʊnt hyːgəl

den Leibling weit von Haus.
den liːplɪŋ vaet fɔn haos.

Ihr lieben, holden Musen,
iːr liːbən, hɔldən muːzən,

wann ruh ich ihr am Busen
van ruː |ɪç |iːr |am buːzən

auch endlich wieder aus?
|aox |ɛntlɪç viːdər |aos.

Schubert   Der Tod und das Mädchen
                der toːt |ʊnt das mɛːtçən

Vorüber, ach!   vorüber geh, wilder Knochenmann!
fɔryːbər, ax   fɔryːbər geː, vɪldər knɔxənman.

Ich bin noch jung, geh, Lieber!
ɪç bɪn nɔx jʊŋ, geː, liːbər.

und rühre mich nicht an.
ʊnt ryːrə mɪç nɪçt |an.

Gieb deine Hand, du schön und zart Gebild!
giːp daenə hant, duː ʃøːn |ʊnt tsart gəbɪlt.

bin Freund und komme nicht zu strafen.
bɪn frɔønt ʊnt kɔmə nɪçt tsuː ʃtraːfən.

Sei gutes Muts! ich bin nicht wild,
zae guːtəs muːts ɪç bɪn nɪçt vɪlt,

sollst sanft in meinen Armen schlafen!
zɔlst zanft |ɪn maenən |armən ʃlaːfən.

Schubert   Der Wanderer
             der vandərər

Ich komme vom Gebirge her,
ɪç kɔmmə fɔm gəbɪrgə heːr,

es dampft das Tal, es braust das Meer.
ɛs dampft das tɑːl, ɛs brɑʊst das meːr.

Ich wandle still, bin wenig froh,
ɪç vandlə ʃtɪl, bɪn veːnɪç froː,

und immer fragt der Seufzer: wo? immer wo?
ʊnt |ɪmmər frɑːkt der zɔøftsər, voː |ɪmmər voː.

Die Sonne dünkt mich hier so kalt,
di zɔnnə dʏŋkt mɪç hiːr zoː kalt,

die Blüte welk, das Leben alt,
di blyːtə vɛlk, das leːbən |alt,

und was sie reden, leerer Schall,
ʊnt vas ziː reːdən, leːrər ʃal,

ich bin ein Fremdling überall.
ɪç bɪn |aen frɛmtlɪŋ |yːbər|al.

Wo bist du, wo bist du
voː bɪst duː, voː bɪst duː

mein geliebtes Land?
maen gəliːptəs lant.

gesucht, geahnt, und nie gekannt!
gəzuxt, gə|ɑːnt, ʊnt niː gəkant.

Das Land, das Land so hoffnungsgrün,
das lant, das lant zoː hɔfnʊŋsgryːn,

das Land, wo meine Rosen blühn,
das lant, voː maenə roːzən blyːn,

wo meine Freunde wandeln gehn,
voː maenə frɔøndə vandəln geːn,

wo meine Toten auferstehn das Land,
voː maenə toːtən |aof|ɛrʃteːn das lant,

167

das meine Sprache spricht,
das maenə ʃpraːxə ʃprɪçt,

o Land, wo bist du?
oː lant, voː bɪst duː.

Ich wandle still, bin wenig froh,
ɪç vandlə ʃtil, bɪn veːnɪç froː,

und immer fragt der Seufzer: wo? immer wo?
ʊnt |ɪmmər fraːkt der zɔøftsər, voː ɪmmər voː.

Im Geisterhauch tönt's mir zurück:
ɪm gaestərhaox tøːnts miːr tsurʏk,

"Dort, wo du nicht bist, dort ist das Gluck!"
dɔrt, voː duː nɪçt bɪst, dɔrt |ɪst das glʏk.

Schubert   Der Wegweiser
               der veːkvaezər

Was vermeid ich denn die Wege,
vas fɛrmaet |ɪç dɛn di veːgə,

wo die andern Wandrer gehn,
voː di |andərn vandrər geːn,

suche mir versteckte Stege
zuxə miːr fɛrʃtɛktə ʃteːgə

durch verschneite Felsenhöhn?
dʊrç fɛrʃnaetə fɛlzənhøːn.

Habe ja doch nichts begangen,
haːbə jaː dɔx nɪçts bəgaŋən,

dass ich Menschen sollte scheun,
das |ɪç mɛnʃən zɔltə ʃɔøn,

welch ein törichtes Verlangen
vɛlç |aen tøːrɪçtəs fɛrlaŋən

treibt mich in die Wüstenein?
traept mɪç |ɪn di vɪstənaen.

Weiser stehen auf den Wegen,
vaezər ʃteːən |aof den veːgən,

168

weisen auf die Städte zu,
vaezən |ɑof di ʃtɛtə tsuː,

und ich wandre sonder Massen,
ʊnt |ɪç vandrə zɔndər masən,

ohne Ruh, und suche Ruh.
oːnə ruː, ʊnt zuçə ruː.

Einen Weiser seh ich stehen
aenən vaezər zeː |ɪç ʃteːən

unverrückt vor meinem Blick;
|ʊnfɛrrʏkt foːr maenəm blɪk,

eine Strasse muss ich gehen,
aenə ʃtrɑːsə mʊs |ɪç geːən,

die noch keiner ging zurück.
di nɔx kaenər gɪŋ tsurʏk.

Schubert   Die Allmacht
              di |almaxt

Gross ist Jehova, der Herr!
groːs |ɪst jeːhoːva, der hɛr.

denn Himmel und Erde verkünden seine Macht.
dɛn hɪmməl |ʊnt |eːrdə fɛrkʏndən zaenə maxt.

Du hörst sie im brausenden Sturm,
duː høːrst ziː |ɪm brɑozəndən ʃtʊrm,

in des Waldstroms laut aufrauschenden Ruf;
ɪn dɛs valt ʃtroːms lɑot |ɑofrɑoʃəndən ruːf,

gross ist Jehova, der Herr, gross ist seine Macht.
groːs |ɪst jeːhoːva, der hɛr, groːs |ɪst zaenə maxt.

Du hörst sie in des grünenden Waldes Gesäusel,
duː høːrst ziː |ɪn dɛs gryːnəndən valdəs gəzɔøzəl,

siehst sie in wogender Saaten Gold,
ziːst ziː |ɪn voːgəndər zɑːtən gɔlt,

in lieblicher Blumen glühendem Schmelz,
ɪn liːplɪçər bluːmən glyːəndəm ʃmɛlts,

im Glanz des sternebesäeten Himmels.
ɪm glants dɛs ʃtɛrnəbəzɛːətən hɪmməls.

Furchtbar tönt sie im Donnergeroll
fʊrçtbaːr tøːnt ziː |ɪm dɔnnərgərɔl

und flammt in des Blitzes
|ʊnt flamt |ɪn dɛs blɪtsəs

schnell hinzuckendem Flug,
ʃnɛl hɪntsʊkəndəm fluːk,

doch kündet das pochende Herz
dɔx kyndət das pɔxəndə hɛrts

dir fühlbarer noch Jehovas Macht,
diːr fyːlbarər nɔx jeːhoːvas maxt,

des ewigen Gottes,
dɛs |eːvɪgən gɔtəs,

blickst du flehend empor
blɪkst duː fleːənt |ɛmpoːr

und hoffst auf Huld und Erbarmen.
|ʊnt hɔfst |aof hʊlt |ʊnt |ɛrbarmən.

Gross ist Jehova, der Herr!
groːs |ɪst jeːhoːva, der her.

Schubert   Die Forelle
             di fɔrɛllə

In einem Bächlein helle, da schoss in froher Eil
ɪn |aenəm bɛçlaen hɛllə, daː ʃɔs |ɪn froːər |ael

die launische Forelle vorüber wie ein Pfeil.
di laonɪʃə fɔrɛllə fɔryːbər viː |aen pfael.

Ich stand an dem Gestade und sah in süsser Ruh
ɪç stant |an dem gəʃtaːdə |ʊnt zaː |ɪn zyːsər ruː

des muntern Fischleins Bade
dɛs mʊntərn fɪʃlaens baːdə

im klaren Bächlein zu.
|ɪm klɑːrən bɛçlaen tsuː.

Ein Fischer mit der Rute wohl an dem Ufer stand,
aen fɪʃər mɪt der ruːtə voːl |an dem |uːfər ʃtant,

und sah's mit kaltem Blute,
ʊnt zɑːs mɪt kaltəm bluːtə,

wie sich das Fischlein wand.
viː zɪç das fɪʃlaen vant.

So lang' dem Wasser Helle,
zoː laŋ dem vasər hɛllə,

so dacht ich, nicht gebricht,
zoː daxt |ɪç, nɪçt gəbrɪçt,

so fängt er die Forelle mit seiner Angel nicht.
zoː fɛŋt |er di fɔrɛllə mɪt zaenər |aŋəl nɪçt.

Doch endlich ward dem Diebe die Zeit zu lang.
dɔx |ɛntlɪç vart dem diːbə di tsaet tsuː laŋ.

Er macht das Bächlein tückisch trübe,
ɛr maxt das bɛçlaen tʏkɪʃ tryːbə,

und eh ich es gedacht,
ʊnt |eː |ɪç |ɛs gədaxt,

so zuckte seine Rute,
zoː tsʊktə zaenə ruːtə,

das Fischlein zappelt dran,
das fɪʃlaen tsapəlt dran,

und ich mit regem Blute sah die Betrogne an.
ʊnt |ɪç mɪt reːgəm bluːtə zɑː di bətroːgnə |an.

Schubert   Die junge Nonne
              di jʊŋə nɔnnə

Wie braust durch die Wipfel der heulende Sturm!
viː braost dʊrç di vɪpfəl der hɔʏləndə ʃtʊrm.

Es klirren die Balken, es zittert das Haus!
ɛs klɪrrən di balkən, ɛs tsɪtərt das haos.

171

Es rollet der Donner, es leuchtet der Blitz,
ɛs rɔllət der dɔnnər, ɛs lɔ͜ø͡çtət der blɪts,

und finster die Nacht, wie das Grab!
ʊnt fɪnstər di naxt, viː das grɑːp.

Immerhin, immerhin,
ɪmmerhɪn, ɪmmərhɪn,

so tobt' es auch jungst noch in mir!
zoː toːpt |ɛs |a͡ox jʏŋst nɔx |ɪn miːr.

Es brauste das Leben, wie jetzo der Sturm,
ɛs bra͡ostə das leːbən, vi jɛ͡tso der ʃtʊrm,

es bebten die Glieder, wie jetzo das Haus,
ɛs beːptən di gliːdər, vi jɛ͡tso das ha͡os,

es flammte die Liebe, wie jetzo der Blitz,
ɛs flamtə di liːbə, viː jɛ͡tso der blɪts,

und finster die Brust, wie das Grab.
ʊnt fɪnstər di brʊst, viː das grɑːp.

Nun tobe, du wilder, gewaltger Sturm,
nuːn toːbə, duː vɪldər, gəvaltgər ʃtʊrm,

im Herzen ist Friede, im Herzen ist Ruh,
ɪm hɛrtsən |ɪst friːdə, ɪm hɛrtsən |ɪst ruː,

des Bräutigams harret die liebende Braut,
dɛs brɔ͡øtɪgams harrət di liːbəndə bra͡ot,

gereinigt in prüfender Glut der ewigen,
gəra͡enɪkt |ɪn pryːfəndər gluːt der |eːvɪgən,

ewigen Liebe getraut.
eːvɪgən liːbə gətra͡ot.

Ich harre, mein Heiland!   mit sehnendem Blick!
ɪç harrə, ma͡en ha͡elant.   mɪt zeːnəndəm blɪk.

komm, himmlischer Bräutigam, hole die Braut,
kɔm, hɪmlɪʃər brɔ͡øtɪgam, hoːlə di bra͡ot,

erlöse die Seele von irdischer Haft!
ɛrlø͡ːzə di zeːlə fɔn |ɪrdɪʃər haft.

Horch, friedlich ertönet das Glöcklein vom Turm!
hɔrç, friːtlɪç ˈɛrtøːnət das glœklaen fɔm tʊrm.

Es lockt mich das süsse Getön
ɛs lɔkt mɪç das zyːsə gətøːn

allmächtig zu ewigen Höhn! Alleluja!
ˈalmɛçtɪk tsuː ˈeːvɪgən høːn. alləluːja.

Schubert   Die Liebe hat gelogen
              di liːbə hat gəloːgən

Die Liebe hat gelogen,
di liːbə hat gəloːgən,

die Sorge lastet schwer,
di zɔrgə lastət ʃveːr,

betrogen, ach! betrogen
bətroːgən, ax. bətroːgən

hat alles mich umher!
hat ˈalləs mɪç ˈʊmheːr.

Es fliessen heisse Tropfen
ɛs fliːsən haesə trɔpfən

die Wange stets herab,
di vaŋə ʃteːts hɛrap,

lass ab, mein Herz, zu klopfen,
las ˈap, maen hɛrts, tsuː klɔpfən,

du armes Herz, lass ab!
duː ˈarməs hɛrts, las ˈap.

Schubert   Die Post
              di pɔst

Von der Strasse her ein Posthorn klingt.
fɔn der ʃtraːsə heːr ˈaen pɔsthɔrn klɪŋkt.

Was hat es, dass es so hoch aufspringt, mein Herz?
vas hat ˈɛs, das ˈɛs zoː hoːx ˈaofʃprɪŋt, maen hɛrts.

Die Post bringt keinen Brief für dich.
di pɔst brɪŋt kaenən briːf fyːr dɪç.

173

Was drängst du denn so wunderlich, mein Herz?
vas drɛŋst duː dɛn zoː vʊndərlɪç, maen hɛrts.

Nun ja, die Post kommt aus der Stadt,
nuːn jaː, di pɔst kɔmt |aos der ʃtat,

wo ich ein liebes Liebchen hatt, mein Herz!
voː |ɪç |aen liːbəs liːpçen hat, maen hɛrts.

Willst wohl einmal hinübersehn
vɪlst voːl |aenmaːl hɪnyːbərzeːn

und fragen, wie es dort mag gehn, mein Herz?
|ʊnt fraːgən, viː |ɛs dɔrt maːk geːn, maen hɛrts.

Schubert   Du bist die Ruh
                duː bɪst di ruː

Du bist die Ruh, der Friede mild,
duː bɪst di ruː, der friːdə mɪlt,

die Sehnsucht du, und was sie stillt.
di zeːnzʊxt duː, ʊnt vas ziː ʃtɪlt.

Ich weihe dir voll Lust Und Schmerz
ɪç vaeə diːr fɔl lʊst |ʊnt ʃmɛrts

zur Wohnung hier mein Aug und Herz.
tsur voːnʊŋ hiːr maen |aok |ʊnt hɛrts.

Kehr ein bei mir, und schliesse du
keːr |aen bae miːr, |ʊnt ʃliːsə duː

still hinter dir die Pforten zu.
ʃtɪl hɪntər diːr di pfɔrtən tsuː.

Treib andern Schmerz aus dieser Brust!
traep |andərn ʃmɛrts |aos diːzər brʊst.

voll sei dies Herz von deiner Lust.
fɔl zae diːs hɛrts fɔn daenər lʊst.

Dies Augenzelt, von deinem Glanz
diːs |aogəntsɛlt, fɔn daenəm glants

allein erhellt, o füll es ganz!
|allaen |ɛrhɛlt, oː fʏl |ɛs gants.

Schubert   Eifersucht und Stolz
                aefərzʊçt |ʊnt ʃtɔlts

Wohin so schnell, so kraus und wild,
vohɪn zo: ʃnɛl, zo: kraos |ʊnt vɪlt,

main lieber Bach?
maen li:bər bax.

eilst du voll Zorn dem frechen Bruder Jäger nach?
aelst du: fɔl tsɔrn dem frɛçən bru:dər jɛ:gər na:x.

Kehr um, und schilt erst deine Müllerin
ke:r |ʊm, ʊnt ʃɪlt |e:rst daenə mʏllərɪn

für ihren leichten, losen,
fy:r |i:rən laeçtən, lo:zən,

kleinen Flattersinn, kehr um!
klaenən flatərzɪn, ke:r|ʊm.

Sahst du sie gestern Abend nicht am Tore stehn,
za:st du: zi: gɛstərn |a:bənt nɪçt |am to:rə ʃte:n,

mit langem Halse nach der grossen Strasse sehn?
mɪt laŋəm halzə nax der gro:sən ʃtra:sə ze:n.

Wenn von dem Fang der Jäger
vɛn fɔn dem faŋ der jɛ:gər

lustig zieht nach Haus,
lʊstɪç tsi:t na:x haos,

da steckt kein sittsam Kind
da: ʃtɛkt kaen zɪtzam kɪnt

den Kopf zum Fenster 'naus.
den kɔpf tsum fɛnstər naos.

Geh, Bächlein, hin und sag ihr das;
ge:, bɛçlaen, hɪn |ʊnt za:k |i:r das,

doch sag ihr nicht, hörst du, kein Wort,
dɔx za:k |i:r nɪçt, hø:rst du:, kaen vɔrt,

von meinem traurigen Gesicht; sag ihr:
fɔn maenəm traorɪgən gəzɪçt, za:k |i:r,

175

Er schnitzt bei mir sich eine Pfeif aus Rohr,
eːr ʃnɪtst bae miːr zɪç |aenə pfaef |aos roːr,

und bläst den Kindern schöne Tänz
ʊnt blɛːst den kɪndərn ʃøːnə tɛnts

und Lieder vor, sag ihr's!
|ʊnt liːdər foːr, zaːk |iːrs.

Schubert   Fischerweise
                fɪʃərvaezə

Den Fischer fechten Sorgen
den fɪʃər fɛçtən zɔrgən

und Gram und Leid nicht an,
|ʊnt graːm |ʊnt laet nɪçt |an,

er löst am frühen Morgen
eːr løːst |am fryːən mɔrgən

mit leichtem Sinn den Kahn.
mɪt laeçtəm zɪn den kaːn.

Da lagert rings noch Friede
daː laːgərt rɪŋs nɔx friːdə

auf Wald und Flur und Bach,
|aof valt |ʊnt fluːr |ʊnt bax,

er ruft mit seinem Liede die goldne Sonne wach.
eːr ruːft mɪt zaenəm liːdə di gɔldnə zɔnnə vax.

Er singt zu seinem Werke
eːr zɪŋt tsuː zaenəm vɛrkə

aus voller frischer Brust,
|aos fɔllər frɪʃər brʊst,

die Arbeit gibt ihm Stärke,
di |arbaet giːpt |iːm ʃtɛrkə,

die Stärke Lebenslust.
di ʃtɛrkə leːbənslʊst.

Bald wird ein bunt Gewimmel
balt vɪrt |aen bʊnt gəvɪmməl

in allen Tiefen laut,
|ɪn |allən tiːfən laot,

und plätschert durch den Himmel,
ʊnt plɛtʃərt dʊrç den hɪmməl,

der sich im Wasser baut.
der zɪç |ɪm vasər baot.

Doch wer ein Netz will stellen,
dɔx veːr |aen nɛts vɪl ʃtɛllən,

braucht Augen klar und gut,
braoxt |aogən klaːr |ʊnt guːt,

muss heiter gleich den Wellen
mʊs haetər glaeç den vɛllən

und frei sein wie die Flut;
|ʊnt frae zaen viː di fluːt,

dort angelt auf der Brücke
dɔrt |aŋəlt |aof der brʏkə

die Hirtin, schlauer Wicht!
di hɪrtɪn, ʃlaoər vɪçt.

gib auf nur deine Tücke,
giːp |aof nuːr daenə tʏkə

den Fisch betrügst du nicht!
deːn fɪʃ bətryːkst duː nɪçt.

Schubert   Frühlingsglaube
              fryːlɪŋsglaobə

Die linden Lüfte sind erwacht,
di lɪndən lʏftə zɪnt |ɛrvaxt,

sie säuseln und wehen Tag und Nacht,
ziː zɔøzəln |ʊnt veːən taːk |ʊnt naxt,

sie schaffen an allen Enden.
ziː ʃafən |an |allən |ɛndən.

O frischer Duft, o neuer Klang!
oː frɪʃər dʊft, |oː nɔøər klaŋ.

177

Nun, armes Herze, sei nicht bang!
nuːn, ǀarmas hɛrtsə, zaɪ nɪçt baŋ.

nun muss sich alles wenden.
nuːn mʊs zɪç ǀalləs vɛndən.

Die Welt wird schöner mit jedem Tag,
di vɛlt vɪrt ʃøːnər mɪt jeːdəm taːk,

man weiss nicht, was noch werden mag,
man vaes nɪçt, vas nɔx veːrdən maːk,

das Blühen will nicht enden, es will nicht enden;
das blyːən vɪl nɪçt ǀɛndən, ǀɛs vɪl nɪçt ǀɛndən,

es blüht das fernste, tiefste Thal:
ɛs blyːt das fɛrnstə, tiːfstə taːl,

Nun, armes Herz, vergiss der Qual!
nuːn, ǀarmas hɛrts, fɛrgɪs der kvaːl.

Nun muss sich alles wenden.
nuːn mʊs zɪç ǀalləs vɛndən.

Schubert   Frühlingstraum
                fryːlɪŋstraom

Ich träumte von bunten Blumen,
ɪç trɔømtə fɔn bʊntən bluːmən,

so wie sie wohl blühen im Mai,
zoː viː ziː voːl blyːən ǀɪm mae,

ich träumte von grünen Wiesen,
ɪç trɔømtə fɔn gryːnən viːzən,

von lustigem Vogelgeschrei.
fɔn lʊstɪgəm foːgəlgəʃrae.

Und als die Hähne krähten,
ʊnt ǀals di hɛːnə krɛːtən,

da ward mein Auge wach;
daː vart maen ǀaogə vax,

da war es kalt und finster,
daː vaːr ǀɛs kalt ǀʊnt fɪnstər,

178

es schrieen die Raben vom Dach.
ɛs ʃriːən di raːbən fɔm dax.

Doch an den Fensterscheiben,
dɔx |an den fɛnstərʃaebən,

wer malte die Blätter da?
veːr maltə di blɛtər daː.

Ihr lacht wohl über den Träumer,
iːr laxt voːl |yːbər den trɔømər,

der Blumen im Winter sah?
der bluːmən |ɪm vɪntər zaː.

Ich träumte von Lieb um Liebe,
ɪç trɔømtə fɔn liːp |um liːbə,

von einer schönen Maid,
fɔn |aenər ʃøːnən maet,

von Herzen und von Küssen,
fɔn hɛrtsən |unt fɔn kʏsən,

von Wonne und Seligkeit.
fɔn vɔnnə |unt zeːlɪçkaet.

Und als die Hähne krähten,
unt |als di hɛːnə krɛːtən,

da ward mein Herze wach;
daː vart maen hɛrtsə vax,

nun sitz ich hier alleine
nuːn zɪts |ɪç hiːr |allaenə

und denke dem Traume nach.
|unt dɛŋkə dem traomə nax.

Die Augen schliess ich wieder,
di |aogən ʃliːs |ɪç viːdər,

noch schlägt das Herz so warm.
nɔx ʃlɛːkt das hɛrts zoː varm.

Wann grünt ihr Blätter am Fenster?
van gryːnt |iːr blɛtər |am fɛnstər.

wann halt ich mein Liebchen im Arm?
van halt |ɪç maen liːpçen |ɪm |arm.

Schubert   Ganymed
            ganime̱ːt

Wie im Morgenglanze du rings mich anglühst,
viː |ɪm mo̱rgənglantse duː rɪŋs mɪç |angly̱ːst,

Frühling, Geliebter!
fry̱ːlɪŋ, gəli̱ːptər.

Mit tausendfacher Liebeswonne
mɪt ta̱ozəntfaxər li̱ːbəsvɔnnə

sich an mein Herze drängt
zɪç |an ma̱en hɛrtsə drɛŋt

deiner ewigen Wärme heilig Gefühl,
da̱enər |e̱ːvɪgən vɛrmə ha̱elɪç gəfy̱ːl,

unendliche Schöne!
un|ɛntlɪçə ʃø̱ːnə.

Dass ich dich fassen möcht in diesen Arm!
das |ɪç dɪç fa̱sən mœçt |ɪn di̱ːzən |arm.

Ach, an deinem Busen lieg ich und schmachte,
ax, |an da̱enəm bu̱ːzən li̱ːk |ɪç |unt ʃma̱xtə,

und deine Blumen,
unt da̱enə blu̱ːmən,

dein Gras drängen sich an mein Herz.
da̱en graːs drɛŋən zɪç |an ma̱en hɛrts.

Du kühlst den brennenden Durst meines Busens,
duː ky̱ːlst den brɛ̱nnəndən durst ma̱enəs bu̱ːzəns,

lieblicher Morgenwind,
li̱ːplɪçər mo̱rgənvɪnt,

ruft drein die Nachtigall
ru̱ːft dra̱en di na̱xtigal

liebend nach mir aus dem Nebeltal.
li̱ːbənt naːx miːr |aos dem ne̱ːbəltaːl.

Ich komm! ich komme' ach! wohin?
ɪç kɔm,   ɪç kɔmme, ax, vohɪ̱n.

180

Hinauf strebt's, hinauf!
hɪnɑof ʃtreːpts, hɪnɑof.

Es schweben die Wolken abwärts,
ɛs ʃveːbən di vɔlkən |apvɛrts,

die Wolken neigen sich der sehnenden Liebe.
di vɔlkən naegən zɪç der zeːnəndən liːbə.

Mir! in eurem Schosse aufwärts!
miːr, ɪn |ɔørəm ʃoːsə |ɑofvɛrts,

umfangend umfangen!
ʊmfaŋɛnt |ʊmfaŋən.

aufwärts an deinen Busen, all'liebender Vater!
ɑofvɛrts |an daenən buːzən, alliːbəndər fɑːtər.

Schubert   Gretchen am Spinnrade
                grɛːtçən |am ʃpɪnrɑːdə

Meine Ruh ist hin, mein Herz ist schwer;
maenə ruː |ɪst hɪn, maen hɛrts |ɪst ʃveːr,

ich finde sie nimmer und nimmermehr.
ɪç fɪndə ziː nɪmmər |ʊnt nɪmmərmeːr.

Wo ich ihn nicht hab, ist mir das Grab,
voː |ɪç |iːn nɪçt hɑːp, ɪst miːr das grɑːp,

die ganze Welt ist mir vergällt.
di gantsə vɛlt |ɪst miːr fɛrgɛlt.

Mein armer Kopf ist mir verrückt,
maen |armər kɔpf |ɪst miːr fɛrrʏkt,

main armer Sinn ist mir zerstückt.
maen |armər zɪn |ɪst miːr tsɛrʃtʏkt.

Meine Ruh ist hin, mein Herz ist schwer;
maenə ruː |ɪst hɪn, maen hɛrts |ɪst ʃveːr,

ich finde sie nimmer und nimmermehr.
ɪç fɪndə ziː nɪmmər |ʊnt hɪmmərmeːr.

Nach ihm nur schau ich zum Fenster hinaus,
nɑːx |iːm nuːr ʃɑo |ɪç tsum fɛnstər hɪnɑos,

181

nach ihm nur geh ich aus dem Haus.
naːx |iːm nuːr geː |ɪç |ɑos dem hɑos.

sein hoher Gang, sein' edle Gestalt,
zaen hoːər gaŋ, zaen |eːdlə gəʃtalt,

seines Mundes Lächeln, seiner Augen Gewalt,
zaenəs mʊndəs lɛçəln, zaenər |ɑogən gəvalt,

und seiner Rede Zauberfluss,
ʊnt zaenər reːdə tsɑobərflʊs,

sein Händedruck, und ach! sein Kuss!
zaen hɛndədrʊk, ʊnt |ax,   zaen kʊs.

Meine Ruh ist hin, mein Herz ist schwer;
maenə ruː |ɪst hɪn, maen hɛrts |ɪst ʃveːr,

ich finde sie nimmer und nimmermehr.
ɪç fɪndə ziː nɪmmər |ʊnt nɪmmərmeːr.

Mein Busen drängt sich nach ihm hin.
maen buːzən drɛŋt zɪç naːx |iːm hɪn.

Ach! dürft ich fassen und halten ihn!
ax, dʏrft |ɪç fasən |ʊnt haltən |iːn.

und küssen ihn, so wie ich wollt,
ʊnt kʏsən |iːn, zoː viː |ɪç vɔlt,

an seinen Küssen vergehen sollt,
an zaenən kʏsən fɛrgeːən zɔlt,

o könnt ich ihn küssen, so wie ich wollt,
oː kœnt |ɪç |iːn kʏsən, zoː viː |ɪç vɔlt,

an seinen Küssen vergehen sollt!
an zaenən kʏsən fɛrgeːən zɔlt.

Schubert   Heiden-Röslein
              haedən røːzlaen

Sah ein Knab ein Röslein stehn,
zɑː |aen knɑːp |aen røːzlaen ʃteːn,

Röslein auf der Heiden,
røːzlaen |ɑof der haedən,

182

war so jung und morgenschön, lief er schnell,
vɑːr zoː juŋ |unt mɔrgənʃøːn, liːf eːr ʃnəl,

es nah zu sehn, sah's mit vielen Freuden.
ɛs nɑː tsuː zeːn, zɑːs mɪt fiːlən frɔ̯øːdən.

Röslein rot, Röslein auf der Heiden.
rø̯øːzlaen roːt, rø̯øːzlaen |ɑof der haɪdən.

Knabe sprach: ich breche dich,
knɑ̯ɑːbə ʃprɑːx, |ɪç brɛçə dɪç,

Röslein auf der Heiden!
rø̯øːzlaen |ɑof der hae̯dən.

Röslein sprach: ich steche dich,
rø̯øːzlaen ʃprɑːx, |ɪç stɛçə dɪç,

dass du ewig denkst an mich,
das duː |e̯ːvɪç dɛŋkst |an mɪç,

und ich will's nicht leiden.
unt |ɪç vɪls nɪçt lae̯dən.

Und der wilde Knabe brach
unt der vɪ̯ldə knɑːbə brɑːx

's Roslein auf der Heiden;
srø̯øːzlaen |ɑof der hae̯dən,

Röslein wehrte sich und stach,
rø̯øːzlaen veːrtə zɪç |unt ʃtɑːx,

half ihr doch kein Weh und Ach,
half |iːr dɔx kae̯n veː |unt |ax,

musst es eben leiden.
must |ɛs |e̯ːbən lae̯dən.

Schubert   Ihr Bild
              iːr bɪlt

Ich stand in dunkeln Traümen
ɪç ʃtant |in duŋkəln tro̯øːmən

und starrt' ihr Bildnis an,
|unt ʃtart |iːr bɪ̯ldnɪs |an,

und das geliebte Antlitz heimlich
ʊnt das gəliːptə |antlɪts haemlɪç

zu leben begann.
tsu leːbən bəgan.

Um ihre Lippen zog sich ein Lächeln wunderbar,
ʊm |iːrə lɪpən tsoːk zɪç aen lɛçəln vʊndərbaːr,

und wie von Wehmuthsthränen erglänzte
ʊnt viː fɔn veːmʊtstrɛːnən |ɛrglɛntstə

ihr Augenpaar.
|iːr |aogənpaːr.

Auch meine Thränen flossen
aox maenə trɛːnən flɔsən

mir von den Wangen herab-
miːr fɔn den vaŋən hɛrap

und ach! ich kann es nicht glauben,
ʊnt |ax, ɪç kan |ɛs nɪçt glaobən,

dass ich dich verloren hab!
das |ɪç dɪç fɛrloːrən haːp.

Schubert   Jägers Abendlied
                jɛːgərs |abəntliːt

Im Felde schleich ich still und wild,
ɪm fɛldə ʃlaeç |ɪç ʃtɪl |ʊnt vɪlt,

gespannt mein Feuerrohr,
gəʃpant maen fɔøərroːr,

da schwebt so licht dein liebes Bild,
daː ʃveːpt zoː lɪçt daen liːbəs bɪlt,

dein süsses Bild mir vor.
daen zyːsəs bɪlt miːr foːr.

Du wandelst jetzt wohl still und mild
duː vandəlst jɛtst voːl ʃtɪl |ʊnt mɪlt

durch Feld und liebes Thal,
dʊrç fɛlt |ʊnt liːbəs taːl,

184

und, ach, mein schnell verrauschend Bild
ʊnt, ax, maen ʃnɛl fɛrraoʃənt bɪlt

stellt sich dir's nicht einmal?
ʃtɛlt zɪç diːrs nɪçt |aenmaːl.

Mir ist es, denk ich nur an dich,
miːr |ɪst |ɛs, dɛŋk |ɪç nuːr |an dɪç,

als in den Mond zu sehn,
als |ɪn den moːnt tsuː zeːn,

ein stiller Friede kommt auf mich,
aen ʃtɪllər friːdə kɔmt |aof mɪç,

weiss nicht, wie mir geschehn.
vaes nɪçt, viː miːr gəʃeːn.

Schubert   Lachen und Weinen
                laxən |ʊnt vaenən

Lachen und Weinen zu jeglicher Stunde
laxən |ʊnt vaenən tsuː jeːklɪçər ʃtʊndə

ruht bei der Lieb auf so mancherlei Grunde.
ruːt bae der liːp |aof zoː mançərlae grʊndə.

Morgens lacht' ich vor Lust,
mɔrgəns laxt |ɪç foːr lʊst,

und warum ich nun weine
ʊnt varʊm |ɪç nuːn vaenə

bei des Abendes Scheine,
bae dɛs |aːbəndəs ʃaenə,

ist mir selb' nicht bewusst.
ɪst miːr zɛlp nɪçt bəvʊst.

Weinen und Lachen zu jeglicher Stunde,
vaenən |ʊnt laxən tsuː jeːklɪçər ʃtʊndə,

ruht bei der Lieb auf so mancherlei Grunde.
ruːt bae der liːp |aof zoː mançərlae grʊndə.

Abends weint' ich vor Schmerz;
aːbənts vaent |ɪç foːr ʃmɛrts,

185

und warum du erwachen kannst
ʊnt varʊm duː |ɛrvaxən kanst

am Morgen mit Lachen,
|am mɔrgən mɪt laxən,

muss ich dich fragen, o Herz.
mʊs |ɪç |dɪç fraːgən, oː hɛrts.

Schubert   Liebesbotschaft
                 liːbəsboːtʃaft

Rauschendes Bächlein, so silbern und hell,
raʊʃəndəs bɛçlaen, zoː zɪlbərn |ʊnt hɛl,

eilst zur Geliebten so munter und schnell?
aelst tsur gəliːptən zoː mʊntər |ʊnt ʃnɛl.

ach, trautes Bächlein, mein Bote sei du;
ax, traotəs bɛçlaen, maen boːtə zae duː,

bringe die Grüsse des Fernen ihr zu.
brɪŋə di gryːsə dɛs fɛrnən |iːr tsuː.

All ihre Blumen im Garten gepflegt,
al |iːrə bluːmən ɪm gartən gəpfleːkt,

die sie so lieblich am Busen trägt,
di ziː zoː liːplɪç |am buːzən trɛːkt,

und ihre Rosen in purpurner Glut,
ʊnt |iːrə roːzən |ɪn pʊrpurnər gluːt,

Bächlein erquicke mit kühlender Flut.
bɛçlaen |ɛrkvɪkə mɪt kyːləndər fluːt.

Wenn sie am Ufer, in Träume versenkt,
vɛn ziː |am |uːfər, ɪn trɔømə fɛrzɛŋkt,

meiner gedenkend, das Köpfchen hängt,
maenər gədɛŋkənt, das kœpfçən hɛŋt,

tröste die Süsse mit freundlichem Blick,
trøːstə di zyːsə mɪt frɔøntlɪçəm blɪk,

denn der Geliebte kehrt bald zurück.
dɛn der gəliːptə keːrt balt tsurʏk.

186

Neigt sich die Sonne mit röthlichem Schein,
naekt zɪç di zɔnnə mɪt rø:tlɪcəm ʃaen,

wiege das Liebchen in Schlummer ein.
vi:gə das li:pçən |ɪn ʃlʊmmər |aen.

Rausche sie murmelnd in süsse Ruh,
raoʃə zi: mʊrməlnt |ɪn zy:sə ru:,

flüstre ihr Träume der Liebe zu.
flʏstrə |i:r trø:mə der li:bə tsu:.

Schubert   Lied der Mignon
              li:t der miɲɔ̃

Nur wer die Sehnsucht kennt,
nu:r ve:r di ze:nzʊxt kɛnt,

weiss, was ich leide!
vaes, vas |ɪç laedə.

Allein und abgetrennt von aller Freude,
allaen |ʊnt |apgətrɛnt fɔn |allər frɔ̈ødə,

seh ich ans Firmament nach jener Seite.
ze: |ɪç |ans fɪrmamɛnt nax je:nər zaetə.

Ach! der mich liebt und kennt,
ax,   der mɪç li:pt |ʊnt kɛnt,

ist in der Weite.
ɪst |ɪn der vaetə.

Es schwindelt mir, es brennt mein Eingeweide.
ɛs ʃvɪndəlt mi:r, ɛs brɛnt maen |aengəvaedə.

Schubert   Litanei
              litanae

Ruhn in Frieden alle Seelen,
ru:n |ɪn fri:dən |allə ze:lən,

die vollbracht ein banges Quälen,
di fɔlbraxt |aen baŋəs kvɛ:lən,

die vollendet süssen Traum,
di fɔl|ɛndət zy:sən traom,

187

lebenssatt, geboren kaum,
leːbənsat, gəboːrən kɑom,

aus der Welt hinüber schieden:
ɑos der vɛlt hɪnyːbər ʃiːdən,

alle Seelen ruhn in Frieden!
allə zeːlən ruːn |ɪn friːdən.

Liebevoller Mädchen Seelen,
liːbəfɔllər mɛːtçən zeːlən,

deren Thränen nicht zu zählen,
deːrən trɛːnən nɪçt tsuː tsɛːlən,

die ein falscher Freund verliess,
di |aen falʃər frɔønt fɛrliːs,

und die blinde Welt verstiess:
ʊnt di blɪndə vɛlt fɛrʃtiːs,

alle, die von hinnen schieden,
allə, di fɔn hɪnnən ʃiːdən,

alle Seelen ruhn in Frieden!
allə zeːlən ruːn |ɪn friːdən.

Und die nie der Sonne lachten,
ʊnt di niː der zɔnnə laxtən,

unterm Mond auf Dornen wachten,
ʊntərm moːnt |ɑof dɔrnən vaxtən,

Gott im reinen Himmelslicht
gɔt ɪm raenən hɪmməlslɪçt

einst zu sehn von Angesicht:
aenst tsuː zeːn fɔn |angəsɪçt,

alle, die von hinnen schieden,
allə, di fɔn hɪnnən ʃiːdən,

alle Seelen ruhn in Frieden!
allə zeːlən ruːn |ɪn friːdən.

188

Schubert   Nacht und Träume
            naxt |ʊnt trɔ͜ømə

Heilge Nacht, du sinkest nieder;
ha͜elgə naxt, duː zɪŋkəst niːdər,

nieder wallen auch die Träume,
niːdər vallən |a͜ox di trɔ͜ømə,

wie dein Mondlicht durch die Räume,
viː da͜en moːntlɪçt dʊrç di rɔ͜ømə,

durch der Menschen stille, stille Brust.
dʊrç der mɛnʃən stɪllə, ʃtɪllə brʊst.

Die belauschen sie mit Lust;
di bəla͜oʃən ziː mɪt lʊst,

rufen, wenn der Tag erwacht:
ruːfən, vɛn der taːk |ɛrvaxt,

Kahre wieder, heilge Nacht!
keːrə viːdər, ha͜elgə naxt.

holde Träume, kehret wieder!
hɔldə trɔ͜ømə, keːrət viːdər.

Schubert   Rastlose Liebe
            rastloːzə liːbə

Dem Schnee, dem Regen, dem Wind entgegen,
dem ʃneː, dem reːgən, dem vɪnt |ɛntgeːgən,

im Dampf der Klüfte, durch Nebeldüfte immer zu!
ɪm dampf der klʏftə, dʊrç neːbəldʏftə |ɪmmər tsuː.

ohne Rast und Ruh!
oːnə rast |ʊnt ruː.

Lieber durch Leiden wollt ich mich schlagen,
liːbər dʊrç la͜edən vɔlt |ɪç mɪç ʃlaːgən,

als so viel Freuden des lebens ertragen.
als zoː fiːl frɔ͜ødən dɛs leːbəns |ɛrtraːgən.

Alle das Neigen von Herzen zu Herzen,
alləs das na͜egən fɔn hɛrtsən tsuː hɛrtsən,

189

ach, wie so eigen schaffet es Schmerzen!
ax, vi: zo: |aegən ʃafət |es ʃmɛrtsən.

Wie, soll ich fliehn? Wälderwärts ziehn?
vi:, zol |ɪç fli:n.   vɛldərvɛrts tsi:n.

Alles vergebens!
_alləs fɛrge:bəns.

Krone des Lebens, Glück ohne Ruh,
kro:nə dɛs le:bəns, glʏk |o:nə ru:,

Liebe bist du, o Liebe bist du!
li:bə bɪst du:, o: li:bə bɪst du:.

Schubert   Sei mir gegrüsst
               zae mi:r gəgry:st

O du Entrissne mir und meinem Kusse,
o: du: |ɛntrɪsnə mi:r |unt maenəm kusə,

sei mir gegrüsst, sei mir geküsst!
zae mi:r gəgry:st, zae mi:r gəkyst.

Erreichbar nur meinem Sehnsuchtsgrusse,
ɛrraeçbar nu:r maenəm ze:nzuxtsgru:sə,

sei mir gegrüsst, sei mir geküsst!
zae mi:r gəgry:st, zae mi:r gəkyst.

Du von der Hand der Liebe diesem Herzen Gegebne,
du: fɔn der hant der li:bə di:zəm hɛrtsən gəge:bnə,

du von dieser Brust Genommne mir!
du: fɔn di:zər brust gənɔmnə mi:r.

mit diesem Tränengusse
mɪt di:zəm trɛ:nəngusə

sei mir gegrüsst, sei mir geküsst!
zae mi:r gəgry:st, zae mi:r gəkyst.

Zum Trotz der Ferne, die sich, feindlich trennend,
tsum trɔts der fɛrnə, di zɪç, faentlɪç trɛnənt,

hat zwischen mich und dich gestellt;
hat tsvɪʃən mɪç |unt dɪç gəʃtɛlt,

dem Neid der Schicksalsmächte zum Verdrusse
dem naet der ʃɪkzalzmɛçtə tsum fɛrdrusə

sei mir gegrüsst, sei mir geküsst!
zae miːr gəgryːst, zae miːr gəkʏst.

Wie du mir je im schönsten Lenz der Liebe
viː duː miːr jeː |ɪm ʃøːnstən lɛnts der liːbə

mit Gruss und Kuss entgegenkamst,
mɪt gruːs |unt kus |ɛntgeːgənkaːmst,

mit meiner Seele glühendstem Ergusse
mɪt maenər zeːlə glyːəntstəm |ɛrgusə

sei mir gegrüsst, sei mir geküsst!
zae miːr gəgryːst, zae miːr gəkʏst.

Ein Hauch der Liebe tilget Räum' und Zeiten,
aen haox der liːbə tɪlgət rɔøm |unt tsaetən,

ich bin bei dir, du bist bei mir,
ɪç bɪn bae diːr, duː bɪst bae miːr,

ich halte dich in dieses Arms Umschlusse,
ɪç haltə dɪç |ɪn diːzəs |arms |umʃlusə,

sei mir gegrüsst, sei mir geküsst!
zae miːr gəgryːst, zae miːr gəkʏst.

Schubert   Ständchen
                ʃtɛntçən

Leise flehen meine Lieder durch
laezə fleːən maenə liːdər durç

die Nacht zu dir;
di naxt tsuː diːr,

in den stillen Hain hernieder,
ɪn den ʃtɪllən haen hɛrniːdər,

Liebchen, komm zu mir!
liːpçən, kɔm tsuː miːr.

Flüsternd schlanke Wipfel
flʏstərnt ʃlaŋkə vɪpfəl

191

rauschen in des Mondes Licht,
raoʃən |ɪn dɛs mo̱ːndəs lɪçt,

des Verräthers feindlich Lauschen
dɛs fɛrre̱ːtərs fa̱entlɪç laoʃən

fürchte, Holde, nicht.
fy̱rçtə, hɔldə, nɪçt.

Hörst die Nachtigallen schlagen?
hø̱ːrst di naxtɪgallən ʃlaːgən.

ach! sie flehen dich,
ax, ziː fle̱ːən dɪç,

mit der Töne sussen Klagen flehen sie für mich.
mɪt der tø̱ːnə zy̱ːsən kla̱ːgən fle̱ːən ziː fyːr mɪç.

Sie verstehn des Busens Sehnen,
ziː fɛrʃte̱ːn dɛs bu̱ːzəns ze̱ːnən,

kennen Liebesschmerz,
kɛnnən li̱ːbəsʃmɛrts,

rühren mit den Silbertönen jedes weiche Herz.
ry̱ːrən mɪt den zɪlbərtø̱ːnən je̱ːdəs va̱eçə hɛrts.

Lass auch dir die Brust bewegen,
las |aox diːr di brust bəve̱ːgən,

Liebchen, höre mich!
li̱ːpçən, hø̱ːrə mɪç.

bebend harr ich dir entgegen!
be̱ːbənt har |ɪç diːr |ɛntge̱ːgən.

komm, beglücke mich!
kɔm, bəgly̱kə mɪç.

Schubert   Ungeduld
              u̱ngədʊlt

Ich schnitt' es gern in alle Rinden ein,
ɪç ʃnɪt |ɛs gɛrn |ɪn |allə rɪndən |aen,

ich grüb es gern in jeden Kieselstein,
ɪç gry̱ːp |ɛs gɛrn |ɪn je̱ːdən ki̱ːzəlʃtaen,

ich möcht es sä'n auf jedes frische Beet
ıç mœçt |ɛs zɛːn |aof jeːdəs frıʃə beːt

mit Kressensamen, der es schnell verrät,
mıt krɛsənzaːmən, der |ɛs ʃnɛl fɛrrɛːt,

auf jeden weissen Zettel möcht ich's schreiben:
aof jeːdən vaesən tsɛtəl mœçt |ıçs ʃraebən,

Dein ist mein Herz, dein ist mein Herz
daen |ıst maen hɛrts, daen |ıst maen hɛrts

und soll es ewig, ewig bleiben!
unt zɔl |ɛs |eːvıç, eːvıç blaebən.

Ich möcht mir ziehen einen jungen Staar,
ıç mœçt miːr tsiːən |aenən juŋən ʃtaːr,

bid dass er spräch die Worte rein und klar,
bıs das _eːr ʃprɛç di vɔrtə raen |unt klaːr,

bis er sie spräch mit meines Mundes Klang,
bıs |eːr ziː ʃprɛç mıt maenəs mundəs klaŋ,

mit meines Herzens vollem, heissen Drang;
mıt maenəs hɛrtsəns fɔlləm, haesən draŋ,

dann säng er hell durch ihre Fensterscheiben:
dan zɛŋ |eːr hɛl durç |iːrə fɛnstərʃaebən,

Dein ist mein Herz. . .
daen |ıst maen hɛrts . . .

Den Morgenwinden möcht ich's hauchen ein,
den mɔrgənvındən mœçt |ıçs haoxən |aen,

ich möcht es säuseln durch den regen Hain;
ıç mœçt |ɛs zɔøzəln durç den reːgən haen,

o, leuchtet' es aus jedem Blumenstern!
oː, lɔøçtət |ɛs |aos jeːdəm bluːmənʃtɛrn.

trüg es der Duft zu ihr von nah und fern!
tryːk |ɛs der duft tsuː |iːr fɔn naː |unt fɛrn.

ihr Wogen, könnt ihr nichts als Räder treiben?
iːr voːgən, kœnt |iːr nıçts |als rɛːdər traebən.

Ich meint, es müsst in meinen Augen stehn,
ɪç maent, ɛs mʏst |ɪn maenən |aogən ʃteːn,

auf meinen Wangen müsst man's brennen sehn,
aof maenən vaŋən mʏst mans brɛnnən zeːn,

zu lesen wär's auf meinem stummen Mund,
tsuː leːzən vɛːrs |aof maenəm ʃtummən munt,

ein jeder Atemzug gäb's laut ihr kund;
aen jeːdər |aːtəmtsuːk gɛːps laot |iːr kunt,

und sie merkt nichts von all dem bangen Treiben.
unt ziː mɛrkt nɪçts fɔn |al dem baŋən traebən.

Dein ist mein Herz . . .
daen |ɪst maen hɛrts . . .

Schubert   Wanderers Nachtlied
              vandərərs naxtliːt

Über allen Gipfeln ist Ruh,
yːbər |allən gɪpfəln |ɪst ruː,

in allen Wipfeln spürest du
ɪn |allən vɪpfəln ʃpyːrəst duː

kaum einen Hauch;
kaom |aenən haox,

die Vöglein schweigen,
di føːglaen ʃvaegən,

schweigen im Walde.
ʃvaegən |ɪm valdə.

Warte nur, balde ruhest du auch.
vartə nuːr, baldə ruːəst duː |aox.

Schubert   Wiegenlied
              viːgənliːt

Schlafe, schlafe, holder, süsser Knabe,
ʃlaːfə, ʃlaːfə, hɔldər, zyːsər knaːbə,

leise wiegt dich deiner Mutter Hand;
laezə viːkt dɪç daenər mutər hant,

194

sanfte Ruhe, milde Labe
zanftə ruːə, mɪldə laːbə

bringt dir schwebend dieses Wiegenband.
brɪŋt diːr ʃveːbənt diːzəs viːɡənbant.

Schlafe, schlafe in dem süssen Grabe,
ʃlaːfə, ʃlaːfə |ɪn dem zyːsən graːbə,

noch beschutzt dich deiner Mutter Arm;
nɔx bəʃʏtst dɪç daenər mutər |arm,

alle Wünsche, alle Habe
alə vʏnʃə, alə haːbə

fasst sie liebend, alle liebewarm.
fast ziː liːbənt, alə liːbəvarm.

Schlafe in der Flaumen Schosse,
ʃlaːfə |ɪn der flaomən ʃoːsə,

noch umtönt dich lauter Liebeston,
nɔx |umtøːnt dɪç laotər liːbəstoːn,

eine Lilie, eine Rose,
aenə liːljə, aenə roːzə,

nach dem Schlafe werd sie dir zum Lohn.
nax dem ʃlaːfə veːrt ziː diːr tsum loːn.

Schubert   Wohin?
             vohɪn.

Ich hört ein Bächlein rauschen
ɪç høːrt |aen bɛçlaen raoʃən

wohl aus dem Felsenquell,
voːl |aos dem fɛlzənkvɛl,

hinab zum Tale rauschen so frisch und wunderhell.
hɪnap tsum taːlə raoʃən zoː frɪʃ |unt vundərhɛl.

Ich weiss nicht, wie mir wurde,
ɪç vaes nɪçt, viː miːr vurdə,

nicht, wer den Rat mir gab,
nɪçt, veːr den raːt miːr gaːp,

ich musste auch hinunter mit meinem Wanderstab.
ıç mʊstə |aox hınʊntər mıt maenəm vandərʃtaːp.

Hinunter und immer weiter,
hınʊntər |ʊnt |ımmər vaetər,

und immer dem Bache nach,
|ʊnt |ımmər dem baxə nax,

und immer frischer rauschte
ʊnt |ımmər frıʃər raoʃtə

und immer heller der Bach.
|ʊnt |ımmər hɛllər der bax.

Ist das denn meine Strasse?
ıst das dɛn maenə ʃtrasə.

O Bächlein, sprich, wohin?
oː bɛçlaen, ʃprıç, vohın.

du hast mit deinem Rauschen
duː hast mıt daenəm raoʃən

mir ganz berauscht den Sinn.
miːr gants bəraoʃt den zın.

Was sag ich denn vom Rauschen?
vas zaːk |ıç dɛn fɔm raoʃən.

das kann kein Rauschen sein:
das kan kaen raoʃən zaen,

Es singen wohl die Nixen tief unten ihren Reihn.
ɛs zıŋən voːl di nıksən tiːf |ʊntən |iːrən raen.

Lass singen, Gesell, lass rauschen,
las zıŋən, gəzɛl, las raoʃən,

und wandre fröhlich nach!
ʊnt vandrə frøːlıç nax.

Es gehn ja Mühlenräder in jedem klaren Bach.
ɛs geːn jaː myːlənrɛːdər |ın jeːdəm klaːrən bax.

Schumann   Dein Angesicht
               daen |angəzɪçt

Dein Angesicht, so lieb und schön,
daen |angəzɪçt, zo: li:p |unt ʃø:n,

das hab' ich jüngst im Traum geseh'n,
das hɑ:p |ɪç jʏŋst |ɪm trɑom gəzə:n,

es ist so mild und engelgleich,
ɛs |ɪst zo: mɪlt |unt |ɛŋəlglaeç,

und doch so bleich, so schmerzenreich.
unt dɔx zo: blaeç, zo: ʃmɛrtsənraeç.

Und nur die Lippen, die sind roth;
unt nu:r di lɪpən, di zɪnt ro:t,

bald aber küsst sie bleich der Tod.
balt |ɑ:bər kʏst zi: blaeç der to:t.

Erlöschen wird das Himmelslicht,
ɛrlœʃən vɪrt das hɪmməslɪçt,

das aus den frommen Augen bricht.
das |ɑos den frɔmmən |ɑogən brɪçt.

Schumann   Der Nussbaum
               der nusbɑom

Es grünet ein Nussbaum vor dem Haus,
ɛs gry:nət |aen nusbɑom fo:r dem hɑos,

duftig, luftig breitet er blätt'rig die Äste aus.
duftɪç, luftɪç braetət |e:r blɛtrɪç di |ɛstə |ɑos.

Viel liebliche Blüthen stehen d'ran;
fi:l li:plɪçə bly:tən ʃte:ən dran,

linde Winde kommen, sie herzlich zu umfah'n.
lɪndə vɪndə kɔmmən, zi: hɛrtslɪç tsu: |umfɑ:n.

Es flüstern je zwei zu zwei gepaart,
ɛs flʏstərn je: tsvae tsu: tsvae gəpɑ:rt,

neigend, beugend zierlich zum Kusse
naegənt, bøgənt tsi:rlɪç tsum kusə

197

die Häuptchen zart.
di hɔ̈øptçən tsart.

Sie flüstern von einem Mägdlein,
ziː flystərn fɔn |aenəm mɛːktlaen,

das dächte die Nächte und Tage lang,
das dɛçtə di nɛçtə |unt taːgə laŋ,

wusste, ach! selber nicht, was.
vustə, ax.   zɛlbər nɪçt, vas.

Sie flüstern, wer mag versteh'n
ziː flystərn, veːr maːk fɛrʃteːn

so gar leise Weis'?
zoː gɑːr laezə vaes.

flüstern vom Bräut'gam und nächstem Jahr.
flystərn fɔm brɔ̈øtgam |unt nɛçstəm jɑːr.

Das Mägdlein horchet, es rauscht im Baum,
das mɛːktlaen hɔrçət, ɛs rɑoʃt |ɪm bɑom,

sehnend, wähnend sinkt es
zeːnənt, vɛːnənt zɪŋkt |ɛs

lächelnd in Schlaf und Traum.
lɛçəlnt |ɪn ʃlɑːf |unt trɑom.

Schumann   Frauenliebe und -Leben
              frɑoənliːbə |unt leːbən

              1. Seit ich ihn gesehen
                 zaet |ɪç |iːn gəzeːən

Seit ich ihn gesehen,
zaet |ɪç |iːn gəzeːən,

glaub' ich blind zu sein;
glɑop |ɪç blint tsuː zaen,

wo ich hin nur blicke,
voː |ɪç hɪn nuːr blɪkə,

seh' ich ihn allein;
zeː |ɪç |iːn |allaen,

wie im wachen Traume
viː |ɪm vaxən traomə

schwebt sein Bild mir vor,
ʃveːpt zaen bɪlt miːr foːr,

taucht aus tiefstem Dunkel
taoxt |aos tiːfstəm duŋkəl

heller, heller nur empor.
hɛller, hɛllər nuːr |empoːr.

Sonst ist licht- und farblos
zɔnst |ɪst lɪçt |unt farbloːs

alles um mich her,
|alləs |um mɪç heːr,

nach der Schwestern Spiele
naːx der ʃvɛstərn ʃpiːlə

nicht begehr' ich mehr,
nɪçt bəgeːr |ɪç meːr,

möchte lieber weinen,
mœçtə liːbər vaenən,

still im Kämmerlein;
ʃtɪl |ɪm kɛmmərlaen,

seit ich ihn gesehen,
zaet |ɪç |iːn gəzeːən,

glaub' ich blind zu sein.
glaop |ɪç blɪnt tsuː zaen.

Schumann   Frauenliebe und -Leben

            2. Er, der Herrlichste von allen
                eːr, der hɛrlɪçstə fɔn |allən

Er, der Herrlichste von allen,
eːr, der hɛrlɪçstə fɔn |allən,

wie so milde, wie so gut!
viː zoː mɪldə, viː zoː guːt.

Holde Lippen, klares Auge,
hɔlde lɪpən, klaːrəs |aogə,

heller Sinn und fester Muth.
hɛllər zɪn |unt fɛstər muːt.

So wie dort in blauer Tiefe,
zoː viː dɔrt |ɪn blaoər tiːfə,

hell und herrlich, jener Stern,
hɛl |unt hɛrlɪç, jeːnər ʃtɛrn,

also Er an meinem Himmel,
alzo eːr |an maenəm hɪmməl,

hell und herrlich, hehr und fern.
hɛl |unt hɛrlɪç, heːr |unt fɛrn.

Wandle, wandle deine Bahnen,
vandlə, vandlə daenə baːnən,

nur betrachten deinen Schein,
nuːr bətraxtən daenən ʃaen,

nur in Demuth ihn betrachten,
nuːr |ɪn deːmuːt |iːn bətraxtən,

selig nur, und traurig sein!
zeːlɪç nuːr, unt traorɪç zaen.

Höre nicht mein stilles Beten,
høːrə nɪçt maen ʃtɪlləs beːtən,

deinem Glücke nur geweiht;
daenəm glʏkə nuːr gəvaet,

darfst mich, nied're Magd, nicht kennen,
darfst mɪç, niːdrə maːkt, nɪçt kɛnnən,

hoher Stern der Herrlichkeit.
hoːər ʃtɛrn der hɛrlɪçkaet.

Nur die Würdigste von allen
nuːr di vʏrdɪçstə fɔn |allən

darf beglucken deine Wahl,
darf beglʏkən daenə vaːl,

und ich will die Hohe segnen
ʊnt |ɪç vɪl di hoːə zeːgnən

viele tausendmal.
fiːlə tɑozəntmaːl.

Will mich freuen dann und weinen,
vɪl mɪç frɔøən dan |ʊnt vaenən,

selig, selig bin ich dann,
zeːlɪç, zeːlɪç bɪn |ɪç dan,

sollte mir das Herz auch brechen,
zɔltə miːr das hɛrts |ɑox brɛçən,

brich, o Herz, was liegt daran?
brɪç, |oː hɛrts, vas liːkt daran.

Schumann   Frauenliebe und -Leben

         3.   Ich kann's nicht fassen
            ɪç kans nɪçt fasən

Ich kann's nicht fassen, nicht glauben,
ɪç kans nɪçt fasən, nɪçt glɑobən,

es hat ein Traum mich berückt;
ɛs hat aen trɑom mɪç bərʏkt,

wie hätt' er doch unter allen
viː hɛt |eːr dɔx |ʊntər |allən

mich Arme erhöht und beglückt?
mɪç |armə |ɛrhøːt |ʊnt bəglʏkt.

Mir war's, er habe gesprochen:
miːr vaːrs, eːr haːbə gəʃprɔxən,

"Ich bin auf ewig dein,"
ɪç bɪn |ɑof |eːvɪç daen,

mir war's ich träume noch immer,
miːr vaːrs |ɪç trɔømə nɔx |immər,

es kann ja nimmer so sein.
ɛs kan jaː nɪmmər zoː zaen.

O lass im Traume mich sterben,
oː lass |ɪm traomə mɪç ʃtɛrbən,

gewieget an seiner Brust,
ɡəviːɡət |an zaenər brust,

den seligen Tod mich schlürfen
den zeːlɪɡən toːt mɪç ʃlyrfən

in Thränen unendlicher Lust.
|ɪn trɛːnən |un|ɛntlɪçər lust.

Schumann   Frauenliebe und -Leben

4. Der Ring
der rɪŋ

Du Ring an meinem Finger,
duː rɪŋ |an maenəm fɪŋər,

mein goldenes Ringelein,
maen ɡɔldənəs rɪŋəlaen,

ich drücke dich fromm an die Lippen,
ɪç drykə dɪç frɔm |an di lɪpən,

an das Herze mein.
an das hɛrtsə maen.

Ich hatt' ihn ausgeträumet,
ɪç hat |iːn |aosɡətrɔømət,

der Kindheit friedlich schönen Traum,
der kɪnthaet friːtlɪç ʃøːnən traom,

ich fand allein mich, verloren
ɪç fant |allaen mɪç, fɛrloːrən

im öden, unendlichen Raum.
|ɪm |øːdən, un|ɛntlɪçən raom.

Du Ring an meinem Finger,
duː rɪŋ |an maenəm fɪŋər,

da hast du mich erst belehrt,
daː hast duː mɪç |eːrst bəleːrt,

hast meinem Blick erschlossen
hast maenəm blɪk |ɛrʃlɔsən

des Lebens unendlichen, tiefen Wert.
dɛs leːbəns |un|ɛntlɪçən, tiːfən veːrt.

Ich will ihm dienen, ihm leben,
ɪç vɪl |iːm diːnən, iːm leːbən,

ihm angehören ganz,
iːm |angəhøːrən gants,

hin selber mich geben und finden
hɪn zɛlbər mɪç geːbən |unt fɪndən

verklärt mich in seinem Glanz.
fɛrklɛːrt mɪç |ɪn zaenəm glants.

Schumann   Frauenliebe und -Leben

        5. Helft mir, ihr Schwestern
            hɛlft miːr, iːr ʃvɛstərn

Helft mir, ihr Schwestern,
hɛlft miːr, |iːr ʃvɛstərn,

freundlich mich schmucken,
frɔøntlɪç mɪç ʃmʏkən,

dient der Glücklichen heute, mir!
diːnt der glʏklɪçən hɔøtə, miːr.

Windet geschäftig mir um die Stirne
vɪndət gəʃɛftɪç miːr |um di ʃtɪrnə

noch der blühenden Myrthe Zier.
nɔx der blyːəndən mʏrtə tsiːr.

Als ich befriedigt, freudigen Herzens,
als |ɪç bəfriːdɪçt, frɔødɪgən hɛrtsəns,

sonst dem Geliebten im Arme lag,
zɔnst dem gəliːptən |ɪm |armə laːk,

immer noch rief er, Sehnsucht im Herzen,
ɪmmər nɔx riːf |eːr, zeːnzuxt |ɪm hɛrtsən,

203

ungeduldig den heutigen Tag.
ungəduldɪç den hɔøtɪgən tɑːk.

Helft mir, ihr Schwestern, helft mir verscheuchen
hɛlft miːr, |iːr ʃvɛstərn, hɛlft miːr fɛrʃɔøçən

eine thörichte Bangigkeit;
aenə tøːrɪçtə baŋɪçkaet,

dass ich mit klarem Aug' ihn empfange,
das |ɪç mɪt klɑːrəm |aok |iːn |ɛmpfaŋə,

ihn, die Quelle der Freudigkeit.
iːn, di kvɛllə der frɔødɪçkaet.

Bist, mein Geliebter, du mir erschienen,
bɪst, maen gəliːptər, duː miːr |ɛrʃiːnən,

giebst du mir, Sonne, deinen Schein?
giːpst duː miːr, zɔnnə, daenən ʃaen.

Lass mich in Andacht, lass mich in Demuth,
las mɪç |ɪn |andaxt, las mɪç |ɪn deːmuːt,

lass mich verneigen, dem Herren mein.
las mɪç fɛrnaegən, dem hɛrrən maen.

Streuet ihm, Schwestern, streuet ihm Blumen,
ʃtrɔøət iːm, ʃvɛstərn, ʃtrɔøət |iːm bluːmən,

bringet ihm knospende Rosen dar.
brɪŋət |iːm knɔspəndə roːzən dɑːr.

Aber euch, Schwestern, grüss' ich mit Wehmuth,
ɑːbər |ɔøç, ʃvɛstərn, gryːs |ɪç mɪt veːmuːt,

freudig scheidend aus eurer Schaar.
frɔødɪç ʃaedənt |aos |ɔørər ʃɑːr.

Schumann   Frauenliebe und -Leben

       6. Süsser Freund
           zyːsər frɔønt

Süsser Freund, du blickest mich verwundert an,
zyːsər frɔønt, duː blɪkəst mɪç fɛrvundərt |an,

kannst es nicht begreifen, wie ich weinen kann;
kanst |ɛs nɪçt bəgraefən, viː |ɪç vaenən kan,

lass der feuchten Perlen ungewohnte Zier
las der fɔøçtən pɛrlən |ungəvoːntə tsiːr

freudig hell erzittern in dem Auge mir.
frɔødɪç hɛl |ɛrtsɪtərn |ɪn dem |aogə miːr.

Wie so bang mein Busen, wie so wonnevoll!
viː zoː baŋ maen buːzən, viː zo vɔnnəfɔl.

wüsst' ich nur mit Worten, wie ich's sagen soll;
vyːst |ɪç nuːr mɪt vɔrtən, viː ɪçs zaːgən zɔl,

komm und birg dein Antlitz hier an meiner Brust,
kɔm |unt bɪrk daen |antlɪts hiːr |an maenər brust,

will in's Ohr dir flüstern alle meine Lust.
vɪl |ɪns |oːr diːr flystərn |allə maenə lust.

Weisst du nun die Thranen, die ich weinen kann,
vaest duː nuːn di trɛːnən, di |ɪç vaenən kan,

sollst du nicht sie sehen du geliebter Mann!
zɔlst duː nɪçt ziː zeːən, duː gəliːptər man.

Bleib an meinem Herzen, fühle dessen Schlag,
blaep |an maenəm hɛrtsən, fyːlə dɛsən ʃlaːk,

dass ich fest und fester nur dich drücken mag.
das |ɪç fɛst |unt fɛstər nuːr dɪç drykən maːk.

Hier an meinem Bette hat die Wiege Raum,
hiːr |an maenəm bɛtə hat diː viːgə raom,

wo sie still verberge meinen holden Traum;
voː ziː ʃtɪl fɛrbɛrgə maenən hɔldən traom,

kommen wird der Morgen, wo der Traum erwacht,
kɔmmən vɪrt der mɔrgən, voː der traom |ɛrvaxt,

und daraus dein Bildnis mir entgegen lacht.
unt daraos daen bɪltnɪs miːr |ɛntgeːgən laxt.

205

Schumann   Frauenliebe und -Leben

7. An meinem Herzen
an maenəm hɛrtsən

An meinem Herzen, an meiner Brust,
an maenəm hɛrtsən, |an maenər brʊst,

du meine Wonne, du meine Lust!
duː maenə vɔnnə, duː maenə lʊst.

Das Glück ist die Liebe, die Lieb' ist das Glück,
das glʏk |ɪst di liːbə, di liːp |ɪst das glʏk,

ich hab's gesagt und nehm's nicht zurück.
ɪç haːps gəzaːkt ʊnt neːms nɪçt tsurʏk.

Hab' überschwenglich mich geschätzt,
haːp |yːbərʃvɛŋlɪç mɪç gəʃɛtst,

bin überglücklich aber jetzt.
bɪn |yːbərglʏklɪç |aːbər jɛtst.

Nur die da säugt, nur die da liebt
nuːr di daː zɔøkt, nuːr di daː liːpt

das Kind, dem sie die Nahrung gibt;
das kɪnt, dem ziː di naːrʊŋ giːpt,

nur eine Mutter weiss allein,
nuːr |aenə mʊtər vaes |allaen,

was lieben heisst und glücklich sein.
vas liːbən haest |ʊnt glʏklɪç zaen.

O wie bedaur' ich doch den Mann,
oː viː bədaor |ɪç dɔx den man,

der Mutterglück nicht fühlen kann!
der mʊtərglʏk nɪçt fyːlən kan.

Du lieber, lieber Engel du,
duː liːbər, liːbər |ɛŋəl duː,

du schauest mich an und lächelst dazu!
duː ʃaoəst mɪç |an |ʊnt lɛçəlst datsuː.

An meinem Herzen, an meiner Brust,
an maenəm hɛrtsən, an maenər brʊst,

du meine Wonne, du meine Lust!
duː maenə vɔnnə, duː maenə lʊst.

Schumann   Frauenliebe und -Leben

8. Nun hast du mir
      nuːn hast duː miːr

Nun hast du mir den ersten Schmerz gethan,
nuːn hast duː miːr den |eːrstən ʃmɛrts gəta̲ːn,

der aber traf.
der |aːbər traːf.

Du schläfst, du harter, unbarmherz'ger Mann,
duː ʃlɛːfst, duː hartər, ʊnbarmhɛrtsgər man,

den Todesschlaf.
den to̲ːdəsʃlaːf.

Es blicket die Verlass'ne vor sich hin,
ɛs blɪ̲kət di fɛrlasnə foːr zɪç hɪn,

die Welt ist leer, ist leer.
di vɛlt |ɪst leːr, ɪst leːr.

Geliebet hab' ich und gelebt,
geli̲ːbət haːp |ɪç |ʊnt gəle̲ːpt,

ich bin nicht lebend mehr.
ɪç bɪn nɪçt le̲ːbənt meːr.

Ich zieh' mich in mein Inn'res still zurück,
ɪç tsiː mɪç |ɪn maen |ɪnrəs ʃtɪl tsurʏk,

der Schleier fällt,
der ʃlaeər fɛlt,

da hab' ich dich und mein verlornes Glück,
daː haːp |ɪç dɪç |ʊnt maen fɛrlo̲ːrnəs glʏk,

du meine Welt!
duː maenə vɛlt.

Schumann   Dichterliebe
                dɪçtərliːbə

         1. Im wunderschönen Monat Mai
            ɪm vʊndərʃøːnən moːnat mae

Im wunderschönen Monat Mai,
ɪm vʊndərʃøːnən moːnat mae,

als alle Knospen sprangen,
als |allə knɔspən ʃpraŋən,

da ist in meinem Herzen
daː |ɪst |ɪn maenəm hɛrtsən

die Liebe aufgegangen.
di liːbə |aofgəgaŋən.

Im wunderschönen Monat Mai,
ɪm vʊndərʃøːnən moːnat mae,

als alle Vögel sangen,
als |allə føːgəl zaŋən,

da hab' ich ihr gestanden
daː haːp |ɪç |iːr gəʃtandən

mein Sehnen und Verlangen.
maen zeːnən |ʊnt fɛrlaŋən.

Schumann   Dichterliebe

         2. Aus meinen Thränen spriessen
            aos maenən trɛːnən ʃpriːsən

Aus mainen Thränen spriessen
aos maenən trɛːnən ʃpriːsən

viel blühende Blumen hervor,
fiːl blyːəndə bluːmən hɛrfoːr,

und meine Seufzer werden
ʊnt maenə zɔøftsər veːrdən

ein Nachtigallenchor.
|aen naxtigallənkoːr.

Und wenn du mich lieb hast, Kindchen,
ʊnt vɛn duː mɪç liːp hast, kɪntçən,

schenk' ich dir die Blumen all',
ʃɛŋk |ɪç diːr di bluːmən |al,

und vor deinem Fenster soll klingen
ʊnt foːr daenəm fɛnstər zɔl klɪŋən

das Lied der Nachtigall.
das liːt der naxtigal.

Schumann   Dichterliebe

                3. Die Rose, die Lilie
                    di roːzə, di liːljə

Die Rose, die Lilie, die Taube, die Sonne,
di roːzə, di liːljə, di taobə, di zɔnnə,

die liebt ich einst alle in Liebeswonne.
di liːpt |ɪç |aenst |allə |in liːbəsvɔnnə.

Ich lieb' sie nicht mehr, ich liebe alleine
ɪç liːp ziː nɪçt meːr, |ɪç liːbə |allaenə

die Kleine, die Feine, die Reine, die Eine;
di klaenə, di faenə, di raenə, di |aenə,

sie selber, aller Liebe Wonne,
ziː zɛlbər, allər liːbə vɔnnə,

ist Rose und Lilie und Taube und Sonne,
ɪst roːzə |ʊnt liːljə |ʊnt taobə |ʊnt zɔnnə,

ich liebe alleine die Kleine,
ɪç liːbə |allaenə di klaenə,

die Feine, die Reine, die Eine!
di faenə, di raenə, di |aenə.

4. Wenn ich in deine Augen seh'
    vɛn |ɪç |ɪn daenə |aogən ze:

Wenn ich in deine Augen seh',
vɛn |ɪç |ɪn daenə |aogən ze:,

so schwindet all' mein Leid und Weh;
zo: ʃvɪndət |al maen laet |unt ve:,

doch wenn ich küsse deinen Mund,
dɔx vɛn |ɪç kʏsə daenən munt,

so werd ich ganz und gar gesund.
zo: vɛrt |ɪç gants |unt ga:r gəzunt.

Wenn ich mich lehn' an deine Brust,
vɛn |ɪç mɪç le:n |an daenə brust,

kommt's über mich wie Himmelslust;
kɔmts |y:bər mɪç vi: hɪmməlslust,

doch wenn du sprichst: ich liebe dich!
dɔx vɛn du: ʃprɪçst, ɪç li:bə dɪc.

so muss ich weinen bitterlich.
zo: mus |ɪç vaenən bɪtərlɪç.

5. Ich will meine Seele tauchen
    ɪç vɪl maenə ze:lə taoxən

Ich will meine Seele tauchen
ɪç vɪl maenə ze:lə taoxən

in den Kelch der Lilie hinein;
|ɪn den kɛlç der li:ljə hɪnaen,

die Lilie soll klingend hauchen
di li:ljə zɔl klɪŋənt haoxən

ein Lied von der Liebsten mein.
|aen li:t fɔn der li:pstən maen.

Das Lied soll schauern und beben,
das liːt zɔl ʃaʊ̯ərn |ʊnt beːbən,

wie der Kuss von ihrem Mund,
viː der kʊs fɔn |i̱ːrəm mʊnt,

den sie mir einst gegeben
den ziː mi̱ːr |aenst gəge̱ːbən

in wunderbar süsser Stund'!
|ɪn vʊn̪dərbaːr zyːsər ʃtʊnt.

Schumann   Dichterliebe

                6.   Im Rhein
                     ɪm ra̱en

Im Rhein, im heiligen Strome,
ɪm ra̱en, ɪm ha̱elɪgən ʃtro̱ːmə,

da spiegelt sich in den Well'n,
daː ʃpi̱ːgəlt zɪç |ɪn den vɛln.

mit seinem grossen Dome,
mɪt za̱enəm gro̱ːsən do̱ːmə,

das grosse, heilige Cöln.
das gro̱ːsə, ha̱elɪgə kœln.

Im Dom, da steht ein Bildniss,
ɪm do̱ːm, daː ʃteːt |aen bɪltnɪs,

auf goldenem Leder gemalt;
a̱of gɔ̱ldənəm le̱ːdər gəma̱lt,

in meines Lebens Wildniss
ɪn ma̱enəs le̱ːbəns vɪltnɪs

hat's freundlich hinein gestrahlt.
hats frɔ̱øntlɪç hɪna̱en gəʃtra̱ːlt.

Es schweben Blumen und Eng'lein
ɛs ʃveːbən blu̱ːmən |ʊnt |ɛŋla̱en

um unsre liebe Frau;
|ʊm |ʊnzrə li̱ːbə fra̱o,

die Augen, die Lippen,
di |a͜ogən, di lɪpən,

die Lippen, die Wänglein,
di lɪpən, di vɛŋlaen,

die gleichen der Liebsten genau.
di glaeçən der li:pstən gəna͜o.

Schumann   Dichterliebe

7. Ich grolle nicht
ɪç grɔllə nɪçt

Ich grolle nicht, und wenn das Herz auch bricht,
ɪç grɔllə nɪçt, |unt vɛn das hɛrts |a͜ox brɪçt,

ewig verlor'nes Lieb, ich grolle nicht.
e:vɪç fɛrlo:rnəs li:p, |ɪç grɔllə nɪçt.

Wie du auch strahlst in Diamantenpracht,
vi: du: |a͜ox ʃtra:lst |ɪn diamantənpraxt,

es fällt kein Strahl in deines Herzens Nacht,
ɛs fɛlt kaen ʃtra:l |ɪn daenəs hɛrtsəns naxt,

das weiss ich längst.
das vaes |ɪç lɛŋst.

Ich grolle nicht und wenn das Herz auch bricht.
ɪç grɔllə nɪçt |unt vɛn das hɛrts |a͜ox brɪçt.

Ich sah dich ja im Traume,
ɪç za: dɪç ja: |ɪm tra͜omə,

und sah die Nacht in deines Herzens Raume,
unt za: di naxt |ɪn daenəs hɛrtsəns ra͜omə,

und sah die Schlang', die dir am Herzen frisst,
unt za: di ʃlaŋ, di di:r |am hɛrtsən frɪst,

ich sah, mein Lieb, wie sehr du elend bist.
ɪç za:, maen li:p, vi: ze:r du: |e:lənt bɪst.

Ich grolle nicht.
ɪç grɔllə nɪçt.

212

Schumann   Dichterliebe

8. Und wüssten's die Blumen
    ʊnt vʏstəns di bluːmən

Und wüssten's die Blumen, die kleinen,
ʊnt vʏstəns di bluːmən, di klaenən,

wie tief verwundet mein Herz,
viː tiːf fɛrvʊndət maen hɛrts,

sie würden mit mir weinen,
ziː vʏrdən mɪt miːr vaenən,

zu heilen meinen Schmerz.
tsuː haelən maenən ʃmɛrts.

Und wüssten's die Nachtigallen,
ʊnt vʏstəns di naxtigallən,

wie ich so traurig und krank,
viː |ɪç zoː traorɪç |ʊnt kraŋk,

sie liessen fröhlich erschallen
ziː liːsən frøːlɪç |ɛrʃallən

erquickenden Gesang.
ɛrkvɪkəndən gəzaŋ.

Und wüssten sie mein Wehe,
ʊnt vʏstən ziː maen veːə,

die goldenen Sternelein,
di gɔldənən ʃtɛrnəlaen,

sie kämen aus ihrer Höhe,
ziː kɛːmən |aos |iːrər høːə,

und sprächen Trost mir ein.
ʊnt ʃprɛçən troːst miːr |aen.

Sie alle können's nicht wissen,
ziː |allə kœnnəns nɪçt vɪsən,

nur Eine kennt meinen Schmerz;
nuːr |aenə kɛnt maenən ʃmɛrts,

213

sie hat ja selbst zerrissen,
zi: hat ja: zɛlpst tsɛrrɪsən,

zerrissen mir das Herz.
tsɛrrɪsən mi:r das hɛrts.

Schumann   Dichterliebe

        9. Das ist ein Flöten und Geigen
            das |ɪst |aen flø:tən |ʊnt gaegən

Das ist ein Flöten und Geigen,
das |ɪst |aen flø:tən |ʊnt gaegən,

Trompeten schmettern darein;
trɔmpe:tən ʃmɛtərn daraen,

da tanzt wohl den Hochzeitreigen
dɑ: tantst vo:l den hɔxtsaetraegən

die Herzallerliebste mein.
di hɛrts|allərli:pstə maen.

Das ist ein Klingen und Dröhnen,
das |ɪst |aen klɪŋən |ʊnt drø:nən,

ein Pauken und ein Schalmei'n;
|aen paokən |ʊnt |aen ʃalmaen,

dazwischen schluchzen und stöhnen
datsvɪʃən ʃluxtsən |ʊnt ʃtø:nən

die lieblichen Engelein.
di li:plɪçən |ɛŋəlaen.

Schumann   Dichterliebe

        10. Hör' ich das Liedchen klingen
             hø:r |ɪç das li:tçən klɪŋən

Hör' ich das Liedchen klingen
hø:r |ɪç das li:tçən klɪŋən,

das einst die Liebste sang,
das |aenst di li:pstə zaŋ,

214

so will mir die Brust zerspringen
zoː vɪl miːr di brust tsɛrʃprɪŋən

von wildem Schmerzensdrang.
fɔn vɪldəm ʃmɛrtsənsdraŋ.

Es treibt mich ein dunkles Sehnen
ɛs traept mɪç |aen duŋkləs zeːnən

hinauf zur Waldeshöh',
hɪnaof tsuːr valdəshøː,

dort löst sich auf in Thränen
dɔrt løːst zɪç |aof |ɪn trɛːnən

mein übergrosses Weh'.
maen |yːbərgroːsəs veː.

Schumann   Dichterliebe

            11. Ein Jüngling liebt ein Mädchen
                 aen jʏŋlɪŋ liːpt aen mɛːtçen

Ein Jüngling liebt ein Mädchen,
aen jʏŋlɪŋ liːpt |aen mɛːtçən,

die hat einen Andern erwählt;
di hat |aenən |andərn |ɛrvɛːlt,

der And're liebt eine Andre
der |andrə liːpt |aenə |andrə

und hat sich mit dieser vermählt.
unt hat zɪç mɪt diːzər fɛrmɛːlt.

Das Mädchen nimmt aus Aerger
das mɛːtçən nɪmt |aos |ɛrgər

den ersten besten Mann,
den |eːrstən bɛstən man,

der ihr in den Weg gelaufen;
der |iːr |ɪn den veːk gəlaofən,

der Jüngling ist übel d'ran.
der jʏŋlɪŋ |ɪst |yːbəl dran.

215

Es ist eine alte Geschichte,
ɛs |ɪst |aenə |altə gəʃɪçtə,

doch bleibt sie immer neu;
dɔx blaept ziː |ɪmmər nɔ́ø,

und wem sie just passiret,
ʊnt veːm ziː jʊst pasíːrət,

dem bricht das Herz entzwei.
dem brɪçt das hɛrts |ɛntsvae.

Schumann   Dichterliebe

12.   Am leuchtenden Sommermorgen
          am lɔ́øçtəndən zɔ́mmərmɔrgən

Am leuchtenden Sommermorgen
am lɔ́øçtəndən zɔ́mmərmɔrgən

geh ich im Garten herum.
geː |ɪç |ɪm gartən hɛrʊm.

Es flüstern und sprechen die Blumen,
ɛs flýstərn |ʊnt ʃprɛ́çən di blúːmən,

ich aber wandle stumm.
ɪç |aːbər vándlə ʃtʊm.

Es flüstern und sprechen die Blumen,
ɛs flýstərn |ʊnt ʃprɛ́çən di blúːmən,

und schau'n mitleidig mich an:
ʊnt ʃáon mɪ́tlaedɪç mɪç |an,

Sei unsrer Schwester nicht böse,
zae |ʊnzrər ʃvɛstər nɪçt bǿːzə,

du trauriger, blasser Mann.
duː tráorɪgər blásər man.

216

Schumann   Dichterliebe

13.   Ich hab' im Traum geweinet
ıç haːp |ım traom gəvaenət

Ich hab' im Traum geweinet,
ıç haːp |ım traom gəvaenət,

mir träumte, du lägest im Grab.
miːr trɔømtə, duː lɛːgəst |ım graːp.

Ich wachte auf, und die Thräne
ıç vaxtə |aof, unt di trɛːnə

floss noch von der Wange herab.
flɔs nɔx fɔn der vaŋə hɛrap.

Ich hab' im Traum geweinet,
ıç haːp |ım traom gəvaenət,

mir träumt', du verliessest mich.
miːr trɔømt, duː fɛrliːsəst mıç.

Ich wachte auf, und ich weinte
ıç vaxtə |aof, unt |ıç vaentə

noch lange bitterlich.
nɔx laŋə bıtərlıç.

Ich hab' im Traum geweinet,
ıç haːp |ım traom gəvaenət,

mir träumte, du wärst mir noch gut.
miːr trɔømtə, duː vɛːrst miːr nɔx guːt.

Ich wachte auf, und noch immer
ıç vaxtə |aof, unt nɔx |ımmər

strömt meine Thränenflut.
ʃtrøːmt maenə trɛːnənfluːt.

217

Schumann   Dichterliebe

14.   Allnächtlich im Traume
     alnɛçtlɪç |ɪm trɑɔmə

Allnächtlich im Traume seh' ich dich,
alnɛçtlɪç |ɪm trɑɔmə ze: |ɪç dɪç,

und sehe dich freundlich grüssen,
ʊnt ze:ə dɪç frɔ̯øntlɪç gry:sən,

und laut aufweinend stürz' ich mich
ʊnt lɑot |ɑofvaenənt ʃtʏrts |ɪç mɪç

zu deinen süssen Füssen.
tsu: daenən zy:sən fy:sən.

Du siehest mich an wehmüthiglich
du: zi:əst mɪç |an ve:mytɪklɪç

und schüttelst das blonde Köpfchen;
ʊnt ʃʏtəlst das blɔndə kœpfçən,

aus deinen Augen schleichen sich
ɑos daenən |ɑogən ʃlaeçən zɪç

die Perlenthränentröpfchen.
di pɛrləntrɛ:nəntrœpfçən.

Du sagst mir heimlich ein leises Wort,
du: zɑːkst miːr haemlɪç |aen laezəs vɔrt,

und giebst mir den Strauss von Cypressen.
ʊnt giːpst miːr den ʃtrɑos fɔn tsy:prɛsən.

Ich wache auf, und der Strauss ist fort,
ɪç vaxə |ɑof, ʊnt der ʃtrɑos |ɪst fɔrt,

und's Wort hab' ich vergessen.
ʊnts vɔrt hɑːp |ɪç fɛrgɛsən.

Schumann   Dichterliebe

15. Aus alten Märchen winkt es
ɑos |altən mɛrçən vɪŋkt |ɛs

Aus alten Märchen winkt es
ɑos |altən mɛrçən vɪŋkt |ɛs

hervor mit weisser Hand,
hɛrfoːr mɪt vaesər hant,

da singt es und da klingt es
dɑː zɪŋt |ɛs |ʊnt dɑː klɪŋt |ɛs

von einem Zauberland;
fɔn |aenəm tsɑobərlant,

wo bunte Blumen blühen
voː bʊntə bluːmən blyːən

im gold'nen Abendlicht,
|ɪm gɔldnən |ɑːbəntlɪçt,

und lieblich duftend glühen,
ʊnt liːplɪç dʊftənt glyːən,

mit bräutlichem Gesicht;
mɪt brɔøtlɪçəm gəzɪçt,

und grüne Bäume singen
ʊnt gryːnə bɔømə zɪŋən

uralte Melodei'n,
|uːr|altə melodaən,

die Lüfte heimlich klingen,
ɹi lʏftə haemlɪç klɪŋən,

und Vögel schmettern drein;
ʊnt føːgəl ʃmɛtərn draen,

und Nebelbilder steigen
ʊnt neːbəlbɪldər ʃtaegən

wohl aus der Erd' hervor,
voːl |ɑos der eːrt hɛrfoːr,

219

und tanzen luft'gen Reigen
ʊnt ta̱ntsən lʊftgən ra̱egən

im wunderlichen Chor;
|ɪm vʊ̱ndərlɪçən koːr,

und blaue Funken brennen
ʊnt bla̱ʊə fʊŋkən brɛ̱nnən

an jedem Blatt und Reis,
|an je̱ːdəm blat |ʊnt ra̱es,

und rothe Lichter rennen
ʊnt ro̱ːtə lɪçtər rɛnnən

im irren, wirren Kreis;
ɪm |ɪrrən, vɪrrən kra̱es,

und laute Quellen brechen
ʊnt la̱otə kvɛ̱llən brɛ̱çən

aus wildem Marmorstein,
|a̱os vɪldəm ma̱mɔrʃtaen,

und seltsam in den Bächen
ʊnt zɛ̱ltzam |ɪn den bɛ̱çən

strahlt fort der Wiederschein.
ʃtraːlt fɔrt der viːdərʃaen.

Ach! könnt' ich dorthin kommen,
ax. kœnt |ɪç dɔ̱rthɪn kɔ̱mmən,

und dort mein Herz erfreu'n,
|ʊnt dɔrt ma̱en hɛrts |ɛrfrɔ̱øn,

und aller Qual entnommen,
ʊnt |a̱llər kvaːl |ɛntnɔ̱mmən,

und frei und selig sein!
ʊnt fra̱e |ʊnt ze̱ːlɪç za̱en.

Ach, jenes Land der Wonne,
ax. je̱ːnəs lant der vɔ̱nnə,

das seh' ich oft im Traum,
das zeː |ɪç |ɔft |ɪm tra̱om,

doch kommt die Morgensonne,
dɔx kɔmt di mɔrgənzɔnnə,

zerfliesst's wie eitel Schaum.
tsɛrfliːsts viː |aetəl ʃa͜om.

Schumann   Dichterliebe

          16.   Die alten, bösen Lieder
              di |altən, bø̠ːzən li̠ːdər

Die alten, bösen Lieder,
di |altən, bø̠ːzən li̠ːdər,

die Träume bös' und arg,
di trɔ͜ømə bø̠ːz |unt |ark,

die lasst uns jetzt begraben,
di last |uns jɛtst bəgraːbən,

holt einen grossen Sarg.
hoːlt |aenən gro̠ːsən zark.

Hinein leg' ich gar Manches,
hɪnaen leːk |ɪç gɑːr man̠çəs,

doch sag' ich noch nicht was;
dɔx zɑːk |ɪç nɔx nɪçt vas,

der Sarg muss sein noch grösser
der zark mus zaen nɔx grø̠ːsər

wie's Heidelberger Fass.
viːs hae̠dəlbɛrgər fas.

Und holt eine Todtenbahre,
unt hoːlt |aenə to̠ːtənbɑːrə,

von Brettern fest und dick;
fɔn brɛ̠tərn fɛst |unt dɪk,

auch muss sie sein noch länger,
ɑ͜ox mus ziː zaen nɔx lɛŋər,

als wie zu Mainz die Brück'.
als viː tsuː ma̠ents di brʏk.

221

Und holt mir auch zwölf Riesen,
unt hoːlt miːr |ɑox tsvœlf riːzən,

die müssen noch stärker sein,
di mʏsən nɔx ʃtɛrkər zaen,

als wie der starke Christoph,
als viː der ʃtarkə krɪstɔf,

im Dom zu Cöln am Rhein.
ɪm doːm tsuː kœln |am raen.

Die sollen den Sarg forttragen,
di zɔlən den zark fɔrttrɑːgən,

und senken in's Meer hinab;
unt zɛŋkən |ɪns meːr hɪnap,

denn solchem grossen Sarge
dɛn zɔlçəm groːsən zargə

gebührt ein grosses Grab.
gəbyːrt |aen groːsəs grɑːp.

Wisst ihr, warum der Sarg wohl
vɪst |iːr, varum der zark voːl

so gross und schwer mag sein?
zoː groːs |unt ʃveːr mɑːk zaen.

Ich senkt' auch meine Liebe
ɪç zɛŋkt |ɑox maenə liːbə

und meinen Schmerz hinein.
|unt maenən ʃmɛrts hɪnaen.

Schumann   Die beiden Grenadiere
                di baedən grenadiːrə

Nach Frankreich zogen zwei Grenadier',
nax fraŋkraeç tsoːgən tsvae grenadiːr,

die waren in Russland gefangen.
di vɑːrən |ɪn ruslant gəfaŋən.

Und als sie kamen in's deutsche Quartier,
unt |als ziː kɑːmən |ɪns dɔøtʃə kvartiːr,

sie liessen die Köpfe hangen.
zi: li:sən di kœpfə haŋən.

Da hörten sie Beide die traurige Mähr',
da: hœrtən zi: baedə di traorɪgə mɛ:r,

dass Frankreich verloren gegangen,
das fraŋkraeç fɛrlo:rən gəgaŋən,

besiegt und geschlagen das tapfere Heer,
bəzi:kt |ʊnt gəʃla:gən das tapfərə he:r,

und der Kaiser gefangen.
ʊnt der kaezər gəfaŋən.

Da weinten zusammen die Grenadier'
da: vaentən tsuzammən di grenadi:r

wohl ob der kläglichen Kunde.
vo:l |ɔp der klɛ:klɪçən kʊndə.

Der Eine sprach: "Wie weh' wird mir,
der |aenə ʃpra:x, vi: ve: vɪrt mi:r,

wie brennt meine alte Wunde!"
vi: brɛnt maenə |altə vʊndə.

Der Andre sprach: "Das Lied ist aus,
der |andrə ʃpra:x, das li:t |ɪst |aos,

auch ich möcht' mit dir sterben,
aox |ɪç mœçt mɪt di:r stɛrbən,

doch hab' ich Weib und Kind zu Haus,
dɔx ha:p |ɪç vaep |ʊnt kɪnt tsu: haos,

die ohne mich verderben."
di |o:nə mɪç fɛrdɛrbən.

"Was schert mich Weib, was schert mich Kind,
vas ʃe:rt mɪç vaep, vas ʃe:rt mɪç kɪnt,

ich trage weit besser Verlangen;
ɪç tra:gə vaet bɛsər fɛrlaŋən,

lass sie betteln gehn, wenn sie hungrig sind-
las zi: bɛtəln ge:n, vɛn zi: hʊŋrɪç zɪnt

223

mein Kaiser, mein Kaiser gefangen!
maen kaezər, maen kaezər gəfaŋən.

Gewähr' mir, Bruder, eine Bitt':
gəvε:r mi:r, bru:dər, aenə bɪt,

Wenn ich jetzt sterben werde,
vεn |ɪç jεtst ʃtεrbən ve:rdə,

so nimm meine Leiche nach Frankreich mit,
zo: nɪm maenə laeçə nax fraŋkraeç mɪt,

begrab' mich in Frankreichs Erde.
bəgra:p mɪç |ɪn fraŋkraeçs |e:rdə.

Das Ehrenkreuz am rothen Band
das |e:rənkrɔøts |am ro:tən bant

sollst du auf's Herz mir legen;
zɔlst du: |aofs hεrts mi:r le:gən,

die Flinte gieb mir in die Hand,
di flɪntə gi:p mi:r |ɪn di hant,

und gürt' mir um den Degen.
unt gʏ:rt mi:r |um den de:gən.

So will ich liegen und horchen still,
zo: vɪl |ɪç li:gən |unt hɔrçən ʃtɪl,

wie ein Schildwach', im Grabe,
vi: |aen ʃɪltvax, |ɪm gra:bə,

bis einst ich höre Kanonengebrüll
bɪs |aenst |ɪç hø:rə kano:nəngəbrʏl

und wiehernder Rosse Getrabe.
|unt vi:ərndər rɔsə gətra:bə.

Dann reitet mein Kaiser wohl über mein Grab,
dan raetət maen kaezər vo:l |y:bər maen gra:p,

viel Schwerter klirren und blitzen,
fi:l ʃvεrtər klɪrrən |unt blɪtsən,

dann steig' ich gewaffnet hervor aus dem Grab-
dan ʃtaek |ɪç gəvafnət hεrfo:r |aos dem gra:p

den Kaiser, den Kaiser zu schützen!"
den kaezər, den kaezər tsu: ʃʏtsən.

224

Schumann   Die Lotosblume
                di lo̱ːtɔsbluːmə

Die Lotosblume ängstigt
di lo̱ːtɔsbluːmə |ɛŋstɪkt

sich vor der Sonne Pracht,
zɪç foːr der zo̱nnə praxt,

und mit gesenktem Haupte
ʊnt mɪt gəze̱ŋktəm hɑoptə

erwartet sie träumend die Nacht.
ɛrva̱rtət ziː trɔ̱ømənt di naxt.

Der Mond, der ist ihr Buhle,
der moːnt, der |ɪst |iːr bu̱ːlə,

er weckt sie mit seinem Licht,
eːr vɛkt ziː mɪt zaenəm lɪçt,

und ihm entschleiert sie freundlich
ʊnt |iːm |ɛntʃla̱eərt ziː frɔ̱øntlɪç

ihr frommes Blumengesicht.
iːr fro̱mməs bluːməngəzɪçt.

Sie blüht und glüht und leuchtet,
ziː blyːt |ʊnt glyːt |ʊnt lɔ̱øçtət,

und starret stumm in die Höh';
ʊnt ʃta̱rrət ʃtʊm |ɪn di høː,

sie duftet und weinet und zittert
ziː du̱ftət |ʊnt va̱enət |ʊnt tsɪ̱ttərt

vor Liebe und Liebesweh.
foːr li̱ːbə |ʊnt li̱ːbəsveː.

Schumann   Du bist wie eine Blume
                duː bɪst viː |aenə blu̱ːmə

Du bist wie eine Blume,
duː bɪst viː |aenə blu̱ːmə,

so hold und schön und rein;
zoː hɔlt |ʊnt ʃøːn |ʊnt ra̱en,

225

ich schau' dich an, und Wehmuth
ɪç ʃao dɪç |an, |ʊnt veːmʊt

schleicht mir in's Herz hinein.
ʃlaeçt miːr |ins hɛrts hɪnaen.

Mir ist, als ob ich die Hände
miːr |ɪst, als |ɔp |ɪç di hɛndə

auf's Haupt dir legen sollt',
|aofs haopt diːr leːgən zɔlt,

betend, dass Gott dich erhalte
beːtənt, das gɔt dɪç |ɛrhaltə

so rein und schön und hold.
zoː raen |ʊnt ʃøːn |ʊnt hɔlt.

Schumann   Mondnacht
               moːntnaxt

Es war, als hätt' der Himmel
ɛs vaːr, |als hɛt der hɪmməl

die Erde still geküsst,
di eːrdə ʃtɪl gəkʏst.

dass sie im Blüthenschimmer
das ziː |ɪm blyːtənʃɪmmər

von ihm nur träumen müsst'.
fɔn |iːm nuːr trɔ͜ømən mʏst.

Die Luft ging durch die Felder,
di lʊft gɪŋ dʊrç di fɛldər,

die Ähren wogten sacht,
di |ɛːrən voːktən zaxt,

es rauschten leis' die Wälder,
ɛs raoʃtən laes di vɛldər,

so sternklar war die Nacht.
zoː ʃtɛrnklaːr vaːr di naxt.

Und meine Seele spannte
ʊnt maenə zeːlə ʃpantə

226

weit ihre Flügel aus,
vaet |iːrə flyːgəl |aos,

flog durch die stillen Lande,
floːk durç di ʃtɪllən landə,

als flöge sie nach Haus.
als fløːgə ziː naːx haos.

Schumann   Stille Thränen
                 ʃtɪllə trɛːnən

Du bist vom Schlaf erstanden
duː bɪst fɔm ʃlaːf |ɛrʃtandən

und wandelst durch die Au,
|unt vandəlst durç di |ao,

da liegt ob allen Landen
daː liːkt |ɔp |allən landən

der Himmel wunderblau.
der hɪmməl vundərblao.

So lang du ohne Sorgen
zoː laŋ duː |oːnə zɔrgən

geschlummert schmerzenlos,
gəʃlummərt ʃmɛrtsənloːs,

der Himmel bis zum Morgen
der hɪmməl bɪs tsum mɔrgən

viel Thränen niedergoss.
fiːl trɛːnən niːdərgɔs.

In stillen Nächten weinet
ɪn stɪllən nɛçtən vaenət

oft mancher aus den Schmerz,
|ɔft mançər |aos den ʃmɛrts,

und morgens dann ihr meinet,
unt mɔrgəns dan |iːr maenət,

stets fröhlich sei sein Herz.
ʃteːts frøːlɪç zae zaen hɛrts.

227

Schumann   Volksliedchen
           fɔlksliːtçən

Wenn ich früh in den Garten geh'
vɛn |ɪç fryː |ɪn den gartən geː

in meinem grünen Hut,
|ɪn maenəm gryːnən huːt,

ist mein erster Gedanke,
ɪst maen |eːrstər gədaŋkə,

was nun mein Liebster tut?
vas nuːn maen liːpstər tuːt.

Am Himmel steht kein Stern,
am hɪmməl ʃteːt kaen ʃtɛrn,

den ich dem Freund nicht gönnte.
den |ɪç dem frɔønt nɪçt gœntə.

Mein Herz gäb' ich ihm gern,
maen hɛrts gɛːp |ɪç |iːm gɛrn,

wenn ich's herausthun könnte.
vɛn |ɪçs hɛraostuːn kœntə.

Schumann   Wanderlied
           vandərliːt

Wohlauf! noch getrunken den funkelnden Wein!
voːl|aof, nɔx gətruŋkən den fuŋkəlndən vaen.

Ade nun, ihr Lieben! geschieden muss sein.
adeː nuːn, iːr liːbən. gəʃiːdən mʊs zaen.

Ade nun, ihr Berge, du väterlich Haus!
adeː nuːn, iːr bɛrgə, duː fɛːtərlɪç haos.

Es treibt in die Ferne mich mächtig hinaus.
ɛs traept |ɪn di fɛrnə mɪç mɛçtɪk hɪnaos.

Die Sonne, sie bleibet am Himmel nicht steh'n,
di zɔnnə, ziː blaebət |am hɪmməl nɪçt ʃteːn,

es treibt sie, durch Länder und Meere zu geh'n.
ɛs traept ziː, dʊrç lɛndər |unt meːrə tsuː geːn.

Die Woge nicht haftet am einsamen Strand,
di voːgə nɪçt haftət |am |aenzɑːmən ʃtrant,

die Stürme, sie brausen mit Macht durch das Land.
di ʃtʏrmə, ziː braozən mɪt maxt dʊrç das lant.

Mit eilenden Wolken der Vogel dort zieht
mit |aelədən vɔlkən der foːgəl dɔrt tsiːt

und singt in der Ferne ein heimathlich Lied.
|ʊnt zɪŋt |ɪn der fɛrnə |aen haematlɪç liːt.

So treibt es den Burschen durch Wälder und Feld,
zoː traept |ɛs den bʊrʃən dʊrç vɛldər |ʊnt fɛlt,

zu gleichen der Mutter, der wandernden Welt.
tsuː glaeçən der mʊtər, der vandərndən vɛlt.

Da grüssen ihn Vögel bekannt über'm Meer,
daː gryːsən |iːn føːgəl bəkant |yːbərm meːr,

sie flogen von Fluren der Heimath hieher;
siː floːgən fɔn fluːrən der haemat hiːhɛr,

da duften die Blumen vertraulich um ihn,
dɑː dʊftən di bluːmən fɛrtraolɪç |ʊm |iːn,

sie trieben vom Lande die Lüfte dahin.
ziː triːbən fɔm landə di lʏftə dahɪn.

Die Vögel, die kennen sein väterlich Haus,
di føːgəl, di kɛnnən zaen fɛːtərlɪç haos,

die Blumen, die pflanzt er der Liebe zum Strauss,
di bluːmən, di pflantst |eːr der liːbə tsum ʃtraos,

und Liebe, die folgt ihm, sie geht ihm zur Hand:
ʊnt liːbə, di fɔlkt |iːm, ziː geːt |iːm tsur hant,

so wird ihm zur Heimath das ferneste Land.
zoː vɪrt |iːm tsur haemat das fɛrnəstə lant.

Wohlauf! noch getrunken den funkelnden Wein!
voːl|aof. nɔx gətrʊŋkən den fʊŋkəlndən vaen.

Ade nun, ihr Lieben! geschieden muss sein.
adeː nuːn, iːr liːbən, gəʃiːdən mʊs zaen.

229

Ade nun, ihr Berge, du väterlich Haus!
adeː nuːn, iːr bɛrgə, duː fɛːtərlɪç haos.

Es treibt in die Ferne mich mächtig hinaus!
ɛs traept |ɪn di fɛrnə mɪç mɛçtɪk hɪnaos.

Schumann   Widmung
                vɪdmuŋ

Du meine Seele, du mein Herz,
duː maenə zeːlə, duː maen hɛrts,

du meine Wonn', o du mein Schmerz,
duː maenə vɔn, |oː duː maen ʃmɛrts,

du meine Welt, in der ich lebe,
duː maenə vɛlt, |ɪn der |ɪç leːbə,

mein Himmel du, darein ich schwebe,
maen hɪmməl duː, daraen |ɪç ʃveːbə,

o du mein Grab, in das hinab
oː duː maen graːp, ɪn das hɪnap

ich ewig meinen Kummer gab!
|ɪç |eːvɪç maenən kummər gaːp.

Du bist die Ruh', du bist der Frieden,
duː bɪst di ruː, duː bɪst der friːdən,

du bist vom Himmel mir beschieden.
duː bɪst fɔm hɪmməl miːr bəʃiːdən.

Dass du mich liebst, macht mich mir werth,
das duː mɪç liːpst, maxt mɪç miːr veːrt,

dein Blick hat mich vor mir verklärt,
daen blɪk hat mɪç foːr miːr fɛrklɛːrt,

du hebst mich liebend über mich,
duː heːpst mɪç liːbənt |yːbər mɪç,

mein guter Geist, mein bess'res Ich!
maen guːtər gaest, maen bɛsrəs |ɪç.

230

Strauss   Allerseelen
            allərzeːlən

Stell' auf den Tisch die duftenden Reseden,
ʃtɛl |ɑof den tɪʃ di duftəndən rəzeːden,

die letzten roten Astern trag' herbei,
di lɛtstən roːtən |astərn traːk hɛrbae,

und lass uns wieder von der Liebe reden,
unt las |uns viːdər fɔn der liːbə reːdən,

wie einst im Mai.
viː |aenst |ɪm mae.

Gieb mir die Hand, dass ich sie heimlich drücke,
giːp miːr di hant, das |ɪç ziː haemlɪç drʏkə,

und wenn man's sieht, mir ist es einerlei,
unt vɛn mans ziːt, miːr |ɪst |ɛs |aenərlae,

gieb mir nur einen deiner süssen Blicke,
giːp miːr nuːr |aenən daenər zyːsən blɪkə,

wie einst im Mai.
viː |aenst |ɪm mae.

Es blüht und duftet heut' auf jedem Grabe,
ɛs blyːt |unt duftət hɔøt |ɑof jeːdəm graːbə,

ein Tag im Jahr ist ja den Toten frei,
aen taːk |ɪm jaːr |ɪst jaː den toːtən frae,

komm an mein Herz, dass ich dich wieder habe
kɔm |an maen hɛrts, das |ɪç dɪç viːdər haːbə

wie einst im Mai.
viː |aenst |ɪm mae.

Strauss   Breit über mein Haupt
            braet |yːbər maen hɑopt

Breit über mein Haupt dein schwarzes Haar,
braet |yːbər maen hɑopt daen ʃvartsəs haːr,

neig' zu mir dein Angesicht,
naek tsuː miːr daen |angəzɪçt,

231

da strömt in die Seele so hell
dɑ: ʃtrømt |ɪn di ze̱:lə zo: hɛl

und klar mir deiner Augen Licht.
|ʊnt klɑ:r mi:r daenər |ɑogən lɪçt.

Ich will nicht droben der Sonne Pracht,
ɪç vɪl nɪçt dro̱:bən der zo̱nnə praxt,

noch der Sterne leuchtenden Kranz,
nɔx der ʃtɛrnə lɔ̱øçtəndən krants,

ich will nur deiner Locken Nacht
ɪç vɪl nu:r daenər lɔkən naxt

und deiner Blicke Glanz.
|ʊnt daenər blɪkə glants.

Strauss   Cäcilie
             tsɛtsi̱:ljə

Wenn du es wüsstest, was träumen heisst
vɛn du: |ɛs vy̱stəst, vas trɔømən haest

von brennenden Küssen, von Wandern
fɔn brɛnnəndən ky̱sən, fɔn vandərn

und Ruhen mit der Geliebten,
|ʊnt ru̱:ən mɪt der gəli̱:ptən,

Aug' in Auge und kosend und plaudernd,
ɑok |ɪn |ɑogə |ʊnt ko̱:zənt |ʊnt plɑodərnt,

wenn du es wüsstest, du neigtest dein Herz!
vɛn du: |ɛs vy̱stəst, du: naektəst daen hɛrts.

Wenn du es wüsstest, was bangen heisst
vɛn du: |ɛs vy̱stəst, vas baŋən haest

in einsamen Nächten, umschauert vom Sturm,
|ɪn |aenzamən nɛ̱çtən, ʊmʃɑoərt fɔm ʃturm,

da niemand tröstet milden Mundes
dɑ: ni̱:mant trø̱:stət mɪldən mʊndəs

die kampfmüde Seele,
di kampfmy̱:də ze̱:lə,

232

wenn du es wüsstest, du kämest zu mir.
vɛn duː |ɛs vy̆stest, duː kɛːməst tsuː miːr.

Wenn du es wüsstest, was leben heisst,
vɛn duː |ɛs vy̆stəst, was leːbən haest,

umhaucht von der Gottheit weltschaffendem Atem,
ʊmhɑoxt fɔn der gɔthaet vɛltʃafəndəm |ɑːtəm,

zu schweben empor, lichtgetragen,
tsuː ʃveːbən |ɛmpoːr, lɪçtgətrɑːgən,

zu seligen Höh'n,
tsuː zeːlɪgən høːn,

wenn du es wüsstest, du lebtest mit mir.
vɛn duː |ɛs vy̆stəst, duː leːptəst mit miːr.

Strauss   Die Nacht
             di naxt

Aus dem Walde tritt die Nacht,
ɑos dem valdə trɪt di naxt,

aus den Bäumen schleicht sie leise,
ɑos den bɔø̆mən ʃlaeçt ziː laezə,

schaut sich um in weitem Kreise, nun gib acht.
ʃɑot zɪç |ʊm |ɪn vaetəm kraezə, nuːn giːp |axt.

Alle Lichter dieser Welt,
allə lɪçtər diːzər vɛlt,

alle Blumen, alle Farben löscht sie aus
allə bluːmən, allə farbən lœʃt ziː |ɑos

und stiehlt die Garben weg vom Feld.
|ʊnt ʃtiːlt di garbən vɛk fɔm fɛlt.

Alles nimmt sie, was nur hold,
alləs nɪmt ziː, vas nuːr hɔlt,

nimmt Silber weg des Stroms,
nɪmt das zɪlbər vɛk dɛs ʃtroːms,

nimmt vom Kupferdach des Doms weg das Gold.
nɪmt fɔm kʊpfərdax dɛs doːms vɛk das gɔlt.

Ausgeplündert steht der Strauch, rücke näher,
ɑosgəplʏndərt ʃteːt der ʃtrɑox, rʏkə nɛːər,

Seel' an Seele; o die Nacht, mir bangt,
zeːl |an zeːlə, oː di naxt, miːr baŋt,

sie stehle dich mir auch.
ziː ʃteːlə dɪç miːr |ɑox.

Strauss   Heimkehr
               haemkeːr

Leiser schwanken die Äste,
laezər ʃvaŋkən di |ɛstə,

der Kahn fliegt uferwärts,
der kɑːn fliːkt |uːfərvɛrts,

heim kehrt die Taube zum Neste,
haem keːrt di tɑobə tsum nɛstə,

zu dir kehrt heim mein Herz.
tsuː diːr keːrt haem maen hɛrts.

Genug am schimmernden Tage,
gənuːk |am ʃɪmmərndən tɑːgə,

wenn rings das Leben lärmt,
vɛn rɪŋs das leːbən lɛrmt,

mit irrem Flügelschlage ist es
mɪt |ɪrrəm flyːgəlʃlɑːgə |ɪst |ɛs

in's Weite geschwärmt.
|ɪns vaetə gəʃvɛrmt.

Doch nun die Sonne geschieden
dɔx nuːn di zɔnnə gəʃiːdən

und Stille sich senkt auf den Hain,
ʊnt ʃtɪllə zɪç zɛŋkt |ɑof den haen,

fühlt es: bei dir ist der Frieden,
fyːlt |ɛs, bae diːr |ɪst der friːdən,

die Ruh' bei dir allein.
di ruː bae diːr |allaen.

234

Strauss   Heimliche Aufforderung
            haemlɪçə |aoffɔrdərʊŋ

Auf, hebe die funkelnde Schale empor zum Mund,
aof, heːbə di fʊŋkəlndə ʃaːlə |empoːr tsum mʊnt,

und trinke beim Freudenmahle dein Herz gesund.
ʊnt trɪŋkə baem frɔ͜ødənmaːlə daen hɛrts gəzʊnt.

Und wenn du sie hebst, so winke mir heimlich zu,
ʊnt vɛn duː ziː heːpst, zoː vɪŋkə miːr haemlɪç tsuː,

dann lächle ich und dann trinke ich still wie du...
dan lɛçlə |ɪç |ʊnt dan trɪŋkə |ɪç ʃtɪl viː duː

und still gleich mir betrachte um uns
|ʊnt ʃtɪl glaeç miːr bətraxtə |ʊm |ʊns

das Heer der trunknen Schwätzer-
das heːr der trʊŋknən ʃvɛtsər

verachte sie nicht zu sehr.
fɛr|axtə ziː nɪçt tsuː zeːr,

Nein, hebe die blinkende Schale, gefüllt mit Wein,
naen, heːbə di blɪŋkəndə ʃaːlə, gəfʏlt mɪt vaen,

und lass beim lärmenden Mahle sie glücklich sein.
|ʊnt las baem lɛrməndən maːlə ziː glʏklɪç zaen.

Doch hast du das Nahl genossen, den Durst gestillt,
dɔx hast duː das maːl gənɔsən, den dʊrst gəʃtɪlt,

dann verlasse der lauten Genossen
dan fɛrlasə der laotən gənɔsən

festfreudiges Bild
fɛstfrɔ͜ødɪgəs bɪlt

und wandle hinaus in den Garten zum Rosenstrauch,
ʊnt vandlə hɪnaos |ɪn den gartən tsum roːzənʃtraox,

dort will ich dich dann erwarten
dɔrt vɪl |ɪç dɪç dan |ɛrvartən

nach altem Brauch,
nax |altəm braox,

235

und will an die Brust dir sinken,
ʊnt vɪl |an di brust diːr zɪŋkən,

eh' du's gehofft,
eː duːs gəhɔft,

und deine Küsse trinken, wie ehmals oft
ʊnt daenə kʏsə trɪŋkən, viː |eːmals |ɔft

und flechten in deine Haare der Rose Pracht
|ʊnt flɛçtən |ɪn daenə haːrə der roːzə praxt

o komm, du wunderbare ersehnte Nacht!
oː kɔm, duː vʊndərbarə |ɛrzeːntə naxt.

Strauss   Kornblumen
             kɔrnbluːmən

Kornblumen nenn' ich die Gestalten,
kɔrnbluːmən nɛn |ɪç di gəʃtaltən,

die milden mit den blauen Augen,
di mɪldən mɪt den blaoən |aogən,

die, anspruchslos, in stillem Walten
di, |anʃpruxsloːs, |ɪn ʃtɪlləm valtən

den Thau des Friedens, den sie saugen
den tao dɛs friːdəns, den ziː zaogən

aus ihren eignen, klaren Seelen,
|aos |iːrən |aegnən, klaːrən zeːlən,

mittheilen allem, dem sie nah'n,
mɪttaelən |alləm, dem ziː naːn,

bewusstlos der Gefühlsjuwelen,
bəvʊstloːs der gəfyːlsjuveːlən,

die sie von Himmelshand empfah'n.
di ziː fɔn hɪmməlshant |ɛmpfaːn.

Dir wird so wohl in ihrer Nähe,
diːr vɪrt zoː voːl |ɪn |iːrər nɛːə,

als gingst du durch ein Saatgefilde,
als gɪŋst duː dʊrç |aen zaːtgəfɪldə,

236

durch das der Hauch des Abends wehe,
durç das der ha͜ox dɛs |ɑːbənts veːə,

voll frommen Friedens und voll Milde.
fɔl frɔmmən friːdəns |ʊnt fɔl mɪldə.

Strauss   Morgen!
            mɔrgən

Und morgen wird die Sonne wieder scheinen
ʊnt mɔrgən vɪrt di zɔnnə viːdər ʃa͜enən

und auf dem Wege, den ich gehen werde,
ʊnt |a͜of dem veːgə, den |ɪç geːən veːrdə,

wird uns, die Glücklichen, sie wieder einen
vɪrt |ʊns, di glʏklɪçən, ziː viːdər |a͜enən

inmitten dieser sonnenatmenden Erde...
|ɪnmɪtən diːzər zɔnnən|ɑːtməndən |eːrdə

und zu dem Strand, dem weiten, wogenblauen,
ʊnt tsuː dem ʃtrant, dem va͜etən, voːgənbla͜oən,

werden wir still und langsam niedersteigen,
veːrdən viːr ʃtɪl |ʊnt laŋzam niːdərʃta͜egən,

stumm werden wir uns in die Augen schauen,
ʃtʊm veːrdən viːr |ʊns |ɪn di |a͜ogən ʃa͜oən,

und auf uns sinkt des Glückes stummes Schweigen.
ʊnt |a͜of |ʊns zɪŋt dɛs glʏkəs ʃtʊmməs ʃva͜egən.

Strauss   Nachtgang
            naxtgaŋ

Wir gingen durch die stille, milde Nacht,
viːr gɪŋən durç di ʃtɪllə, mɪldə naxt,

dein Arm in meinem, dein Auge in meinem.
da͜en |arm |ɪn ma͜enəm, da͜en |a͜ogə |ɪn ma͜enəm.

Der Mond goss silbernes Licht über dein Angesicht,
der moːnt gɔs zɪlbərnəs lɪçt |yːbər da͜en |angəzɪçt,

wie auf Goldgrund ruhte dein schönes Haupt.
viː |a͜of gɔltgrunt ruːtə da͜en ʃøːnəs ha͜opt.

237

Und du erschienst mir wie eine Heilige,
ʊnt duː |ɛrʃiːnst miːr viː |aenə haelɪgə,

mild und gross und seelenübervoll,
mɪlt |ʊnt groːs |ʊnt zeːlən|yːbərfɔl,

heilig und rein, wie die liebe Sonne.
haelɪç |ʊnt raen, viː di liːbə zɔnnə.

Und in die Augen schwoll mir
ʊnt |ɪn di |aogən ʃvɔl miːr

ein warmer Drang wie Tränenahnung.
aen varmər draŋ viː trɛːnən|aːnʊŋ.

Fester fasst' ich dich und küsste,
fɛstər fast |ɪç dɪç |ʊnt kʏstə,

küsste dich ganz leise.   Meine Seele weinte.
kʏstə dɪç gants laezə.   maenə zeːlə vaentə.

Strauss   Ständchen
              ʃtɛntçən

Mach' auf, mach' auf, doch leise, mein Kind,
max |aof, max |aof, dɔx laezə, maen kɪnt,

um Keinen vom Schlummer zu wecken;
ʊm kaenən fɔm ʃlʊmmər tsuː vɛkən,

kaum murmelt der Bach, kaum zittert im Wind
kaom mʊrməlt der bax, kaom tsɪtərt |ɪm vɪnt

ein Blatt an den Büschen und Hecken.
|aen blat |an den byʃən |ʊnt hɛkən.

Drum leise, mein Mädchen, dass nichts sich regt,
drʊm laezə, maen mɛːtçən, das nɪçts zɪç reːkt,

nur leise die Hand auf die Klinke gelegt.
nuːr laezə di hant |aof di klɪŋkə gəleːkt.

Mit Tritten wie Tritte der Elfen so sacht,
mɪt trɪtən viː trɪtə der |ɛlfən zoː zaxt,

um über die Blumen zu hüpfen,
ʊm |yːbər di bluːmən tsuː hʏpfən,

238

flieg' leicht hinaus in die Mondscheinnacht
fliːk laeçt hɪnɑos |ɪn di moːntʃaennaxt

zu mir in den Garten zu schlüpfen.
tsuː miːr |ɪn den gartən tsuː ʃlʏpfən.

Rings schlummern die Blüthen am rieselnden Bach
rɪŋs ʃlʊmmərn di blyːtən |am riːzəlndən bax

und duften im Schlaf, nur die Liebe ist wach!
|ʊnt dʊftən |ɪm ʃlaːf, nuːr di liːbə |ɪst vax.

Sitz' nieder, hier dämmert's geheimnissvoll
zɪts niːdər, hiːr dɛmmərts gehaemnɪsfɔl

unter den Lindenbäumen, die Nachtigall
|ʊntər den lɪndənbɔømən, di naxtigal

uns zu Haüpten soll von uns'ren Küssen träumen,
|ʊns tsuː hɔøptən zɔl fɔn |ʊnzrən kʏsən trɔømən,

und die Rose, wenn sie am Morgen erwacht,
ʊnt di roːzə, vɛn ziː |am mɔrgən |ɛrvaxt,

hoch glühn von den Wonneschauern der Nacht.
hoːx glyːn fɔn den vɔnnəʃaoərn der naxt.

Strauss   Traum durch die Dämmerung
             trɑom dʊrç di dɛmmərʊŋ

Weite Wiesen im Dämmergrau;
vaetə viːzən |ɪm dɛmmərgrɑo,

die Sonne verglomm, die Sterne ziehn,
di zɔnnə fɛrglɔm, di ʃtɛrnə tsiːn,

nun geh' ich hin zu der schönsten Frau,
nuːn geː |ɪç hɪn tsuː der ʃøːnstən frɑo,

weit über Wiesen im Dämmergrau,
vaet |yːbər viːzən |ɪm dɛmmərgrɑo,

tief in den Busch von Jasmin.
tiːf |ɪn den bʊʃ fɔn jasmiːn.

Durch Dämmergrau in der Liebe Land;
dʊrç dɛmmərgrɑo |ɪn der liːbə lant,

ich gehe nicht schnell, ich eile nicht;
ɪç geːə nɪçt ʃnɛl, ɪç |aelə nɪçt,

mich zieht ein weiches sammtenes Band
mɪç tsiːt |aen vaeçəs zamtənəs bant

durch Dämmergrau in der Liebe Land,
dʊrç dɛmmərgraо |ɪn der liːbə lant,

in ein blaues, mildes Licht.
|ɪn |aen blaоəs, mɪldəs lɪçt.

Strauss   Wiegenlied
               viːgənliːt

Träume, träume, du, mein süsses Leben,
trɔømə, trɔømə, duː, maen zyːsəs leːbən,

von dem Himmel, der die Blumen bringt.
fɔn dem hɪmməl, der di bluːmən brɪŋt.

Blüten schimmern da, die beben
blyːtən ʃɪmmərn daː, di beːbən

von dem Lied, das deine Mutter singt.
fɔn dem liːt, das daenə mʊtər zɪŋt.

Träume, träume, Knospe meiner Sorgen,
trɔømə, trɔømə, knɔspə maenər zɔrgən,

von dem Tage, da die Blume spross;
fɔn dem taːgə, daː di bluːmə ʃprɔs,

von dem hellen Blütenmorgen,
fɔn dem hɛllən blyːtənmɔrgən,

da dein Seelchen sich der Welt erschloss.
daː daen zeːlçən zɪç der vɛlt |ɛrʃlɔs.

Träume, träume, Blüte meiner Liebe,
trɔømə, trɔømə, blyːtə maenər liːbə,

von der stillen, von der heil'gen Nacht,
fɔn der ʃtɪllən, fɔn der haelgən naxt,

da die Blume seiner Liebe
dɑː di bluːmə zaenər liːbə

diese Welt zum Himmel mir gemacht.
diːzə vɛlt tsum hɪmməl miːr gəmaxt.

(By permission of Vera Tügel, Copyright owner.)

Strauss   Wie sollten wir geheim sie halten
             viː zɔltən viːr gəhaem ziː haltən

Wie sollten wir geheim sie halten,
viː zɔltən viːr gəhaem ziː haltən,

die Seligkeit, die uns erfüllt?
di zeːlɪçkaet, di |uns |ɛrfylt.

Nein, bis in seine tiefsten Falten
naen, bɪs |ɪn zaenə tiːfstən faltən

sei allen unser Herz enthüllt!
zae |allən |unzər hɛrts |ɛnthylt.

Wenn zwei in Liebe sich gefunden
vɛn tsvae |ɪn liːbə zɪç gəfundən

geht Jubel hin durch die Natur,
geːt juːbəl hɪn durç di natuːr,

in längern wonnevollen Stunden
ɪn lɛŋərn vɔnnəfɔllən ʃtundən

legt sich der Tag auf Wald und Flur.
leːkt zɪç der tɑːk |aof valt |unt fluːr.

Selbst aus der Eiche morschem Stamm,
zɛlpst |aos der |aeçə mɔrʃəm ʃtam,

die ein Jahrtausend überlebt,
di |aen jɑːrtaozənt |yːbərleːpt,

steigt neu des Wipfels grüne Flamme
ʃtaekt nɔø dɛs vɪpfəls gryːnə flammə

und rauscht von Jugendlust durchbebt.
|unt raoʃt fɔn juːgəntlust durçbeːpt.

Zu höherm Glanz und Dufte brechen
tsuː høːərm glants |unt duftə brɛçən

die Knospen auf beim Glück der Zwei
di knɔspən |aof baem glʏk der tsvae

und süsser rauscht es in den Bächen
|unt zyːsər raoʃt |es |ın den bɛçən

und reicher blüht und reicher glänzt der Mai.
|unt raeçər blyːt |unt raeçər glɛntst der mae.

Strauss   Zueignung
             tsuaegnuŋ

Ja, du weisst es, theure Seele,
jaː, duː vaest |es, tɔørə zeːlə,

dass ich fern von dir mich quäle,
das |ıç fɛrn fɔn diːr mıç kvɛːlə,

Liebe macht die Herzen krank, habe Dank.
liːbə maxt di hɛrtsən kraŋk, haːbe daŋk.

Einst hielt ich, der Freiheit Zecher,
aenst hiːlt |ıç, der fraehaet tsɛçər,

hoch den Amethisten Becher
hoːx den |amətıstən bɛçər

und du segnetest den Trank, habe Dank.
|unt duː zeːgnətəst den traŋk, haːbə daŋk.

Und beschworst darin die Bösen,
unt bəʃvoːrst darın di bøːzən,

bis ich, was ich nie gewesen,
bıs |ıç, vas |ıç niː gəveːzən,

heilig an's Herz dir sank, habe Dank.
haelıç |ans hɛrts diːr zaŋk, haːbə daŋk.

Wagner   Allmächt'ge Jungfrau, "Tannhäuser"
              almɛçtgə juɲfrɑo   tanhɔøzər

Allmächt'ge Jungfrau, hör' mein Flehen!
almɛçtgə juɲfrɑo, høːr maen fleː‿ən.

Zu dir, Gepries'ne, rufe ich!
tsuː diːr, gəpriːsnə, ruːfə |ɪç.

Lass mich im Staub vor dir vergehen,
las mɪç |ɪm ʃtɑop foːr diːr fɛrgeː‿ən,

o! nimm von dieser Erde mich!
oː, nɪm fɔn diːzər |eːrdə mɪç.

Mach' dass ich rein und engelgleich
max das |ɪç raen |unt |ɛɲəlglaeç

eingehe in dein selig Reich!
|aengeː‿ə |ɪn daen zeːlɪç raeç.

Wenn je, in thör'gem Wahn befangen,
vɛn jeː, ɪn tøːrgəm vɑːn bəfaɲən,

mein Herz sich abgewandt von dir,
maen hɛrts zɪç |apgəvant fɔn diːr,

wenn je ein sündiges Verlangen,
vɛn jeː |aen zʏndɪgəs fɛrlaɲən,

ein weltlich Sehnen keimt' in mir:
aen vɛltlɪç zeːnən kaemt |ɪn miːr,

so rang ich unter tausend Schmerzen,
soː raɲ |ɪç |untər tɑozənt ʃmɛrtsən,

dass ich es töd' in meinem Herzen.
das |ɪç |ɛs tøːt |ɪn maenəm hɛrtsən.

Doch, konnt' ich jeden Fehl nicht büssen,
dɔx, kɔnt |ɪç jeːdən feːl nɪçt byːsən,

so nimm dich gnädig meiner an!
zoː nɪm dɪç gnɛːdɪç maenər |an.

Dass ich mit demuthvollem Grüssen
das |ɪç mɪt deːmutfɔlləm gryːsən

243

als würd'ge Magd dir nahen kann:
als vʏrdgə maːkt diːr naːən kan,

um deiner gnadenreichste Huld
ʊm daenər gnaːdənraeçstə hʊlt

nur anzuflehn für seine Schuld!
nuːr |antsufleːn fyːr zaenə ʃʊlt.

Wagner   Dich, theure Halle, "Tannhäuser"
        dɪç, tɔ̸rə halə   tanhɔ̸zər

Dich, theure Halle, grüss' ich wieder,
dɪç, tɔ̸rə halə, gryːs |ɪç viːdər,

froh grüss' ich dich, geliebter Raum!
froː gryːs |ɪç dɪç, gəliːptər raom.

In dir ersachen seine Lieder
ɪn diːr |ɛrwaxən zaenə liːdər

und wecken mich aus düst'rem Traum.
|ʊnt vɛkən mɪç |aos dyːstrəm traom.

Da er aus dir geschieden,
daː eːr |aos diːr gəʃiːdən,

wie öd' erschienst du mir!
viː ø̸t |ɛrʃiːnst duː miːr.

Aus mir entfloh der Frieden,
aos miːr |ɛntfloː der friːdən,

die Freude zog aus dir!
di frɔ̸də tsoːk |aos diːr.

Wie jetzt mein Busen hoch sich hebet,
viː jɛtst maen buːzən hoːx zɪç heːbət,

so scheinst du jetzt mir stolz und hehr;
zoː ʃaenst duː jɛtst miːr ʃtɔlts |ʊnt heːr,

der mich und dich so neu belebet,
der mɪç |ʊnt dɪç zoː nɔ̸ bəleːbət,

nicht weilt er ferne mehr!
nɪçt vaelt |eːr fɛrnə meːr.

Sei mir gegrüsst, sei mir gegrüsst!
zae miːr gəgryːst, zae miːr gəgryːst.

Du, theure Halle, sei mir gegrüsst!
duː tɔ̈ːrə hallə, zae miːr gəgryːst.

Wagner   Du bist der Lenz, "Die Walkure"
              duː bɪst der lɛnts, di valkyːrə

Du bist der Lenz, nach dem ich verlangte
duː bɪst der lɛnts, nax dem |ɪç fɛrlaŋtə

in frostigen Winters Frist.
|ɪn frɔstɪgən vɪntərs frɪst.

Dich grüsste mein Herz mit heiligem Grau'n,
dɪç gryːstə maen hɛrts mɪt haelɪgəm graon,

als dein Blick zuerst mir erblühte.
als daen blɪk tsu|eːrst miːr |ɛrblyːtə.

Fremdes nur sah ich von je,
frɛmdəs nuːr zɑː |ɪç fɔn jeː,

freundlos war mir das Nahe;
frɔ̈ntloːs vɑːr miːr das nɑːə,

als hätt' ich nie es gekannt,
als hɛt |ɪç niː |ɛs gəkant,

war, was immer mir kam.
vɑːr, vas |ɪmmər miːr kɑːm.

Doch dich kannt' ich deutlich und klar:
dɔx dɪç kant |ɪç dɔ̈tlɪç |unt klɑːr,

als mein Auge dich sah, war'st du mein Eigen:
als maen |aogə dɪç zɑː, varst duː maen |aegən,

was im Busen ich barg, was ich bin,
was |ɪm buːzən |ɪç bark, vas |ɪç bɪn,

hell wie der Tag taucht' es mir auf,
hɛl viː der tɑːk taoxt |ɛs miːr |aof,

wie tönender Schall schlug's an mein Ohr,
viː tɔ̈ːnəndər ʃal ʃluːks |an maen |oːr,

245

als in frostig öder Fremde
als |ın frɔstıç |ø:dər frɛmdə

zuerst ich den Freund ersah.
tsu|e:rst |ıç den frɔ͜ønt |ɛrzɑ:.

Wagner   Einsam in trüben Tagen, "Lohengrin"
          a͟enzam |ın try:bən tɑ͜:gən, lo͜:əngrın

Einsam in trüben Tagen
a͟enzam |ın try:bən tɑ͜:gən

hab' ich zu Gott gefleht,
hɑ:p |ıç tsu: gɔt gəfle͟:t,

des Herzens tiefstes Klagen
dɛs hɛrtsəns ti͟:fstəs klɑ͟:gən

ergoss ich im Gebet,
|ɛrgɔs |ıç |ım gəbe͟:t,

da drang aus meinem Stöhnen
dɑ: draŋ |aos maenəm ʃtø͟:nən

ein Laut so klagevoll,
|aen la͟ot zo: klɑ͟:gəfɔl,

der zu gewalt'gem Tönen
der tsu: gəva͟ltgəm tø͟:nən

weit in die Lüfte schwoll:
va͟et |ın di ly͟ftə ʃvɔl,

ich hört' ihn fernhin hallen,
ıç hø͟:rt |i:n fɛrnhın ha͟llən,

bis kaum mein Ohr er traf;
bıs ka͟om maen |o:r |e:r trɑ:f,

mein Aug' ist zugefallen,
maen a͟ok |ıst tsu͟gəfallən,

ich sank in süssen Schlaf.
ıç zaŋk |ın zy͟:sən ʃlɑ:f.

In lichter Waffen Scheine ein Ritter nahte da,
ın lı͟çtər va͟fən ʃaenə |aen rı͟tər nɑ͟:tə dɑ:,

so tugendlicher Reine ich keinen noch ersah.
zoː tuːgəntlɪçər raenə |ɪç kaenən nɔx |eːrzaː.

Ein golden Horn zur Hüften,
aen gɔldən hɔrn tsur hʏftən,

gelehnet auf sein Schwert,
gəleːnət aof zaen ʃveːrt,

so trat er aus den Lüften zu mir,
zoː traːt |eːr |aos den lʏftən tsuː miːr,

der Recke werth,
der rɛkə vert,

mit züchtigem Gebahren gab Tröstung er mir ein:
mɪt tsʏçtɪgəm gəbaːrən gaːp trœstʊŋ |eːr miːr aen,

des Ritters will, ich wahren,
dɛs rɪtərs vɪl |ɪç vaːrən,

er soll mein Streiter sein!
eːr zɔl maen ʃtraetər zaen.

Hört, was dem Gottgesandten ich biete für Gewähr:
høːrt, vas dem gɔtgəzantən |ɪç biːtə fyːr gəvɛːr,

in meines Vaters Landen die Krone trage er,
ɪn maenəs faːtərs landən di kroːnə traːgə |eːr,

mich glücklich soll ich preisen,
mɪç glʏklɪç zɔl |ɪç praezən,

nimmt er mein Gut dahin,
nɪmt |eːr maen guːt dahɪn,

will er Gemahl mich heissen,
vɪl |eːr gəmaːl mɪç haesən,

geb' ich ihm, was ich bin!
geːp |ɪç iːm, vas |ɪç bɪn.

Wagner   Morgenlich leuchtend, "Die Meistersinger"
               mɔrgənlıç lɔøçtənt   di maestərzıŋər

Morgenlich leuchtend im rosigen Schein,
mɔrgənlıç lɔøçtənt |ım roːzıgən ʃaen,

von Blüth' und Duft geschwellt die Luft,
fɔn blyːt |unt duft gəʃvɛlt di luft,

voll aller Wonnen nie ersonnen,
fɔl |allər vɔnnən niː |ɛrzɔnnən,

ein Garten lud mich ein,
aen gartən luːt mıç |aen,

dort unter einem Wunderbaum,
dɔrt |untər |aenəm vundərbɑom,

von Früchten reich behangen,
fɔn fryçtən raeç bəhaŋən,

zu schau'n im sel'gen Liebestraum,
tsuː ʃɑon |ım zeːlgən liːbəstrɑom,

was höchstem Lustverlangen Erfüllung kühn verhiess,
was høːçstəm lustfɛrlaŋən ɛrfylluŋ kyːn fɛrhiːs,

das schönste Weib, Eva, im Paradies!
das ʃøːnstə vaep, eːva, ım paradiːs.

Abendlich dämmernd umschloss mich die Nacht;
ɑːbəntlıç dɛmmərnt |umʃlɔs mıç di naxt,

auf steilem Pfad war ich genaht
ɑof ʃtaeləm pfɑːt vɑːr |ıç gənɑːt

zu einer Quelle reiner Welle,
tsuː |aenər kvɛllə raenər vɛllə,

die lockend mir gelacht:
di lɔkənt miːr gəlaxt,

dort unter einem Lorbeerbaum,
dɔrt |untər |aenəm lɔrbeːrbɑom,

von Sternen hell durchschienen,
fɔn ʃtɛrnən hɛl durçʃiːnən,

248

ich schaut' im wachen Dichtertraum,
ɪç ʃaot |ɪm vaxən dɪçtərtraom,

von heilig holden Mienen,
fɔn haelɪç hɔldən miːnən,

mich netzend mit dem edlen Nass,
mɪç nɛtsənt mɪt dem |eːdlən nas,

das hehrste Weib: die Muse des Parnass!
das heːrstə vaep, di muːzə dɛs parnas.

Huldreichster Tag,
hultraeçstər taːk,

dem ich aus Dichter's Traum erwacht!
dem |ɪç |aos dɪçtərs traom ɛrvaxt.

Dass ich erträumt, das Paradies,
das |ɪç |ɛrtrɔømt, das paradiːs,

in himmlisch neu verklärter Pracht
ɪn hɪmlɪʃ nɔø fɛrklɛrtər praxt

hell vor mir lag, dahin lachend
hɛl foːr miːr laːk, dahɪn laxənt

nun der Quell den Pfad mir wies;
nuːn der kvɛl den pfaːt miːr viːs,

die, dort geboren, mein Herz erkoren,
di, dɔrt gəboːrən, maen hɛrts |ɛrkoːrən,

der Erde lieblichstes Bild,
der |eːrdə liːplɪçstəs bɪlt,

als Muse mir geweit, so heilig
als muːzə miːr gəvaet, zoː haelɪç

ernst als mild, ward kühn von mir gefreit;
ɛrnst |als mɪlt, vart kyːn fɔn miːr gəfraet,

am lichten Tag der Sonnen,
am lɪçtən taːk der zɔnnən,

durch Sanges Sieg gewonnen:
durç zaŋəs ziːk gəvɔnnən,

Parnass und Paradies!
parnas |ʊnt paradiːs.

Wagner   O du mein holder Abenstern, "Tannhäuser"
          oː duː maen hɔldər |aːbəntʃtɛrn, tanhɔøzər

Wie Todesahnung Dämm'rung deckt die Lande;
viː toːdəs|aːnʊŋ dɛmrʊŋ dɛkt di landə,

umhüllt das Thal mit schwärzlichem Gewande,
ʊmhʏlt das taːl mɪt ʃvɛrtslɪçəm gəvandə,

der Seele, die nach jenen Hön'n verlangt,
der zeːlə, di nax jeːnən høːn fɛrlaŋt,

vor ihrem Flug durch Nacht und Grausen bangt.
foːr |iːrəm fluːk dʊrç naxt |ʊnt graozən baŋt.

Da scheinest du, o! lieblichster der Sterne,
daː ʃaenəst duː, oː, liːplɪçstər der ʃtɛrnə,

dein sanftes Licht entsendest du der Ferne,
daen zanftəs lɪçt |ɛntzɛndəst duː der fɛrnə,

die nächt'ge Dämm'rung theilt dein lieber Strahl,
di nɛçtgə dɛmrʊŋ taelt daen liːbər ʃtraːl,

und freundlich zeigst du den Weg aus dem Thal.
ʊnt frɔøntlɪç tsaekst duː den veːk |aos dem taːl.

O du mein holder Abendstern,
oː duː maen hɔldər |aːbəntʃtɛrn,

wohl grüsst' ich immer dich so gern;
voːl gryːst |ɪç |ɪmmər dɪç zoː gɛrn,

vom Herzen, das sie nie verrieth,
fɔm hɛrtsən, das ziː niː fɛrriːt,

grüsse sie, wenn sie vorbei dir zieht,
gryːsə ziː, vɛn ziː fɔrbae diːr tsiːt,

250

wenn sie entschwebt dem Thal der Erden,
vɛn ziː |ɛntʃveːpt dem taːl der |eːrdən,

ein sel'ger Engel dort zu werden.
aen zeːlgər |ɛŋəl dɔrt tsuː veːrdən.

Wagner   Träume
                troͼmə

Sag, welch wunderbare Träume
zaːk, vɛlç vʊndərbaːrə troͼmə

halten meinen Sinn umfangen,
haltən maenən zɪn |umfaŋən,

dass sie nicht wie leere Schäume
das ziː nɪçt viː leːrə ʃoͼmə

sind in ödes Nichts vergangen?
zɪnt ɪn |øːdəs nɪçts fɛrgaŋən.

Träume, die in jeder Stunde,
troͼmə, di |ɪn jeːdər ʃtʊndə,

jedem Tage schöner blüh'n,
jeːdəm taːgə ʃøːnər blyːn,

und mit ihrer Himmelskunde
ʊnt mɪt |iːrər hɪmməlskʊndə

selig durch's Gemüte ziehn?
zeːlɪç dʊrçs gəmyːtə tsiːn.

Träume, die wie hehre Strahlen
troͼmə, di viː heːrə ʃtraːlən

in die Seele sich versenken,
|ɪn di zeːlə zɪç fɛrzɛŋkən,

dort ein ewig Bild zu malen:
dɔrt |aen |eːvɪç bɪlt tsuː maːlən,

Allvergessen, Eingedenken!
alfɛrgɛsən, aengədɛŋkən.

Träume, wie wenn Frühlingssonne
troͼmə, viː vɛn fryːlɪŋszɔnnə

aus dem Schnee die Blüten ′küsst,
|ɑos dem ʃneː di blyː̯tən kʏst,

dass zu nie geahnter Wonne
das tsuː niː gə|ɑːntər vɔnnə

sie der neue Tag begrüsst,
ziː der nɔø̯ə tɑːk bəgryː̯st,

dass sie wachsen, dass sie blühen,
das ziː vak̲sən, das ziː blyː̯ən,

träumend spenden ihren Duft,
trɔø̯mənt ʃpɛndən |iːrən dʊft,

sanft an deiner Brust verglühen,
zanft |an da̲enər brʊst fɛrglyː̯ən,

und dann sinken in die Gruft.
ʊnt dan zɪ̲ŋkən |ɪn di grʊft.

Wagner   Winterstürme wichen dem Wonnemond,
              vɪntərʃtʏrmə vɪ̯çən dem vɔnnəmoːnt

              "Die Walküre"
               di valky̲ːrə

Winterstürme wichen dem Wonnemond,
vɪntərʃtʏrmə vɪ̯çən dem vɔnnəmoːnt,

in mildem Lichte leuchtet der Lenz;
ɪn mɪ̲ldəm lɪçtə lɔø̯çtət der lɛnts,

auf linden Lüften, leicht und lieblich,
ɑof lɪ̲ndən ly̲ftən, la̲eçt |ʊnt liːplɪç,

Wunder webend er sich wiegt;
vʊndər veːbənt |eːr zɪç viːkt,

durch Wald und Auen weht sein Athem,
dʊrç valt |ʊnt |ɑo̲ən veːt za̲en |ɑːtəm,

weit geöffnet lacht sein Aug';
va̲et gə|ø̲fnət laxt za̲en |ɑok,

aus sel'ger Vöglein Sange süss er ′tönt,
ɑos zeː̲lgər føː̲glaen zaŋə zyːs |eːr tøːnt,

252

holde Düfte haucht er aus;
hɔldə dʏftə hɑoxt |eːr |ɑos,

seinem warmen Blut entblühen wonnige Blumen,
zaenəm varmən bluːt |ɛntblyːən vɔnnɪɡə kluːmən,

Keim und Spross entspringt seiner Kraft.
kaem |ʊnt ʃprɔs |ɛntʃprɪŋt zaenər kraft.

Mit zarter Waffen Zier bezwingt er die Welt,
mɪt tsartər vafən tsiːr bətsvɪŋkt |eːr di vɛlt,

Winter und Sturm wichen der starken Wehr:
vɪntər |ʊnt ʃtʊrm vɪçən der ʃtarkən veːr,

wohl musste den tapfern Streichen
voːl mʊstə den tapfərn ʃtraeçən

die strenge Thüre auch weichen,
di ʃtrɛŋə tyːrə |ɑox vaeçən,

die trotzig und starr uns trennte von ihm.
di trɔtsɪç |ʊnt ʃtar |ʊns trɛntə fɔn |iːm.

Zu seiner Schwester schwang er sich her;
tsuː zaenər ʃvɛstər ʃvaŋ |eːr zɪç heːr,

die Liebe lockte den Lenz:
di liːbə lɔktə den lɛnts,

in uns'rem Busen barg sie sich tief;
ɪn |ʊnzrəm buːzən bark ziː zɪç tiːf,

nun lacht sie selig dem Licht.
nuːn laxt ziː zeːlɪç dem lɪçt.

Die bräutliche Schwester befreite der Bruder;
di brɔøtlɪçə ʃvɛstər bəfraetə der bruːdər,

zertrümmert liegt, was je sie getrennt;
tsɛrtrʏmmərt liːkt, vas jeː ziː gətrɛnt,

jauchzend grüsst sich das junge Paar:
jɑoxtsənt gryːst zɪç das jʊŋə pɑːr,

vereint sind Liebe und Lenz!
fɛr|aent zɪnt liːbə |ʊnt lɛnts.

Weber   Leise, leise, fromme Weise,
           laezə, laezə, frɔmmə vaezə

          "Der Freischütz"
           der fraeʃʏts

Wie nahte mir der Schlummer
viː naːtə miːr der ʃlʊmmər

bevor ich ihn gesehn?
befoːr |ɪç |iːn gəzeːn.

Ja, Liebe pflegt mit Kummer
jaː, liːbə pfleːkt mɪt kʊmmər

stets Hand in Hand zu gehn.
ʃteːts hant |ɪn hant tsuː geːn.

Ob Mond auf seinem Pfad wohl lacht?
ɔp moːnt |aof zaenəm pfaːt voːl laxt.

Wie schön die Nacht!
viː ʃøːn di naxt.

Leise, fromme Weise,
laezə, frɔmmə vaezə,

schwing dich auf zum Sternenkreise!
ʃvɪŋ dɪç |aof tsum ʃtɛrnənkraezə.

Lied erschalle, feiernd walle
liːt |ɛrʃallə, faeərnt vallə

mein Gebet zur Himmelshalle!
maen gəbeːt tsur hɪmməlshallə.

O wie hell die gold'nen Sterne,
oː viː hɛl di gɔldnən ʃtɛrnə,

mit wie reinem Glanz sie glühn!
mɪt viː raenəm glants ziː glyːn.

Nur dort in der Berge Ferne
nuːr dɔrt |ɪn der bɛrgə fɛrnə

scheint ein Wetter aufzuziehn,
ʃaent |aen vɛtər |aoftsutsiːn,

dort am Wald auch schwebt ein Heer
dɔrt |am valt |aox ʃveːpt |aen heːr

dunkler Wolken dumpf und schwer.
duŋklər vɔlkən dumpf |unt ʃveːr.

Zu dir wende ich die Hände,
tsuː diːr vɛndə |ɪç di hɛndə,

Herr, ohn' Anfang und ohn' Ende.
hɛr, oːn |anfaŋ |unt |oːn |ɛndə.

Vor Gefahren uns zu wahren,
foːr gəfaːrən |uns tsuː vaːrən,

sende deine Engelschaaren!
zɛndə daenə |ɛŋəlʃaːrən.

Alles pflegt schon längst der Ruh!
alləs pfleːkt ʃoːn lɛŋst der ruː.

Trauter Freund, wo weilest du?
traotər frɔønt, voː vaeləst duː.

Ob mein Ohr auch eifrig lauscht,
ɔp maen |oːr |aox |aefrɪç laoʃt,

nur der Tannen Wipfel rauscht,
nuːr der tannən vɪpfəl raoʃt,

nur das Birkenlaub im Hain
nuːr das bɪrkənlaop |im haen

flüstert durch die hehre Stille,
flʏstərt durç di heːrə ʃtɪllə,

nur die Nachtigall und Grille
nuːr di naxtigal |unt grɪllə

scheint der Nachtluft sich zu freu'n.
ʃaent der naxtluft zɪç tsuː frɔøn.

Doch wie! täuscht mich nicht mein Ohr?
dɔx viː, tɔøʃt mɪç nɪçt maen |oːr.

Dort klingt's wie Schritte!
dɔrt klɪŋts viː ʃrɪtə.

Dort aus der Tannen Mitte
dɔrt |ɑos der tannən mɪtə

kommt was hervor! Er ist's!
kɔmt vas hɛrfɔr. eːr |ɪsts.

die Flagge der Liebe mag weh'n!
di flagə der liːbə maːk veːn.

Dein Mädchen wacht noch in der Nacht!
daen mɛːtçən vaxt nɔx |ɪn der naxt.

Er scheint mich noch nicht zu sehn.
eːr ʃaent mɪç nɔx nɪçt tsuː zeːn.

Gott! täuscht das Licht des Mond's mich nicht,
gɔt. tɔøʃt das lɪçt dɛs moːnts mɪç nɪçt,

so schmückt ein Blumenstrauss den Hut!
zoː ʃmʏkt |aen bluːmənʃtraos den huːt.

Gewiss, er hat den besten Schuss gethan;
gəvɪs, eːr hat den bɛstən ʃus getɑːn,

das kündet Glück für morgen an!
das kʏndət glʏk fyːr mɔrgən |an.

O süsse Hoffnung! Neu belebter Muth!
oː syːsə hɔfnuŋ. nɔø bəleːptər muːt.

All' meine Pulse schlagen,
al maenə pulsə ʃlɑːgən,

und das Herz wallt ungestüm
unt das hɛrts valt |ungəʃtyːm

süss entzückt entgegen ihm!
zyːs |ɛnttsʏkt |ɛntgeːgən |iːm.

Konnt' ich das zu hoffen wagen?
kɔnt |ɪç das tsuː hɔfən vɑːgən.

Ja! es wandte sich das Glück
jɑː ɛs vantə zɪç das glʏk

zu dem theuren Freund zurück,
tsuː dem tɔørən frɔønt tsurʏk,

will sich morgen treu bewähren!
vɪl zɪç mɔrgən trɔ̸ bəvɛːrən.

Ist's nicht Täuschung, ist's nicht Wahn?
ɪsts nɪçt tɔ̸ʃʊŋ,   ɪsts nɪçt vɑːn.

Himmel, nimm des Dankes Zähren
hɪmməl, nɪm dɛs daŋkəs tsɛːrən

für dies Pfand der Hoffnung an!
fyːr diːs pfant der hɔfnʊŋ |an.

Wolf, H.   Alle gingen, Herz zur Ruh
              alə gɪŋən, hɛrts, tsur ruː

Alle gingen, Herz, zur Ruh,
alə gɪŋən, hɛrts, tsur ruː,

Alle schlafen, nur nicht du.
alə ʃlɑːfən, nuːr nɪçt duː.

Denn der hoffnungslose Kummer
dɛn der hɔfnʊŋsloːzə kʊmmər

scheucht von deinem Bett den Schlummer,
ʃɔ̸çt fɔn daenəm bɛt den ʃlʊmmər,

und dein Sinnen schweift in stummer
ʊnt daen zɪnnən ʃvaeft |ɪn ʃtʊmmər

Sorge seiner Liebe zu.
zɔrgə zaenər liːbə tsuː.

Wolf, H.   Anakreons Grab
              anɑːkreɔns grɑːp

Wo die Rose hier blüht,
voː di roːzə hiːr blyːt,

wo Reben und Lorbeer sich schlingen,
voː reːbən |ʊnt lɔrbeːr zɪç ʃlɪŋən,

wo das Turtelchen lockt,
voː das tʊrtəlçən lɔkt,

wo sich das Grillchen ergötzt,
voː zɪç das grɪlçən |ɛrgœtst,

257

welch ein Grab ist hier,
vɛlç |aen grɑːp |ɪst hiːr,

das alle Götter mit Leben
das |allə gœtər mɪt leːbən

schön bepflanzt und geziert?
ʃøːn bəpflantst |ʊnt gətsiːrt.

Es ist Anakreons Ruh.
ɛs |ɪst |anɑːkreɔns ruː.

Frühling, Sommer und Herbst
fryːlɪŋ, zɔmmər |ʊnt hɛrpst

genoss der glückliche Dichter;
gənɔs der glʏklɪçə dɪçtər,

vor dem Winter hat ihn endlich
foːr dem vɪntər hat |iːn |ɛntlɪç

der Hügel geschützt.
der hyːgəl gəʃʏtst.

Wolf, H.   Auch kleine Dinge
             ɑox klaenə dɪŋə

Auch kleine Dinge können uns entzücken,
ɑox klaenə dɪŋə kœnnən |ʊns |ɛnttsʏkən,

auch kleine Dinge können theuer sein.
ɑox klaenə dɪŋə kœnnən tɔøər zaen.

Bedenkt, wie gern wir uns mit Perlen schmücken,
bədɛŋkt, viː gɛrn viːr |ʊns mɪt pɛrlən ʃmʏkən,

sie werden schwer bezahlt und sind nur klein.
ziː vɛrdən ʃveːr bətsɑːlt |ʊnt zɪnt nuːr klaen.

Bedenkt, wie klein ist die Olivenfrucht,
bədɛŋkt, viː klaen |ɪst di |oliːvənfruxt,

und wird um ihre Güte doch gesucht.
ʊnt vɪrt |ʊm |iːrə gyːtə dɔx gəzuːxt.

Denkt an die Rose nur, wie klein sie ist,
dɛŋkt |an di roːzə nuːr, viː klaen ziː |ıst,

und duftet doch so lieblich, wie ihr wisst.
ʊnt dʊftət dɔx zoː liːplıç, viː |iːr vıst.

Wolf, H.   Auf dem grünen Balkon
                aof dem gryːnən balkɔ̃

Auf dem grünen Balkon mein Mädchen
aof dem gryːnən balkɔ̃ maen mɛːtçən

schaut nach mir durchs Gitterlein.
ʃaot nax miːr dʊrçs gıtərlaen.

Mit den Augen blinzelt sie freundlich,
mıt den |aogən blıntsəlt ziː frɔøntlıç,

mit dem Finger sagt sie mir: Nein!
mıt dem fıŋər zaːkt ziː miːr, naen.

Glück, das nimmer ohne Wanken
glʏk, das nımmər |oːnə vaŋkən

junger Liebe folgt hienieden,
juŋər liːbə fɔlkt hiniːdən,

hat mir eine Lust beschieden,
hat miːr |aenə lʊst bəʃiːdən,

und auch da noch muss ich schwanken.
ʊnt |aox daː nɔx mʊs |ıç ʃvaŋkən.

Schmeicheln hör ich oder Zanken,
ʃmaeçəln høːr |ıç |oːdər tsaŋkən,

komm ich an ihr Fensterlädchen.
kɔm |ıç |an |iːr fɛnstərlɛːtçən.

Immer nach dem Brauch der Mädchen
ımmər nax dem braox der mɛːtçən

träuft ins Gluck ein bisschen Pein:
trɔøft |ıns glʏk |aen bısçən paen,

Mit den Augen blinzelt sie freundlich,
mıt den |aogən blıntsəlt ziː frɔøntlıç,

259

mit dem Finger sagt sie mir: Nein!
mɪt dem fɪŋər zaːkt ziː miːr, naen.

Wie sich nur in ihr vertragen
viː zɪç nuːr |ɪn |iːr fɛrtraːgən

ihre Kälte, meine Gluth?
|iːrə kɛltə, maenə gluːt.

Weil in ihr mein Himmel ruht,
vael |ɪn |iːr maen hɪmməl ruːt,

seh ich Trüb und Hell sich jagen.
zeː |ɪç tryːp |ʊnt hɛl zɪç jaːgən.

In den Wind gehn meine Klagen,
ɪn den vɪnt geːn maenə klaːgən,

dass noch nie die süsse Kleine
das nɔx niː di zyːsə klaenə

ihre Arme schlang um meine;
|iːrə |armə ʃlaŋ |ʊm maenə,

doch sie hält mich hin so fein,
dɔx ziː hɛlt mɪç hɪn zoː faen,

mit den Augen blinzelt sie freundlich,
mɪt den |aogən blɪntsəlt ziː frɔøntlɪç,

mit dem Finger sagt sie mir: Nein!
mɪt dem fɪŋər zaːkt ziː miːr, naen.

Wolf, H.   Auf ein altes Bild
                aof |aen |altəs bɪlt

In grüner Landschaft Sommerflor,
ɪn gryːnər landʃaft zɔmmərfloːr,

bei kühlem Wasser, Schilf und Rohr,
bae kyːləm vasər, ʃɪlf |ʊnt roːr,

schau, wie das Knäblein sündelos
ʃao, viː das knɛːplaen zyndəloːs

frei spielet auf der Jungfrau Schoss!
frae ʃpiːlət |aof der jʊŋfrao ʃoːs.

Und dort im Walde wonnesam,
unt dɔrt |ɪm valdə vɔnnəzaːm,

ach, grünet schon des Kreuzes Stamm!
ax, gryːnət ʃoːn dɛs krɔøtsəs ʃtam.

Wolf, H.   Das verlassene Mägdlein
           das fɛrlasənə mɛːktlaen

Früh, wann die Hähne krähn,
fryː, van di hɛːnə krɛːn,

eh die Sternlein schwinden,
eː di ʃtɛrnlaen ʃvɪndən,

muss ich am Herde stehn,
mʊs |ɪç |am heːrdə ʃteːn,

muss Feuer zünden.
mʊs fɔøər tsʏndən.

Schön ist der Flammen Schein,
ʃøːn |ɪst der flammən ʃaen,

es springen die Funken;
ɛs ʃprɪŋən di fʊŋkən,

ich schaue so darein,
ɪç ʃaoə zoː daraen,

in Leid versunken.
ɪn laet fɛrzʊŋkən.

Plötzlich, da kommt es mir,
plœtslɪç, daː kɔmt |ɛs miːr,

treuloser Knabe,
trɔøloːzər knaːbə,

dass ich die Nacht von dir
das |ɪç di naxt fɔn diːr

geträumet habe.
gətrɔømət haːbə.

Träne auf Träne dann
trɛːnə |aof trɛːnə dan

stürzet hernieder;
ʃtʏrtsət hɛrniːdər,

so kommt der Tag heran-
zoː kɔmt der tɑːk hɛran

o ging er wieder!
oː gɪŋ |eːr viːdər.

Wolf, H.   Er ist's
             ɛr |ɪsts

Frühling lässt sein blaues Band
fryːlɪŋ lɛst zaen blɑoəs bant

wieder flattern durch die Lüfte;
viːdər flatərn dʊrç di lʏftə,

süsse, wohlbekannte Düfte
zyːsə, voːlbəkantə dʏftə

streifen ahnungsvoll das Land.
ʃtraefən |ɑːnʊŋsfɔl das lant.

Veilchen träumen schon,
faelcən trɔømən ʃoːn,

wollen blade kommen.
vɔlən baldə kɔmmən.

Horch, von fern ein leiser Harfenton!
hɔrç, fɔn fɛrn |aen laezər harfəntoːn.

Frühling, ja du bist's!
fryːlɪŋ, jɑː duː bɪsts.

Dich hab ich vernommen,
dɪç hɑːp |ɪç fɛrnɔmmən,

ja du bist's!
jɑː duː bɪsts.

Wolf, H.   Fussreise
            fuːsraezə

Am frisch geschnittnen Wanderstab,
am frɪʃ gəʃnɪtnən vandərʃtaːp,

wenn ich in der Frühe
vɛn |ɪç |ɪn der fryːə

so durch Wälder ziehe, Hügel auf und ab:
zoː durç vɛldər tsiːə, hyːgəl |aof |unt |ap,

dann, wie's Vöglein im Laube
dan, viːs føːglaen |ɪm laobə

singet und sich rührt,
zɪŋət |unt zɪç ryːrt,

oder wie die goldne Traube
oːdər viː di gɔldnə traobə

Wonnegeister spürt in der ersten Morgensonne:
vɔnnəgaestər ʃpyːrt |ɪn der |eːrstən mɔrgənzɔnnə,

so fühlt auch mein alter, lieber Adam Herbst-
zoː fyːlt |aox maen |altər, liːbər |aːdəm hɛrpst

und Frühlingsfieber, gottbeherzte,
unt fryːlɪŋsfiːbər, gɔtbəhɛrtstə,

nie verscherzte Erstlings - Paradieseswonne.
niː fɛrʃɛrtstə |ɛrstlɪŋs   paradiːzəsvɔnnə.

Also bist du nicht so schlimm, o alter Adam,
alzo bɪst duː nɪçt zoː ʃlɪm, oː |altər |aːdam,

wie die strengen Lehrer sagen;
viː di ʃtrɛŋən leːrər zaːgən,

liebst und lobst du immer doch,
liːpst |unt loːpst duː |ɪmmər dɔx,

singst und preisest immer noch,
zɪŋst |unt praezəst |ɪmmər nɔx,

wie an ewig neuen Schöpfungstagen,
viː |an |eːvɪç nɔøən ʃœpfuŋstaːgən,

263

deinen lieben Schöpfer und Erhalter.
daenən liːbən ʃœpfər |ʊnt |ɛrhaltər.

Möcht es dieser geben, und mein ganzes Leben
mœçt |ɛs diːzər geːbən, ʊnt maen gantsəs leːbən

wär im leichten Wanderschweisse
vɛːr |ɪm laeçtən vandərʃvaesə

eine solche Morgenreise!
|aenə zɔlçə mɔrgənraezə.

Wolf, H.   Gebet
                gəbeːt

Herr! schicke was du willt,
hɛr.   ʃɪkə vas duː vɪlt,

ein Liebes oder Leides;
aen liːbəs |oːdər laedəs,

ich bin vergnügt, dass beides
ɪç bɪn fɛrgnyːkt, das baedəs

aus deinen Händen quillt.
|aos daenən hɛndən kvɪlt.

Wollest mit Freuden
vɔləst mɪt frɔødən

und wollest mit Leiden
|ʊnt vɔləst mɪt laedən

mich nicht überschütten!
mɪç nɪçt |yːbərʃytən.

Doch in der Mitten
dɔx |ɪn der mɪtən

liegt holdes Bescheiden.
liːkt hɔldəs bəʃaedən.

Wolf, H.   Gesang Weylas
              gəzaŋ vaelas

Du bist Orplid, mein Land!
duː bɪst |ɔrpliːt maen lant.

das ferne leuchtet;
das fɛrnə lɔøçtət,

vom Meere dampfet dein besonnter Strand
fɔm meːrə dampfət daen bəzɔntər ʃtrant

den Nebel, so der Götter Wange feuchtet.
den neːbəl, zoː der gœtər vaŋə fɔøçtət.

Uralte Wasser steigen
uːr|altə vasər ʃtaegən

verjüngt um deine Hüften, Kind!
fɛrjyŋt |um daenə hyftən, kɪnt.

Vor deiner Gottheit beugen
foːr daenər gɔthaet bɔøgən

sich Könige, die deine Wärter sind.
zɪç køːnɪgə, di daenə vɛrtər zɪnt.

Wolf, H.   Gesegnet sei
              gəzeːgnət zae

Gesegnet sei, durch den die Welt entstund;
gəzeːgnət zae, dʊrç den di vɛlt |entʃtʊnt,

wie trefflich schuf er sie nach allen Seiten!
viː trɛflɪç ʃuːf |eːr ziː nax |allən zaetən.

Er schuf das Meer mit endlos tiefem Grund,
eːr ʃuːf das meːr |mɪt |entloːs tiːfəm grʊnt,

er schuf die Schiffe, die hinübergleiten,
eːr ʃuːf di ʃɪfə, di hɪnyːbərglaetən,

er schuf das Paradies, mit ew'gem Licht,
eːr ʃuːf das paradiːs, mɪt |eːvgəm lɪçt,

er schuf die Schönheit und dein Angesicht.
eːr ʃuːf di ʃøːnhaet |unt daen |angəzɪçt.

265

Wolf, H.   Ich hab in Penna
                ıç haːp |ın p̱ɛnna

Ich hab in Penna einen Liebsten wohnen,
ıç haːp |ın p̱ɛnna |aenən liːpstən vo̱ːnən,

in der Maremmenebne einen andern,
ın der marɛmmən|eːbnə |aenən |andərn,

einen im schönen Hafen von Ancona,
aenən |ım ʃøːnən haːfən fɔn aŋko̱na,

zum vierten muss ich nach Viterbo wandern;
tsum fiːrtən mus |ıç nax vite̱rbo va̱ndərn,

ein andrer wohnt in Casentino dort,
aen |andrər vo̱ːnt |ın kazɛnti̱ːno dɔrt,

der nächste lebt mit mir am selben Ort,
der nɛ̱çstə leːpt mıt miːr̥ |am zɛlbən |ɔrt,

und wieder einen hab ich in Magione,
unt vi̱ːdər |aenən haːp |ıç |ın madʒo̱ne

vier in La Fratta, zehn in Castiglione.
fiːr |ın la fratta, tseːn |ın kasti̱ʎone.

Wolf, H.   In dem Schatten meiner Locken
                ın dem ʃa̱tən ma̱enər lɔ̱kən

In dem Schatten meiner Locken
ın dem ʃatən maenər lɔkən

schlief mir mein Geliebter ein.
ʃliːf miːr maen gəli̱ːptər |aen.

Weck ich ihn nun auf? Ach nein!
vɛk |ıç |i̱ːn nuːn |a̱of. ax na̱en.

Sorglich strählt ich meine krausen
zɔrklıç ʃtrɛːlt |ıç maenə kra̱ozən

Locken täglich in der Frühe,
lɔkən tɛ̱ːklıç |ın der fry̱ːə,

doch umsonst ist meine Mühe,
dɔx |umzo̱nst |ıst ma̱enə my̱ːə,

weil die Winde sie zerzausen.
ve͟el di vɪndə ziː tsɛrtsɑozən.

Lockenschatten, Windessausen
lɔ͟kənʃatən, vɪndəszɑozən

schläferten den Liebsten ein.
ʃlɛfərtən den li͟ːpstən |aen.

Weck ich ihn nun auf? Ach nein!
vɛk |ɪç |iːn nuːn |ɑof. ax na͟en.

Hören muss ich, wie ihn gräme,
hø͟ːrən mʊs |ɪç, viː |iːn grɛ͟ːmə,

dass er schmachtet schon so lange,
das |eːr ʃma͟xtət ʃoːn zoː laŋə,

dass ihm Leben geb und nehme
das |iːm le͟ːbən geːp |ʊnt ne͟ːmə

diese meine braune Wange.
di͟ːzə maenə brɑonə vaŋə.

Und er nennt mich seine Schlange,
ʊnt |eːr nɛnt mɪç za͟enə ʃla͟ŋə,

und doch schlief er bei mir ein.
ʊnt dɔx ʃliːf |eːr ba͟e miːr |aen.

Weck ich ihn nun auf? Ach nein!
vɛk |ɪç |iːn nuːn |ɑof. ax na͟en.

Wolf, H.   In der Frühe
              ɪn der fry͟ːə

Kein Schlaf noch kühlt das Auge mir,
kaen ʃlaːf nɔx kyːlt das |ɑogə miːr,

dort gehet schon der Tag herfür
dɔrt ge͟ːət ʃoːn der taːk hɛrfy͟ːr

an meinem Kammerfenster.
|an ma͟enəm ka͟mmərfɛnstər.

Es wühlet mein verstörter Sinn
ɛs vy͟ːlət ma͟en fɛrʃtœ͟rtər zɪn

noch zwischen Zweifeln her und hin
nɔx tsvɪʃən tsvaefəln heːr |ʊnt hɪn

und schaffet Nachtgespenster.
|ʊnt ʃafət naxtgəʃpɛnstər.

Ängst'ge, quäle dich nicht länger,
ɛŋstgə, kvɛːlə dɪç nɪçt lɛŋər,

meine Seele!
maenə zeːlə.

Freu dich! Schon sind da und dorten
frɔø dɪç. ʃoːn zɪnt daː ʊnt dɔrtən

Morgenglocken wach geworden.
mɔrgənglɔkən vax gəvɔrdən.

Wolf, H.   Mausfallen-Sprüchlein
               maosfallən-ʃpryçlaen

Kleine Gäste, kleines Haus,
klaenə gɛstə, klaenəs haos,

liebe Mäusin, oder Maus,
liːbə mɔøzɪn, |oːdər maos,

stelle dich nur kecklich ein
ʃtɛllə dɪç nuːr kɛklɪç |aen

heute Nacht bei Mondenschein!
hɔøtə naxt bae moːndənʃaen.

Mach aber die Tür fein hinter dir zu,
max |aːbər di tyːr faen hɪntər diːr tsuː,

hörst du? hörst du?
høːrst duː, høːrst duː.

Dabei hüte dein Schwänzchen!
dabae hyːtə daen ʃvɛntsçən.

hörst du? hörst du? Dein Schwänzchen?
høːrst duː, høːrst du. daen ʃvɛntsçən.

Nach Tische singen wir,
naːx tɪʃə zɪŋən viːr,

268

nach Tische springen wir
nɑːx tɪʃə sprɪŋən viːr

und machen ein Tänzchen, ein Tänzchen!
|ʊnt maxən |aen tɛntsçən, aen tɛntsçən.

Witt, witt! Witt, witt!
vɪt, vɪt,   vɪt, vɪt.

Meine alte Katze tanzt wahrscheinlich mit,
maenə |altə katsə tantst vɑːrʃaenlɪç mɪt,

hörst du? hörst du?
høːrst duː. høːrst duː.

Wolf, H.   Nimmersatte Liebe
               nɪmmərzatə liːbə

So ist die Lieb!
zoː |ɪst di liːp.

Mit Küssen nicht zu stillen:
mɪt kʏsən nɪçt tsuː ʃtɪllən,

wer ist der Tor und will ein Sieb
veːr |ɪst der toːr |ʊnt vɪl aen ziːp

mit eitel Wasser füllen?
mɪt |aetəl vasər fʏllən.

Und schöpfst du an die tausend Jahr,
ʊnt ʃœpfst duː |an di taozənt jɑːr,

und küssest ewig, ewig gar,
ʊnt kʏsəst |eːvɪç, eːvɪç gɑːr,

du tust ihr nie zu Willen.
duː tuːst |iːr niː tsuː vɪllən.

Die Lieb, die Lieb hat alle Stund
di liːp, di liːp hat |allə ʃtʊnt

neu wunderlich Gelüsten;
nɔø vʊndərlɪç gəlʏstən,

wir bissen uns die Lippen wund,
viːr bɪsən |ʊns di lɪpən vʊnt,

269

da wir uns heute küssten.
daː viːr |uns hɔøtə kʏstən.

Das Mädchen hielt in guter Ruh,
das mɛːtçən hiːlt |ɪn guːtər ruː,

wie's Lämmlein unterm Messer;
viːs lɛmlaen |untərm mɛsər,

ihr Auge bat: nur immer zu,
iːr |aogə bat, nuːr |ɪmmər tsuː,

je weher, desto besser!
jeː veːər, dɛsto bɛsər.

So ist die Lieb, und war auch so,
zoː |ɪst di liːp, unt vaːr |aox zoː,

wie lang es Liebe gibt,
viː laŋ |ɛs liːbə giːpt,

und anders war Herr Salomo,
unt |andərs vaːr hɛr zaːlomo,

der Weise, nicht verliebt.
der vaezə, nɪçt fɛrliːpt.

Wolf, H.   Nun wandre, Maria
                nuːn vandrə, mariːa

Nun wandre, Maria, nun wandre nur fort.
nuːn vandrə, mariːa, nuːn vandrə nuːr fɔrt.

Schon krähen die Hähne, und nah ist der Ort.
ʃoːn krɛːən di hɛːnə, unt naː |ɪst der |ɔrt.

Nun wandre, Geliebte, du Kleinod mein,
nuːn vandrə, gəliːptə, duː klaenoːt maen,

und balde wir werden in Bethlehem sein.
unt baldə viːr veːrdən |ɪn beːthlehɛm zaen.

Dann ruhest du fein und schlummerst dort.
dan ruːəst duː faen |unt ʃlummərst dɔrt.

Schon krähen die Hähne, und nah ist der Ort.
ʃoːn krɛːən di hɛːnə, unt naː |ɪst der |ɔrt.

Wohl seh ich, Herrin, die Kraft dir schwinden;
voːl zeː |ɪç, hɛrrɪn, di kraft diːr ʃvɪndən,

kann deine Schmerzen, ach, kaum verwinden.
kan daenə ʃmɛrtsən, |ax, kɑom fɛrvɪndən.

Getrost! wohl finden wir Herberg dort;
gətroːst. voːl fɪndən viːr hɛrbɛrk dɔrt,

schon krähn die Hähne und nah ist der Ort.
ʃoːn krɛːn di hɛːnə |unt naː |ɪst der |ɔrt.

Wär erst bestanden dein Stündlein, Marie,
vɛːr |eːrst bəʃtandən daen ʃtʏntlaen, mariː,

die gute Botschaft gut lohnt ich sie.
di guːtə boːtʃaft guːt loːnt |ɪç ziː.

Das Eselein hie gäb ich drum fort!
das |eːzəlaen hiː gɛːp |ɪç drum fɔrt.

Schon krähen die Hähne,
ʃoːn krɛːən di hɛːnə,

komm, nah ist der Ort.
kɔm naː |ɪst der ɔrt.

Wolf, H.   Schlafendes Jesuskind
                ʃlaːfəndəs jeːzuskɪnt

Sohn der Jungfrau, Himmelskind!
zoːn der juŋfrao, hɪmməlskɪnt.

am Boden auf dem Holz der Schmerzen
am boːdən |aof dem hɔlts der ʃmɛrtsən

eingeschlafen,
|aengəʃlaːfən,

das der fromme Meister
das der frɔmmə maestər

sinnvoll spielend deinen leichten
zɪnfɔl ʃpiːlənt daenən laeçtən

Träumen unterlegte;
trɔømən |untərleːktə,

Blume du, noch in der Knospe
bluːmə duː, nɔx |ɪn der knɔspe

dämmernd eingehüllt
dɛmmərnt |aengəhʏlt

die Herrlichkeit des Vaters!
di hɛrlɪçkaet des faːtərs.

O wer sehen könnte,
oː veːr zeːən kœntə,

welche Bilder hinter dieser Stirne,
vɛlçə bɪldər hɪntər diːzər ʃtɪrnə,

diesen schwarzen Wimpern,
diːzən ʃvartsən vɪmpərn,

sich in sanftem Wechsel malen!
zɪç |ɪn zanftəm vɛksəl maːlən.

Sohn der Jungfrau, Himmelskind!
zoːn der juŋfrao, hɪmməlskɪnt.

Wolf, H.   Über Nacht
              yːbər naxt

Über Nacht, über Nacht
yːbər naxt, yːbər naxt

kommt still das Leid,
kɔmt stɪl das laet,

und bist du erwacht,
unt bɪst duː |ɛrvaxt,

o traurige Zeit,
oː traorɪgə tsaet,

du grüssest den dämmernden Morgen
duː gryːsəst den dɛmmərndən mɔrgən

mit Weinen und mit Sorgen.
mɪt vaenən |unt mɪt zɔrgən.

Über Nacht, über Nacht
yːbər naxt, yːbər naxt

272

kommt still das Glück,
kɔmt ʃtɪl das glʏk,

und bist du erwacht, o selig Geschick,
unt bɪst duː |ɛrvaxt, oː zeːlɪç gəʃɪk,

der düstre Traum ist zerronnen,
der dyːstrə traom |ɪst tsɛrrɔnnən,

und Freude ist gewonnen.
|unt frɔødə |ɪst gəvɔnnən.

Über Nacht, über Nacht
yːbər naxt, yːbər naxt

kommt Freud und Leid,
kɔmt frɔøt |unt laet,

und eh du's gedacht,
unt |eː duːs gədaxt,

verlassen dich beid
fɛrlasən dɪç baet

und gehen dem Herrn zu sagen,
unt geːən dem hɛrn tsuː zaːgən,

wie du sie getragen.
viː duː ziː gətraːgən.

Wolf, H.   Verborgenheit
                fɛrbɔrgənhaet

Lass, o Welt, o lass mich sein!
las, oː vɛlt, oː las mɪç zaen.

locket nicht mit Liebesgaben,
lɔkət nɪçt mɪt liːbəsgaːbən,

lasst dies Herz alleine haben
last diːs hɛrts |allaenə haːbən

seine Wonne, seine Pein!
zaenə vɔnnə, zaenə paen.

Was ich traure, weiss ich nicht,
vas |ɪç traorə, vaes |ɪç nɪçt,

273

es ist unbekanntes Wehe;
ɛs |ɪst |ʊnbəkantəs ve:ə,

immerdar durch Tränen sehe
ɪmmərda:r dʊrç trɛ:nən ze:ə

ich der Sonne liebes Licht.
|ɪç der zɔnnə li:bəs lɪçt.

Oft bin ich mir kaum bewusst
ɔft bɪn |ɪç mi:r kɑom bəvʊst

und die helle Freude zücket
ʊnt di hɛllə frɔ:ødə tsʏkət

durch die Schwere, so mich drücket,
dʊrç di ʃve:rə, zo: mɪç drʏkət,

wonniglich in meiner Brust.
vɔnɪklɪç |ɪn maenər brʊst.

Wolf, H.   Zur Ruh, zur Ruh!
              tsu:r ru:, tsu:r ru:

Zur Ruh, zur Ruh ihr müden Glieder!
tsu:r ru:, tsu:r ru: |i:r my:dən gli:dər

schliesst fest euch zu, ihr Augenlider!
ʃli:st fɛst |ɔ:øç tsu:, i:r |ɑogənli:dər.

ich bin allein, fort ist die Erde;
ɪç bɪn |allaen, fɔrt |ɪst di |e:rdə,

Nacht muss es sein, dass Licht mir werde,
naxt mʊs |ɛs zaen, das lɪçt mi:r ve:rdə,

o führt mich ganz, ihr innern Mächte!
o: fy:rt mɪç gants, i:r |ɪnnərn mɛçtə.

hin zu dem Glanz der tiefsten Nächte.
hɪn tsu: dem glants der ti:fstən nɛçtə.

Fort aus dem Raum der Erdenschmerzen,
fɔrt |ɑos dem rɑom der |e:rdənʃmɛrtsən,

durch Nacht und Traum zum Mutterherzen!
dʊrç naxt |ʊnt trɑom tsum mʊtərhɛrtsən.

274

PHONETIC TRANSCRIPTION OF FRENCH SONGS AND ARIAS

Pierre Delattre and Berton Coffin

Open Syllabication

The most characteristic feature of French is that all syllables tend to open, that is, tend to end in a vowel: <u>Avec une amie</u> is pronounced [a – vɛ – ky – na – mi]. English speakers, on the contrary, tend to close all syllables with a consonant: <u>Eat at eight</u> is pronounced by an American [it – æt – eit]. To help avoid such closing of syllables, we have transcribed all syllables as <u>open</u>; we have even separated the final phonetic consonant from the preceding vowel: <u>il observe</u>   [i – lɔ – bsɛ – rv].

Stress and Rhythm

The place of stress is always the same in French - the last syllable of a long word or a group of words: Mes am<u>is</u>, mes meilleurs am<u>is</u>. What makes those last syllables stand out is not an increase of force (intensity, loudness) but an increase of length (duration). In fact, all syllables have equal force and all but the last have equal duration. This sort of stress and rhythm pattern should agree very naturally with singing. No special marking is necessary.

The "mute e"

The ə as in <u>demi</u> [demi] is an unstable vowel which falls or remains according to very involved rules <u>in speech.</u> In singing, however, two statements will suffice.

a. Within a word, before a consonant, it is always sung as a syllable: re-ve-nez.
b. Final after a consonant (tou<u>te</u>), or after a vowel (la vi<u>e</u>), it can fall [tut la vi] or remain and be sung [tu tə la vi əl , at the fancy of the poet or composer (poetic license). Even if the same words occurred two lines apart, the ə could remain once and be dropped the next. Therefore, follow the phonetic transcription.

Liaison

Symbols used in the following explanation:
a. Compulsory liaison = ‿
b. Optional liaison = ↲
c. Forbidden liaison = /
(cf. <u>Principes de Phonétique du Français,</u> chart of <u>Liaison, p. 39.</u>)

Another unstable sound peculiar to French is the consonant of liaison, as in mes amis /auront/attendu. Final consonants that are mute in the isolated word can at times be pronounced with the vowel that begins the next word - at times but not always. It is most useful to know which liaisons are quite forbidden:

a. between two words not closely connected: ils vont/ils viennent...
b. after a singular noun: un soldat/anglais, une maison/ immense.
c. after et: et/ils chantent
d. before the numbers un, huit, onze: cent/un.
e. before an aspirate h: les/haches.

Other liaisons are either compulsory (i.e., article, or adjective before a noun, personal pronoun before or after a verb), or optional. The latter are done more or less frequently depending on (a) the grammatical relation between the two words (in the above example, auront/attendu is more frequent than amis/auront) and (b) the degree of formality (in formal style, both could be made, but especially auront/ attendu).

In the phonetic transcriptions for singing, we omitted all the forbidden liaison, and a small portion of the optional ones - just those which we judged would sound much too stuffy.

Nasality

In French, vowel nasality is "distinctive": whether you say [pɛ] paix or [pɛ̃] pain makes a difference in meaning. Every vowel must therefore be completely nasal: mon [mɔ̃], or completely free from nasality: ami [ami], année [a ne]. If the vowel is nasal, do not pronounce at all the nasal consonant that follows: mondain [mɔ̃ dɛ̃]. The n's are absolutely silent.

Value of the phonetic symbols used in the
transcription of French

Phonetic Symbols	Sounds as derived from English sounds	As found in French words
VOWELS		
ɑ	father, arm	âme . . . am
a	father, with tongue more fronted, about central	Madame . . . madam
e	say, but without diphthongization	nez . . . ne

276

ɛ	sell	plaire . . . plɛr
i	see, but more close	qui . . . ki
o	no, but without dipthongization	nos . . . no
ɔ	law, taught, open midway between a and o	porte . . . pɔrt
u	soon, but more close	jour . . . ʒur
ø	no, for lip rounding, but with tongue tip fronted to touch the lower teeth	deux . . . dø
œ	law, floor, for lip rounding, but with tongue tip fronted nearly enough to touch the lower teeth	fleur . . . flœr
y	do, for lip rounding, but with tongue tip fronted to touch firmly the lower teeth and mass of tongue raised forward.	du . . . dy
ã	somewhat like pond when the n is not pronounced	dans . . . dã
ɛ̃	somewhat like bent when the n is not pronounced	pain . . . pɛ̃
ɔ̃	somewhat like haunt when the n is not pronounced	non . . . nɔ̃
œ̃	somewhat like hunt when the n is not pronounced	un . . . œ̃
ə	the, but with more lip rounding. Same as œ of French fleur, but somewhat weaker, shorter. In speech it can often disappear, but very seldom in singing.	petit . . . pəti

CONSONANTS

b	bay	bonne . . . bon
d	day, with tongue more fronted, touching upper teeth	dans . . . dã
f	fate	fille . . . fij
g	gate	garçon . . . garsɔ̃
k	key, without aspiration	comme . . . kɔm
l	leave, more fronted, tongue touching upper teeth, always clear, even after a vowel	livre . . . livr

CONSONANTS continued

m	<u>m</u>i<u>n</u>e	<u>maison</u> . . . mɛzõ
n	<u>n</u>i<u>n</u>e	<u>n</u>ouveau . . . nuvo
ɲ	<u>pinion</u>, with tongue more fronted, touching upper teeth	ga<u>gn</u>er . . . gaɲe
p	<u>p</u>a<u>y</u>, without aspiration	<u>p</u>etit . . . pəti
r	tongue tip flap (more lightly rolled than in Italian) is preferred <u>in singing</u> to pharyngeal friction of spoken French.	<u>r</u>ue . . . ry
s	<u>s</u>ore, more fronted than in English	<u>s</u>œur . . . sœr
ʃ	<u>sh</u>ore, more fronted than in English, lips rounded	<u>ch</u>ez . . . ʃe
t	<u>t</u>ile, without aspiration and with tongue more fronted touching upper teeth	<u>t</u>able . . . tabl
v	<u>v</u>ile	<u>v</u>ous . . . vu
ʒ	<u>rouge</u>, <u>garage</u>, <u>regime</u>, with tongue more fronted	<u>j</u>e . . . ʒə
j	<u>y</u>es, be<u>y</u>ond	réveil<u>l</u>é . . . reveje
w	<u>w</u>e, a<u>w</u>ay	<u>ou</u>i . . . wi
ɥ	<u>w</u>e, but with tongue tip fronted to touch lower teeth	<u>h</u>uit . . . ɥit

Bachelet   Chère Nuit
baʃle   ʃɛr nɥi

Voici l'heure bientôt.
vwa si lœ rə bjɛ̃ to.

Derrière la colline
dɛ rjɛ rə la kɔ li nə,

Je vois le soleil qui décline
ʒə vwa lə sɔ lɛ jki de kli nə,

Et cache ses rayons jaloux.
e ka ʃə se rɛ jɔ̃ ʒa lu.

J'entends chanter l'âme des choses
ʒɑ̃ tɑ̃ ʃɑ̃ te la mə de ʃo zə,

Et les narcisses et les roses
e le na rsi sə ze le ro zə

M'apportent des parfums plus doux!
ma pɔ rtə de pa rfœ̃ ply du!

Chère nuit aux clartés sereines,
ʃɛ rə nɥi o kla rte sə rɛ nə,

Toi qui ramènes Le tendre amant,
twa ki ra mɛ nə lə tɑ̃ dra mɑ̃,

Ah! descends et voile la terre
ɑ dɛ sɑ̃ ze vwa lə la tɛ rə,

De ton mystère, Calme et charmant.
də tɔ̃ mi stɛ rə, ka lme ʃa rmɑ̃.

Mon bonheur renaît sous ton aile,
mɔ̃ bɔ nœ rrə nɛ su tɔ̃ nɛ lə,

O nuit plus belle Que les beaux jours:
o nɥi ply bɛ lə kə le bo ʒu r:

Ah! lève-toi! Pour faire encore
ɑ lɛ və twa! pu rfɛ rɑ̃ ko rə

Briller l'aurore De mes amours!
bri je lo rɔ rə, də me za mu r!

Berlioz   L'absence
bɛrljoz   l absɑ̃s

Reviens, reviens, ma bien aimée!
rə vjɛ̃ rə vjɛ̃, ma bjɛ̃ ne me ə!

279

Comme une fleur loin du soleil,
kɔ my nə flœ r, lwɛ̃ dy sɔ lɛ j,

La fleur de ma vie est fermée
la flœ rdə ma vi ɛ, fɛ rme ə,

Loin de ton sourire vermeil.
lwɛ̃ də tɔ̃ su ri rə vɛ rmɛ j.

Entre nos coeurs quelle distance!
ɑ̃ trə no kœ rkɛ lə di stɑ̃ sə!

Tant d'espace entre nos baisers!
tɑ̃ dɛ spa sɑ̃ trə no bɛ ze!

O sort amer! ô dure absence!
o sɔ ra mɛ r! o dy ra psɑ̃ sə!

O grand désirs inapaisés!
o grɑ̃ de zi ri na pɛ ze!

D'ici là-bas que de campagnes,
di si la bɑ kə də kɑ̃ pa ɲə,

Que de villes et de hameaux,
kə də vi lə e də a mo,

Que de vallons et de montagnes,
kə də va lɔ̃ e də mɔ̃ ta ɲə,

A lasser le pied des chevaux!
a lɑ se lə pje de ʃə vo!

Bizet Habanera, from "Carmen"
bizɛ abanera karmɛn

L'amour est un oiseau rebelle
la mu rɛ tœ̃ nwa zo rə bɛ lə

Que nul ne peut apprivoiser,
kə ny lnə pø ta pri vwa ze,

Et c'est bien en vain qu'on l'appelle,
e sɛ bjɛ̃ nɑ̃ vɛ̃ kɔ̃ la pɛ lə,

S'il lui convient de refuser.
si llɥi kɔ̃ vjɛ̃ də rə fy ze

Rien n'y fait, menace ou prière,
rjɛ̃ ni fɛ, mə na su pri jɛ rə,

L'un parle bien, l'autre se tait;
lœ̃ pa rlə bjɛ̃ lo trə sə tɛ;

Et c'est l'autre que je préfère
e sɛ lo trə kə ʒə pre fɛ rə,

Il n'a rien dit; mais il me plait.
i lna rjɛ̃ di mɛ zi lmə plɛ.

L'amour est enfant de Bohême,
la mu rɛ tã fã də bo ɛ m,

Il n'a jamais, jamais connu de loi,
i lna ʒa mɛ ʒa mɛ ko ny də lwa,

Si tu ne m'aimes pas, je t'aime;
si ty nə mɛ mə pa, ʒə tɛ mə;

Si je t'aime, prends garde à toi!
si ʒə tɛ mə prã ga rda twa!

Mais si je t'aime, si je t'aime, prends garde à toi!
mɛ si ʒə tɛ mə, si ʒə tɛ mə prã ga rda twa!

L'oiseau que tu croyais surprendre
lwa zo kə ty krwa jɛ sy rprã drə

Battit de l'aile et s'envola;
ba ti də lɛ le sã vɔ la;

L'amour est loin, tu peux l'attendre;
la mu rɛ lwɛ̃, ty pø la tã drə;

Tu ne l'attends plus, il est la!
ty nə la tã ply i lɛ la!

Tout autour de toi vite, vite,
tu to tu rdə twa vi tə vi tə,

Il vient, s'en va, puis il revient;
i lvjɛ̃, sã va pɥi zi lrə vjɛ̃

Tu crois le tenir, il t'évite;
ty krwa lə tə ni r, i lte vi tə;

Tu crois l'éviter, il te tient!
ty krwa le vi te, i ltə tjɛ̃!

Bizet   Je dis que rien ne m'épouvante, from "Carmen"
bizɛ   ʒə di kə rjɛ̃ nə mepuvãt   karmɛn

C'est des contrebandiers le refuge ordinaire.
sɛ de kõ trə bã dje lə rə fy ʒo rdi nɛ rə.

Il est ici, je le verrai
i lɛ ti si ʒə lə vɛ re,

Et le devoir que m'imposa sa mère
e lə də vwa rkə mɛ̃ po za sa mɛ rə,

Sans trembler je l'accomplirai.
sã trã ble ʒə la kõ pli re.

Je dis, que rien ne m'épouvante
ʒə di kə rjɛ̃ nə me pu vã tə,

Je dis, hélas! que je réponds de moi;
ʒə di e lɑs, kə ʒə re põ də mwa;

Mais j'ai beau faire la vaillante,
mɛ ʒe bo fɛ rə la va jã tə,

Au fond du coeur je meurs d'effroi!
o fõ dy kœ r, ʒə mœ rdɛ frwa!

Seule en ce lieu sauvage,
sœ lã sə ljø so va ʒə,

Toute seule j'ai peur, mais j'ai tort d'avoir peur;
tu tə sœ lə ʒe pœ r, mɛ ʒe tɔ rda vwa rpœ r;

Vous me donnerez du courage,
vu mə dɔ nə re dy ku ra ʒə,

Vous me protégerez, Seigneur!
vu mə prɔ te ʒə re sɛ ɲœ r!

Je vais voir de près cette femme
ʒə vɛ vwa rdə prɛ sɛ tə fa mə,

Dont les artifices maudits
dõ le za rti fi sɛ mo di,

Ont fini par faire un in-fâme
õ fi ni pa rfɛ rœ̃ nɛ̃ fɑ mə,

De celui que j'aimais jadis!
də sə lɥi kə ʒe mɛ ʒa di!

Elle est dangereuse elle est belle!
ɛ lɛ dã ʒə rø zə, ɛ lɛ bɛ lə!

Mais je ne veux pas avoir peur! Non – – –
mɛ ʒə nə vø pa za vwa rpœ r!   nõ – – –

282

Je parlerai haut devant elle
ʒə pa rlə re o də vã tɛ lə,

Ah! vous me protégerez! donnez moi du courage!
a!　　　 vu mə prɔ te ʒə re! dɔ ne mwa dy ku ra ʒə!

Bizet　　　La fleur que tu m'avais jetée, from "Carmen"
bizɛ　　　 la flœr kə ty m avɛ ʒəte　　　　　karmɛn

La fleur que tu m'avais jetée,
la flœ rkə ty ma vɛ ʒə te ə,

Dans ma prison m'était restée,
dã ma pri zɔ̃ me tɛ rɛ ste ə,

Flétrie et sèche, cette fleur
fle tri e sɛ ʃə sɛ tə flœ r,

Gardait toujours sa douce odeur;
ga rdɛ tu ʒu rsa du so dœ r;

Et pendant des heures entières,
e pã dã de zœ rə zã tjɛ rə,

Sur mes yeux, fermant mes paupières,
sy rme zjø fɛ rmã me po pjɛ rə,

De cette odeur je m'enivrais
də sɛ to dœ rʒə mã ni vrɛ,

Et dans la nuit je te voyais!
e dã la nɥi ʒə tə vwa jɛ!

Je me prenais à te maudire,
ʒə mə prə nɛ a tə mo di rə,

A te détester, à me dire:
a tə de tɛ ste a mə di rə:

Pourquoi faut il que le destin
pu rkwa fo ti lkə lə dɛ stɛ̃,

L'ait mise là sur mon chemin!
lɛ mi zə la, sy rmɔ̃ ʃə mɛ̃!

Puis je m'accusais de blasphème,
pɥi, ʒə ma ky zɛ də bla sfɛ mə,

Et je ne sentais en moi même,
e ʒə nə sã tɛ zã mwa mɛ mə,

283

Je ne sentais qu'un seul désir,
ʒə nə sã tɛ kœ̃ sœ lde zi r,

un seul désir, un seul espoir:
œ̃ sœ lde zi r, œ̃ sœ lɛ spwa r:

Te revoir, ô Carmen, oui, te revoir!
tə rə vwa ro ka rmɛ n, wi tə rə vwa r!

Car tu n'avais eu qu'a paraître,
ka rty na vɛ zy ka pa rɛ trə,

Qu'à jeter un regard sur moi,
ka ʒə te œ̃ rə ga rsy rmwa,

Pour t'emparer de tout mon être,
pu rtã pa re də tu mõ nɛ trə,

O ma Carmen!   Et j'étais une chose à toi!
o ma ka rmɛ n! e ʒe tɛ zy nə ʃo za twa!

Carmen, je t'aime!
ka rmɛ n, ʒə tɛ mə!

Bizet   Ouvre ton coeur
bizɛ   uvrə tõ kœr

La marguerite a fermé sa corolle,
la ma rgə ri t, a fɛ rme sa kɔ rɔ lə,

L'ombre a fermé les yeux du jour.
lõ bra fɛ rme le zjø dy ʒu r.

Belle, me tiendras tu parole?
bɛ lə, mə tjɛ̃ dra ty pa rɔ lə?

Ouvre ton coeur à mon amour.
u vrə tõ kœ ra mõ na mu r.

O jeune ange, à ma flamme,
o ʒœ nã ʒa ma fla mə,

Qu'un rêve charme ton sommeil,
kœ̃ rɛ və ʃa rmə tõ sɔ mɛ j,

Je veux reprendre mon âme,
ʒə vø rə prã drə mõ nɑ mə,

Ouvre ton coeur, ô jeune ange, à ma flamme,
u vrə tõ kœ ro ʒœ nã ʒa ma fla mə

Comme une fleur s'ouvre au soleil!
kɔ my nə flœ r, su vro sɔ lɛ j

Bizet   Seguidilla, from "Carmen"
bizɛ   segidija   karmɛn

Près des remparts de Séville,
prɛs de rɑ̃ pa rdə se vi lə,

Chez mon ami Lillas Pastia
ʃe mɔ̃ na mi li la pa stja

J'irai danser la Séguedille
ʒi re dɑ̃ se la se gə di j

Et boire du Manzanilla.
e bwa rə dy mɑ̃ za ni ja.

J'irai chez mon ami Lillas Pastia
ʒi re ʃe mɔ̃ na mi li la pa stja.

Oui, mais toute seule on s'ennuie,
wi, mɛ tu tə sœ lɔ̃ sɑ̃ nɥi ə,

Et les vrais plaisirs sont à deux;
e le vrɛ plɛ zi rsɔ̃ ta dø;

Donc, pour me tenir compagnie,
dɔ̃ k, pu rmə tə ni rkɔ̃ pa ɲi ə,

J'emmènerai mon amoureux!
ʒɑ̃ mɛ nə re mɔ̃ na mu rø!

Mon amoureux il est au diable,
mɔ̃ na mu rø, i lɛ to dja blə,

Je l'ai mis à la porte hier!
ʒə le mi a la pɔ rtə jɛ r!

Mon pauvre coeur très consolable,
mɔ̃ po vrə kœ rtrɛ kɔ̃ sɔ la blə,

Mon coeur est libre comme l'air!
mɔ̃ kœ rɛ li brə kɔ mə lɛ r!

J'ai des galants à la douzaine,
ʒe de ga lɑ̃ a la du zɛ nə,

Mais ils ne sont pas à mon gré.
mɛ i lnə sɔ̃ pa za mɔ̃ gre.

Voici la fin de la semaine:
vwa si la fɛ̃ də la sə mɛ nə:

Qui veut m'aimer? je l'aimerai!
ki vø mɛ me? ʒə lɛ mə re!

Qui veut mon âme? Elle est à prendre!
ki vø mɔ̃ na mɛ lɛ ta prɑ̃ drə!

Vous arrivez au bon moment!
vu za ri ve o bɔ̃ mɔ mɑ̃!

Je n'ai guère le temps d'attendre,
ʒə ne gɛ rə lə tɑ̃ da tɑ̃ drə,

Car avec mon nouvel amant, . . .
ka ra vɛ kmɔ̃ nu vɛ la mɑ̃, . . .

Bizet   Votre toast, je peux vous le rendre, from "Carmen"
bizɛ   vɔtrə tost ʒə pø vu lə rɑ̃dr   karmɛn

Votre toast, je peux vous le rendre,
vɔ trə to st, ʒə pø vu lə rɑ̃ drə,

Señors, señors, car avec les soldats
se ɲɔ rsɛ ɲɔ r, ka ra vɛ kle sɔ lda,

Oui, les Toréros, peuvent s'entendre;
wi le tɔ re ro, pœ və sɑ̃ tɑ̃ drə;

Pour plaisirs, pour plaisirs, ils ont les combats!
pu rplɛ zi rpu rplɛ si r, i lzɔ̃ le kɔ̃ ba!

Le cirque est plein, c'est jour de fête!
lə si rkɛ plɛ̃ sɛ ʒu rdə fɛ tə!

Le cirque est plein du haut en bas;
lə si rkɛ plɛ̃ dy o tɑ̃ ba;

Les spectateurs, perdant la tête,
le spɛ kta tœ r, pɛ rdɑ̃ la tɛ tə,

Les spectateurs s'interpellent à grand fracas!
le spɛ kta tœ r, sɛ̃ tɛ rpɛ lə ta grɑ̃ fra ka!

Apostrophes, cris et tapage
a pɔ strɔ fə kri ze ta pa ʒə,

Poussés jusques à la fureur!
pu se ʒy skə za la fy rœ r!

286

Car c'est la fête du courage!
ka rsɛ la fɛ tə dy ku ra ʒə!

C'est la fête des gens de coeur!
sɛ la fɛ tə de ʒɑ̃ də kœ r!

Allons! en garde! ah!
a lɔ̃! ɑ̃ ga rdə! a!

Toréador, en garde!
tɔ re a dɔ r ɑ̃ ga rdə!

Et songe bien, oui, songe en combattant,
e sɔ̃ ʒə bjɛ̃ wi sɔ̃ ʒɑ̃ kɔ̃ ba tɑ̃,

Qu'un oeil noir te regarde, Et que l'amour t'attend,
kœ̃ nœ jnwa rtə rə ga rd, e kə la mu rta tɑ̃,

Toréador, l'amour t'attend!
tɔ re a dɔ r, la mu rta tɑ̃!

Tout d'un coup, on fait silence...
tu dœ̃ ku, ɔ̃ fɛ si lɑ̃ sə...

Ah! que se passe-t-il?
a kə sə pa sə ti l?

Plus de cris, c'est l'instant!
ply də kri sɛ lɛ̃ stɑ̃!

Le taureau s'élance En bondissant hors du Toril!
lə tɔ ro se lɑ̃ sɑ̃ bɔ̃ di sɑ̃ ɔ rdy tɔ ri l!

Il s'élance, il entre, il frappe!
i lse lɑ̃ sə, i lɑ̃ tri lfra pə!

un cheval roule, Entraînant un Picador,
œ̃ ʃə va lru lə, ɑ̃ trɛ nɑ̃ tœ̃ pi ka dɔ r,

" Ah! bravo! Toro! " hurle la foule!
a bra vo tɔ ro! y rlə la fu lə!

Le taureau va, il vient, et frappe encor!
lə tɔ ro va, i lvjɛ̃, e fra pɑ̃ kɔ r!

En secouant ses banderilles,
ɑ̃ sə ku ɑ̃ se bɑ̃ də ri jə,

Plein de fureur, il court! Le cirque est plein de sang!
plɛ̃ də fy rœ r, i lku r! lə si rkɛ plɛ̃ də sɑ̃!

On se sauve, on franchit les grilles!
ɔ̃ sə so v, ɔ̃ frɑ̃ ʃi le gri jə!

C'est ton tour maintenant!   Allons! en garde! ah!
sɛ tɔ̃ tu rmɛ̃ tə nɑ̃! a lɔ̃! ɑ̃ ga rdə! a!

Charpentier Depuis le jour, from "Louise"
ʃarpɑ̃tje   dəpчi lə ʒur   luiz

Depuis le jour où je me suis donnée,
də pчi lə ʒu r, u ʒə mə sчi dɔ ne ə,

Toute fleurie semble ma destinée.
tu tə flœ ri ə sɑ̃ blə ma dɛ sti ne ə.

Je crois rêver sous un ciel de féerie,
ʒə krwa rɛ ve, su zœ̃ sjɛ ldə fe ri ə,

l'âme encore grisée de ton premier baiser!
la mɑ̃ kɔ rə gri ze ə, də tɔ̃ prə mje bɛ ze!

Quelle belle vie! Mon rêve n'était pas un rêve!
kɛ lə bɛ lə vi ə! mɔ̃ rɛ və ne tɛ pa zœ̃ rɛ və!

Ah! je suis heureuse!
a! ʒə sчi zø rø zə!

L'amour étend sur moi ses ailes!
la mu re tɑ̃ sy rmwa se zɛ lə!

Au jardin de mon coeur chante une joie nouvelle!
o ʒa rdɛ̃ də mɔ̃ kœ r, ʃɑ̃ ty nə ʒwa nu vɛ lə!

Tout vibre, tout se réjouit de mon triomphe!
tu vi brə tu sə re ʒu i də mɔ̃ tri jɔ̃ fə!

Autour de moi tout est sourire, lumière et joie!
o tu rdə mwa tu tɛ su ri rə, ly mjɛ re ʒwa ə!

et je tremble délicieusement
e ʒə trɑ̃ blə, de li si ø zə mɑ̃

au souvenir charmant du premier jour d'amour!
o su və ni rʃa rmɑ̃, dy prə mje ʒu rda mu r!

Je suis heureuse! trop heureuse.
ʒə sчi zø rø zə! trɔ pø rø zə.

288

Chausson   Les Papillons
ʃosɔ̃   le papijɔ̃

Les papillons couleur de neige
le pa pi jɔ̃ ku lœ rdə nɛ ʒə,

Volent par essaims sur la mer;
vɔ lə pa rɛ sɛ̃ sy rla mɛ r;

Beaux papillons blancs,
bo pa pi jɔ̃ blɑ̃,

quand pourrai-je Prendre le bleu chemin de l'air!
kɑ̃ pu rɛ ʒə prɑ̃ drə lə blø ʃə mɛ̃ də lɛ r!

Savez-vous, ô belle des belles,
sa ve vu, o bɛ lə de bɛ lə,

Ma bayadère aux yeux de jais,
ma ba ja dɛ ro zjø də ʒɛ,

S'ils me voulaient prêter leurs ailes,
si lmə vu lɛ prɛ te lœ rzɛ lə,

Dites, savez vous où j'irais?
di tə sa ve vu u ʒi rɛ?

Sans prendre un seul baiser aux roses,
sɑ̃ prɑ̃ drœ̃ sœ lbɛ ze o ro zə,

A travers vallons et forêts
a tra vɛ rva lɔ̃ ze fɔ rɛ,

J'irais à vos lèvres mi closes,
ʒi rɛ za vo lɛ vrə mi klo zə,

Fleur de mon âme, et j'y mourrais.
flœ rdə mɔ̃ nɑ mə, e ʒi mu rrɛ.

Chausson   Le Temps des lilas
ʃosɔ̃   lə tɑ̃ de lila

Le temps des lilas et le temps des roses
lə tɑ̃ de li la e lə tɑ̃ de ro zə

Ne reviendra plus à ce printemps-ci;
nə rə vjɛ̃ dra ply a sə prɛ̃ tɑ̃ si;

Le temps des lilas et le temps des roses
lə tɑ̃ de li la e lə tɑ̃ de ro zə

Est passé le temps des oeillets aussi.
ɛ pa se, lə tɑ̃ de zœ jɛ o si.

289

Le vent a changé, les cieux sont moroses,
lə vã a ʃã ʒe, le sjø sõ mo ro zə,

Et nous n'irons plus courir, et cueillir
e nu ni rõ ply ku ri r, e kœ ji r

Les lilas en fleur et les belles roses;
le li la zã flœ re le bɛ lə ro zə;

Le printemps est triste et ne peut fleurir.
lə prɛ̃ tã ɛ tri stə nə pø flœ ri r.

Oh! joyeux et doux printemps de l'année,
o ʒwa jø ze du prɛ̃ tã də la ne ə,

Qui vins, l'an passé, nous ensoleiller;
ki vɛ̃ lã pa se, nu zã sɔ lɛ je;

Notre fleur d'amour est si bien fanée.
nɔ trə flœ rda mu rɛ si bjɛ̃ fa ne ə.

Las! que ton baiser ne peut l'éveiller!
lɑs! kə tõ bɛ ze nə pø le vɛ je!

Et toi, que fais tu? pas de fleurs écloses,
e twa, kə fɛ ty? pa də flœ rze klo zə,

Point de gai soleil ni d'ombrages frais;
pwɛ̃ də ge sɔ lɛ jni dõ bra ʒə frɛ;

Le temps des lilas et le temps des roses
lə tã de li la e lə tã de ro zə,

Avec notre amour est mort à jamais.
a vɛ knɔ tra mu rɛ mɔ ra ʒa mɛ.

Debussy   Recit et Air de Lia from "L'Enfant Prodigue"
dəbysi   resi e ɛr də lia   l ãfã prɔdig

L'année en vain chasse l'année!
la ne ə ã vɛ̃ ʃa sə la ne ə!

A chaque saison ramenée,
a ʃa kə sɛ zõ ra mə ne ə,

Leurs jeux et leurs ébats m'attristent malgré moi;
lœ rʒø e lœ rze ba ma tri stə ma lgre mwa;

Ils rouvrent ma blessure et mon chagrin s'accroît...
i lru vrə ma blɛ sy rə, e mõ ʃa grɛ̃ sa krwa...

290

Je viens chercher la grève solitaire...
ʒə vjɛ̃ ʃɛ rʃe la grɛ və so li tɛ rə...

Douleur involontaire!   Efforts superflus!
du lœ rɛ̃ vɔ lɔ̃ tɛ rə!   ɛ fɔ rsy pɛ rfly!

Lia pleure toujours l'enfant qu'elle n'a plus!
li a, plœ rə tu ʒu r, lɑ̃ fɑ̃ kɛ lə na ply!

Azaël! Azaël!   Pourquoi m'as-tu quittée?
a za ɛ l! a za ɛ l! pu rkwa ma ty ki te ə?

En mon coeur maternel ton image est restée.
ɑ̃ mɔ̃ kœ rma tɛ rnɛ l, tɔ̃ ni ma ʒe rɛ ste.

Azaël! Azaël!   Pourquoi m'as-tu quittée?
a za ɛ l! a za ɛ l! pu rkwa ma ty ki te ə?

Cependant les soirs étaient doux,
sə pɑ̃ dɑ̃ le swa re tɛ du,

Dans la plaine d'ormes plantée,
dɑ̃ la plɛ nə dɔ rmə plɑ̃ te ə,

Quand, sous la charge récoltée,
kɑ̃ su la ʃa rʒə re kɔ lte ə,

On ramenait les grands boeufs roux.
ɔ̃ ra mə nɛ le grɑ̃ bø ru.

Lorsque la tâche était finie,
lɔ rskə la tɑ ʃe tɛ fi ni,

Enfants, vieillards et serviteurs,
ɑ̃ fɑ̃, vjɛ ja re sɛ rvi tœ r,

Ouvriers des champs ou pasteurs,
u vri je de ʃɑ̃ u pa stœ r,

Louaient, de Dieu la main bénie.
lu ɛ, də djø la mɛ̃ be ni ə,

Ainsi les jours suivaient les jours
ɛ̃ si le ʒu rsɥi vɛ le ʒu r

Et dans la pieuse famille,
e dɑ̃ la pi ø zə fa mi jə,

Le jeune homme et la jeune fille
lə ʒœ nɔ mə, e la ʒœ nə fi j

Echangeaient leurs chastes amours.
e ʃã ʒɛ lœ rʃa stə za mu r.

D'autres ne sentent pas le poids de la vieillesse;
do trə nə sã tə pa lə pwa, də la vjɛ jɛ sə;

Heureux dans leurs enfants,
ø rø dã lœ rzã fã,

Ils voient couler les ans
i lvwa ku le le zã

sans regret comme sans tristesse...
sã rə grɛ kɔ mə sã tri stɛ sə...

Aux coeurs inconsolés que les temps sont pesants!...
o kœ rɛ̃ kõ sɔ le, kə le tã sõ pə zã!...

Azaël! Azaël! Pourquoi m'as-tu quittée?
a za ɛ l! a za ɛ l! pu rkwa ma ty ki te ə?

Debussy   Beau soir
dəbysi   bo swar

Lorsque au soleil couchant les rivières sont roses,
lɔ rsko sɔ lɛ jku ʃã, le ri vjɛ rə sõ ro zə,

Et qu'un tiède frisson court sur les champs de blé.
e kœ̃ tjɛ də fri sõ ku rsy rle ʃã də ble.

Un conseil d'être heureux semble sortir des choses
œ̃ kõ sɛ jdɛ trø rø sã blə sɔ rti rde ʃo zə

Et monter vers le coeur troublé
e mõ te vɛ rlə kœ rtru ble

Un conseil de goûter le charme d'être au monde
œ̃ kõ sɛ jdə gu te lə ʃa rmə dɛ tro mõ də

Cependant qu'on est jeune et que le soir est beau,
sə pã dã kõ nɛ ʒœ ne kə lə swa rɛ bo,

Car nous nous en allons, Comme s'en va cette onde;
ka rnu nu zã na lõ, kɔ mə sã va sɛ tõ də;

Elle à la mer, Nous au tombeau.
ɛ la la mɛ r, nu o tõ bo

Debussy   C'est l'Extase
dəbysi   sɛ l ekstɑz

C'est l'extase langoureuse
sɛ lɛ kstɑ zə lɑ̃ gu rø zə

C'est la fatigue amoureuse
sɛ la fa ti ga mu rø zə

C'est tous les frissons des bois
sɛ tu le fri sɔ̃ de bwa

Parmi l'étreinte des brises
pa rmi le trɛ̃ tə de bri zə

C'est, vers les ramures grises,
sɛ, vɛ rle ra my rə gri zə,

Le chœur des petites voix.
lə kœ rde pə ti tə vwa.

O le frêle et frais murmure
o lə frɛ le frɛ my rmy rə

Cela gazouille et susurre,
sə la ga zu je sy sy rə,

Cela ressemble au cri doux.
sə la rə sɑ̃ blo kri du.

que l'herbe agitée expire.
kə lɛ rba ʒi te ɛ kspi rə.

Tu dirais, sous l'eau qui vire
ty di rɛ, su lo ki vi rə

Le roulis sourd des cailloux.
lə ru li su rde ka ju.

Cette âme qui se lamente
sɛ tɑ mə ki sə la mɑ̃ tə

En cette plainte dormante
ɑ̃ sɛ tə plɛ̃ tə dɔ rmɑ̃ tə

C'est la nôtre, n'est-ce pas?
sɛ la no trə, nɛ sə pa?

La mienne, dis, et la tienne
la mjɛ nə, di, e la tjɛ nə

Dont s'exhale l'humble antienne
dɔ̃ sɛ gza lə lœ̃ blɑ̃ tjɛ nə

Par ce tiède soir, tout bas.
pa rsə tjɛ də swa r, tu bɑ.

293

Debussy   Chevaux de bois
dəbysi   ʃəvo d bwa

Tournez, tournez, bons chevaux de bois
tu rne, tu rne, bɔ̃ ʃə vo də bwa

Tournez, cent tours, tournez mille tours
tu rne sɑ̃ tu r, tu rne mi lə tu r

Tournez souvent et tournez toujours
tu rne su vɑ̃ e tu rne tu ʒu r

Tournez tournez au son des hautbois.
tu rne tu rne o sɔ̃ de o bwa.

L'enfant tout rouge et la mère blanche
lɑ̃ fɑ̃ tu ru ʒə, e la mɛ rə blɑ ʃə

Le gars en noir et la fille en rose
lə gɑ ɑ̃ nwa re la fi jɑ̃ ro zə

L'une à la chose et l'autre à la pose,
ly na la ʃo ze lo tra la po zə,

Chacun se paie un sou de dimanche
ʃa kœ̃ sə pɛ œ̃ su də di mɑ̃ ʃə

Tournez, tournez, chevaux de leur coeur,
tu rne, tu rne, ʃə vo də lœ rkœ r,

Tandis qu'autour de tous vos tournois
tɑ̃ di ko tu rdə tu vo tu rnwa

Clignote l'oeil du filou sournois
kli ɲo tə lœ jdy fi lu su rnwa

Tournez au son du piston vainqueur!
tu rne o sɔ̃ dy pi stɔ̃ vɛ̃ kœ r!

C'est étonnant comme ça vous soûle
sɛ te tɔ nɑ̃ kɔ mə sa vu su lə

D'aller ainsi dans ce cirque bête:
da le ɛ̃ si dɑ̃ sə si rkə bɛ tə:

Rien dans le ventre et mal dans la tête,
rjɛ̃ dɑ̃ lə vɑ̃ tre ma ldɑ̃ la tɛ tə,

Du mal en masse et du bien en foule
dy ma lɑ̃ ma se dy bjɛ̃ ɑ̃ fu lə

Tournez dadas, sans qu'il soit besoin
tu rne da da, sɑ̃ ki lswa bə zwɛ̃

D'user jamais de nuls éperons
dy ze ʒa me də ny lze pə rɔ̃

294

Pour commander à vos galops ronds.
pu rkɔ mã de, a vo ga lo rɔ̃,

Tournez, tournez, sans espoir de foin
tu rne, tu rne, sã zɛ spwa rdə fwɛ̃

Et dépêchez, chevaux de leur âme
e de pe ʃe, ʃə vo də lœ ra mə

Déjà voici que sonne à la soupe
de ʒa vwa si kə sɔ na la su pə

La nuit qui tombe et chasse la troupe
la nɥi ki tɔ̃ be ʃa sə la tru pə

De gais buveurs que leur soif affame.
də gɛ by vœ rkə lœ rswa fa fa mə.

Tournez, tournez! Le ciel en velours
tu rne, tu rne! lə sjɛ lã və lu r

D'astres en or se vêt lentement,
da strə zã nɔ rsə vɛ lã tə mã,

L'Eglise tinte un glas tristement.
le gli zə tɛ̃ tœ̃ gla tri stə mã.

Tournez au son joyeux des tambours, tournez.
tu rne o sɔ̃ ʒwa jø de tã bu r, tu rne.

Debussy   Clair de lune
dəbysi   klɛr də lyn

Votre âme est un paysage choisi
vɔ tra mɛ tœ̃ pe i za ʒə ʃwa zi

Que vont charmants masques et bergamasques
kə vɔ̃ ʃa rmã ma skə ze bɛ rga ma skə

Jouant du luth et dansant et quasi
ʒu ã dy ly te dã sã, e ka zi

tristes sous leurs déguisements fantasques,
tri stə, su lœ rde gi zə mã fã ta skə,

Tout en chantant sur le mode mineur
tu tã ʃã tã sy rlə mo də mi nœ r

L'amour vainqueur et la vie opportune,
la mu rvɛ̃ kœ re la vi ɔ pɔ rty nə,

Ils n'ont pas l'air de croire à leur bonheur,
i lnɔ̃ pa lɛ rdə krwa ra lœ rbɔ nœ r,

Et leur chanson se mêle au clair de lune,
e lœ rʃɑ̃ sɔ̃ sə mɛ lo klɛ rdə ly nə,

Au calme clair de lune triste et beau,
o ka lmə klɛ rdə ly nə, tri ste bo,

Qui fait rêver les oiseaux dans les arbres
ki fɛ rɛ ve le zwa zo dɑ̃ le za rbrə

Et sangloter d'extase les jets d'eau
e sɑ̃ glɔ te dɛ ksta zə le ʒɛ do

Les grands jets d'eau sveltes parmi les marbres.
le grɑ̃ ʒɛ do svɛ ltə pa rmi le ma rbrə.

Debussy   De Fleurs (Proses Lyriques)
dəbysi   də flœr   proz lirik

Dans l'ennui si désolément vert de la serre de douleur,
dɑ̃ lɑ̃ nɥi, si de zɔ le mɑ̃ vɛ r də la sɛ rə də du lœ r,

les Fleurs enlacent mon coeur de leurs tiges méchantes.
le flœ rzɑ̃ la sə mɔ̃ kœ r, də lœ rti ʒə me ʃɑ̃ tə.

Ah! quand reviendront autour de ma tête les chères mains
ɑ kɑ̃ rə vjɛ̃ drɔ̃ o tu rdə ma tɛ tə, le ʃɛ rə mɛ̃

si tendrement désenlaceuses?
si tɑ̃ drə mɑ̃ de zɑ̃ la sø zə?

Les grand Iris violets violèrent méchamment tes yeux,
le grɑ̃ di ri svjɔ le, vjɔ lɛ rə me ʃa mɑ̃ te zjø,

en semblant les refléter, Eux, qui furent l'eau du songe
ɑ̃ sɑ̃ blɑ̃ le rə fle te, ø ki fy rə lo dy sɔ̃ ʒə

où plongèrent mes rêves
u plɔ̃ ʒɛ rə me rɛ və,

si doucement enclos en leur couleur;
si du sə mɑ̃ tɑ̃ klo ɑ̃ lœ rku lœ r;

Et les lys, blancs jets d'eau de pistils embaumés,
e le li s, blɑ̃ ʒe do də pi sti lɑ̃ bo me,

ont perdu leur grâce blanche
ɔ̃ pɛ rdy lœ rgrɑ sə blɑ̃ ʃə

296

Et ne sont plus que pauvres malades sans soleil!
e nə sõ ply kə po vrə ma la də sã sɔ lɛ j!

Soleil! ami des fleurs mauvaises,
sɔ lɛ j! a mi de flœ rm vɛ zə,

Tueur de rêves! Tueur d'illusions ce pain béni
ty œ rdə rɛ və! ty œ rdi ly zjõ, sə pɛ̃ be ni

des âmes misérables!   Venez!
de zɑ mə mi ze ra blə! və ne!

Les mains salvatrices Brisez les vitres de mensonge,
le mɛ̃ sa lva tri sə, bri ze le vi trə də mã sõ ʒə,

Brisez les vitres de maléfice, mon âme meurt de
bri ze le vi trə də ma le fi sə, mõ nɑ mə mœ rdə

trop de soleil!   Mirages!
trɔ də sɔ lɛ j!   mi ra ʒə!

Plus ne refleurira la joie de mes yeux
ply nə rə flœ ri ra la ʒwa də me zjø

Et mes mains sont lasses de prier,
e me mɛ̃ sõ lɑ sə də pri je,

Mes yeux sont las de pleurer!
me zjø sõ lɑ də plœ re!

Eternellement ce bruit fou des pétales noirs
e tɛ rnɛ lə mã, sə brɥi fu de pe ta lə nwa r

de l'ennui tombant goutte à goutte sur ma tête
də lã nɥi tõ bã gu ta gu tə, sy rma tɛ tə

Dans le vert de la serre de douleur!
dã lə vɛ rdə la sɛ rə də du lœ r!

Debussy   De Grève (Proses Lyriques)
dəbysi   də grɛv   proz lirik

Sur la mer les crépuscules tombent,
sy rla mɛ rle kre py sky lə tõ bə,

Soie blanche effilée.
swa blã ʃe fi le ə.

Les vagues comme de petites folles Jasent,
le va gə kɔ mə də pə ti tə fɔ lə ʒɑ zə,

petites filles sortant de l'école,
pə ti tə fi jə sɔ rtɑ̃ də le kɔ lə,

Parmi les froufrous de leur robe,
pa rmi le fru fru də lœ rrɔ bə,

Soie verte irisée!
swa vɛ rti ri ze ə!

Les nuages, graves voyageurs,
le ny a ʒə, grɑ və vwa ja ʒœ r,

se concertent sur le prochain orage,
sə kɔ̃ sɛ rtə sy rlə prɔ ʃɛ nɔ ra ʒə,

Et c'est un fond vraiment trop grave
e sɛ tœ̃ fɔ̃ vrɛ mɑ̃ trɔ grɑ və

à cette anglaise aquarelle.
a sɛ tɑ̃ glɛ za kwa rɛ lə.

Les vagues, les petites vagues,
le va gə, le pe ti tə va gə,

ne savent plus où se mettre,
nə sa və ply u sə mɛ trə.

car voici la méchante averse,
ka rvwa si la me ʃɑ̃ ta vɛ rsə,

Frou frous de jupes envolées,
fru fru də ʒy pə zɑ̃ vɔ le ə,

Soie verte affolée.
swa vɛ rta fɔ le ə.

Mais la lune, compatissante à tous!
mɛ la ly nə, kɔ̃ pa ti sɑ̃ ta tu s!

Vient apaiser ce gris conflit
vjɛ̃ ta pɛ ze sə gri kɔ̃ fli

Et caresse lentement ses petites amies
e ka rɛ sə lɑ̃ tə mɑ̃ se pə ti tə za mi

qui s'offrent comme lèvres aimantes
ki sɔ frə kɔ mə lɛ vrə zɛ mɑ̃ tə

A ce tiède et blanc baiser.
a sə tjɛ de de blɑ̃ bɛ ze.

Puis, Plus rien Plus que les cloches attardées
pɥi, ply rjɛ̃, ply kə le klɔ ʃə za ta rde ə

des flottantes églises!
de flɔ tɑ̃ tə ze gli zə!

Angélus des vagues, Soie blanche apaisée!
ã ʒe ly sde va gə, swa blã ʃa pɛ ze ə!

Debussy   De Rêve (Proses Lyriques)
dəbysi   də rɛv   proz lirik

La nuit a des douceurs de femme
la nɥi a de du sœ rdə ʃa mə

Et les vieux arbes, sous la lune d'or, Songent!
e le vjø za rbrə su la ly nə dɔ r, sõ ʒə!

A Celle qui vient de passer la tête emperlée,
a sɛ lə ki vjɛ̃ də pa se, la tɛ tã pɛ rle ə,

Maintenant navrée, à jamais navrée,
mɛ̃ tə nã na vre ə, a ʒa mɛ na vre ə,

Ils n'ont pas su lui faire signe.
i lnõ pa sy lɥi fɛ rə si ɲə.

Toutes! Elles ont passé: les Frêles, les Folles,
tu tə!   ɛ lə zõ pɑ se, le frɛ lə, le fɔ lə,

Semant leur rire au gazon grêle, aux brises frôleuses
sə mã lœ rri ro ga zõ grɛ lə, o bri zə fro lø zə

la caresse charmeuse des hanches fleurissantes.
la ka rɛ sə ʃa rmø zə, de ã ʃə flœ ri sã tə.

Hélas! de tout ceci, plus rien qu'un blanc frisson.
e la s, də tu sə si, ply rjɛ̃ kœ̃ blã fri sõ.

Les vieux arbres sous la lune d'or pleurent
le vjø za rbrə su la ly nə dɔ r, plœ rə

leurs belles feuilles d'or!
lœ rbɛ lə fœ jə dɔ r!

Nul ne leur dédiera plus la fierté
ny lnə lœ rde di ra ply, la fjɛ rte

des casques d'or
de ka skə dɔ r

Maintenant ternis, à jamais ternis.
mɛ̃ tə nã tɛ rni, a ʒa mɛ tɛ rni.

Les chevaliers sont morts Sur le chemin du Grâal!
le ʃə va lje sõ mɔ r, sy rlə ʃə mɛ̃ dy grɑ l!

La nuit a des douceurs de femme, Das mains semblent
la nɥi a de du sœ rdə fa mə, de mɛ̃, sɑ̃ blə

frôler les âmes, mains si folles, si frêles,
fro le le zɑ mə, mɛ̃ si fɔ lə, si frɛ lə,

Au temps où les épées chantaient pour Elles!
o tɑ̃ u le ze pe ə, ʃɑ̃ tɛ pu rɛ lə!

D'étranges soupirs s'élèvent sous les arbres.
de trɑ̃ ʒə su pi r, se lɛ və su le zɑ rbrə.

Mon âme c'est du rêve ancien qui t'étreint!
mɔ̃ nɑ mə sɛ dy rɛ vɑ̃ sjɛ̃, ki te trɛ̃!

Debussy   De Soir (Proses Lyriques)
dəbysi   də swar   proz lirik

Diamanche sur les villes, Dimanche dans les coeurs!
di mɑ̃ ʃə sy rle vi lə, di mɑ̃ ʃə dɑ̃ le kœ r!

Diamanche chez les petites filles chantant
di mɑ̃ ʃə ʃe le pə ti tə fi jə ʃɑ̃ tɑ̃

d'une voix informée des rondes obstinées
dy nə vwa ɛ̃ fɔ rme, de rɔ̃ də zo psti ne ə

ou de bonnes Tours n'en ont plus que pour quelques jours!
u də bɔ nə tu r, nɑ̃ nɔ̃ ply kə pu rkɛ lkə ʒu r!

Dimanche, les gares sont folles!
di mɑ̃ ʃə, le ga rə sɔ̃ fɔ lə!

Tout le monde appareille pour des banlieues d'aventure
tu lə mɔ̃ da pa rɛ jə, pu rde bɑ̃ ljø da vɑ̃ ty rə

en se disant adieu avec des gestes éperdus!
ɑ̃ sə di zɑ̃ a djø, a vɛ kde ʒɛ stə ze pɛ rdy!

Dimanche les trains vont vite,
di mɑ̃ ʃə, le trɛ̃ vɔ̃ vi tə,

dévorés par d'insatiables tunnels;
de vɔ re pa rdɛ̃ sa sja blə ty nɛ l;

Et les bons signaux des routes échangent d'un oeil unique
e le bɔ̃ si ɲo de ru tə, e ʃɑ̃ ʒə dœ̃ nœ jy ni kə

des impressions toutes mécaniques.
de zɛ̃ prɛ si jɔ̃, tu tə me ka ni kə.

300

Dimanche, dans le bleu de mes rêves
di mã ʃə, dã lə blø də me rɛ və

Où mes pensées tristes de feux d'artifices manqués
u me pã se tri stə, də fø da rti fi sə mã ke

Ne veulent plus quitter le deuil
nə vœ lə ply ki te lə dœ j

de vieux Dimanches trépassés.
de vjø di mã ʃə, tre pa se.

Et la nuit à pas de velours vient endormir
e la nɥi a pɑ də və lu r, vjɛ̃ tã dɔ rmi r

le beau ciel fatigué, et c'est Dimanche
lə bo sjɛ lfa ti ge, e sɛ di mã ʃə,

dans les avenues d'étoiles;
dã le za və ny de twa lə;

la Vierge or sur argent
la vjɛ rʒə ɔ rsy ra rʒã

laisse tomber les fleurs de sommeil!
lɛ sə tõ be, le flœ rdə so mɛ j!

Vite, les petits anges Dépassez les hirondelles
vi tə, le pə ti zã ʒə, de pa se le zi rõ dɛ lə,

afin de vous coucher forts d'absolution!
a fɛ̃ də vu ku ʃe, fɔ rda pso ly si jõ!

Prenez pitié des villes, Prenez pitié des coeurs,
prə ne pi tje de vi lə, prə ne pi tje de kœ r,

Vous, la Vierge or sur argent!
vu la vjɛ rʒə, ɔ rsy ra rʒã!

Debussy   En sourdine
dəbysi   ã surdin

Calmes dans le demi—jour
ka lmə dã lə də mi ʒu r

Que les branches hautes font,
kə le brã ʃə o tə fõ,

Pénétrons bien notre amour
pe ne trõ bjɛ̃ no tra mu r

301

De ce silence profond.
də sə si lɑ̃ sə prɔ fɔ̃.

Fondons nos âmes, nos coeurs
fɔ̃ dɔ̃ no zɑ mə, no kœ r

et nos sens extasiés,
e no sɑ̃ sɛ ksta zi e,

Parmi les vagues langueurs
pa rmi le va gə lɑ̃ gœ r

Des pins et des arbousiers.
de pɛ̃ e de za rbu zje.

Ferme tes yeux à demi,
fɛ rmə te zjø a də mi,

Croise tes bras sur ton sein,
krwa zə te bra sy rtɔ̃ sɛ̃,

Et de ton coeur endormi
e də tɔ̃ kœ rɑ̃ dɔ rmi

Chasse à jamais tout dessein.
ʃa sa ʒa mɛ tu dɛ sɛ̃.

Laissons-nous persuader
lɛ sɔ̃ nu pɛ rsy a de

Au souffle berceur et doux
o su flə bɛ rsœ re du

Qui vient à tes pieds rider
ki vjɛ̃ a te pje ri de

Les ondes de gazon roux.
le zɔ̃ də də ga zɔ̃ ru.

Et quand solennel, le soir,
e kɑ̃ sɔ la nɛ llə swa r,

Des chênes noirs tombera,
de ʃɛ nə nwa rtɔ̃ bə ra,

Voix de notre désespoir,
vwa də no trə de zɛ spwa r,

Le rossignol chantera.
lə rɔ si ɲɔ lʃɑ̃ tə ra.

Debussy   Fantoches
dəbysi   fãtoʃ

Scaramouche et Pulcinella
ska ra mu ʃe py lsi nɛ la

Qu'un mauvais dessein rassembla
kœ̃ mɔ vɛ dɛ sɛ̃ ra sã bla

Gesticulent noirs sous la lune. la la la...
ʒɛ sti ky lə nwa rsu la ly nə. la la la...

Cependant l'excellent docteur Bolonais
sə pã dã lɛ ksɛ lã dɔ ktœ rbɔ lɔ nɛ

Cueille avec lenteur des simples
kœ ja vɛ klã tœ rde sɛ̃ plə

Parmi l'herbe brune.
pa rmi lɛ rbə bry nə.

Lors sa fille, piquant minois
lɔ rsa fi jə, pi kã mi nwa

Sous la charmille, en tapinois,
su la ʃa rmi jə, ã ta pi nwa,

Se glisse demi—nue la la la
sə gli sə də mi ny ə la la lą

En quête de son beau pirate espagnol,
ã kɛ tə də sõ bo pi ra tɛ spa ɲo l,

Dont un amoureux rossignol
dõ tœ̃ na mu rø rɔ si ɲo l

Clame la détresse à tue—tête.
kla mə la de trɛ sa ty tɛ tə.

Debussy   Green
dəbysi   grin

Voici des fruits, des fleurs, des feuilles et des branches,
vwa si de frɥi, de flœ r, de fœ jə ze de brã ʃə,

Et puis voici mon coeur, qui ne bat que pour vous;
e pɥi vwa si mõ kœ r, ki nə ba kə pu rvu;

Ne le déchirez pas avec vos deux mains blanches,
nə lə de ʃi re pa, a vɛ kvo dø mɛ̃ blã ʃə,

Et qu'à vos yeux si beaux l'humble présent soit doux.
e ka vo zjø si bo, lœ̃ blə pre zã swa du.

303

J'arrive tout couvert encore de rosée
ʒa ri və tu ku vɛ rɑ̃ ko rə də ro ze ə

Que le vent du matin vient glacer à mon front,
kə lə vɑ̃ dy ma tɛ̃ vjɛ̃ gla se à mɔ̃ frɔ̃,

Souffrez que ma fatigue à vos pieds reposée
su fre kə ma fa ti gə, a vo pje rə po ze ə

Rêve des chers instants qui la délasseront.
rɛ və de ʃɛ rzɛ̃ stɑ̃ ki la de lɑ sə rɔ̃.

Sur votre jeune sein, laissez rouler ma tête.
sy rvɔ trə ʒœ nə sɛ̃, lɛ se ru le ma tɛ tə.

Toute sonore encore de vos derniers baisers.
tu tə sɔ nɔ rɑ̃ ko rə, də vo dɛ rnje bɛ ze.

Laissez-la s'apaiser de la bonne tempête,
lɛ se la sa pɛ ze də la bo nə tɑ̃ pɛ tə,

Et que je dorme un peu puisque vous reposez.
e kə ʒə dɔ rmœ̃ pø, pɥi skə vu rə po ze.

Debussy   Harmonie du soir
dəbysi   armoni dy swar

Voici venir les temps où vibrant sur sa tige
vwa si və ni rle tɑ̃ u vi brɑ̃ sy rsa ti ʒə

Chaque fleur s'évapore ainsi qu'un encensoir;
ʃa kə flœ rse va pɔ rɛ̃ si kœ̃ nɑ̃ sɑ̃ swa r;

Les sons et les parfums tournent dans l'air du soir;
le sɔ̃ ze le pa rfœ̃ tu rnə dɑ̃ lɛ rdy swa r;

Valse mélancolique et langoureux vertige,
va lsə me lɑ̃ kɔ li ke lɑ̃ gu rø vɛ rti ʒə,

Chaque fleur s'évapore ainsi qu'un encensoir;
ʃa kə flœ rse va pɔ rɛ̃ si kœ̃ nɑ̃ sɑ̃ swa r;

Le violon frémit comme un coeur qu'on afflige,
lə vi o lɔ̃ fre mi kɔ mœ̃ kœ rkɔ̃ na fli ʒə,

Valse mélancolique et langoureux vertige,
va lsə me lɑ̃ kɔ li ke lɑ̃ gu rø vɛ rti ʒə,

Le ciel est triste et beau comme un grand reposoir
lə sjɛ lɛ tri ste bo kɔ mœ̃ grɑ̃ rə po zwa r   .

304

Le violon frémit comme un coeur qu'on afflige;
lə vi o lɔ̃ fre mi ko mœ̃ kœ rkɔ̃ na fli ʒə;

Un coeur tendre, qui hait le néant vaste et noir!
œ̃ kœ rtɑ̃ drə, ki ɛ lə ne ɑ̃ va ste nwa r!

Le ciel est triste et beau comme un grand reposoir;
lə sjɛ lɛ tri ste bo kɔ mœ̃ grɑ̃ rə po zwa r;

Le soleil s'est noyé dans son sang qui se fige...
lə so lɛ jsɛ nwa je dɑ̃ sɔ̃ sɑ̃ ki sə fi ʒə...

Un coeur tendre, qui hait le néant vaste et noir,
œ̃ kœ rtɑ̃ drə, ki ɛ lə ne ɑ̃ va ste nwa r,

Du passé lumineux recueille tout vestige
dy pa se ly mi nø rə kœ jə tu vɛ .sti ʒə

Le soleil s'est noyé dans son sang qui se fige
lə so lɛ jsɛ nwa je dɑ̃ sɔ̃ sɑ̃ ki sə fi ʒə

Ton souvenir en moi luit comme un ostensoir.
tɔ̃ su və ni rɑ̃ mwa lɥi, ko mœ̃ no stɑ̃ swa r.

Debussy   Il pleure dans mon coeur
debysi   il plœr dɑ̃ mɔ̃ kœr

Il pleure dans mon coeur
i lplœ rə dɑ̃ mɔ̃ kœ r

comme il pleut sur la ville.
kɔ mi lplø sy rla vi lə.

Quelle est cette langueur
kɛ lɛ sɛ tə lɑ̃ gœ r

Qui pénètre mon coeur?
ki pe nɛ trə mɔ̃ kœ r?

O bruit doux de la pluie
o brɥi du də la plɥi ə

Par terre et sur les toits!
pa rtɛ re sy rle twa!

Pour un coeur qui s'ennuie
pu rœ̃ kœ rki sɑ̃ nɥi ə

O le bruit de la pluie!
o lə brɥi də la plɥi!

Il pleure sans raison
i lpœ rə sɑ̃ rɛ zɔ̃

Dans ce coeur qui s'écoeure.
dɑ̃ sə kœ rki se kœ rə.

Quoi! nulle trahison?
kwa! ny lə tra i zɔ̃?

Ce deuil est sans raison.
sə dœ j ɛ sɑ̃ rɛ zɔ̃.

C'est bien la pire peine
sɛ bjɛ̃ la pi rə pɛ nə

De ne savoir pourquoi,
də nə sa vwa rpu rkwa,

sans amour et sans haine,
sɑ̃ za mu re sɑ̃ ɛ nə,

Mon coeur a tant de peine.
mɔ̃ kœ ra tɑ̃ də pɛ nə.

Debussy   L'échelonnement des haies
dəbysi   l eʃlɔnmɑ̃ de ɛ

L'échelonnement des haies
le ʃə lɔ nə mɑ̃ de ɛ

Moutonne à l'infini, mer
mu tɔ na lɛ̃ fi ni, mɛ r

Claire dans le brouillard clair
klɛ rə dɑ̃ lə bru ja rklɛ r

Qui sent bon les jeunes baies.
ki sɑ̃ bɔ̃ le ʒœ nə bɛ.

Des arbres et des moulins
de za rbrə ze de mu lɛ̃

Sont légers sur le vert tendre
sɔ̃ le ʒe sy rlə vɛ rtɑ̃ drə

Où vient s'ébattre et s'étendre
u vjɛ̃ se ba tre se tɑ̃ drə

L'agilité des poulains.
la ʒi li te de pu lɛ̃.

Dans ce vague d'un Dimanche
dã sə va gə dœ̃ di mã ʃə

Voici se jouer aussi
vwa si sə ʒu e o si,

De grandes brebis aussi
də grã də brə bi o si

Douces que leur laine blanche.
du sə kə lœ rlɛ nə blã ʃə.

Tout à l'heure déferlait
tu ta lœ rə de fɛ rlɛ

L'onde roulée en volutes
lɔ̃ də, ru le ə ã vo ly tə

De cloches comme des flûtes
də klɔ ʃə kɔ mə de fly tə

Dans le ciel comme du lait.
dã lə sjɛ l, kɔ mə dy lɛ.

Debussy   Les cloches
dəbysi   le klɔʃ

Les feuilles s'ouvraient sur le bord des branches,
le fœ jə su vrɛ sy r lə bo rde brã ʃə,

Délicatement,
de li ka tə mã,

Les cloches tintaient, légères et franches,
le klɔ ʃə tɛ̃ tɛ le ʒɛ rə ze frã ʃə,

Dans le ciel clément.
dã lə sjɛ lkle mã.

Rythmique et fervent comme une antienne,
ri tmi ke fɛ rvã kɔ my nã ti ɛ nə,

Ce lointain appel
sə lwɛ̃ tɛ na pɛ l

Me remémorait la blancheur chrétienne,
mə rə me mɔ rɛ la blã ʃœ rkre tjɛ nə,

Des fleurs de l'autel.
de flœ rdə lo tɛ l.

307

Ces cloches parlaient d'heureuses années,
se klɔ ʃə pa rlɛ dø rø zə za ne ə,

Et dans le grand bois
e dɑ̃ lə grɑ̃ bwa

Semblaient reverdir les feuilles fanées
sɑ̃ blɛ rə vɛ rdi rle fœ jə fa ne ə,

Des jours d'autrefois.
de ʒu rdo trə fwa.

Debussy   L'ombre des arbres
dəbysi   l ɔ̃brə de zarbr

L'ombre des arbres dans la rivière embrumée
lɔ̃ brə de za rbrə dɑ̃ la ri vjɛ rɑ̃ bry me ə,

Meurt comme de la fumée,
mœ rkɔ mə də la fy me ə,

Tandis qu'en l'air, parmi les ramures réelles
tɑ̃ di kɑ̃ lɛ r, pa rmi le ra my rə re ɛ lə,

Se plaignent les tourterelles
sə plɛ ɲə le tu rtə rɛ lə,

Combien ô voyageur, ce paysage blême
kɔ̃ bjɛ̃, o vwa ja ʒœ r, sə pe i za ʒə blɛ mə,

Te mira blême toi—même
tə mi ra blɛ mə twa mɛ mə,

Et que tristes pleuraient dans les hautes feuillées,
e kə tri stə plœ rɛ dɑ̃ le o tə fœ je ə,

Tes espérances noyées.
te zɛ spe rɑ̃ sə, nwa je ə.

Debussy   Mandoline
dəbysi   mɑ̃dɔlin

Les donneurs de sérénades
le dɔ nœ rdə se re na də,

Et les belles écouteuses
e le bɛ lə ze ku tø zə,

308

Echangent des propos fades
e ʃɑ̃ ʒə de prɔ po fa də

Sous les ramures chanteuses.
su le ra my rə ʃɑ̃ tø zə.

C'est Tircis et c'est Aminte,
sɛ ti rsi se sɛ ta mɛ̃ tə,

Et c'est l'éternel Clitandre,
e sɛ le tɛ rnɛ lkli tɑ̃ drə,

Et c'est Damis qui pour mainte
e sɛ da mi ski pu rmɛ̃ tə

Cruelle fait maint vers tendre.
kry ɛ lə fɛ mɛ̃ vɛ rtɑ̃ drə.

Leurs courtes vestes de soie,
lœ rku rtə vɛ stə də swa,

Leurs longues robes à queues,
lœ rlɔ̃ gə ro bə za kø,

Leur élégance, leur joie
lœ re le gɑ̃ sə, lœ rʒwa

Et leurs molles ombres bleues,
e lœ rmɔ lə zɔ̃ brə blø,

Tourbillonnent dans l'extase
tu rbi jɔ nə dɑ̃ lɛ ksta zə,

D'une lune rose et grise,
dy nə ly nə ro ze gri zə,

Et la mandoline jase,
e la mɑ̃ dɔ li nə ʒa zə

parmi les frissons de brise La, la...
pa rmi le fri sɔ̃ də bri zə la, la...

Debussy   Nuit d'étoiles
dəbysi   nɥi d etwal

Nuit d'étoiles sous tes voiles,
nɥi de twa lə, su te vwa lə,

Sous ta brise et tes parfums,
su ta bri ze te pa rfœ̃,

Triste lyre qui soupire,
tri stə li rə, ki su pi rə,

Je rêve aux amours défunts.
ʒə rɛ vo za mu rde fœ̃.

La sereine mélancolie
la sə rɛ nə me lɑ̃ kɔ li ə

Vient éclore au fond de mon coeur,
vjɛ̃ te klɔ ro fɔ̃ də mɔ̃ kœ r,

Et j'entends l'âme de ma mie
e ʒɑ̃ tɑ̃, la mə də ma mi ə

Tressaillir dans le bois rêveur.
trɛ sa ji rdɑ̃ lə bwa rɛ vœ r.

Je revois à notre fontaine
ʒə rə vwa za nɔ trə fɔ̃ tɛ nə

Tes regards bleus comme les cieux,
te rə ga rblø kɔ mə le sjø,

Cette rose, c'est ton haleine,
sɛ tə ro zə, sɛ tɔ̃ na lɛ nə,

Et ces étoiles sont tes yeux.
e sɛ ze twa lə sɔ̃ te zjø.

Debussy   Romance
dəbysi   rɔmɑ̃s

L'âme évaporée et souffrante,
la me va pɔ re e su frɑ̃ tə,

L'âme douce, l'âme odorante,
la mə du sə, la mɔ dɔ rɑ̃ tə,

Des lis divins que j'ai cueillis
de li sdi vɛ̃, kə ʒe kœ ji

Dans le jardin de ta pensée,
dɑ̃ lə ʒa rdɛ̃, də ta pɑ̃ se,

Où donc les vents l'ont-ils chassée,
u dɔ̃ kle vɑ̃ lɔ̃ ti lʃa se,

Cette âme adorable des lis?
sɛ ta ma dɔ ra blə de li s?

N'est-il plus un parfum qui reste
nɛ ti lply zœ̃ pa rfœ̃ ki rɛ stə

De la suavité céleste,
də la sy a vi te se lɛ stə,

Des jours où tu m'enveloppais
de ʒu ru ty mɑ̃ və lɔ pɛ,

D'une vapeur surnaturelle,
dy nə va pœ rsy rna ty rɛ lə,

Faite d'espoir, d'amour fidèle,
fɛ tə dɛ spwa r, da mu rfi dɛ lə,

De béatitude et de paix?
də be a ti ty d, e də pɛ?

Debussy   Spleen
dəbysi   splin

Les roses étaient toutes rouges,
le ro zə ze tɛ tu tə ru ʒə,

Et les lierres étaient tout noirs.
e le ljɛ rə ze tɛ tu nwa r.

Chère, pour peu que tu te bouges,
ʃɛ rə, pu rpø kə ty tə bu ʒə,

Renaissent tous mes désespoirs.
rə nɛ sə tu me de zɛ spwa r.

Le ciel était trop bleu, trop tendre,
lə sjɛ le tɛ tro blø tro tɑ̃ drə,

La mer trop verte et l'air trop doux.
la mɛ rtro vɛ rte lɛ rtro du.

Je crains toujours, ce qu'est d'attendre!
ʒə krɛ̃ tu ʒu r, sə kɛ da tɑ̃ drə!

Quelque fuite atroce de vous.
kɛ lkə fɥi ta tro sə də vu.

Du houx à la feuille vernie
dy u a la fœ jə vɛ rni,

Et du luisant buis je suis las
e dy lɥi zɑ̃ bɥi ʒə sɥi lɑ,

Et de la campagne infinie,
e də la kã pa ɲɛ̃ fi ni ə,

Et de tout, fors de vous. Hélas!
e də tu, fɔ rdə vu. e lɑ!
   (s not pronounced here, archaic
      to rime with <u>las</u>.)

Delibes   Bell Song, from "Lakmé"
dəlib   lakme

Ah, Où va la jeune Indoue, Fille des Parias,
a u va la ʒœ nɛ̃ du ə, fi jə de pa ri ja,

Quand la lune se joue dans les grands mimosas?
kã la ly nə sə ʒu ə, dã le grã mi mo za?

Elle court sur la mousse et ne se souvient pas
ɛ lə ku rsy rla mu sə, e nə sə su vjɛ̃ pa,

Que partout on repousse l'enfant des Parias.
kə pa rtu õ rə pu sə, lã fã de pa ri ja.

Le long des lauriers roses, Rêvant de douces choses,
lə lõ de lɔ rje ro zə, rɛ vã də du sə ʃo zə,

Ah! Elle passe sans bruit Et riant à la nuit!
a ɛ lə pɑ sə sã brɥi, e ri jã ta la nɥi!

Là–bas dans la forêt plus sombre, Quel est ce voyageur perdu?
la bɑ dã la fɔ rɛ ply sõ brə, kɛ lɛ sə vwa ja ʒœ rpɛ rdy?

Autour de lui des yeux brillent dans l'ombre,
o tu rdə lɥi de zjø bri jə dã lõ brə,

Il marche encore au hasard, éperdu
i lma rʃã kɔ rə o a za r, e pɛ rdy,

Les fauves rugissent de joie,
le fo və ry ʒi sə də ʒwa ə,

Ils vont se jeter sur leur proie,
i lvõ sə ʒə te sy rlœ rprwa ə,

La jeune fille accourt et brave leurs fureurs:
la ʒœ nə fi ja ku r, e bra və lœ rfy rœ r,

Elle a dans sa main la baguette,
ɛ la dã sa mɛ̃ la ba gɛ tə,

312

Où tinte la clochette, des charmeurs! Ah!
u tɛ̃ tə la klɔ ʃɛ tə, de ʃa rmœ r!   a!

L'étranger la regarde, Elle reste éblouie.
le trɑ̃ ʒe la rə ga rdə, ɛ lə rɛ ste blu i ə.

Il est plus beau que les Rajahs!
i lɛ ply bo kə le ra ʒa!

Il rougira, S'il sait qu'il doit la vie
i lru ʒi ra, si lsɛ ki ldwa la vi ə,

A la fille des Parias.
a la fi jə de pa ri ja.

Mais lui, l'endormant dans un rêve,
mɛ lɥi lɑ̃ dɔ rmɑ̃ dɑ̃ zœ̃ rɛ və,

Jusque dans le ciel il l'enlève,
ʒy skə dɑ̃ lə sjɛ li llɑ̃ lɛ və,

En lui disant: ta place est là!
ɑ̃ lɥi di zɑ̃, ta pla sɛ la!

C'était Vishnou fils de Brahma!
se tɛ vi ʃnu, fi sdə bra ma!

Depuis ce jour au fond des bois,
də pɥi sə ʒu ro fɔ̃ de bwa,

Le voyageur entend parfois
lə vwa ja ʒœ rɑ̃ tɑ̃ pa rfwa,

Le bruit léger de la baguette,
lə brɥi le ʒe də la ba gɛ tə,

Où tinte la clochette, des charmeurs!
u tɛ̃ tə la klɔ ʃɛ tə, de ʃa rmœ r

Delibes   Bonjour, Suzon!
dəlib   bɔ̃ʒur syzɔ̃

Bonjour, Suzon, ma fleur des bois!
bɔ̃ ʒu rsy zɔ̃ ma flœ rde bwa!

Es-tu toujours la plus jolie?
ɛ ty tu ʒu rla ply ʒɔ li ə

Je reviens tel que tu me vois,
ʒə rə vjɛ̃ tɛ lkə ty mə vwa,

D'un grand voyage en Italie.
dœ̃ grã vwa ja ʒã ni ta li ə.

Du paradis j'ai fait le tour.
dy pa ra di ʒe fɛ lə tu r.

J'ai fait des vers, j'ai fait l'amour,
ʒe fɛ de vɛ rʒe fɛ la mu r,

Mais que t'importe?
mɛ kə tɛ̃ pɔ rtə?

Je passe devant ta maison, Ouvre ta porte!
ʒə pɑ sə də vã ta mɛ zɔ̃, u vrə ta pɔ rtə!

Je t'ai vue au temps des lilas,
ʒə te vy o tã de li lɑ,

Ton coeur joyeux venait d'éclore.
tɔ̃ kœ rʒwa jø və nɛ de klɔ rə,

Et tu disais, je ne veux pas qu'on m'aime encore.
e ty di zɛ, ʒə nə vø pa kɔ̃ mɛ mã kɔ rə.

Qu'as tu fait depuis mon départ?
ka ty fɛ də pɥi mɔ̃ de pa r?

Qui part trop tôt revient trop tard.
ki pa rtrɔ to rə vjɛ̃ trɔ ta r.

Mais que m'importe?
mɛ kə mɛ̃ pɔ rtə?

Delibes   Les filles de Cadix
dəlib   le fij də kadiks

Nous venions de voir le taureau,
nu və njɔ̃ də vwa rlə tɔ ro,

Trois garçons, trois fillettes,
trwa ça rsɔ̃ trwa fi jɛ tə,

Sur la pelouse il faisait beau,
sy rla pə lu zi lfə zɛ bo,

Et nous dansions un boléro Au son des castagnettes:
e nu dã sjɔ̃ zœ̃ bɔ le ro, o sɔ̃ de ka sta ɲɛ tə,

Dites—moi, voisin, Si j'ai bonne mine,
di tə mwa vwa zɛ̃, si ʒe bɔ nə mi n,

314

Et si ma basquine Va bien ce matin.
e si ma ba ski nə va bjɛ̃ sə ma tɛ̃.

Vous me trouvez la taille fine? ah!
vu mə tru ve la ta jə fi nə? ɑ!

Les filles de Cadix aiment assez cela, ah! la ra la.
le fi jə də ka di ksɛ mə ta se sə la, ɑ la ra la

Et nous dansions un boléro Un soir, c'était dimanche.
e nu dɑ̃ sjɔ̃ zɶ̃ bɔ le ro ɶ̃ swa rse tɛ di mɑ̃ ʃə.

Vers nous s'en vient un hidalgo,
vɛ rnu sɑ̃ vjɛ̃ tɶ̃ i da lgo,

Cousu d'or, la plume au chapeau,
ku zy dɔ rla ply mo ʃa po,

Et le poing sur la hanche: Si tu veux de moi,
e lə pwɛ̃ sy rla ɑ̃ ʃə, si ty vø də mwa,

Brune au doux sourire, Tu n'as qu'à le dire.
bry no du su ri rə, ty na ka lə di rə

Cet or est à toi. Passez votre chemin beau sire,
sɛ tɔ rɛ ta twa. pa se vɔ trə ʃə mɛ̃ bo si rə,

Les filles de Cadix n'entendent pas cela,
le fi jə də ka di ksnɑ̃ tɑ̃ də pa sə la,

la ra la, ah.
la ra la, ɑ.

Duparc   Chanson triste
dypark   ʃɑ̃sɔ̃ trist

Dans ton coeur dort un clair de lune,
dɑ̃ tɔ̃ kɶ rdɔ rɶ̃ klɛ rdə ly nə,

un doux clair de lune d'été,
ɶ̃ du klɛ rdə ly nə de te,

Et pour fuir la vie importune,
e pu rfɥi rla vi ɛ̃ pɔ rty nə,

Je me noierai dans ta clarté.
ʒə mə nwa re, dɑ̃ ta kla rte.

J'oublierai les douleurs passées
ʒu bli re le du lɶ rpa se ə,

Mon amour; quand tu berceras
mõ na mu r; kã ty bɛ rsə ra

Mon triste coeur et mes pensées
mõ tri stə kœ re me pã se ə,

Dans le calme aimant de tes bras!
dã lə ka lmɛ mã də te bra!

Tu prendras ma tête malade
ty prã dra ma tɛ tə ma la də,

Oh! quelquefois sur tes genoux,
o kɛ lkə fwa sy rte ʒə nu,

Et lui diras une ballade,
e lɥi di ra y nə ba la də,

Une ballade, qui semblera parler de nous,
y nə ba la də, ki sã blə ra pa rle də nu,

Et dans tes yeux pleins de tristesses,
e dã te zjø plɛ̃ də tri stɛ sə,

Dans tes yeux alors je boirai
dã te zjø a lɔ rʒə bwa re,

Tant de baisers et de tendresses,
tã də bɛ ze e də tã drɛ sə,

Que peut-être je guérirai.
kə pø tɛ trə ʒə ge ri re.

Duparc   Extase
dypark   ɛkstaz

Sur un lys pâle mon coeur dort
sy rœ̃ li spɑ lə, mõ kœ rdɔ r,

D'un sommeil doux comme la mort,
dœ̃ so mɛ jdu kɔ mə la mɔ r,

Mort exquise, mort parfumée
mɔ rɛ kski zə, mɔ rpa rfy me ə,

Du souffle de la bien-aimée.
dy su flə də la bjɛ̃ ne me ə.

Sur ton sein pâle mon coeur dort
sy rtõ sɛ̃ pɑ lə, mõ kœ rdɔ r,

D'un sommeil doux comme la mort.
dœ̃ sɔ mɛ jdu kɔ mə la mɔ r.

Duparc　　　　Le Manoir de Rosemonde
dypark　　　　lə manwar də rozmɔ̃d

De sa dent soudaine et vorace,
də sa dɑ̃ su dɛ ne vɔ ra sə,

Comme un chien l'amour m'a mordu.
kɔ mœ̃ ʃjɛ̃ la mu rma mɔ rdy.

En suivant mon sang répandu,
ɑ̃ sɥi vɑ̃ mɔ̃ sɑ̃ re pɑ̃ dy,

Va, tu pourras suivre ma trace.
va, ty pu ra sɥi vrə ma tra sə.

Prends un cheval de bonne race,
prɑ̃ zœ̃ ʃə va ldə bɔ nə ra sə,

Pars, et suis mon chemin ardu,
pa r, e sɥi mɔ̃ ʃə mɛ̃ a rdy,

Fondrière ou sentier perdu,
fɔ̃ dri jɛ ru sɑ̃ tje pɛ rdy,

Si la course ne te harasse!
si la ku rsə nə tə a ra sə!

En passant par où j'ai passé,
ɑ̃ pa sɑ̃ pa ru ʒe pa se,

Tu verras que seul et blessé,
ty vɛ ra, kə sœ l, e blɛ se,

J'ai parcouru ce triste monde,
ʒe pa rku ry sə tri stə mɔ̃ də,

Et qu'ainsi je m'en fus mourir Bien loin,
e kɛ̃ si ʒə mɑ̃ fy mu ri r, bjɛ̃ lwɛ̃,

sans découvrir Le bleu manoir de Rosemonde.
sɑ̃ de ku vri r, lə blø ma nwa rdə ro zə mɔ̃ də.

Duparc   L'invitation au voyage
dypark   l ɛ̃vitasjɔ̃ o vwajaʒ

Mon enfant, ma soeur, Songe à la douceur
mɔ̃ nɑ̃ fɑ̃, ma sœ r, sɔ̃ ʒa la du sœ r,

D'aller là—bas vivre ensemble, Aimer à loisir,
da le la bɑ vi vrɑ̃ sɑ̃ blə, ɛ me a lwa zi r,

Aimer et mourir Au pays qui te ressemble!
ɛ me e mu ri r, o pe i ki tə rə sɑ̃ blə!

Les soleils mouillés De ces ciels brouillés
le sɔ lɛ jmu je, də se sjɛ lbru je,

Pour mon esprit ont les charmes Si mystérieux
pu rmɔ̃ nɛ spri ɔ̃ le ʃa rmə, si mi ste ri jø,

De tes traîtres yeux, Brillant à travers leurs larmes.
də te trɛ trə zjø, bri jɑ̃ ta tra vɛ rlœ rla rmə.

Là, tout n'est qu'ordre et beauté, Luxe, calme et volupté!
la, tu nɛ kɔ rdre bo te, ly ksə, ka lmə, e vɔ ly pte!

Vois sur ces canaux Dormir ces vaisseaux
vwa sy rse ka no dɔ rmi rse vɛ so,

Dont l'humeur est vagabonde;
dɔ̃ ly mœ rɛ va ga bɔ̃ də;

C'est pour assouvir Ton moindre désir
sɛ pu ra su vi rtɔ̃ mwɛ̃ drə de zi r,

Qu'ils viennent du bout du monde.
ki lvjɛ nə dy bu dy mɔ̃ də.

Les soleils couchants Revêtent les champs,
le sɔ lɛ jku ʃɑ̃, rə vɛ tə le ʃɑ̃,

Les canaux, la ville entière, D'hyacinthe et d'or;
le ka no, la vi lɑ̃ tjɛ rə, di a sɛ̃ te dɔ r;

Le monde s'endort Dans une chaude lumière!
lə mɔ̃ də sɑ̃ dɔ r, dɑ̃ zy nə ʃo də ly mjɛ rə!

Là, tout n'est qu'ordre et beauté,
la, tu nɛ kɔ rdre bo te,

Luxe, calme et volupté!
ly ksə, ka lmə, e vɔ ly pte!

Duparc   Phidylé
dypark   fidile

L'herbe est molle au sommeil
lɛ rbɛ mɔ lo sɔ mɛ j,

318

sous les frais peupliers,
su le frɛ pœ pli je,

Aux pentes des sources moussues,
o pɑ̃ tə de su rsə mu sy ə,

Qui dans les prés en fleurs
ki dɑ̃ le pre zɑ̃ flœ r,

germant par mille issues,
ʒɛ rmɑ̃ pa rmi li sy ə,

Se perdent sous les noirs halliers.
sə pɛ rdə su le nwa ra lje.

Repose, ô Phidylé.
rə po zə, o fi di le.

Midi sur les feuillages Rayonne,
mi di sy rle fœ ja ʒə rɛ jɔ n,

et t'invite au sommeil.
e tɛ̃ vi to sɔ mɛ j.

Par le trèfle et le thym, seules,
pa rlə trɛ fle lə tɛ̃, sœ lə,

en plein soleil,
ɑ̃ plɛ̃ sɔ lɛ j,

Chantent les abeilles volages;
ʃɑ̃ tə le za bɛ jə vɔ la ʒə;

Un chaud parfum circule au détour des sentiers,
œ̃ ʃo pa rfœ̃ si rky lo de tu rde sɑ̃ tje,

La rouge fleur des blés s'incline,
la ru ʒə flœ rde ble sɛ̃ kli nə,

Et les oiseaux, rasant de l'aile la coline,
e le zwa zo ra zɑ̃ də lɛ lə la kɔ li nə,

Cherchent l'ombre des églantiers.
ʃɛ rʃə lɔ̃ brə de ze glɑ̃ tje.

Repose, ô Phidylé, Repose, ô Phidylé.
rə po zə, o fi di le, rə po zə, o fi di le.

Mais, quand l'Astre incliné sur sa courbe éclatante,
mɛ kɑ̃ la strɛ̃ kli ne, sy rsa ku rbe kla tɑ̃ tə,

Verra ses ardeurs s'apaiser,
vɛ ra se za rdœ rsa pɛ ze,

Que ton plus beau sourire
kə tɔ̃ ply bo su ri r

et ton meilleur baiser Me récompensent,
e tõ mɛ jœ rbɛ ze, mə re kõ pã sə,

me récompensent de l'attente!
mə re kõ pã sə, də la tã tə!

Duparc   Soupir
dypark   supir

Ne jamais la voir ni l'entendre,
nə ʒa mɛ la vwa rni lã tã drə,

Ne jamais tout haut la nommer,
nə ʒa mɛ tu o la nɔ me,

Mais, fidèle, toujours l'attendre, Toujours l'aimer.
mɛ fi dɛ lə tu ʒu rla tã drə, tu ʒu rlɛ me.

Ouvrir les bras, et, las d'attendre,
u vri rle bra e lɑ da tã drə,

Sur le néant les refermer,
sy rlə ne ã le rə fɛ rme,

Mais encor, toujours les lui tendre, Toujours l'aimer.
mɛ zã ko r, tu ʒu rle lɥi tã drə, tu ʒu rlɛ me.

Ah! ne pouvoir que les lui tendre,
a nə pu vwa rkə le lɥi tã drə,

Et dans les pleurs se consumer,
e dã le plœ rsə kõ sy me,

Mais ces pleurs toujours lés répandre,
mɛ se plœ r, tu ʒu rle re pã drə,

Toujours l'aimer.
tu ʒu rlɛ me.

Fauré   Après un rêve
fore   aprɛ zœ̃ rɛv

Dans un sommeil que charmait ton image
dã zœ̃ sɔ mɛ jkə ʃa rmɛ tõ ni ma ʒə,

Je rêvais le bonheur, ardent mirage;
ʒə rɛ vɛ lə bɔ nœ r a rdɑ̃ mi ra ʒə;

Tes yeux étaient plus doux, ta voix pure et sonore.
te zjø e tɛ ply du ta vwa py re sɔ nɔ rə.

Tu rayonnais comme un ciel éclairé par l'aurore;
ty rɛ jɔ nɛ kɔ mœ̃ sjɛ le klɛ re pa rlɔ rɔ rə;

Tu m'appelais, et je quittais la terre
ty ma pə lɛ e ʒə ki tɛ la tɛ rə,

Pour m'enfuir avec toi vers la lumière;
pu rmɑ̃ fɥi ra vɛ ktwa vɛ rla ly mjɛ rə;

Les cieux pour nous entr'ouvraient leurs nues,
le sjø pu rnu ɑ̃ tru vrɛ lœ rny ə,

Splendeurs inconnues, lueurs divines entrevues...
splɑ̃ dœ rzɛ̃ kɔ ny ə, ly œ rdi vi nə zɑ̃ trə vy ə...

Hélas! Hélas, triste réveil des songes!
e lɑ se lɑ s, tri stə re vɛ jde sɔ̃ ʒə!

Je t'appelle, ô nuit, rends-moi tes mensonges;
ʒə ta pɛ lo nɥi rɑ̃ mwa te mɑ̃ sɔ̃ ʒə;

Reviens, reviens radieuse,
rə vjɛ̃, rə vjɛ̃ ra di ø zə,

Reviens, ô nuit mystérieuse!
rə vjɛ̃, o nɥi mi ste ri ø zə!

Fauré   Au bord de l'eau
fɔre   o bɔr də l o

S'asseoir tous deux au bord du flot qui passe,
sa swa rtu dø o bɔ ˌrdy flo ki pa sə,

Le voir passer;
lə vwa rpa se;

Tous deux s'il glisse un nuage en l'espace,
tu dø si lgli sœ̃ ny a ʒɑ̃ lɛ spa sə,

Le voir glisser;
lə vwa rgli se;

A l'horizon s'il fume un toit de chaume,
a lɔ ri zɔ̃ si lfy mœ̃ twa də ʃo mə,

Le voir fumer;
lə vwa rfy me

Aux alentours, si quelque fleur embaume,
o za lã tu r, si kɛ lkə flœ rã bo mə,

S'en embaumer;
sã nã bo me;

Entendre au pied du saule où l'eau murmure,
ã tã dro pje dy so lu lo my rmy rə,

L'eau murmurer,
lo my rmy re,

Ne pas sentir tant que ce rêve dure
nə pa sã ti rtã kə sə rɛ və dy rə,

Le temps durer,
lə tã dy re,

Mais n'apportant de passion profonde
mɛ na po rtã də pa si õ prɔ fõ də,

Qu'à s'adorer,
ka sa dɔ re

Sans nul souci des querelles du monde,
sã ny lsu si, de kə rɛ lə dy mõ də,

Les ignorer,
le zi ɲo re,

Et seuls tous deux devant tout ce qui lasse,
e sœ ltu dø də vã tu sə ki la sə,

Sans se lasser;
sã sə la se;

Sentir l'amour devant tout ce qui passe,
sã ti rla mu rdə vã tu sə ki pa sə,

Ne point passer!
nə pwɛ̃ pa se!

Fauré   Aurore
fore   ɔrɔr

Des jardins de la nuit s'envolent les étoiles.
de ʒa rdɛ̃ də la nɥi sã vɔ lə le ze twa lə.

322

Abeilles d'or qu'attire un invisible miel;
a bɛ jə dɔ rka ti rɛ̃ nɛ̃ vi zi blə mjɛ l;

Et l'aube, au loin, tendant la candeur de ses toiles,
e lo bo lwɛ̃ tɑ̃ dɑ̃ la kɑ̃ dœ rdə se twa lə,

trame de fils d'argent le manteau bleu du ciel.
tra mə də fi lda rʒɑ̃ lə mɑ̃ to blø dy sjɛ l.

Du jardin de mon coeur qu'un rêve lent enivre,
dy ʒa rdɛ̃ də mɔ̃ kœ r kɛ̃ rɛ və lɑ̃ ɑ̃ ni vrə,

S'envolent mes désirs sur les pas du matin,
sɑ̃ vɔ lə me de zi r, sy rle pɑ dy ma tɛ̃,

Comme un essaim léger qu'à l'horizon de cuivre,
kɔ mɛ̃ nɛ sɛ̃ le ʒe ka lɔ ri zɔ̃ də kɥi vrə,

appelle un chant plaintif, éternel et lointain.
a pɛ lɛ̃ ʃɑ̃ plɛ̃ ti f, e tɛ rnɛ le lwɛ̃ tɛ̃.

Ils volent à tes pieds, astres chassés des nues,
i lvɔ lə ta te pje a strə ʃa se de ny ə,

Exilés du ciel d'or où fleurit ta beauté,
ɛ gzi le dy sjɛ ldɔ ru flœ ri ta bo te,

Et, cherchant jusqu'à toi des routes inconnues,
e ʃɛ rʃɑ̃ ʒy ska twa de ru tə zɛ̃ kɔ ny ə,

Mêlent au jour naissant leur mourante clarté.
mɛ lə to ʒu rnɛ sɑ̃ lœ rmu rɑ̃ tə kla rte.

Fauré   Automne
fore   otɔn

Automne au ciel brumeux, aux horizons navrants,
o tɔ no sjɛ lbry mø, o zɔ ri zɔ̃ na vrɑ̃,

Aux rapides couchants, aux aurores pâlies,
o ra pi də ku ʃɑ̃, o zɔ ro rə pɑ li ə,

Je regarde couler comme l'eau du torrent,
ʒə rə ga rdə ku le kɔ mə lo dy tɔ rɑ̃,

Tes jours faits de mélancolie.
te ʒu rfɛ də me lɑ̃ kɔ li ə.

Sur l'aile des regrets, mes esprits emportés,
sy rlɛ lə de rə grɛ me zɛ spri zɑ̃ pɔ rte,

323

Comme s'il se pouvait que notre âge renaisse,
kɔ mə si lsə pu vɛ kə nɔ tra ʒə rə nɛ sə,

Parcourent en rêvant les coteaux enchantés,
pa rku rə tɑ̃ rɛ vɑ̃ le kɔ to zɑ̃ ʃɑ̃ te,

Où, jadis, sourit ma jeunesse!
u ʒa di ssu ri ma ʒœ nɛ sə!

Je sens au clair soleil du souvenir vainqueur,
ʒə sɑ̃ o klɛ rsɔ lɛ jdy su və ni rvɛ̃ kœ r,

Refleurir en bouquet les roses déliées,
rə flœ ri rɑ̃ bu kɛ le ro zə de li e ə,

Et monter à mes yeux des larmes, qu'en mon coeur
e mɔ̃ te a me zjø de la rmə kɑ̃ mɔ̃ kœ r,

Mes vingt ans avaient oubliées!
me vɛ̃ tɑ̃ a vɛ tu bli je ə!

Fauré   En prière
fore   ɑ̃ prijɛr

Si la voix d'un enfant peut monter jusqu'à Vous,
si la vwa dœ̃ nɑ̃ fɑ̃ pø mɔ̃ te ʒy ska vu,

O mon Père,
o mɔ̃ pɛ rə,

Écoutez de Jésus, devant Vous à genoux,
e ku te də ʒe zy də vɑ̃ vu a ʒə nu,

La prière!
la pri jɛ rə!

Si Vous m'avez choisi pour enseigner vos lois
si vu ma ve ʃwa zi, pu rɑ̃ sɛ ɲe vo lwa

sur la terre,
sy rla tɛ rə,

Je saurai Vous servir, auguste Roi des rois,
ʒə sɔ re vu sɛ rvi ro gy stə rwa de rwa,

O Lumiére!
o ly mjɛ rə!

Sur mes lèvres, Seigneur,
sy rme lɛ vrə sɛ ɲœ r,

324

mettez la vérité Salutaire,
mɛ te la ve ri te sa ly tɛ rə,

Pour que celui qui doute,
pu rkə sə lyi ki du t,

avec humilité, Vous révère!
a vɛ ky mi li te vu re vɛ rə!

Ne m'abandonnez pas,
nə ma bɑ̃ dɔ ne pa,

donnez-moi la douceur Nécessaire,
dɔ ne mwa la du sœ rne sɛ sɛ rə,

Pour apaiser les maux, soulager la douleur,
pu ra pɛ ze le mo su la ʒe la du lœ r,

la misère!
la mi zɛ rə!

Révélez-Vous à moi, Seigneur en qui je crois,
re ve le vu za mwa, sɛ ɲœ rɑ̃ ki ʒə krwa,

et j'espère
e ʒɛ spɛ rə,

Pour Vous je veux souffrir, et mourir sur la croix,
pu rvu ʒə vø su fri r, e mu ri rsy rla krwa,

Au calvaire!
o ka lvɛ rə!

Fauré   Fleur jetée
fore   flœr ʒəte

Emporte ma folie au gré du vent,
ɑ̃ pɔ rtə ma fɔ li ə o gre dy vɑ̃,

Fleur en chantant cueillie
flœ rɑ̃ ʃɑ̃ tɑ̃ kœ ji ə,

Et jetée en rêvant,
e ʒə te ɑ̃ rɛ vɑ̃,

Emporte ma folie, au gré du vent,
ɑ̃ pɔ rtə ma fɔ li o gre dy vɑ̃,

Comme la fleur fauchée périt l'amour.
kɔ mə la flœ rfo ʃe ə pe ri la mu r.

325

La main qui t'a touchée
la mɛ̃ ki ta tu ʃe ə

Fuit ma main sans retour,
fɥi ma mɛ̃ sɑ̃ rə tu r,

Que le vent qui te séche, ô pauvre fleur,
kə lə vɑ̃ ki tə sɛ ʃə, o po vrə flœ r,

Tout à l'heure si fraiche,
tu ta lœ rə si frɛ ʃə,

Et demain sans couleur,
e də mɛ̃ sɑ̃ ku lœ r,

Que le vent qui te sèche, ô pauvre fleur,
kə lə vɑ̃ ki tə sɛ ʃə, o po vrə flœ r,

Que le vent qui te sèche,
kə lə vɑ̃ ki tə sɛ ʃə,

Sèche mon coeur.
sɛ ʃə mɔ̃ kœ r.

Fauré   Ici—bas
fore   isi bɑ

Ici—bas tous les lilas meurent,
i si bɑ tu le li la mœ rə,

Tout les chants des oiseaux sont courts,
tu le ʃɑ̃ de zwa zo sɔ̃ ku r,

Je rêve aux étés qui demeurent toujours!
ʒə rɛ vo ze te ki də mœ rə tu ʒu r!

Ici—bas les lèvres effleurent
i si bɑ le lɛ vrə zɛ flœ rə,

Sans rien laisser de leur velours,
sɑ̃ rjɛ̃ lɛ se də lœ rvə lu r,

Je rêve aux baisers qui demeurent toujours!
ʒə rɛ vo bɛ ze ki də mœ rə tu ʒu r!

Ici—bas, tous les hommes pleurent
i si bɑ tu le zo mə plœ rə,

Leurs amitiés ou leurs amours,
lœ rza mi tje u lœ rza mu r,

Je rêve aux couples qui demeurent,
ʒə rɛ vo ku plə ki də mœ rə,

Qui demeurent toujours!
ki də mœ rə tu ʒu r!

Fauré   Les berceaux
fɔre   le bɛrso

Le long du Quai, les grands vaisseaux,
lə lɔ̃ dy ke le grɑ̃ vɛ so,

Que la houle incline en silence,
kə la u lɛ̃ kli nɑ̃ si lɑ̃ sə,

Ne prennent pas garde aux berceaux,
nə prɛ nə pa ga rdo bɛ rso,

Que la main des femmes balance.
kə la mɛ̃ de fa mə ba lɑ̃ sə.

Mais viendra le jour des adieux,
mɛ vjɛ̃ dra lə ʒu rde za djø,

Car il faut que les femmes pleurent,
ka ri lfo kə le fa mə plœ rə,

Et que les hommes curieux
e kə le zɔ mə ky ri ø,

Tentent les horizons qui leurrent!
tɑ̃ tə le zɔ ri zɔ̃ ki lœ rə!

Et ce jour-là les grands vaisseaux,
e sə ʒu rla le grɑ̃ vɛ so,

Fuyant le port qui diminue,
fɥi jɑ̃ lə pɔ rki di mi ny ə,

Sentent leur masse retenue
sɑ̃ tə lœ rma sə rə tə ny ə,

Par l'âme des lointains berceaux.
pa rlɑ mə de lwɛ̃ tɛ̃ bɛ rso.

327

Fauré   Les roses d'Ispahan
fɔre   le roz d ispaɑ̃

Les roses d'Ispahan dans leur gaîne de mousse,
le ro zə di spa ɑ̃ dɑ̃ lœ rgɛ nə də mu sə,

Les jasmins de Mossoul, les fleurs de l'oranger,
le ʒa smɛ̃ də mɔ su l, le flœ rdə lɔ rɑ̃ ʒe,

Ont un parfum moins frais, ont une odeur moins douce,
ɔ̃ tœ̃ pa rfœ̃ mwɛ̃ frɛ ɔ̃ ty no dœ rmwɛ̃ du sə,

O blanche Leïlah! que ton souffle léger.
o blɑ̃ ʃə le i la! kə tɔ̃ su flə le ʒe.

Ta lèvre est de corail et ton rire léger
ta lɛ vrɛ də kɔ ra je tɔ̃ ri rə le ʒe,

Sonne mieux que l'eau vive et d'une voix plus douce.
sɔ nə mjø kə lo vi ve dy nə vwa ply du sə.

Mieux que le vent joyeux qui berce l'oranger,
mjø kə lə vɑ̃ ʒwa jø ki bɛ rsə lɔ rɑ̃ ʒe,

Mieux que l'oiseau qui chante au bord d'un nid de mousse.
mjø kə lwa zo ki ʃɑ̃ to bɔ rdœ̃ ni də mu sə.

O Leïlah! depuis que de leur vol léger
o le i la də pɥi kə də lœ rvɔ llə ʒe,

Tous les baisers ont fui de ta lèvre si douce
tu le bɛ ze ɔ̃ fɥi də ta lɛ vrə si du sə,

Il n'est plus de parfum dans le pâle oranger,
i lnɛ ply də pa rfœ̃ dɑ̃ lə pɑ lɔ rɑ̃ ʒe,

Ni de céleste arome aux roses dans leur mousse.
ni də se lɛ sta ro mo ro zə dɑ̃ lœ rmu sə.

Oh! que ton jeune amour, ce papillon léger
o kə tɔ̃ ʒœ na mu r, sə pa pi jɔ̃ le ʒe,

Revienne vers mon coeur d'une aile prompte et douce,
rə vjɛ nə vɛ rmɔ̃ kœ rdy nə lə prɔ̃ te du sə,

Et qu'il parfume encor la fleur de l'oranger,
e ki lpa rfy mɑ̃ kɔ rla flœ rdə lɔ rɑ̃ ʒe,

Les roses d'Ispahan dans leur gaine de mousse.
le ro zə di spa ɑ̃, dɑ̃ lœ rgɛ nə də mu sə.

Fauré   Lydia
fore   lidja

Lydia sur tes roses joues
li di a sy rte ro zə ʒu ə,

Et sur ton col frais et si blanc,
e sy rtɔ̃ kɔ lfrɛ ze si blɑ̃,

Roule étincelant L'or fluide que tu dénoues;
ru le tɛ̃ sə lɑ̃, lɔ rfly i də kə ty de nu ə;

Le jour qui luit est le meilleur,
lə ʒu rki lɥi ɛ lə mɛ jœ r,

Oublions l'éternelle tombe;
u bli jɔ̃ le tɛ rnɛ lə tɔ̃ bə;

Laisse tes baisers, tes baisers de colombe
lɛ sə te bɛ ze, te bɛ ze də kɔ lɔ̃ bə,

Chanter sur ta lèvre en fleur.
ʃɑ̃ te sy rta lɛ vrɑ̃ flœ r.

Un lys caché répand sans cesse
œ̃ li ska ʃe re pɑ̃ sɑ̃ sɛ sə,

Une odeur divine en ton sein;
y no dœ rdi vi nɑ̃ tɔ̃ sɛ̃;

Les délices comme un essaim Sortent de toi,
le de li sə kɔ mœ̃ nɛ sɛ̃ sɔ rtə də twa,

jeune déesse
ʒœ nə de ɛ sə,

Je t'aime et meurs, ô mes amours,
ʒə tɛ me mœ ro me za mu r,

Mon âme en baisers m'est ravie!
mɔ̃ nɑ mɑ̃ bɛ ze mɛ ra vi ə!

O Lydia rends—moi la vie, Que je puisse mourir toujours!
o li di a rɑ̃ mwa la vi ə, kə ʒə pɥi sə mu ri rtu ʒu r!

Fauré   Mai
fore   me

Puisque Mai tout en fleurs dans les prés nous réclame,
pɥi skə me tu tɑ̃ flœ r, dɑ̃ le pre nu re kla mə,

Viens, ne te lasse pas de mêler à ton âme
vjɛ̃ nə tə la sə pa də mɛ le a tɔ̃ nɑ mə,

329

La campagne, les bois, les ombrages charmants,
la kɑ̃ pa ɲə le bwa le zɔ̃ bra ʒə ʃa rmɑ̃,

Les larges clairs de lune au bord des flots dormants;
le la rʒə klɛ rdə ly no bɔ rde flo dɔ rmɑ̃;

Le sentier qui finit où le chemin commence,
lə sɑ̃ tje ki fi ni u lə ʃə mɛ̃ kɔ mɑ̃ sə,

Et l'air, et le printemps et l'horizon immense,
e lɛ re lə prɛ̃ tɑ̃ e lɔ ri zɔ̃ i mɑ̃ sə,

L'horizon que ce monde attache humble et joyeux,
lɔ ri zɔ̃ kə sə mɔ̃ da ta ʃœ̃ ble ʒwa jø,

Comme une lèvre au bas de la robe des cieux.
kɔ my nə lɛ vro ba də la rɔ bə de sjø.

Viens, et que le regard des pudiques étoiles,
vjɛ̃ e kə lə rə ga rde py di kə ze twa lə,

Qui tombe sur la terre à travers tant de voiles
ki tɔ̃ bə sy rla tɛ rə a tra vɛ rtɑ̃ de rwa lə.

Que l'arbre pénétré de parfums et de chants,
kə la rbrə pe ne tre də pa rfœ̃ ze də ʃɑ̃,

Que le souffle embrasé de midi dans les champs,
kə lə su flɑ̃ bra ze də mi di dɑ̃ le ʃɑ̃,

Et l'ombre et le soleil, et l'onde, et la verdure,
e lɔ̃ bre lə sɔ lɛ j, e lɔ̃ de la vɛ rdy rə,

Et le rayonnement de toute la nature,
e lə rɛ jɔ nə mɑ̃, də tu tə la na ty rə,

Fassent épanouir, comme une double fleur,
fa sə te pa nu i r, kɔ my nə du blə flœ r,

La beauté sur ton front et l'amour dans ton coeur!
la bo te sy rtɔ̃ frɔ̃ e la mu rdɑ̃ tɔ̃ kœ r!

Fauré   Nell
fore   nɛl

Ta rose de poupre à ton clair soleil,
ta ro zə də pu rpra tɔ̃ klɛ rsɔ lɛ j,

O Juin, étincelle enivrée,
o ʒɥɛ̃ e tɛ̃ sɛ lɑ̃ ni vre ə,

Penche aussi vers moi ta coupe dorée:
pã ʃo si vɛ rmwa ta ku pə do re ə:

Mon coeur à ta rose est pareil.
mõ kœ ra ta ro zɛ pa rɛ j.

Sous le mol abri de la feuille ombreuse
su lə mɔ la bri də la fœ jõ brø zə,

Monte un soupir de volupté;
mõ tœ̃ su pi rdə vɔ ly pte;

Plus d'un ramier chante au bois écarté,
ply dœ̃ ra mje ʃã to bwa e ka rte,

O mon coeur, sa plainte amoureuse.
o mõ kœ r, sa plɛ̃ ta mu rø zə.

Que ta perle est douce au ciel enflammé,
kə ta pɛ rlɛ du so sjɛ lã fla me,

Etoile de la nuit pensive!
e twa lə də la nɥi pã si və!

Mais combien plus douce est la clarté vive
mɛ kõ bjɛ̃ ply du sɛ la kla rte vi və,

Qui rayonne en mon coeur, en mon coeur charmé!
ki rɛ jɔ nã mõ kœ r, ã mõ kœ rʃa rme!

La chantante mer, le long du rivage,
la ʃã tã tə mɛ rlə lõ dy ri va ʒə,

Taira son murmure éternel,
tɛ ra sõ my rmy re tɛ rnɛ l,

Avant qu'en mon coeur, chère amours, ô Nell,
a vã kã mõ kœ r, ʃɛ ra mu r, o nɛ l,

Ne fleurisse plus ton image!
nə flœ ri sə ply tõ ni ma ʒə!

Fauré   Prison (fɔre − prizõ)
Hahn   D'une prison (an − d yn prizõ)

Le ciel est par dessus le toit, si bleu, si calme...
lə sjɛ lɛ pa rdə sy lə twa, si blø si ka lmə...

Un arbre, par dessus le toît, berce sa palme...
œ̃ na rbrə pa rdə sy lə twa, bɛ rsə sa pa lmə...

La cloche dans le ciel qu'on voit, doucement tinte,
la klɔ ʃə dɑ̃ lə sjɛ lkɔ̃ vwa, du sə mɑ̃ tɛ̃ tə,

Un oiseau sur l'arbre qu'on voit, chante sa plainte...
œ̃ nwa zo sy rla rbrə kɔ̃ vwa, ʃɑ̃ tə sa plɛ̃ tə...

Mon Dieu, mon Dieu! La vie est là simple et tranquille!
mɔ̃ djø, mɔ̃ djø! la vi ɛ la sɛ̃ ple trɑ̃ ki lə!

Cette paisible rumeur là vient de la ville...
sɛ tə pɛ zi blə ry mœ rla vjɛ̃ də la vi lə...

Qu'as-tu fait, ô toi que voilà, pleurant sans cesse
ka ty fɛ o twa kə vwa la, plœ rɑ̃ sɑ̃ sɛ sə,

Dis, qu'as-tu fait, toi que voilà, de ta jeunesse?
di ka ty fɛ, twa kə vwa la, də ta ʒœ nɛ sə?

Fifteenth Century Song   L'Amour de Moi
                           l amur də mwa

L'amour de moi s'y est enclose
la mu rdə mwa si ɛ tɑ̃ klo zə,

Dedans un joli jardinet,
də dɑ̃ zœ̃ ʒo li ʒa rdi nɛ,

Où croît la rose et le muguet
u krwa la ro ze lə my gɛ,

Et aussi fait la passerose.
e o si fɛ la pa sə ro zə.

Ce jardin est bel et plaisant,
sə ʒa rdɛ̃ ɛ bɛ le plɛ zɑ̃,

Il est garni de toutes flours.
i lɛ ga rni də tu tə flu r.

Hélas! il n'est si douce chose
e la si lnɛ si du sə ʃo zə,

Que de ce doux rossignolet
kə də sə du rɔ si ɲo lɛ,

Qui chante au soir, au matinet:
ki ʃɑ̃ to swa r, o ma ti nɛ:

Quand il est las, il se repose.
kɑ̃ ti lɛ lɑ, i lsə rə po zə.

Je l'ai regardée une pose:
ʒə le rə ga rde y nə po zə:

Elle était blanche comme lait
ɛ le tɛ blɑ̃ ʃə kɔ mə lɛ,

Et douce comme un agnelet,
e du sə kɔ mɛ̃ na ɲə lɛ,

Vermeille et fraîche comme rose.
vɛ rmɛ je frɛ ʃə, kɔ mə ro zə.

Fourdrain   Carnaval
furdrɛ̃   karnaval

Carnaval!   Joyeux Carnaval!
ka rna va l!   ʒwa jø ka rna va l!

On s'élance La foule assiège
ɔ̃ se lɑ̃ sə, la fu la sjɛ ʒə,

Des hérauts à pied, à cheval,
de e ro za pje a ʃə va l,

Précédant un riche cortège!   Une fanfare
pre se dɑ̃ tɛ̃ ri ʃə kɔ rtɛ ʒə! y nə fɑ̃ fa rə,

des clameurs s'él vent stridentes, sonores!
de kla mœ rse lɛ və stri dɑ̃ tə, so nɔ rə!

Du haut des chars il pleut des fleurs
dy o de ʃa ri lplø de flœ r,

Et des papiers multicolores Saluez!
e de pa pje my lti ko lo rə, sa ly e!

Voici la Reine tenant sa marotte;
vwa si la rɛ nə tə nɑ̃ sa ma rɔ t,

Elle a sa traine de gala,
ɛ la sa trɛ nə də ga la,

Et des cheveux couleur carotte;
e de ʃə vø ku lœ rka ro tə;

Elle taquine son bouffon
ɛ lə ta ki nə sɔ̃ bu fɔ̃

Dont les lèvres restent muettes,
dɔ̃ le lɛ vrə rɛ stə my ɛ tə,

Elle lui montre comment
ɛ lə lɥi mõ trə kɔ mã

"font" Font font les petites marionettes.
fõ, fõ fõ le pə ti tə ma rjɔ nɛ tə.

Il lui répond: Merci, m'amour;
i llɥi re põ: mɛ rsi, ma mu r;

De ces leçons-là je me passe
də se lə sõ la ʒə mə pa sə,

J'écoute l'âme du faubourg
ʒe ku tə lɑ mə dy fo bu r,

Jusqu'à toi monter dans l'espace.
ʒy ska twa mõ te dã lɛ spa sə.

Je vois là haut, je vois soudain
ʒə vwa la o, ʒə vwa su dɛ̃,

Le soleil s'exalter lui-même
lə sɔ lɛ jsɛ gza lte lɥi mɛ mə,

Reine, il baise ta main
rɛ nə, i lbɛ zə ta mɛ̃,

Et fait flamber ton diadème.
e fɛ flã be, tõ di a dɛ mə.

Fourdrain   Le Papillon
furdrɛ̃   lə papijõ

Gai papillon, papillon d'or
ge pa pi jõ, pa pi jõ dɔ r

Qui t'envoles rapide et frêle,
ki tã vɔ lə ra pi de frɛ lə,

Au bout des doigts je garde encor
o bu de dwa ʒə ga rdã kɔ r,

Un peu de cendre de ton aile!
œ̃ pø də sã drə də tõ nɛ lə!

Tu venais voir la blonde enfant
ty və nɛ vwa rla blõ dã fã,

Qui babille dans ma chambrette,
ki ba bi jə dɑ̃ ma ʃɑ̃ brɛ tə,

Tu venais, Monsieur le passant
ty və nɛ, mə sjø lə pa sɑ̃,

Dire bonjour à ma grisette
di rə bɔ̃ ʒu ra ma gri zɛ tə.

Ah! vraiment elle est bien ta soeur,
a! vrɛ mɑ̃ ɛ lɛ bjɛ̃ ta sœ r,

Comme toi légère et volage,
kɔ mə twa le ʒɛ re vɔ la ʒə,

Elle sait endormir le coeur Et le bercer
ɛ lə sɛ tɑ̃ do rmi rlə kœ re lə bɛ rse,

en un mirage.
ɑ̃ nœ̃ mi ra ʒə.

Mais papillon, dès le printemps,
mɛ pa pi jɔ̃, dɛ lə prɛ̃ tɑ̃,

Elle s'enfuira la méchante,
ɛ lə sɑ̃ fɥi ra la me ʃɑ̃ tə,

Laissant de tous ses grands serments
lɛ sɑ̃ də tu se grɑ̃ sɛ rmɑ̃,

Un peu de poussiére qui chante.
œ̃ pø də pu sjɛ rə, ki ʃɑ̃ tə.

Franck   La procession
frɑ̃k   la prɔsɛsjɔ̃

Dieu s'avance à travers les champs
djø sa vɑ̃ sa tra vɛ rle ʃɑ̃

Par les landes, les prés, les verts taillis de hêtres.
pa rle lɑ̃ də, le pre, le vɛ rta ji də ɛ trə.

Il vient, suivi du peuple, et porté par les prêtres:
i lvjɛ̃, sɥi vi dy pœ plə, e pɔ rte pa rle prɛ trə:

Aux cantiques de l'homme, oiseaux, mêlez vos chants!
o kɑ̃ ti kə də lɔ mə, wa zo, mɛ le vo ʃɑ̃!

On s'arrête. La foule autour d'un chêne antique
õ sa rɛ tə. la fu lo tu rdœ̃ ʃɛ nã ti kə,

S'incline, en adorant, sous l'ostensoir mystique:
sɛ̃ kli nã na dɔ rã, su lo stã swa rmi sti kə:

Soleil! darde sur lui tes longs rayons couchants!
sɔ lɛ jda rdə sy rlɥi, te lõ rɛ jõ ku ʃã!

Aux cantiques de l'homme, oiseaux, mêlez vos chants!
o kã ti kə də lɔ mə, wa zo mɛ le vo ʃã!

Vous, fleurs, avec l'encens exhalez votre arôme!
vu, flœ r, a vɛ klã sã ɛ gza le vɔ tra ro mə!

O fête! tout reluit, tout prie et tout embaume!
o fɛ tə! tu rə lɥi, tu pri e tu tã bo mə!

Dieu s'avance à travers les champs.
djø sa vã sa tra vɛ rle ʃã.

Franck   Le mariage des roses
frãk   lə mariaʒ de roz

Mignonne, sais-tu comment S'épousent les roses?
mi ɲo nə sɛ ty ko mã se pu zə le ro zə?

Ah! cet hymen est charmant, cet hymen est charmant!
a sɛ ti mɛ nɛ ʃa rmã, sɛ ti mɛ nɛ ʃa rmã!

Quelles tendres choses Elles disent en ouvrant
kɛ lə tã drə ʃo zə ɛ lə di zə tã nu vrã

Leurs paupières closes!
lœ rpo pjɛ rə klo zə!

Mignonne, sais-tu comment S'épousent les roses?
mi ɲo nə sɛ ty ko mã se pu zə le ro zə?

Elles disent: aimons nous! Si courte est la vie!
ɛ lə di zə, ɛ mõ nu! si ku rtɛ la vi ə!

Ayons les baisers plus doux, L'âme plus ravie!
ɛ jõ le bɛ ze ply du, la mə ply ra vi ə!

Pendant que l'homme à genoux Doute, espère ou prie!
pã dã kə lo ma ʒə nu du tɛ spɛ ru pri ə!

O mes soeurs, embrassons-nous! Si courte est la vie!
o me sœ r ã bra sõ nu! si ku rtɛ la vi ə!

Crois—moi, mignonne, crois—moi, Aimons—nous comme elles,
krwa mwa mi ɲo nə krwa mwa ɛ mõ nu kɔ me lə,

Vois, le printemps vient à toi, Le printemps vient à toi.
vwa lə prɛ̃ tã vjɛ̃ ta twa, lə prɛ̃ tã vjɛ̃ ta twa.

Et des hirondelles, Aimer est l'unique loi
e de zi rõ dɛ lə ɛ me ɛ ly ni kə lwa

A leurs nids fidèles.
a lœ rni fi dɛ lə.

O ma reine, suis ton roi, Aimons—nous comme elles.
o ma rɛ nə sɥi tõ rwa, ɛ mõ nu kɔ me lə,

Excepté d'avoir aimé, Qu'est-il donc sur terre?
ɛ ksɛ pte da vwa rɛ me, kɛ ti ldõ ksy rtɛ rə?

Votre horizon est fermé Ombre, nuit, mystère!
vɔ trɔ ri zõ ɛ fɛ rme õ brə nɥi mi stɛ rə!

Un seul phare est allumé L'amour nous l'éclaire,
œ̃ sœ lfa rɛ ta ly me, la mu rnu le klɛ rə,

Excepté d'avoir aimé Qu'est-il donc sur terre?
e ksɛ pte da vwa rɛ me, kɛ ti ldõ ksy rtɛ rə?

Franck   Lied
frãk   lid

Pour moi sa main cueillait des roses A ce buisson,
pu rmwa sa mɛ̃ kœ jɛ de ro zə a sə bɥi sõ,

Comme elle encore à peine écloses, Chère moisson.
kɔ mɛ lã kɔ ra pɛ ne klo zə ʃɛ rə mwa sõ.

La gerbe, hélas! en est fanée Comme elle aussi;
la ʒɛ rbe la sã nɛ fa ne ə kɔ mɛ lo si;

La moissonneuse moissonnée Repose ici.
la mwa sɔ nø zə mwa sɔ ne ə rə po zi si.

Mais sur la tombe qui vous couvre, O mes amours!
mɛ sy rla tõ bə ki vu ku vrə, o me za mu r!

Une églantine, qui s'entr'ouvre, Sourit toujours.
y ne glã ti nə ki sã tru vrə, su ri tu ʒu r.

Et sous le buisson qui surplombe, Quand je reviens,
e su lə bɥi sõ ki sy rplõ bə, kã ʒə rə vjɛ̃,

Une voix me dit sous la tombe: "Je me souviens."
y nə vwa mə di su la tõ bə: ӡə mə su vjɛ̃.

Gluck   Divinités du Styx (Alceste)
glyk   divinite dy stiks alsɛst

Divinités du Styx, ministres de la mort,
di vi ni te dy sti ks, mi ni strə də la mɔ r,

je n'invoquerai point, votre pitié cruelle,
ӡə nɛ̃ vɔ kə re pwɛ̃, vɔ trə pi tje kry ɛ lə,

J'enlève un tendre époux à son funeste sort,
ӡɑ̃ lɛ vɛ̃ tɑ̃ dre pu, a sõ fy nɛ stə sɔ r,

mais je vous abandonne une épouse fidèle.
mɛ ӡə vu za bɑ̃ dɔ ny ne pu ӡə fi dɛ lə.

Divinités du Styx, ministres de la mort,
di vi ni te dy sti ks, mi ni strə də la mɔ r,

mourir pour ce qu'on aime est un trop doux effort,
mu ri rpu rsə kõ nɛ mə, ɛ tɛ̃ trɔ du zɛ fɔ r,

une vertu si naturelle, mon coeur est animé
y nə vɛ rty si na ty rɛ lə, mõ kœ rɛ ta ni me,

du plus noble transport!
dy ply nɔ blə trɑ̃ spɔ r!

Je sens une force nouvelle,
ӡə sɑ̃ zy nə fɔ rsə nu vɛ lə,

Je vais où mon amour m'appelle,
ӡə vɛ zu mõ na mu rma pɛ lə,

mon coeur est animé du plus noble transport.
mõ kœ rɛ ta ni me, dy ply nɔ blə trɑ̃ spɔ r.

Gounod   Ah! Je veux vivre, from "Roméo et Juliette"
guno   ɑ ӡə vø vivr   rɔmeo e ӡyljɛt

Ah! Je veux vivre Dans le rêve qui m'enivre
ɑ ӡə vø vi vrə dɑ̃ lə rɛ və ki mɑ̃ ni vrə

Longtemps encor!   Douce flamme, Je te garde
lõ tã zã kɔ r, du sə fla mə ʒə tə ga rdə

dans mon âme Comme un trésor!
dã mõ nɑ mə kɔ mẽ tre zɔ r!

Cette ivresse De jeunesse Ne dure, hélas! qu'un jour.
sɛ ti vrɛ sə də ʒœ nɛ sə, nə dy re lɑ skẽ ʒu r.

Puis vient l'heure Où l'on pleure,
pɥi vjẽ lœ rə u lõ plœ rə,

Le coeur cède à l'amour,
lə kœ rsɛ dɑ la mu r,

Et le bonheur fuit sans retour.
e lə bɔ nœ rfɥi sã rə tu r.

Loin de l'hiver morose
lwẽ də li vɛ rmɔ ro zə,

laisse-moi, laisse-moi sommeiller,
lɛ sə mwa, lɛ sə mwa sɔ mɛ je,

Et respirer la rose,
e rɛ spi re la ro zə,

respirer la rose avant de l'effeuiller.
rɛ spi re la ro za vã də lɛ fœ je.

Reste dans mon âme
rɛ stə dã mõ nɑ mə,

Comme un doux trésor Longtemps encor!
kɔ mẽ du tre zɔ r, lõ tã zã kɔ r!

Gounod   Ah! lève-toi, soleil!, from Roméo et Juliette"
guno   ɑ lɛv twa sɔlɛj   romeo e ʒyljɛt

L'amour! oui, son ardeur a troublé tout mon être!
la mu r! wi, sõ na rdœ ra tru ble tu mõ nɛ trə!

Mais quelle soudaine clarté resplendit
mɛ kɛ lə su dɛ nə kla rte rɛ splã di

à cette fenêtre?
a sɛ tə fə nɛ trə?

C'est là que dans la nuit rayonne sa beauté!
sɛ la kə dã la nɥi rɛ jɔ nə sa bo te!

Ah! lève-toi, soleil! fais pâlir les étoiles
ɑ! lɛ və twa, sɔ lɛ j! fɛ pɑ li rlə ze twa lə,

Qui, dans l'azur sans voiles,
ki, dɑ̃ la zy rsɑ̃ vwa lə,

Brillent au firmament.
bri jə to fi rma mɑ̃.

Ah! lève-toi, parais! Astre pur et charmant!
ɑ! lɛ və twa, pa rɛ! a strɛ py re ʃa rmɑ̃!

Elle rêve! elle dénoue
ɛ lə rɛ və! ɛ lə de nu ə,

Une boucle de cheveux Qui vient caresser sa joue
y nə bu klə də ʃə vø, ki vjɛ̃ ka rɛ se sa ʒu ə,

Amour! porte-lui mes voeux! Elle parle!
a mu r! pɔ rtə lɥi me vø! ɛ lə pa rlə!

Qu'elle est belle!
kɛ lɛ bɛ lə!

Ah! je n'ai rien entendu!
ɑ! ʒə ne rjɛ̃ nɑ̃ tɑ̃ dy!

Mais ses yeux parlent pour elle,
mɛ se zjø pa rlə pu rɛ lə,

Et mon coeur a répondu! Viens, parais!
e mɔ̃ kœ ra re pɔ̃ dy! vjɛ̃, pa rɛ!

Gounod   Avant de quitter ces lieux, from "Faust"
guno   avɑ̃ də kite se ljø   Fr. fɔst Ger. fa̱ost

Avant de quitter ces lieux,
a vɑ̃ də ki te se ljø,

Sol natal des mes aïeux
sɔ lna ta ldə me za jø,

A toi, Seigneur et roi des cieux,
a twa sɛ ɲœ re rwa de sjø,

Ma soeur je confie!
ma sœ rʒə kɔ̃ fi ə!

Daigne de tout danger
dɛ ɲə də tu dɑ̃ ʒe,

Toujours, toujours la protéger,
tu ʒu rtu ʒu rla prɔ te ʒe,

Cette soeur si chérie;
sɛ tə sœ rsi ʃe ri ə;

Daigne la protéger de tout danger.
dɛ ɲə la prɔ te ʒe də tu dã ʒe.

Délivré d'une triste pensée,
de li vre dy nə tri stə pã se ə,

J'irai chercher la gloire au sein des ennemis,
ʒi re ʃɛ rʃe la glwa ro sɛ̃ de zɛ nə mi,

Le premier, le plus brave au fort de la mêlée
lə prə mje lə ply bra vo fɔ rdə la mɛ le ə

J'irai combattre pour mon pays.
ʒi re kɔ̃ ba trə pu rmɔ̃ pe i.

Et si vers lui Dieu me rappelle,
e si vɛ rlɥi djø mə ra pɛ lə,

Je veillerai sur toi fidèle, O Marguerite!
ʒə vɛ jə re sy rtwa fi dɛ lə, o ma rgə ri tə,

...O Roi des cieux, jette les yeux,
   o rwa de sjø ʒɛ tə le zjø,

protège Marguerite, Roi des cieux!
prɔ tɛ ʒə ma rgə ri tə, rwa de sjø!

Gounod   Faites-lui mes aveux, from ''Faust''
guno   fɛtə lɥi me zavø   Fr. fɔst Ger. fa̲ost

Faites-lui mes aveux, Portez mes voeux!
fɛ tə lɥi me za vø pɔ rte me vø!

Fleurs écloses près d'elle, Dites-lui qu'elle est belle,
flœ rze klo zə prɛ dɛ lə, di tə lɥi kɛ lɛ bɛ lə,

Que mon coeur nuit et jour Languit d'amour!
kə mɔ̃ kœ rnɥi te ʒu r, lã gi da mu r!

Révélez à son âme Le secret de ma flamme,
re ve le za sɔ̃ nɑ mə, lə sə kre də ma fla mə,

Qu'il s'exhale avec vous Parfums plus doux!
ki lsɛ gza la vɛ kvu pa rfœ̃ ply du!

341

Fanée! hélas! ce sorcier, que Dieu damne,
fa ne ə! e la ssə sɔ rsje kə djø da nə,

M'a porté malheur!
ma pɔ rte ma lœ r!

Je ne puis, sans qu'elle se fane,
ʒə nə pɥi sã kɛ lə sə fa nə,

Toucher une fleur! Si je trempais mes doigts
tu ʃe ry nə flœ r! si ʒə trã pɛ me dwa

dans l'eau bénite!
dã lo be ni tə!

C'est là que chaque soir vient prier Marguerite!
sɛ la kə ʃa kə swa r, vjɛ̃ pri je ma rgə ri tə!

Voyons maintenant! voyons vite! Elles se fanent?
vwa jɔ̃ mɛ̃ tə nã! vwa jɔ̃ vi tə! ɛ lə sə fa nə?

non! Satan, je ris de toi!
nɔ̃! sa tã, ʒə ri də twa!

C'est en vous que j'ai foi; Parlez pour moi!
sɛ tã vu kə ʒe fwa pa rle pu rmwa!

Qu'elle puisse connaître L'émoi qu'elle a fait naître,
kɛ lə pɥi sə kɔ nɛ trə, le mwa kɛ la fɛ nɛ trə,

Et dont mon coeur troublé N'a point parlé!
e dɔ̃ mɔ̃ kœ rtru ble na pwɛ̃ pa rle!

Si l'amour l'effarouche, Que la fleur sur sa bouche
si la mu rle fa ru ʃə, kə la flœ rsy rsa bu ʃə,

Sache au moins déposer Un doux baiser!
sa ʃo mwɛ̃ de po ze ɶ̃ du bɛ ze!

Gounod   Il était un roi de Thulé, from "Faust"
guno   il etɛ tɛ̃ rwa də tyle   Fr. fɔst Ger. f‿aost

Je voudrais bien savoir quel était ce jeune homme;
ʒə vu drɛ bjɛ̃ sa vwa rkɛ le tɛ sə ʒɶ no mə;

Si c'est un grand seigneur, et comment il se nomme?
si sɛ tɛ̃ grã sɛ ɲœ r, e kɔ mã i lsə nɔ mə?

Il était un Roi de Thulé, Qui, jusqu'à la tombe fidèle,
i le tɛ tɛ̃ rwa də ty le ki, ʒy ska la tɔ̃ bə fi dɛ lə,

Eut, en souvenir de sa belle,
y tɑ̃ su və ni rdə sa bɛ lə,

Une coupe en or ciselé.
y nə ku pɑ̃ nɔ rsi zə le.

Il avait bonne grâce, à ce qu'il m'a semblé.
i la vɛ bɔ nə grɑ sə, a sə ki lma sɑ̃ ble.

Nul trésor n'avait tant de charmes,
ny ltre zɔ rna vɛ tɑ̃ də ʃa rmə,

Dans les grand jours il s'en servait,
dɑ̃ le grɑ̃ ʒu ri lsɑ̃ sɛ rvɛ,

Et chaque fois qu'il y buvait,
e ʃa kə fwɑ ki li by vɛ,

Ses yeux se remplissaient de larmes!
se zjø sə rɑ̃ pli sɛ də la rmə!

Quand il sentit venir la mort,
kɑ̃ ti lsɑ̃ ti və ni rla mɔ r,

Etendu sur sa froide couche,
e tɑ̃ dy sy rsa frwa də ku ʃə,

Pour la porter jusqu'à sa bouche,
pu rla pɔ rte ʒy ska sa bu ʃə,

Sa main fit un suprême effort!
sa mɛ̃ fi tɛ̃ sy prɛ mɛ fɔ r!

Je ne savais que dire, Et j'ai rougi d'abord.
ʒə nə sa vɛ kə di rə, e ʒe ru ʒi da bɔ r.

Et puis, en l'honneur de sa dame,
e pɥi, ɑ̃ lɔ nœ rdə sa da mə,

Il but une dernière fois.
i lby ty nə dɛ rnjɛ rə fwa.

La coupe trembla dans ses doigts,
la ku pə trɑ̃ bla dɑ̃ se dwa,

Et doucement il rendit l'âme!
e du sə mɑ̃ i lrɑ̃ di lɑ mə!

Gounod   Je ris de me voir si belle, from "Faust"
guno   ʒə ri də mə vwar si bɛl Fr. fɔst Ger. fa͟ost

Je ris de me voir Si belle en ce miroir, Ah!
ʒə ri də mə vwa rsi bɛ lɑ̃ sə mi rwa r, ɑ!

343

Est-ce toi, Marguerite, Est-ce toi?
ɛ sə twa, ma rgə ri tə, ɛ sə twa?

Réponds-moi, réponds vite!
re põ mwa, re põ vi tə!

Non! ce n'est plus toi! non,
nõ! sə nɛ ply twa! nõ,

Ce n'est plus ton visage; C'est la fille d'un roi,
sə nɛ ply tõ vi za ʒə; sɛ la fi jə dõ̃ rwa,

Qu'on salue au passage!
kõ sa ly o pa sa ʒə!

Ah s'il était ici! S'il me voyait ainsi!
ɑ si le tɛ ti si! si lmə vwa jɛ tɛ̃ si!

Comme une demoiselle Il me trouverait belle,
kɔ my nə də mwa zɛ lə, i lmə tru və rɛ bɛ lə,

Achevons la métamorphose.
a ʃə võ la me ta mɔ rfo zə.

Il me tarde encor d'essayer Le bracelet et le collier!
il mə ta rdɑ̃ kɔ rdɛ sɛ je lə bra sə le e lə kɔ lje!

Dieu! c'est comme une main, qui sur mon bras se pose!
djø! sɛ kɔ my nə mɛ̃, ki sy rmõ brɑ sə po zə!

Gounod   Le veau d'or est toujours debout, from "Faust"
guno   lə vo dɔr ɛ tuʒur dəbu, Fr. fɔst Ger. fa̠ost

Le veau d'or est toujours debout!
lə vo dɔ rɛ tu ʒu r də bu!

On encense Sa puissance,
õ nɑ̃ sɑ̃ sə sa pɥi sɑ̃ sə,

D'un bout du monde à l'autre bout!
dõ̃ bu dy mõ da lo trə bu!

Pour fêter l'infâme idole,
pu rfɛ te lɛ̃ fa mi do lə,

Rois et peuples confondus,
rwɑ ze pœ plə kõ fõ dy,

Au bruit sombre des écus,
o brɥi sõ brə de ze ky,

Dansent une ronde folle,
dã sə ty nə rɔ̃ də fɔ lə,

Autour de son piédestal!
o tu rdə sɔ̃ pje dɛ sta l!

Et Satan conduit le bal, conduit le bal!
e sa tã kɔ̃ dɥi lə ba l, kɔ̃ dɥi lə ba l!

Le veau d'or est vainqueur des dieux!
lə vo dɔ rɛ vɛ̃ kœ rde djø!

Dans sa gloire Dérisoire,
dã sa glwa rə de ri zwa rə,

Le monstre abject insulte aux cieux!
lə mɔ̃ stra bʒɛ ktɛ̃ sy lto sjø!

Il contemple, ô rage étrange!
i lkɔ̃ tã plo ra ʒe trã ʒə!

A ses pieds le genre humain,
a se pje lə ʒã ry mɛ̃,

Se ruant, le fer en main,
sə ry ã lə fɛ rã mɛ̃,

Dans le sang et dans la fange,
dã lə sã e dã la fã ʒə,

Où brille l'ardent métal!
u bri jə la rdã me ta l!

Et Satan conduit le bal, conduit le bal!
e sa tã kɔ̃ dɥi lə ba l, kɔ̃ dɥi lə ba l!

Gounod   Salut! demeure chaste et pure, from "Faust"
guno   saly dəmœr ʃast e pyr   Fr. fɔst Ger. f<u>ao</u>st

Quel trouble inconnu me pénètre?
kɛl tru blɛ̃ kɔ ny mə pe nɛ trə?

Je sens l'amour s'emparer de mon être!
ʒə sã la mu rsã pa re də mɔ̃ nɛ trə!

O Marguerite, à tes pieds me voici!
o ma rgə ri tə, a te pje mə vwa si!

Salut! demeure chaste et pure,
sa ly də mœ rə ʃa ste py rə,

345

où se devine La présence d'une âme innocente et divine!
u sə də vi nə la pre zɑ̃ sə, dy nɑ mi nɔ sɑ̃ te di vi nə!

Que de richesse en cette pauvreté!
kə də ri ʃɛ sɑ̃ sɛ tə po vrə te!

En ce réduit, que de félicité!
ɑ̃ sə re dɥi kə də fe li si te!

O nature, c'est là que tu la fis si belle!
o na ty rə, sɛ la kə ty la fi si bɛ lə!

C'est là que cette enfant a dormi sous ton aîle,
sɛ la kə sɛ tɑ̃ fɑ̃ a dɔ rmi su tɔ̃ nɛ l,

A grandi sous tes yeux.
a grɑ̃ di su te zjø.

Là que de ton haleine enveloppant son âme,
la kə də tɔ̃ na lɛ nə, ɑ̃ və lɔ pɑ̃ sɔ̃ na mə,

Tu fis avec amour épanouir la femme
ty fi a vɛ ka mu r, e pa nu i rla fa

En cet ange des cieux! C'est là! oui! c'est là!
mɑ̃ sɛ tɑ̃ ʒə de sjø! sɛ la! wi! sɛ la!

Gounod   Sérénade
guno   serenad

Quand tu chantes bercée Le soir entre mes bras,
kɑ̃ ty ʃɑ̃ tə bɛ rse ə lə swa rɑ̃ trə me bra,

Entends-tu ma pensée, Qui te répond tout bas?
ɑ̃ tɑ̃ ty ma pɑ̃ se ə ki tə re pɔ̃ tu ba?

Ton doux chant me rappelle Les plus beaux de mes jours.
tɔ̃ du ʃɑ̃ mə ra pɛ lə le ply bo də me ʒu r.

Ah! Chantez, chantez, ma belle, Chantez, chantez toujours,
a ʃɑ̃ te ʃɑ̃ te ma bɛ lə, ʃɑ̃ te ʃɑ̃ te tu ʒu r,

Chantez, chantez, ma belle, Chantez toujours!
ʃɑ̃ te, ʃɑ̃ te, ma bɛ lə, ʃɑ̃ te tu ʒu r!

Quand tu ris, sur ta bouche L'amour s'épanouit;
kɑ̃ ty ri sy rta bu ʃə la mu rse pa nu i;

Et soudain le farouche Soupçon s'évanouit.
e su dɛ̃ lə fa ru ʃə su psɔ̃ se va nu i.

346

Ah! le rire fidèle Prouve un coeur sans détours.
a lə ri rə fi 'dɛ lə pru vɛ̃ kœ rsɑ̃ de tu r.

Ah! Riez, riez, ma belle, Riez, riez toujours,
a ri je, ri je, ma bɛ lə, ri je, ri je tu ʒu r,

Quand tu dors, calme et pure Dans l'ombre sous mes yeux,
kɑ̃ ty dɔ rka lme py rə dɑ̃ lɔ̃ brə su me zjø,

Ton haleine murmure Des mots harmonieux.
tɔ̃ na lɛ nə my rmy rə de mo za rmɔ ni ø.

Ton beau corps se révèle sans voile et sans atours.
tɔ̃ bo kɔ rsə re vɛ lə sɑ̃ vwa le sɑ̃ za tu r.

Ah! Dormez, dormez, ma belle, Dormez, dormez toujours,
a dɔ rme, dɔ rme, ma bɛ lə, dɔ rme, dɔ rme tu ʒu r,

Dormez, dormez, ma belle, Dormez toujours!
dɔ rme, dɔ rme, ma bɛ lə, dɔ rme tu ʒu r!

Gounod   Si le bonheur à sourire t'invite, from "Faust"
guno   si lə bɔnœr a surir tɛ̃vit Fr. fɔst Ger. fa̱ost

Si le bonheur à sourire t'invite,
si lə bo nœ ra su ri rə tɛ̃ vi tə,

Joyeux alors je sens un doux émoi;
ʒwa jø a lɔ rʒə sɑ̃ zœ̃ du ze mwa;

Si la douleur t'accable, Marguerite,
si la du lœ rta ka blə, mar gə ri tə,

O Marguerite, je pleure alors,
o ma rgə ri tə, ʒə plœ ra lɔ r,

je pleure comme toi!
ʒə plœ rə kɔ mə twa!

Comme deux fleurs sur une même tige,
kɔ mə dø flœ rsy ry nə mɛ mə ti ʒə,

Notre destin suivant le même cours,
nɔ trə dɛ stɛ̃ sɥi vɑ̃ lə mɛ mə ku r,

De tes chagrins en frère je m'afflige,
də te ʃa grɛ̃ ɑ̃ frɛ rə ʒə ma fli ʒə,

O Marguerite, Comme une soeur je t'aimerai toujours!
o ma rgə ri tə, kɔ my nə sœ rʒə tɛ mə re tu ʒu r!

347

Gounod   Vous qui faites l'endormie, "Faust"
guno   vu ki fɛ tə lãdɔrmi Fr. fɔst Ger. f<u>a</u>ost

Vous qui faites l'endormie, N'entendez-vous pas,
vu ki fɛ tə lã dɔ rmi ə, nã tã de vu pɑ,

O Catherine, ma mie, N'entendez-vous pas
o ka tə ri nə ma mi ə, nã tã de vu pɑ

Ma voix et mes pas?
ma vwa e me pɑ?

Ainsi ton galant t'appelle,
ɛ̃ si tõ ga lã ta pɛ lə,

Et ton coeur l'en croit. Ah!
e tõ kœ rlã krwa. ɑ!

N'ouvre ta porte, ma belle,
nu vrə ta pɔ rtə ma bɛ lə,

Que la bague au doigt!
kə la ba go dwa!

Catherine que j'adore, Pourquoi refuser
ka tə ri nə ke ʒa dɔ rə, pu rkwa rə fy ze,

A l'amant qui vous implore,
a la mã ki vu zɛ̃ plɔ rə,

Pourquoi refuser Un si doux baiser?
pu rkwa rə fy ze, œ̃ si du bɛ ze?

Ainsi ton galant supplie, Et ton coeur l'en croit.
ɛ̃ si tõ ga lã sy pli ə, e tõ kœ rlã krwa.

Ah! Ne donne un baiser, ma mie,
ɑ! nə dɔ nœ̃ bɛ ze, ma mi ə,

Que la bague au doigt! Ah!
kə la ba go dwa! ɑ!

Hahn   L'heure exquise
an   l œr ɛkskiz

La lune blanche Luit dans les bois;
la ly nə blã ʃə lɥi dã le bwa;

De chaque branche Part une voix Sous la ramée
də ʃa kə brã ʃə pa ry nə vwa su la ra me ə,

O bienaimée.
o bjɛ̃ nɛ me ə.

348

L'étang reflète, Profond miroir
le tã rə flɛ tə, prɔ fõ mi rwa r,

La silhouette Du saule noir
la si lu ɛ tə dy so lə nwa r

Où le vent pleure Rêvons! c'est l'heure! . . .
u lə vã plœ rə, rɛ võ! sɛ lœ rə! . . .

Un vaste et tendre Apaisement, Semble descendre
œ̃ va ste tã dra pɛ zə mã sã blə dɛ sã drə

Du firmament Que l'astre irise . . .
dy fi rma mã kə la stri ri zə . . .

C'est l'heure exquise.
sɛ lœ rɛ kski zə.

Hahn   Si mes vers avaient des ailes!
an   si me vɛr avɛ de zɛl

Mes vers fuiraient, doux et frêles,
me vɛ rfɥi rɛ du ze frɛ lə,

Vers votre jardin si beau
vɛ rvɔ trə ʒa rdɛ̃ si bo,

Si mes vers avaient des ailes Comme l'oiseau!
si me vɛ ra vɛ de zɛ lə, kɔ mə lwa zo!

Ils voleraient, étincelles,
i lvɔ lə rɛ e tɛ̃ sɛ lə,

Vers votre foyer qui rit
vɛ rvɔ trə fwa je ki ri,

Si mes vers avaient des ailes Comme l'esprit.
si me vɛ ra vɛ de zɛ lə, kɔ mə lɛ spri.

Près de vous, purs et fidèles,
prɛ də vu py re fi dɛ lə,

Ils accourraient, nuit et jour
i lza ku rrɛ, nɥi te ʒu r,

Si mes vers avaient des ailes
si me vɛ ra vɛ de zɛ lə,

Comme l'amour!
kɔ mə la mu r!

Halévy   Si la rigueur, from ''La Juive''
alevi   si la rigœr   la ʒɥiv

Si la rigueur ou la vengeance
si la ri gœ ru la vã ʒã sə,

Leur font haïr ta sainte loi,
lœ rfõ a i rta sɛ̃ tə lwa,

Que le pardon, que la clémence, mon Dieu,
kə lə pa rdõ, kə la kle mã sə, mõ djø,

Les ramène en ce jour vers toi,
le ra mɛ nã sə ʒu rvɛ rtwa,

Rapelons-nous son précepte sacré,
ra pə lõ nu sõ pre sɛ ptə sa kre,

Ouvrons nos bras à l'enfant égaré,
u vrõ no bra a lã fã e ga re,

Nous rappelant son précepte sacré,
nu ra pə lã sõ pre sɛ ptə sa kre,

oh, mon Dieu, les ramène vers toi,
o, mõ djø, le ra mɛ nə vɛ rtwa,

en ce jour vers toi.
ã sə ʒu rvɛ rtwa.

Hüe   A des oiseaux
y   a de zwazo

Bonjour, bonjour les fauvettes,
bõ ʒu rbõ ʒu rle fo vɛ tə,

Bonjour les joyeux pinsons,
bõ ʒu rle ʒwa jø pɛ̃ sõ,

Eveillez les pâquerettes
e vɛ je le pa kə rɛ tə

Et les fleurs des verts buissons!
e le flœ rde vɛ rbɥi sõ!

Toujours votre âme est en fête,
tu ʒu rvɔ tra mɛ tã fɛ tə,

Gais oiseaux qu'on aime à voir,
ge zwa zo kõ nɛ ma vwa r,

350

Pour l'amant et le poète,
pu rla mã e lə pɔ ɛ tə,

Vous chantez matin et soir!
vu ʃã te ma tɛ̃ e swa r!

Mais dans la plaine, il me semble
mɛ dã la plɛ ni lmə sã blə

Qu'on a tendu des réseaux;
kɔ̃ na tã dy de re zo;

Voltigez toujours ensemble:
vɔ lti ʒe tu ʒu rzã sã blə:

En garde, petits oiseaux!
ã ga rdə, pə ti zwa zo!

Penchez-vous sans toucher terre,
pã ʃe vu sã tu ʃe tɛ rə,

Voyez-vous au coin du bois,
vwa je vu o kwɛ̃ dy bwa,

Vous guettant avec mystère,
vu gɛ tã ta vɛ kmi stɛ rə,

Ces enfants à l'oeil sournois?
se zã fã a lœ jsu rnwa?

Ah, bien vite à tire d'aile,
a bjɛ̃ vi ta ti rə dɛ lə,

Fuyez, fuyez leurs appâts;
f чi je, fчi je lœ rza pɑ;

Venez avec l'hirondelle,
və ne a vɛ kli rɔ̃ dɛ lə,

Qui, dans son vol, suit mes pas.
ki dã sɔ̃ vɔ lsчi me pɑ.

Dans mon jardin nulle crainte;
dã mɔ̃ ʒa rdɛ̃ ny lə krɛ̃ tə;

Vous pourrez, d'un bec léger,
vu pu re dœ̃ bɛ kle ʒe,

Piller, piller sans contrainte,
pi je pi je sã kɔ̃ trɛ̃ tə,

Tous les fruits mûrs du verger.
tu le frчi my rdy vɛ rʒe.

Bonsoir, bonsoir les fauvettes,
bɔ̃ swa rbɔ̃ swa rle fo vɛ tə,

351

Bonsoir les joyeux pinsons,
bõ swa rle ʒwa jø pɛ̃ sõ,

Endormez les pâquerettes
ã dɔ rme le pa kə rɛ tə,

Et les fleurs des verts buissons!
e le flœ rde vɛ rbɥi sõ!

Hüe   J'ai pleuré en rêve
y   ʒe plœre ã rɛv

J'ai pleuré en rêve: J'ai rêvé que tu étais morte;
ʒe plœ re ã rɛ və: ʒe rɛ ve kə ty e tɛ mɔ rtə;

Je m'éveillai et les larmes coulèrent de mes joues.
ʒə me vɛ je, e le la rmə ku lɛ rə də me ʒu ə.

J'ai pleuré en rêve: J'ai rêvé que tu me quittais;
ʒe plœ re ã rɛ və: ʒe rɛ ve kə ty mə ki tɛ;

Je m'éveillai et je pleurai amèrement longtemps après.
ʒə me vɛ je, e ʒə plœ re a mɛ rə mã lõ tã za prɛ.

J'ai pleuré en rêve: J'ai rêvé que tu m'aimais encore;
ʒe plœ re ã rɛ və: ʒe rɛ ve kə ty mɛ mɛ zã kɔ rə;

et le torrent de mes larmes coule toujours, toujours.
e lə tɔ rã də me la rmə ku lə tu ʒu r, tu ʒu r.

Koechlin   Si tu le veux
keklɛ̃   si ty lə vø

Si tu le veux, ô mon amour,
si ty lə vø o mõ na mu r

Ce soir dès que la fin du jour Sera venue,
sə swa rdɛ kə la fɛ̃ dy ʒu rsə ra və ny ə,

Quand les étoiles surgiront,
kã le ze twa lə sy rʒi rõ

352

Et mettront des clous d'or au fond
e mɛ trõ de klu dɔ ro fõ

Bleu de la nue,
blø də la ny ə,

Nous partirons seuls tous les deux
nu pa rti rõ sœ ltu le dø,

Dans la nuit brune en amoureux,
dã la nɥi bry nã na mu rø,

Sans qu'on nous voie; Et tendrement je te dirai
sã kõ nu vwa ə; e tã drə mã ʒə te di re,

Un chant d'amour où je mettrai Toute ma joie.
œ̃ ʃã da mu ru ʒə mɛ tre, tu tə ma ʒwa ə.

Mais quand tu rentreras chez toi,
mɛ kã ty rã trə ra ʃe twa,

Si l'on te demande pourquoi,
si lõ tə də mã də pu rkwa,

Mignonne fée, Tes cheveux sont plus fous qu'avant,
mi ɲo nə fe ə, te ʃə vø sõ ply fu ka vã

Tu répondras que seul le vent T'a décoiffée,
ty re põ dra kə sœ llə vã, ta de kwa fe ə,

Si tu le veux, ô mon amour.
si ty lə vø, o mõ na mu r.

Lully   Bois épais
lyli   bwa zepɛ

Bois épais, redouble ton ombre;
bwa ze pɛ, rə du blə tõ nõ brə;

Tu ne saurais être assez sombre,
ty nə sɔ rɛ zɛ tra se sõ brə,

Tu ne peux trop cacher
ty nə pø tro ka ʃe,

Mon malheureux amour.
mõ ma lø rø za mu r.

Je sens un désespoir
ʒə sã zœ̃ de ze spwa r,

Dont l'horreur est extrême,
dõ lɔ rœ re te kstre mə,

Je ne dois plus voir ce que j'aime,
ʒə nə dwa ply vwa rsə kə ʒe mə,

Je ne veux plus souffrir le jour.
ʒə nə vø ply su fri rlə ʒu r.

Martini   Plaisir d'Amour
martini   plezir d amur

Plaisir d'amour ne dure qu'un moment
ple zi rda mu r, nə dy rə kœ̃ mɔ mã,

Chagrin d'amour dure toute la vie
ʃa grɛ̃ da mu r dy rə tu tə la vi ə,

J'ai tout quitté pour l'ingrate Silvie
ʒe tu ki te pu rlɛ̃ gra tə si lvi ə

Elle me quitte et prend un autre amant.
ɛ lə mə ki te prã tœ̃ no tra mã.

Plaisir d'amour ne dure qu'un moment
ple zi rda mu r, nə dy rə kœ̃ mɔ mã

Chagrin d'amour dure toute la vie.
ʃa grɛ̃ da mu rdy rə tu tə la vi ə.

Tant que cette eau coulera doucement
tã kə se to ku lə ra du sə mã,

Vers ce ruisseau qui borde la prairie,
ve rsə rɥi so ki bɔ rdə la pre ri ə,

Je t'aimerai me répétait Silvie.
ʒə te mə re, mə re pe te si lvi ə.

L'eau coule encor, elle a changé pourtant.
lo ku lã kɔ r, e la ʃã ʒe pu rtã.

354

Massenet   Ah! fuyez, douce image, from ''Manon''
masne   ɑ fɥije dus imaʒ   manõ

Je suis seul! Seul enfin! c'est le moment suprême!
ʒə sɥi sœ l! sœ lã fɛ̃! sɛ lə mɔ mã sy prɛ mə!

Il n'est plus rien que j'aime
i lnɛ ply rjɛ̃ kə ʒɛ mə

Que le repos sacré que m'apporte la foi!
kə lə rə po sa kre kə ma pɔ rtə la fwa!

Oui, j'ai voulu mettre Dieu même
wi, ʒe vu ly mɛ trə djø mɛ mə,

Entre le monde et moi!
ã trə lə mõ d, e mwa!

Ah! fuyez, douce image, à mon âme trop chère;
ɑ fɥi je du si ma ʒ, a mõ na mə trɔ ʃɛ rə;

Respectez un repos cruellement gagné,
rɛ spɛ kte zœ̃ rə po kry ɛ lə mã ga ɲe,

Et songez, si j'ai bu dans une coupe amère,
e sõ ʒe, si ʒe by dã zy nə ku pa mɛ rə,

Que mon coeur l'emplirait de ce qu'il a saigné!
kə mõ kœ rlã pli rɛ, də sə ki la sɛ ɲe!

Ah, fuyez! loin de moi!
ɑ, fɥi je! lwɛ̃ də mwa!

Que m'importe la vie et ce semblant de gloire?
kə mɛ̃ pɔ rtə la vi ə e sə sã blã də glwa rə?

Je ne veux que chasser du fond de ma mémoire
ʒə nə vø kə ʃa se dy fõ də ma me mwa rə,

Un nom maudit! ce nom qui m'obsède et pourquoi?
œ̃ nõ mo di! sə nõ, ki mɔ psɛ də, e pu rkwa?

Mon Dieu! De votre flamme
mõ djø! də vɔ trə fla mə,

Purifiez mon âme, Et dissipez à sa lueur
py ri fi e mõ na mə, e di si pe a sa ly œ r,

L'ombre qui passe encor dans le fond de mon coeur!
lõ brə ki pɑ sã kɔ rdã lə fõ də mõ kœ r!

Massenet   Il est doux, il est bon, from ''Hérodiade''
masne   il ɛ du il ɛ bõ   erɔdjad

Celui dont la parole efface toutes peines,
sə lɥi dõ la pa rɔ le fa sə tu tə pɛ nə,

Le Prophète est ici! c'est vers lui que je vais!
lə prɔ fɛ tɛ ti si! sɛ vɛ rlɥi kə ʒə vɛ!

Il est doux, il est bon, sa parole est sereine:
i lɛ du, i lɛ bõ, sa pa rɔ lɛ sə rɛ nə,

Il parle, tout se tait. Plus léger sur la plaine
i lpa rlə, tu sə tɛ, ply le ʒe sy rla plɛ nə,

L'air attentif, passe sans bruit. Il parle!
lɛ ra tã ti ʃpa sə sã brɥi. i lpa rlə!

Ah! quand reviendra-t-il? quand pourrai-je l'entendre?
ɑ kã rə vjẽ dra ti l? kã pu rɛ ʒə lã tã drə?

Je souffrais j'étais seule et mon coeur s'est calmé
ʒə su frɛ, ʒe tɛ sœ le mõ kœ rsɛ ka lme,

En écoutant sa voix mélodieuse et tendre,
ã ne ku tã sa vwa me lɔ di ø ze tã drə,

Mon coeur s'est calmé!
mõ kœ rsɛ ka lme!

Prophète bien aimé, puis-je vivre sans toi!
prɔ fɛ tə bjẽ nɛ me pɥi ʒə vi vrə sã twa!

C'est là! dans ce désert où la foule étonnée
sɛ la! dã sə de ze ru la fu le tɔ ne,

Avait suivi ses pas, Qu'il m'accueillit un jour,
a vɛ sɥi vi se pɑ, ki lma kœ ji tẽ ʒu r,

enfant abandonnée! Et qu'il m'ouvrit ses bras!
ã fã a bã dɔ ne ə! e ki lmu vri se bra!

Massenet   Le Rêve, from "Manon"
masne   lə rɛv   manõ

Instant charmant Où la crainte fait trève,
ẽ stã ʃa rmã u la krẽ tə fɛ trɛ və,

Où nous sommes deux seulement! Tiens, Manon,
u nu sɔ mə dø sœ lə mã, tjẽ, ma nõ,

en marchant Je viens de faire un rêve!
ã ma rʃã, ʒə vjẽ də fɛ rẽ rɛ və!

En fermant les yeux je vois
ã fɛ rmã le zjø ʒə vwa

Là-bas une humble retraite
la ba, y nœ̃ blə rə trɛ tə,

Une maisonnette Toute blanche au fond des bois!
y nə mɛ zo nɛ tə tu tə blɑ̃ ʃo fɔ̃ de bwa!

Sous ces tranquilles ombrages
su se trɑ̃ ki lə zɔ̃ bra ʒə,

Les clairs et joyeux ruisseaux
le klɛ rze ʒwa jø rɥi so,

Où se mirent les feuillages Chantent avec les oiseaux!
u sə mi rə le fœ ja ʒə, ʃɑ̃ tə ta vɛ kle zwa zo!

C'est le paradis! Oh! non!
sɛ lə pa ra di! o nɔ̃

Tout est là triste et morose,
tu tɛ la tri ste mo ro zə,

Car il y manque une chose Il y faut encor Manon!
ka ri li mɑ̃ ky nə ʃo z, i li fo tɑ̃ ko r, ma nɔ̃!

Viens! Là sera notre vie,
vjɛ̃! la sə ra no trə vi ə,

Si tu le veux, ô Manon!
si ty lə vø, o ma nɔ̃!

Massenet   Obéissons, quand leur voix appelle, from "Manon"
masne   ɔbeisɔ̃ kɑ̃ lœr vwa apɛlə   manɔ̃

Obéissons, quand leur voix appelle,
ɔ be i sɔ̃ kɑ̃ lœ rvwa a pɛ lə,

Aux tendres amours toujours!
o tɑ̃ drə za mu rtu ʒu r!

Tant que vous êtes belle, usez sans les compter
tɑ̃ kə vu zɛ tə bɛ ly ze sɑ̃ le kɔ̃ te

vos jours! tous vos jours!
vo ʒu r! tu vo ʒu r!

Profitons bien de la jeunesse,
pro fi tɔ̃ bjɛ̃ də la ʒœ nɛ sə,

Des jours qu'amène le printemps;
de ʒu rka mɛ nə lə prɛ̃ tɑ̃;

357

Aimons, chantons, rions sans cesse,
ɛ mõ, ʃã tõ ri jõ sã sɛ sə,

Nous n'avons encor que vingt ans! Ah!
nu na võ zã kɔ rkə vɛ̃ tã.! ɑ

Le coeur, hélas! le plus fidèle,
lə kœ re lɑ s! lə ply fi dɛ lə,

Oublie en un jour l'amour,
u bli ã nœ̃ ʒu rla mu r,

Et la jeunesse ouvrant son aile A disparu sans retour.
e la ʒœ nɛ su vrã sõ nɛ la di spa ry sã rə tu r.

Bien court, hélas, est le printemps!
bjɛ̃ ku re lɑ sɛ lə prɛ̃ tã!

Massenet   Ouvre tes yeux bleus
masne   uvrə te zjø blø

Ouvre tes yeux bleus, ma mignonne:
u vrə te zjø blø ma mi ɲɔ nə:

Voici le jour.
vwa si lə ʒu r.

Déjà la fauvette fredonne
de ʒa la fo vɛ tə frə dɔ nə,

Un chant d'amour.
œ̃ ʃã da mu r.

L'aurore épanouit la rose:
lo rɔ re pa nu i la ro zə:

Viens avec moi Cueillir la marguerite éclose.
vjɛ̃ za vɛ kmwa, kœ ji rla ma rgə ri te klo zə.

Réveille-toi!
re vɛ jə twa!

A quoi bon contempler la terre Et sa beauté?
a kwa bõ kõ tã ple la tɛ rə, e sa bo te?

L'amour est un plus doux mystère
la mu rɛ tœ̃ ply du mi stɛ rə,

Qu'un jour d'été;
kœ̃ ʒu rde te;

358

C'est en moi que l'oiseau module
sɛ tɑ̃ mwa kə lwa zo mɔ dy

Un chant vainqueur,
lœ̃ ʃɑ̃ vɛ̃ kœ r,

Et le grand soleil qui nous brûle
e lə grɑ̃ sɔ lɛ jki nu bry lə,

Est dans mon coeur!
ɛ dɑ̃ mɔ̃ kœ r!

Massenet   Pleurez! pleurez, mes yeux! , from "Le Cid"
masne   plœre plœre me zjø   lə sid

De cet affreux combat je sors l'âme brisée!
də sɛ ta frø kɔ̃ ba, ʒə sɔ rlɑ me bri ze ə!

Mais enfin je suis libre et je pourrai du moins
mɛ zɑ̃ fɛ̃, ʒə sɥi li brə, e ʒə pu re dy mwɛ̃

Soupirer sans contrainte et souffrir sans témoins.
su pi re sɑ̃ kɔ̃ trɛ̃ t, e su fri rsɑ̃ te mwɛ̃.

Pleurez, mes yeux! tombez triste rosée
plœ re me zjø, tɔ̃ be tri stə ro ze ə

Qu'un rayon de soleil ne doit jamais tarir!
kœ̃ rɛ jɔ̃ də sɔ lɛ jnə dwa ʒa mɛ ta ri r!

S'il me reste un espoir, c'est de bientôt mourir!
si lmə rɛ stœ̃ nɛ spwa r, sɛ də bjɛ̃ to mu ri r!

Pleurez, mes yeux, pleurez toutes vos larmes!
plœ re me zjø, plœ re tu tə vo la rmə!

Mais qui donc a voulu l'éternité des pleurs?
mɛ ki dɔ̃ ka vu ly, le tɛ rni te de plœ r?

O chers ensevelis, trouvez-vous tant de charmes
o ʃɛ rzɑ̃ sə və li, tru ve vu tɑ̃ də ʃa rmə

A léguer aux vivants d'implacables douleurs?
a le ge ro vi vɑ̃ dɛ̃ pla ka blə du lœ r?

Hélas! je me souviens il me disait:
e lɑ sʒə mə su vjɛ̃ i lmə di zɛ,

Avec ton doux sourire
a vɛ ktɔ̃ du su ri rə,

359

Tu ne saurais jamais conduire
ty nə sɔ rɛ ʒa mɛ, kɔ̃ dyi rə

Qu'aux chemins glorieux ou qu'aux sentiers bénis!
ko ʃə mɛ̃ glɔ ri ø, u ko sɑ̃ tje be ni!

Ah! mon père! Hélas!
ɑ mɔ̃ pɛ rə, e la s!

Massenet   Vision fugitive, from "Hérodiade"
masne   vizjɔ̃ fyʒitiv   erɔdjad

Ce breuvage pourrait me donner un tel rêve!
sə brœ va ʒə pu rɛ mə dɔ ne œ̃ tɛ lrɛ və!

Je pourrais la revoir...Contempler sa beauté!
ʒə pu rɛ la rə vwa r, kɔ̃ tɑ̃ ple sa bo te!

Divine volupté à mes regards promise!
di vi nə vɔ ly pte a me rə ga rprɔ mi zə!

Espérance trop brève qui viens bercer mon coeur
ɛ spe rɑ̃ sə trɔ brɛ və, ki vjɛ̃ bɛ rse mɔ̃ kœ r

et troubler ma raison...
e tru ble ma rɛ zɔ̃...

Ah! ne t'enfuis pas, douce illusion!
a! nə tɑ̃ fyi pa, du si ly zi ɔ̃!

Vision fugitive et toujours poursuivie,
vi zi ɔ̃ fy ʒi ti ve tu ʒu rpu rsyi vi ə,

Ange mystérieux qui prends toute ma vie...
ɑ̃ ʒə mi ste ri jø ki prɑ̃ tu tə ma vi ə...

Ah! c'est toi que je veux voir,
a sɛ twa kə ʒə vø vwa r,

O mon amour! ô mon espoir!
o mɔ̃ na mu r! o mɔ̃ nɛ spwa r!

Te presser dans mes bras!
tə prɛ se dɑ̃ me bra!

Sentir battre ton coeur
sɑ̃ ti rba trə tɔ̃ kœ r

D'une amoureuse ardeur!
dy na mu rø za rdœ r!

Puis, mourir enlacés
pɥi mu ri rã la se,

dans une même ivresse,
dã zy nə mɛ mi vrɛ sə,

Pour ces transports, pour cette flamme,
pu rse trã spɔ r, pu rsɛ tə fla mə,

Ah! sans remords et sans plainte
a! sã rə mɔ re sã plɛ̃ tə,

Je donnerais mon âme pour toi,
ʒə dɔ nə rɛ mõ na mə pu rtwa,

mon amour! mon espoir!
mõ na mu r! mõ nɛ spwa r!

Meyerbeer   Ah! mon fils, from "Le Prophète"
Fr. mejɛrbɛr a mõ fis   lə prɔfɛt
Ger. maeɔrbeːr

Ah! mon fils, sois béni!
a mõ fi s, swa be ni!

Ta pauvre mère te fut plus chère
ta po vrə mɛ rə, tə fy ply ʃɛ rə,

que ta Bertha, que ton amour!
kə ta bɛ rta, kə tõ na mu r!

Ah! mon fils! tu viens, hélas!
a mõ fi s! ty vjɛ̃, e la s,

de donner pour ta mère plus que la vie,
də dɔ ne, pu rta mɛ rə, ply kə la vi,

en donnant ton bonheur!
ã dɔ nã tõ bɔ nœ r!

Ah! mon fils! que vers le ciel
a mõ fi s! kə vɛ rlə sjɛ l,

s'élève ma prière,
se lɛ və ma pri jɛ rə,

et sois béni dans le Seigneur! Jean! ah!
e swa be ni dã lə sɛ ɲœ r! ʒã! a!

Offenbach   Les oiseaux dans la charmille, from "Les Contes d'Hoffmann"
ɔfɛnbak   le zwazo dɑ̃ la ʃarmij   le kɔ̃t d ɔfman

Les oiseaux dans la charmille,
le zwa zo dɑ̃ la ʃa rmi jə,

Dans les cieux l'astre du jour,
dɑ̃ le sjø la strə dy ʒu r,

Tout parle à la jeune fille D'amour! Ah!
tu pa rlɑ la ʒœ nə fi jə da mu r! ɑ!

tout parle d'amour! Ah!
tu pa rlə da mu r! ɑ!

Voilà la chanson gentille,
vwa la la ʃɑ̃ sɔ̃ ʒɑ̃ ti jə,

La chanson d'Olympia!
la ʃɑ̃ sɔ̃ dɔ lɛ̃ pi a!

Tout ce qui chante et résonne
tu sə ki ʃɑ̃ te re zɔ nə,

Et soupire, tour à tour,
e su pi rə tu ra tu r,

Emeut son coeur qui frissonne D'amour!
e mø sɔ̃ kœ rki fri sɔ nə da mu r!

Voilà la chanson mignonne, la chanson d'Olympia!
vwa la la ʃɑ̃ sɔ̃ mi ɲɔ nə, la ʃɑ̃ sɔ̃ dɔ lɛ̃ pi a!

Offenbach   Scintille, diamant, from "Les Contes d'Hoffmann"
ɔfɛnbak   sɛ̃tij djamɑ̃   le kɔ̃t d ɔfman

Scintille, diamant, Miroir où se prend l'alouette,
sɛ̃ ti jə di a mɑ̃, mi rwa ru sə prɑ̃ la lu ɛ tə,

Scintille, diamant, fascine, attire-la;
sɛ̃ ti jə di a mɑ̃, fa si na ti rə la;

L'alouette ou la femme A cet appas vainqueur
la lu ɛ tə, u la fa mə, a sɛ ta pɑ vɛ̃ kœ r,

Vont de l'aile ou du coeur;
vɔ̃ də lɛ lu dy kœ r;

L'une y laisse la vie Et l'autre y perd son âme!
ly ni lɛ sə la vi ə, e lo tri pɛ rsɔ̃ nɑ mə!

Beau diamant, attire-la!
bo di a mã, a ti rə la!

Paladilhe   Psyché
paladij   psiʃe

Je suis jaloux, Psyché, de toute la nature!
ʒə sɥi ʒa lu psi ʃe, də tu tə la na ty rə

Les rayons du soleil vous baisent trop souvent,
le rɛ jõ dy so lɛ j, vu bɛ zə tro su vã,

Vos cheveux souffrent trop les caresses du vent.
vo ʃə vø su frə tro le ka rɛ sə dy vã.

Quand il les flatte, j'en murmure!
kã ti lle fla tə, ʒã my rmy rə!

L'air même que vous respirez
lɛ rmɛ mə kə vu rɛ spi re,

Avec trop de plaisir passe sur votre bouche.
a vɛ ktro də plɛ zi rpa sə sy rvo trə bu ʃə.

Votre habit de trop près vous touche!
vo tra bi də tro prɛ vu tu ʃə!

Et sitôt que vous soupirez
e si to kə vu su pi re,

Je ne sais quoi qui m'effarouche
ʒə nə sɛ kwa ki mɛ fa ru ʃə,

Craint, parmi vos soupirs, des soupirs égarés!
krɛ̃, pa rmi vo su pi r, de su pi rze ga re!

Ravel   Chanson à boire (Don Quichotte à Dulcinée)
ravɛl   ʃɑ̃sõ a bwar dõ kiʃot a dylsine

Foin du bâtard, illustre Dame,
fwɛ̃ dy ba ta ri ly strə da mə,

363

Qui pour me perdre à vos doux yeux
ki pu rmə pɛ rdra vo du zjø,

Dit que l'amour et le vin vieux
di kə la mu re lə vɛ̃ vjø,

Mettent en deuil mon coeur, mon âme! Ah!
mɛ tə tɑ̃ dœ jmɔ̃ kœ r, mɔ̃ na mə! ɑ!

Je bois A la joie!
ʒə bwa, a la ʒwa!

La joie est le seul but Où je vais droit...
la ʒwa ɛ lə sœ lby u ʒə vɛ drwa...

lorsque j'ai lorsque j'ai bu!
lɔ rskə ʒe, lɔ rskə ʒe by!

Ah! la joie! Là Je bois A la joie!
a la ʒwa! la, ʒə bwa a la ʒwa!

Foin du jaloux, brune maîtresse,
fwɛ̃ dy ʒa lu bry nə mɛ trɛ sə,

Qui geint, qui pleure et fait serment
ki ʒɛ̃ ki plœ re fɛ sɛ rmɑ̃

D'être toujours ce pâle amant,
dɛ trə tu ʒu rsə pɑ la mɑ̃

Qui met de l'eau dans son ivresse!
ki mɛ də lo dɑ̃ sɔ̃ ni vrɛ sə!

Ah! Je bois à la joie!
ɑ! ʒə bwa, a la ʒwa!

La joie est le seul but Où je vais droit
la ʒwa ɛ lə sœ lbu u ʒə vɛ drwa,

lorsque j'ai bu!
lɔ rskə ʒe by!

Ah! la joie! Là, Je bois A la joie!
a la ʒwa! la, ʒə bwa a la ʒwa!

Ravel   Chanson épique (Don Quichotte a Dulcinée)
ravɛl   ʃɑ̃sɔ̃ epik   dɔ̃ kiʃɔt a dylsine

Bon Saint Michel qui me donnez loisir
bɔ̃ sɛ̃ mi ʃɛ lki mə dɔ ne lwa zi r,

De voir ma Dame et de l'entendre,
də vwa rma da me də lɑ̃ tɑ̃ drə,

Bon Saint Michel qui me daignez choisir
bɔ̃ sɛ̃ mi ʃɛ lki mə dɛ ɲe ʃwa zi r,

Pour lui complaire et la défendre,
pu rlɥi kɔ̃ plɛ re la de fɑ̃ drə,

Bon Saint Michel veuillez descendre
bɔ̃ sɛ̃ mi ʃɛ lvœ je dɛ sɑ̃ drə,

Avec Saint Georges sur l'autel
a vɛ ksɛ̃ ʒɔ rʒə sy rlo tɛ l,

De la Madone au bleu mantel.
də la ma dɔ no blø mɑ̃ tɛ l.

D'un rayon du ciel bénissez ma lame
dœ̃ rɛ jɔ̃ dy sjɛ l, be ni se ma la mə,

Et son égale en pureté Et son égale en piété
e sɔ̃ ne ga lɑ̃ py rə te, e sɔ̃ ne ga lɑ̃ pi e te,

Comme en pudeur et chasteté: Ma Dame,
kɔ mɑ̃ py dœ re ʃa stə te: ma da mə,

(O grands Saint Georges et Saint Michel)
o grɑ̃ sɛ̃ ʒɔ rʒə e sɛ̃ mi ʃɛ l,

L'ange qui veille sur ma veille,
lɑ̃ ʒə ki vɛ jə sy rma vɛ jə,

Ma douce Dame si pareille A Vous,
ma du sə da mə si pa rɛ j, a vu

Madone au bleu mantel! Amen.
ma dɔ no blø mɑ̃ tɛ l! a mɛ n.

Ravel   Chanson romanesque (Don Quichotte a Dulcinée)
ravɛl   ʃɑ̃sɔ̃ romanɛsk   dɔ̃ kiʃɔt a dylsine

Si vous me disiez que la terre
si vu mə di zje kə la tɛ rə,

A tant tourner vous offensa,
a tã tu rne vu zɔ fã sa,

Je lui dépêcherais Pança:
ʒə lɥi de pɛ ʃə rɛ pã sa:

Vous la verriez fixe et se taire.
vu la vɛ rje fi kse sə tɛ rə.

Si vous me disiez que l'ennui
si vu mə di zje kə lã nɥi,

Vous vient du ciel trop fleuri d'astres,
vu vjẽ dy sjɛ ltrɔ flœ ri da strə,

Déchirant les divins cadastres,
de ʃi rã le di vẽ ka da strə,

Je faucherais d'un coup la nuit.
ʒə fo ʃə rɛ dœ̃ ku la nɥi.

Si vous me disiez que l'espace
si vu mə di zje kə lɛ spa sə

Ainsi vidé ne vous plaît point,
ẽ si vi de nə vu plɛ pwẽ,

Chevalierdieu, la lance au poing,
ʃə va lje djø, la lã so pwẽ,

J'étoilerais le vent qui passe.
ʒe twa lə rɛ lə vã ki pa sə.

Mais si vous disiez que mon sang
mɛ si vu di zje kə mõ sã,

Est plus à moi qu'à vous, ma Dame,
ɛ ply za mwa ka vu, ma da mə,

Je blêmirais dessous le blâme,
ʒə blɛ mi rɛ də su lə bla mə,

Et je mourrais, vous bénissant.
e ʒə mu rrɛ vu be ni sã.

O Dulcinée.
o dy lsi ne ə.

Permission for reprinting of the original
lyrics in phonetics granted by Durand et Cie.,
Paris, and Elken-Vogel Co., Inc., Philadelphia,
Pennsylvania.

Ravel   Sainte
ravɛl   sɛ̃t

A la fenêtre recélant
a la fə nɛ trə rə se lɑ̃

Le santal vieux qui se dédore
lə sɑ̃ ta lvjø ki sə de dɔ rə,

De la viole étincelant
də la vi ɔ le tɛ̃ sə lɑ̃

Jadis selon flûte ou mandore.
ʒa di ssə lõ fly tu mɑ̃ dɔ r.

Est la sainte pâle étalant
ɛ la sɛ̃ tə pɑ le ta lɑ̃

Le livre vieux qui se déplie
lə li vrə vjø ki sə de pli ə,

Du Magnificat ruisselant
dy ma ɲi fi ka trɥi sə lɑ̃

Jadis selon vêpre ou complie.
ʒa di ssə lõ vɛ pru kõ pli.

A ce vitrage d'ostensoir
a sə vi tra ʒə dɔ stɑ̃ swa r,

Que frôle une harpe par l'Ange
kə fro ly nə a rpə pa rlɑ̃ ʒə

Formée avec son vol du soir.
fɔ rme a vɛ ksõ vɔ ldy swa r.

Pour la délicate phalange
pu rla de li ka tə fa lɑ̃ ʒə

Du doigt que sans le vieux santal
dy dwa kə sɑ̃ lə vjø sɑ̃ ta l,

Ni le vieux livre elle balance
ni lə vjø li vrɛ lə ba lɑ̃ sə,

Sur le plumage instrumental
sy rlə ply ma ʒɛ̃ stry mɑ̃ ta l,

Musicienne du silence.
my zi si ɛ nə dy si lɑ̃ s.

Saint-Saëns Amour, viens aider, from "Samson et Dalila"
sɛ̃ sɑ̃s   amur vjɛ̃ zɛde   sɑ̃sɔ̃ e dalila

Samson recherchant ma présence,
sɑ̃ sɔ̃ rə ʃɛ rʃɑ̃ ma pre zɑ̃ sə,

Ce soir doit venir en ces lieux.
sə swa rdwa və ni rɑ̃ se ljø.

Voici l'heure de la vengeance
vwa si lœ rə də la vɑ̃ ʒɑ̃ sə

Qui doit satisfaire nos Dieux!
ki dwa sa ti sfɛ rə no djø!

Amour! viens aider ma faiblesse!
a mu rvjɛ̃ zɛ de ma fɛ blɛ sə!

Verse le poison dans son sein!
vɛ rsə lə pwa zɔ̃ dɑ̃ sɔ̃ sɛ̃!

Fais que, vaincu par mon adresse,
fɛ kə vɛ̃ ky pa rmɔ̃ na drɛ sə,

Samson soit enchaîné demain!
sɑ̃ sɔ̃ swa tɑ̃ ʃɛ ne də mɛ̃!

Il voudrait en vain de son âme
i lvu drɛ tɑ̃ vɛ̃ də sɔ̃ na mə,

Pouvoir me chasser, me bannir!
pu vwa rmə ʃa se, mə ba ni r!

Pourrait-il éteindre la flamme
pu rɛ ti le tɛ̃ drə la fla mə

Qu'alimente le souvenir?
ka li mɑ̃ tə lə su və ni r?

Il est à moi! c'est mon esclave!
i lɛ ta mwa! sɛ mɔ̃ nɛ skla və!

Mes frères craignent son courroux;
me frɛ rə krɛ ɲə sɔ̃ ku ru;

Moi, seule entre tous, je le brave,
mwa, sœ lɑ̃ trə tu s, ʒə lə bra və,

Et le retiens à mes genoux!
e lə rə tjɛ̃ za me ʒə nu!

Amour! viens aider ma faiblesse!
a mu rvjɛ̃ zɛ de ma fɛ blɛ sə!

Contre l'amour sa force est vaine;
kɔ̃ trə la mu rsa fɔ rsɛ vɛ nə;

Et lui, le fort parmi les forts,
e lɥi lə fɔ rpa rmi le fɔ r,

368

Lui, qui d'un peuple rompt la chaîne,
lчi ki dœ̃ pœ plə rɔ̃ la ʃɛ nə,

Succombera sous mes efforts!
sy kɔ̃ bə ra su me zɛ fɔ r!

Saint-Saëns Danse Macabre
sɛ̃ sãs   dãs makabr

Zig et zig et zig, La mort en cadence
zi ge zi ge zig la mɔ rã ka dã sə

Frappant une tombe avec son talon,
fra pã ty nə tɔ̃ ba vɛ ksɔ̃ ta lɔ̃,

La mort à minuit joue un air de dance,
la mɔ ra mi nчi ʒu œ̃ nɛ rdə dã sə

Zig et zig et zag, sur son violon.
zi ge zi ge zag sy rsɔ̃ vi ɔ lɔ̃.

Le vent d'hiver souffle, et la nuit est sombre;
lə vã di vɛ rsu fle la nчi ɛ sɔ̃ brə;

Des gémissements sortent des tilleuls;
de ʒe mi sə mã sɔ rtə de ti jœ l;

Les squelettes blancs vont à travers l'ombre,
le skə lɛ tə blã vɔ̃ ta tra vɛ rlɔ̃ brə,

Courant et sautant sous leur grands linceuls.
ku rã te so tã su lœ rgrã lɛ̃ sœ l.

Zig et zig et zig, chacun se trémousse.
zi ge zi ge zig ʃa kœ̃ sə tre mu s

On entend claquer les os des danseurs;
ɔ̃ nã tã kla ke le zo de dã sœ r;

Un couple lascif s'asseoit sur la mousse,
œ̃ ku plə la si fsa swa sy rla mu sə

Comme pour goûter d'anciennes douceurs.
kɔ mə pu rgu te dã sjɛ nə du sœ r.

Zig et zig et zag, la mort continue
zi ge zi ge zag la mɔ rkɔ̃ ti ny ə

De racler sans fin son aigre instrument.
də ra kle sã fɛ̃ sɔ̃ nɛ grɛ̃ stry mã.

Un voile est tombé! La danseuse est nue,
œ̃ vwa lɛ tɔ̃ be! la dã sø ze ny ə

son danseur la serre amoureusement.
sõ dã sœ rla sɛ ra mu rø zə mã.

La dame est, dit-on, marquise ou baronne,
la da mɛ, di tõ, ma rki zu ba rɔ nə,

Et le vert galant un pauvre charron; Horreur!
e lə vɛ rga lã œ̃ po vrə ʃa rõ; ɔ rœ r!

et voilà qu'elle s'abandonne
e vwa la kɛ lə sa bã dɔ nə

Comme si le rustre était un baron.
kɔ mə si lə ry stre tɛ tœ̃ ba rõ.

Zig et zig et zig, quelle sarabande!
zi ge zi ge zig kɛ lə sa ra bã də

Quels cercles de morts se donnant la main!
kɛ lsɛ rklə də mɔ rsə dɔ nã la mɛ̃!

Zig et zig et zag, on voit dans la bande
zi ge zi ge zag õ vwa dã la bã də

Le roi gambader auprès du vilain.
lə rwa gã ba de o prɛ dy vi lɛ̃.

Mais psit! tout à coup on quitte la ronde,
mɛ psi t! tu ta ku, õ ki tə la rõ də,

On se pousse, on fuit, le coq a chanté.
õ sə pu s, õ fɥi, lə kɔ ka ʃã te.

Oh! la belle nuit pour le pauvre monde,
o la bɛ lə nɥi pu rlə po vrə mõ də,

Et vivent la mort et l'égalité!
e vi və la mɔ r, e le ga li te!

Saint-Saëns Mon coeur s'ouvre à ta voix, from "Samson et Dalila"
sɛ̃ sãs   mõ kœr s uvr a ta vwa   sãsõ e dalila

Mon coeur s'ouvre à ta voix comme s'ouvrent les fleurs
mõ kœ rsu vra ta vwa, kɔ mə su vrə le flœ r,

Aux baisers de l'aurore!
o bɛ ze də lo rɔ rə!

Mais, ô mon bien-aimé, pour mieux sécher mes pleurs,
mɛ o mõ bjɛ̃ nɛ me, pu rmjø se ʃe me plœ r,

370

Que ta voix parle encore!
kə ta vwa pa rlã kɔ rə!

Dis—moi, qu'à Dalila tu reviens pour jamais,
di mwa ka da li la, ty rə vjɛ̃ pu rʒa mɛ,

Redis à ma tendresse Les serments d'autrefois,
rə di za ma tã drɛ sə, le sɛ rmã do trə fwa,

ces serments que j'aimais!
se sɛ rmã kə ʒɛ mɛ!

Ah! réponds à ma tendresse,
ɑ re põ za ma tã drɛ sə,

Verse—moi, verse—moi l'ivresse!
vɛ rsə mwa, vɛ rsə mwa li vrɛ sə!

Réponds à ma tendresse!
re põ za ma tã drɛ sə!

Ainsi qu'on voit des blés les épis onduler
ɛ̃ si kõ vwa de ble le ze pi zõ dy le,

Sous la brise légère,
su la bri zə le ʒɛ rə,

Ainsi frémit mon coeur, prêt à se consoler,
ɛ̃ si fre mi mõ kœ r, prɛ ta sə kõ so le,

A ta voix qui m'est chère!
a ta vwa ki mɛ ʃɛ rə!

La flèche est moins rapide à porter le trépas,
la flɛ ʃɛ mwɛ̃ ra pi d, a po rte lə tre pɑ,

Que ne l'est ton amante à voler dans tes bras!
kə nə lɛ tõ na mã ta vo le dã te bra!

Samson! je t'aime!
sã sõ! ʒə tɛ mə!

Saint—Saëns Printemps qui commence, from "Samson et Dalila"
sɛ̃ sãs   prɛ̃tã ki komãs   sãsõ e dalila

Printemps qui commence, Portant l'espérance
prɛ̃ tã ki ko mã sə, po rtã lɛ spe rã sə,

Aux coeurs amoureux, Ton souffle qui passe,
o kœ rza mu rø, tõ su flə ki pa sə,

De la terre efface Les jours malheureux.
də la tɛ rɛ fa sə, le ʒu rma lø rø.

Tout brûle en notre âme Et ta douce flamme
tu bry lɑ̃ no trɑ mə, e ta du sə fla mə

Vient sécher nos pleurs;
vjɛ̃ se ʃe no plœ r;

Tu rends à la terre, Par un doux mystère,
ty rɑ̃ za la tɛ rə, pa rœ̃ du mi stɛ rə,

Les fruits et les fleurs.
le frɥi ze le flœ r.

En vain je suis belle! Mon coeur plein d'amour,
ɑ̃ vɛ̃ ʒə sɥi bɛ lə! mɔ̃ kœ rplɛ̃ da mu r,

Pleurant l'infidèle Attend son retour!
plœ rɑ̃ lɛ̃ fi dɛ lə a tɑ̃ sɔ̃ rə tu r!

Vivant d'espérance, Mon coeur désolé
vi vɑ̃ dɛ spe rɑ̃ sê, mɔ̃ kœ rde zo le,

Garde souvenance Du bonheur passé.
ga rdə su və nɑ̃ sə, dy bo nœ rpa se.

A la nuit tombante J'irai triste amante
a la nɥi tɔ̃ bɑ̃ tə, ʒi re tri sta mɑ̃ tə,

M'asseoir au torrent, L'attendre en pleurant!
ma swa ro to rɑ̃, la tɑ̃ drɑ̃ plœ rɑ̃!

Chassant ma tristesse, S'il revient un jour,
ʃa sɑ̃ ma tri stɛ sə, si lrə vjɛ̃ tœ̃ ʒu r,

à lui ma tendresse Et la douce ivresse
a lɥi ma tɑ̃ drɛ sə, e la du si vrɛ sə

Qu'un brûlant amour Garde à son retour.
kœ̃ bry lɑ̃ ta mu r, ga rda sɔ̃ rə tu r.

Chassant ma tristesse,
ʃa sɑ̃ ma tri stɛ sə,

S'il revient un jour, à lui ma tendresse!
si lrə vjɛ̃ tœ̃ ʒu r, a lɥi ma tɑ̃ drɛ sə!

Et la douce ivresse
e la du si vrɛ sə,

Qu'un brûlant amour Garde à son retour!
kœ̃ bry lɑ̃ ta mu r, ga rda sɔ̃ rə tu r!

Thomas   Connais tu le pays, from "Mignon"
tɔma   kɔnɛ ty lə pei   miɲõ

Connais-tu le pays où fleurit l'oranger,
kɔ nɛ ty lə pe i, u flœ ri lɔ rã ʒe,

Le pays des fruits d'or et des roses vermeilles,
lə pe i de frɥi dɔ r, e de ro zə vɛ rmɛ jə,

Où la brise est plus douce, et l'oiseau plus léger,
u la bri zɛ ply du s, e lwa zo ply le ʒe,

Où dans toute saison butinent les abeilles,
u dã tu tə sɛ zõ, by ti nə le za bɛ jə,

Où rayonne et sourit, comme un bienfait de Dieu,
u rɛ jo ne su ri kɔ mœ̃ bjɛ̃ fɛ də djø,

Un éternel printemps sous un ciel toujours bleu?
œ̃ ne tɛ rnɛ lprɛ̃ tã su zœ̃ sjɛ ltu ʒu rblø?

Hélas! que ne puis-je te suivre
e la skə nə pɥi ʒə tə sɥi vrə,

Vers ce rivage heureux, d'où le sort m'exila!
vɛ rsə ri va ʒø rø du lə sɔ rmɛ gzi la!

C'est là, que je voudrais vivre,
sɛ la kə ʒə vu drɛ vi vrə,

Aimer, aimer et mourir! C'est là! oui, c'est là!
ɛ me, ɛ me re mu ri r! sɛ la! wi sɛ la!

Connais-tu la maison où l'on m'attend là-bas,
kɔ nɛ ty la mɛ zõ, u lõ ma tã la ba,

La salle aux lambris d'or, où des hommes de marbre
la sa lo lã bri dɔ r, u də zo mə də ma rbrə,

M'appellent dans la nuit en me tendant les bras?
ma pɛ lə dã la nɥi, ã mə tã dã le bra?

Et la cour où l'on danse à l'ombre d'un grand arbre?
e la ku ru lõ dã s, a lõ brə dœ̃ grã ta rbrə?

Et le lac transparent, où glissent sur les eaux
e lə la ktrã spa rã, u gli sə sy rle zo,

Mille bateaux légers, pareils à des oiseaux!
mi lə ba to le ʒe, pa rɛ ja de zwa zo!

Vers ce pays lointain d'où le sort m'exila!
vɛ rsə pe i lwɛ̃ tɛ̃ du lə sɔ rmɛ gzi la!

373

Thomas   Elle ne croyait pas, from "Mignon"
tɔma   ɛl nə krwajɛ pa   miɲɔ̃

Elle ne croyait pas, dans sa candeur naïve,
ɛ lə nə krwa jɛ pa, dɑ̃ sa kɑ̃ dœ rna i və,

Que l'amour innocent qui dormait dans son coeur,
kə la mu ri nɔ sɑ̃ ki dɔ rmɛ dɑ̃ sɔ̃ kœ r,

Dût se changer un jour en une ardeur plus vive
dy sə ʃɑ̃ ʒe rœ̃ ʒu rɑ̃ ny na rdœ rply vi və,

Et troubler à jamais son rêve de bonheur.
e tru ble ra ʒa mɛ, sɔ̃ rɛ və də bɔ nœ r.

Pour rendre à la fleur épuisée
pu rrɑ̃ dra la flœ re pɥi ze ə,

Sa fraîcheur, son éclat vermeil,
sa frɛ ʃœ rsɔ̃ ne kla vɛr mɛ j,

O printemps, donne-lui ta goutte de rosée!
o prɛ̃ tɑ̃, dɔ nə lɥi ta gu tə də rɔ ze ə!

O mon coeur, donne-lui ton rayon de soleil!
o mɔ̃ kœ r, dɔ nə lɥi tɔ̃ rɛ jɔ̃ də sɔ lɛ j!

C'est en vain que j'attends un aveu de sa bouche,
sɛ tɑ̃ vɛ̃ kə ʒa tɑ̃ zœ̃ na vø də sa bu ʃə,

Je veux connaître en vain ses secrètes douleurs,
ʒə vø kɔ nɛ trɑ̃ vɛ̃ se sə krɛ tə du lœ r,

Mon regard l'intimide et ma voix l'effarouche,
mɔ̃ rə ga rlɛ̃ ti mi də, e ma vwa le fa ru ʃə,

Un mot trouble son âme et fait couler ses pleurs!
œ̃ mo tru blə sɔ̃ na m, e fɛ ku le se plœ r!

Thomas   Je suis Titania, from "Mignon"
tɔma   ʒə sɥi titanja   miɲɔ̃

Oui! pour ce soir, je suis reine des fées!
wi pu rsə swa r, ʒə sɥi rɛ nə de fe ə!

Voici mon sceptre d'or et voici mes trophées!
vwa si mɔ̃ sɛ ptrə dɔ r, e vwa si me trɔ fe ə!

Je suis Titania la blonde
ʒə sɥi ti ta ni a la blɔ̃ də,

Je suis Titania fille de l'air
ʒə sɥi ti ta ni a fi jə də lɛ r,

En riant je parcours le monde,
ã ri jã ʒə pa rku rlə mõ də,

Plus vive que l'oiseau,
ply vi və kə lwa zo

plus prompte que l'éclair!
ply prõ tə kə le klɛ r!

La troupe folle des lutins suit mon char qui vole et
la tru pə fɔ lə de ly tɛ̃, sɥi mõ ʃa rki vɔ le

dans la nuit Fuit! autour de moi toute ma cour,
dã la nɥi, fɥi, o tu rdə mwa tu tə ma ku r,

court, chantant le plaisir et l'amour.
ku rʃã tã lə plɛ zi re la mu r.

du rayon de Phoebé qui luit!
dy rɛ jõ də fe be ki lɥi!

Parmi les fleurs que l'aurore Fait éclore,
pa rmi le flœ rkə lo rɔ rə fɛ te klɔ rə,

Par les bois et par les prés Diaprés
pa rle bwa e pa rle pre di a pre,

Sur les flots converts d'écume, dans la brume,
sy rle flo ku vɛ rde ky mə dã la bry mə,

On me voit d'un pied léger voltiger!
õ mə vwa dœ̃ pje le ʒe vɔ lti ʒe!

D'un pied léger par les bois, par les prés
dœ̃ pje le ʒe pa rle bwa pa rle pre,

Et dans la brume on me voit voltiger, ah!
e dã la bry mõ mə vwa vɔ lti ʒe, a!

Voilà Titania!   En riant je parcours le monde,
vwa la, ti ta ni a! ã ri jã ʒə pa rku rlə mõ də,

Plus vive que l'oiseau, plus prompte que l'éclair.
ply vi və kə lwa zo ply prõ tə kə le klɛ r!

Je suis Titania, fille de l'air.
ʒə sɥi ti ta ni a fi jə də lɛ r.

Tchaikowsky Adieu, forêts, from "Jeanne d'Arc"
          adjø fɔrɛ   ʒɑn d ark

Oui, Dieu le veut!   Je dois suivre ton ordre,
wi djø lə vø!   ʒə dwa, sɥi vrə tõ nɔ rdrə,

obéir à ton appel, sainte Vierge!
ɔ be i ra tõ na pɛ l, sɛ̃ tə vjɛ rʒə!

Pourquoi, mon coeur, pourquoi bats tu si fort?
pu rkwa mõ kœ r, pu rkwa ba ty si fɔ r?

Pourquoi frémir? L'effroi remplit mon âme!
pu rkwa fre mi r? lɛ frwa rɑ̃ pli mõ na mə!

Adieu, forêts, adieu, prés fleuris, champs d'or,
a djø fɔ rɛ, a djø pre flœ ri ʃɑ̃ dɔ r,

Et vous, paisibles vallons, adieu!
e vu pɛ zi blə va lõ, a djø!

Jeanne aujourd'hui vous dit à jamais adieu.
ʒɑ no ʒu rdɥi vu di ta ʒa mɛ a djø.

Oui, pour toujours, toujours, adieu!
wi, pu rtu ʒu r, tu ʒu r, a djø!

Mes prés fleuris et mes forêts ombreuses,
me pre flœ ri e me fɔ rɛ zõ brø zə,

Vous fleurirez pour d'autres que pour moi.
vu flœ ri re pu rdo trə kə pu rmwa.

Adieu, forêts, eau pure de la source: Je vais partir
a djø fɔ rɛ, o py rə də la su rsə, ʒə vɛ pa rti r,

et ne vous verrai plus, Jeanne vous fuit, et pour jamais.
e nə vu vɛ re ply, ʒɑ nə vu fɥi, e pu rʒa mɛ.

O doux vallon où j'ai connu la joie!
o du va lõ u ʒe kɔ ny la ʒwa ə!

Aujourd'hui je te quitte, doux vallon!
o ʒu rdɥi ʒə tə ki tə, du va lõ!

Et mes agneaux, dans les vertes prairies
e me za ɲo, dɑ̃ le vɛ rtə prɛ ri ə,

demanderont en vain leur guide!
də mɑ̃ də rõ tɑ̃ vɛ̃ lœ rgi də!

Au champ d'honneur je dois guider les braves,
o ʃɑ̃ dɔ nœ r, ʒə dwa gi de le bra və,

cueillir les palmes sanglantes de la victoire!
kœ ji rle pa lmə sɑ̃ glɑ̃ tə də la vi ktwa rə!

Je vais où les voix m'appellent, Voix saintes,
ʒə vɛ u le vwa ma pɛ lə, vwa sɛ̃ tə,

Seigneur, vous voyez au fond de mon âme!
sɛ ɲœ r, vu vwa je zo fɔ̃ də mɔ̃ na mə!

Mon coeur se brise, Mon âme souffre, mon coeur saigne!
mɔ̃ kœ rsə bri zə, mɔ̃ na mə su frə, mɔ̃ kœ rsɛ ɲə!

O monts aimés, adieu, forêts ombreuses,
o mɔ̃ zɛ me, a djø fo rɛ zɔ̃ brø zə,

Et vous, paisibles vallons, adieu!
e vu pɛ zi blə va lɔ̃ a djø!

Jeanne aujourd'hui vous dit à jamais adieu!
ʒɑ no ʒu rdɥi vu di ta ʒa mɛ a djø!

Oui, pour toujours, adieu.
wi pu rtu ʒu r, a djø

Prés fleuris, arbres verts, Si chers à mon enfance,
pre flœ ri a rbrə vɛ r, si ʃɛ ra mɔ̃ nɑ̃ fɑ̃ sə,

Vous fleurissez pour d'autres que pour moi.
vu flœ ri se pu rdo trə kə pu rmwa.

Adieu, mes champs, adieu, vallon, source pure,
a djø me ʃɑ̃ a djø, va lɔ̃ su rsə py rə,

Il faut partir et pour toujours!
i lfo pa rti re pu rtu ʒu r!

Ah! recevez mon éternel adieu!
ɑ! rə sə ve mɔ̃ ne tɛ rnɛ la djø!

INDEX OF TITLES AND FIRST LINES